W9-BCI-513

Cambridge Historical Series

EDITED BY G. W. PROTHERO, F.B.A., LITT.D.

HON. LL.D. OF EDINBURGH AND HARVARD, AND HONORARY FELLOW OF KING'S COLLEGE, CAMBRIDGE

HISTORY OF MODERN FRANCE

IN TWO VOLUMES

Volume I 1815–1852

HISTORY
OF
MODERN FRANCE
1815–1913

BY

EMILE BOURGEOIS

Volume I 1815–1852

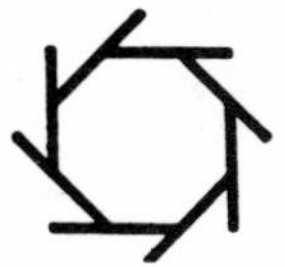

OCTAGON BOOKS

A DIVISION OF FARRAR, STRAUS AND GIROUX

New York 1972

First published 1919

Reprinted 1972
by permission of the Cambridge University Press

OCTAGON BOOKS
A DIVISION OF FARRAR, STRAUS & GIROUX, INC.
19 Union Square West
New York, N. Y. 10003

Reprinted from the original edition in the Wesleyan University Library

Library of Congress Cataloging in Publication Data

Bourgeois, Emile, 1857-1934.
History of modern France, 1815-1913.
Reprint of the 1919 ed., which was issued as no. 7 of the Cambridge historical series.
Bibliography: v. 1, p. ; v. 2, p.
CONTENTS: v. 1. 1815-1852.—v. 2. 1852-1913.
1. France—History—19th century. I. Title.
II. Series: Cambridge historical series, 7.

DC251.B6 1972 944 72-8498
ISBN 0-374-90847-8

Manufactured by Braun-Brumfield, Inc.
Ann Arbor, Michigan

Printed in the United States of America

GENERAL PREFACE

The aim of this series is to sketch the history of Modern Europe, with that of its chief colonies and conquests, from about the end of the fifteenth century down to the present time. In one or two cases the story commences at an earlier date: in the case of the colonies it generally begins later. The histories of the different countries are described, as a rule, separately; for it is believed that, except in epochs like that of the French Revolution and Napoleon I, the connection of events will thus be better understood and the continuity of historical development more clearly displayed.

The series is intended for the use of all persons anxious to understand the nature of existing political conditions. "The roots of the present lie deep in the past"; and the real significance of contemporary events cannot be grasped unless the historical causes which have led to them are known. The plan adopted makes it possible to treat the history of the last four centuries in considerable detail, and to embody the most important results of modern research. It is hoped therefore that the series will be useful not only to beginners but to students who have already acquired some general knowledge of European History. For those who wish to carry their studies further, the bibliography appended to each volume will act as a guide to original sources of information and works of a more special character.

Considerable attention is paid to political geography; and each volume is furnished with such maps and plans as may be requisite for the illustration of the text.

G. W. PROTHERO.

PREFACE

THE author of this work having asked me to write a few words by way of introduction, I readily consent, for I esteem it an honour to have been the means of bringing his book before the British public. It would ill beseem me, as general editor of the series to which it belongs, to praise a work in whose production I have necessarily had some share, however humble; and praise would be superfluous, for I am convinced that the book will amply recommend itself. But it may be interesting to its readers to learn something of the author, and of his high qualifications for the task which, at my invitation, he undertook.

M. Bourgeois began his historical studies as the pupil of Fustel de Coulanges, Ernest Lavisse, and Gabriel Monod. After devoting himself for some years to the teaching of medieval history at the University of Caen, he became a professor at the University of Lyons, where he studied and taught the history of modern France, and the general history of Europe since the seventeenth century. During his residence at Lyons (1885–93), he published three volumes on the diplomacy of the Regent and the Abbé Dubois, George the First and Elizabeth Farnese. This work was "crowned" by the Institute of France. He also edited, with critical notes, the correspondence of Alberoni, Voltaire's *Siècle de Louis XIV*, and Spanheim's *Relation de la Cour de France.* In 1890 he undertook a still more ambitious task—the production of an *Historical Manual on the Foreign Policy of France from Richelieu to the Congress of Berlin.* This work, the ripe fruit of researches in the archives of his own and other countries, pursued during twenty years, has been completed in three volumes. A fourth volume, in which the author hopes to carry the story down to the present day, is in preparation. M. Bourgeois' chapters in the *Cambridge Modern History* (vols. X, XI and XII), on France during the Restoration, the Monarchy of July, the Revolution of 1848, the Second Empire and the Third Republic, are familiar to many readers. From Lyons he passed first to the Ecole Normale Supérieure, and thence to a professorship at the University of Paris, where, as Professor of Diplomatic and Political History, he has prepared many pupils to take a leading part in education and historical science. During the last twenty years he has also taught Modern History at the Ecole des Sciences Politiques—an institution in which most of the higher members of the public services in France, especially of the Corps Diplomatique, receive their training. These professorships he still holds.

In the work before us, M. Bourgeois has traced the lines of that remarkable political evolution through which France has been able to realise the principles and to establish the institutions of democracy—an evolution retarded at one time by the worshippers of the Ancien Régime, at another by the devotees of Napoleonism, and still more by the difficulty of reconciling individual liberty and social progress with the administrative centralisation dear to a people as much in love with order as with liberty. The author has endeavoured to treat the events and the personages of this difficult and complex period with impartiality. If his own predilections and political opinions occasionally make themselves felt, or may be gathered from his survey as a whole, no reasonable person will blame him for that. It is within the province of the historian not only to narrate but to judge. He must present the facts as they are, inventing nothing, concealing nothing, distorting nothing; but, having presented the facts, it is not only his right but his duty to pass judgment upon them. By deciding a case one way or the other—by acquitting or condemning—a judge does not forfeit his claim to impartiality. Justice and indignation are not incompatible.

The historian, in dealing with recent times, finds it at once especially important and unusually hard to write without political bias. That M. Bourgeois has succeeded in this task, I believe his critics will allow. And if there is a peculiar difficulty in writing recent history, arising not only from this cause but also from the fact that many important records and documents are not yet divulged, the attempt to trace its connexion and development enjoys this peculiar advantage, that it opens our eyes to the aims, the motives and the occurrences which have led directly to the events of our own day. Moreover, the evidence of contemporaries is, in all historical epochs, the primary source and the first condition of our knowledge. The learned who study ancient times have to put forth a great effort of sympathy and imagination in order to revive the past and to make the dead bones live. To place oneself in the position of a contemporary is the first requisite if one is to understand the motives and appreciate the actions of men long since buried in the dust of ages. The historian of the 19th century, writing early in the 20th, is called upon to make no such effort. He has seen with his own eyes many of the events which he describes; he has personally known the actors, or has seen and conversed with those who knew them; and what he may lose in perspective or in cool because unconcerned judgment, he more than gains in intimacy and vividness of portraiture.

G. W. PROTHERO.

LONDON,
July, 1917.

TABLE OF CONTENTS

CHAPTER I

The Restoration of the Bourbons

CHAPTER II

Ministry of Villèle

CHAPTER III

The Reign of Charles X

CHAPTER IV

THE EARLY YEARS OF LOUIS PHILIPPE

CHAPTER V

LOUIS PHILIPPE AND THE PARLIAMENTARY BOURGEOISIE

CHAPTER VI

LOUIS PHILIPPE AND THE PARLIAMENTARY OPPOSITION

CHAPTER VII

Louis Philippe and the Eastern Question

CHAPTER VIII

Louis Philippe and Guizot

CHAPTER IX

The Republic and the Democracy

CHAPTER X

The Presidency of Louis Napoleon

CHAPTER XI

The Revision of the Constitution and the Coup d'État

CHAPTER I

THE RESTORATION OF THE BOURBONS

On July 8, 1815, Louis XVIII returned to the Tuileries. The monarchical system which he was bringing back, for the second time since his brother's execution, was not the system that France would have adopted if left to herself. The great majority of Frenchmen, the army, the proletariat, and some even of the representatives of the Liberal bourgeoisie who along with Benjamin Constant, Lanjuinais and Carnot had accepted Napoleon's Charter of 1815, would have remained loyal to the Empire, the heir of the Revolution, through fear of the Ancien Régime, had not Europe willed otherwise. It was the doing of the Allies who had declared war against Napoleon on April 20, 1815, had won the victory of June 18 and invaded France, had brought Louis XVIII from Ghent to Cambrai on June 28, and finally on July 7 had dissolved the Chambers and occupied Paris. France had to submit to the restoration of the Monarchy, as it had to submit to the invasion of its territory by over a million of foreign soldiers, and to its reduction by the treaty of November 20, 1815. Nations which, after welcoming the Revolution, and accepting its benefits, had risen against the domination of a Napoleon, now looked on with approval while their rulers disposed of the French nation as arbitrarily as Napoleon had once disposed of themselves. The violence thus done to France by the foreigner was the enduring cause of the unpopularity and weakness of the Bourbons, who were privy to the act and reaped its fruits.

No doubt Louis XVIII, warned by the catastrophe of the "Hundred Days," and very unwilling to take the road of exile again, was fully alive to the dangerous conditions attending his restoration. He was a prince to whom increasing age and infirmities forbade further adventure, epicurean enough to appreciate and enjoy the advantages of power, and intelligent enough to devise the best means of maintaining it. For this purpose he found his principal resource in the highly centralised administrative system bequeathed to him by the vanquished Napoleon, with which marvellous instrument of authority, altogether superior to the organisation of the old Monarchy, he did not dream of interfering. Nearly all his Ministers had once been intimate co-workers with the Emperor. The first of these was Prince Talleyrand, and next Fouché, in Foreign Affairs and Police; then Baron Louis at Finance, Gouvion St Cyr at the War Office; and in the Home Department lastly, as Minister of Justice, Baron Pasquier, who had been Prefect of Police in 1810. By these selections Louis XVIII indicated his wish to base his executive authority on the men and measures of the previous dynasty. He retained the departmental system with its prefects and sub-prefects, to whom the Communes were administratively subordinate, the judiciary and its courts and jurisdictions under irremovable judges, and a very powerful staff of public officers; the old civil procedure as settled by the Code Napoléon; a secret criminal procedure, and the transfer of the office of Notary or Solicitor by purchase. He maintained the executive authority of the *Conseils de Préfecture* and of the Council of State, the educational monopoly of the State as existing in the Imperial University, and the Legion of Honour; finally he took over the whole system of direct and indirect taxation, of excise, of state monopolies, and of local excise-duties, with all the members of its old staff in their various departments; also the protective duties enacted for the benefit of the great land-owners and manufacturers. Court ceremonial, and even the style of official Art, were left untouched, as if in very truth the Bourbon King had succeeded to the crown of the Empire.

But around the person of Louis XVIII, and even more markedly round the members of his family, his brother, the Comte d'Artois, and the sons of the latter, the Ducs d'Angoulême and de Berry, groups of intriguing Royalists were forming, displeased by this apparent adhesion of the King to the principles, to the men, and to the works of the French Revolution, and burning to restore the privileges of the nobility and the Clergy, in fact the Ancien Régime in its entirety. Already indeed, before the Hundred Days, these Ultras, as they were called, had forced Louis XVIII into excesses which later on he had to repudiate; for in his proclamation of Cambrai he once more promised to observe the Charter of 1814, to forget the past, and to maintain the principles of liberty and equality laid down in 1789. But now they were returning from Ghent, all the more furious after their late reverse, for the presence and encouragement of foreign arms. They had feasted the Prussian troops who occupied Paris, and reckoned for their work of vengeance upon the zealous aid of Fouché. They opened the flood-gates—to use an expression of one of their number, La Bourdonnaye—"to a torrent of deaths, of fetters, of executions," in fact, to a "White Terror." Immediately after July 24, 1815, Fouché had drawn up a list of proscriptions, by which nineteen persons were sent to Courts Martial and others were placed under observation. The number of victims was increased by the savagery in the south of France, especially at Toulouse, where General Ramel was killed, and at Avignon and Nîmes, by the murders of Generals Brune and Lagarde. It was not long before the Jacobin Ministers whom the maddened Royalists had taken into their service became the objects of their suspicion. And when the general elections of July 1815 gave the Ultras a majority of 350 votes out of 420, when a hundred new peers had been nominated in the Upper House, the party of reaction thought itself strong enough to do without Fouché and Talleyrand, known as "vice and crime," who accordingly resigned in Sept. 1815. With a Lower House such as it could not have dared to hope for, a "Chambre introuvable," that party believed itself to be the mistress of France, and on the point of realising the Counter-Revolution of its dreams, without the King's consent, and even against his interests.

No less compromising were the friends that Louis XVIII found among the sovereigns and foreign ministers who had restored him to his throne. True, the Tsar Alexander and the English statesmen had begun by recommending to the King of France the honest as well as prudent application of her Constitutional Charter. But the way adopted by the Congress of Vienna of disposing of nations against their will, forcibly uniting Belgium and Holland, Norwegians and Swedes, restoring Italians to the yoke of Austria, Poles to that of Russia, was not of a nature to inspire confidence in their Liberalism. The proclamation of the Holy Alliance was understood by the French as a threat and reminded them of the Declaration of Pillnitz and the League of Sovereigns against Peoples. This alliance, as conceived by its author, Tsar Alexander, a sovereign who was alike a mystic and a politician, was more or less directed against the Austrian and English statesmen who, at the Congress of Vienna and ever since, had combined to check the ambition of Russia in Poland and in the East. By this Holy Alliance the Tsar hoped to manipulate Europe to his own ends, just as he was now preparing to deal with France; on her he hoped to impose his will through his ambassador, the Corsican Pozzo di Borgo, and the Duc de Richelieu, who had been governor of Odessa, and on the fall of Talleyrand took office (Sept. 26) as Premier. But it was not long before the influence of Metternich, the sworn foe of the Revolution and of the principle of popular liberty which he deemed hostile to Austria, made itself felt. On Nov. 28, 1815, the sovereigns renewed the Treaty of Chaumont, and the Alliance acquired a totally different complexion. Though France had, under compulsion, disbanded her armies, restored the conquered fortresses, paid heavy contributions for the troops of occupation, and submitted to their demands, those for instance of the Prussians, who wanted to blow up the bridge of Jena, or those of Wellington, who had agreed with Blücher as to the restitution of the pictures unclaimed under the treaty of 1814, she still could not endure the thought that her King should countersign the decrees of the Holy Alliance. For all his desire for reconciliation, Louis XVIII found himself by the end of 1815 seriously compromised by the demands of the Royalists and the Allies. "Pillnitz and Coblentz have appeared once more at our gates," said Lafayette.

Luckily for the King, the Opposition was weak and unorganised. The rural population, weary of revolution, and exhausted by war, submitted in silence to the yoke of the great proprietors and the bureaucracy. The inhabitants of the towns and the students, though probably less docile, had great difficulty in finding exponents of their opinions in the Press or in Parliament. Paul-Louis Courier had not begun to issue his pamphlets; Lafayette had sought the seclusion of his country-house at Lagrange. Benjamin Constant was in England, Manuel in Brussels. Beneath the watchful eye of a very active secret police, and under the fear of punishment, the democrats who would have been willing enough to join the disbanded Bonapartists did not venture to demonstrate or to combine.

The impotence to which the nation was thus reduced may have relieved the apprehensions of Louis XVIII, and it naturally emboldened the royalist Ultras. It seemed to warrant them in hoping and daring anything and everything. The majority which they commanded in the "incredible" Chamber enabled them to curtail even the precarious liberty given by the Charter. A Law of Dec. 4, 1815, inspired by memories of the Revolutionary tribunals and of the special courts of the Empire, set up in every department military courts or commissions, with exceptional jurisdiction. The evidence was taken by a Colonel as Provost-Marshal and one civilian judge; and their judgments, after having been put into legal form by the President and four judges of the ordinary courts, were to be carried out in 24 hours without appeal on law or fact. Not long before, the Chamber had made use of its first meetings to confer on the King the power of suspending the liberty of the individual (on Oct. 27) and of the Press (on Nov. 3, 1815), by a series of measures as to seditious writings and acts, which constituted a positive Statute of High Treason, with penalties of death, banishment, and confiscation of goods for the very slightest infraction.

After passing these laws, the Royalists proceeded to acts. The one act which gives the most accurate measure of their revengefulness was the condemnation of Marshal Ney by the Chamber of Peers and his execution in Paris on Dec. 7, 1815. Not long after this, a savage law of proscription sent into exile Carnot, Cambon, David Cambacérès, Maret, Savary, Soult, Clauzel, Drouet d'Erlon, Count Lobau, men whose services had been the glory of the Convention and the Empire. Generals of less fame, but innocent of any crime, though Republicans, were summoned before the Courts Martial, or the Mixed Military Courts. The Institute was purged by the expulsion of Lakanal, Garat, Monge, Grégoire, and Cardinal Maury; the Polytechnic School was broken up. The universities and schools were placed under the dominion of the Clergy.

The heads of the Church ruled both the State and the Chambers through the medium of the "Congregation," a body affiliated to the Jesuits, whose clerical members, grouped into "Missions," inflamed the religious passions of the people. "In that year"—Royer-Collard used to say—"one had to be a Royalist to have the right to think and even to live."

Excesses of this sort were bound in the long run to imperil the stability of a shaky and hardly-restored throne. Unpopular already on account of his alliance with foreigners, the King now ran the risk of becoming an object of hatred. This bloodthirsty reaction, this violent return to the Ancien Régime, was not only unwelcome to the King, but might well provoke another revolution. Had not Napoleon been safe in St Helena, the Hundred Days might have been repeated. At Grenoble a conspiracy was started by certain retired soldiers, headed by a lawyer of Dauphiny named Didier, in favour of the King of Rome; but the ill-concerted attempt was easily put down by bloody executions at Grenoble in May and June 1816, at Lyons, and in Paris, where the Generals Mouton-Duvernet, Charton, and Bonnaire were sacrificed to the fury of the Royalists. None the less were these movements of revolt a warning to Louis XVIII. The challenges of the Ultras were met by the pamphlets of Paul-Louis Courier, an ex-officer under the Empire, and the lyrics of Béranger, the poet-laureate of Imperial glories. Warned by Decazes, his Minister of Police, the King was beginning to dread the zeal of his lieges more than the plots of his foes.

Nothing was more curious than the tactics of the Royalists when faced by the resistance of the King: Chateaubriand invented a formula for them in his "Essay on Monarchy." In order to force the King and his Ministers to lend themselves to the royalist attempts to return to the Ancien Régime, they claimed in the name of constitutional liberty the right to make violent attacks in the Chambers and in the Press. They charged with despotism an administration more moderate than themselves in order to browbeat them into passing a Finance Act restoring to the Clergy the property given up by the Pope at the Concordat. In Parliament a serious quarrel occurred on the introduction by the Minister, Vaublanc, of a Franchise Bill which was intended to cut down the influence of the rabid Royalists by means of partial elections and indirect representation. The result was not to the advantage of the King, who was obliged to dismiss M. de Vaublanc (May 1816). The royalist journals, the *Drapeau Blanc, Quotidienne, Gazette de France, Conservateur,* taking their cue from de Bonald, La Bourdonnaye, Villèle, Corbière, and the *Débats*, which had adopted the views of Chateaubriand, demanded in the name of liberty the submission of the Crown to the exigences of a royalist and religious reaction. A little more, and Louis XVIII would have been charged with tyranny for trying to protect his subjects against it.

All Royalists however did not agree with the Ultras; there were some Liberals amongst them, who thought it both right and possible to combine a regard for the nation with monarchic convictions, and deemed that they might well serve the King, without upsetting the whole of France. And it was fortunate for Louis XVIII, at that critical moment, that these Liberals were men endowed alike with character and with talent, whose eloquence was the glory of the parliamentary debates of the day. The chief and centre of their group was Royer-Collard, a mighty orator, who very soon made good his position through his eminence as a philosopher, his political past under the Directory, and his influence on the students of the Sorbonne. The vigorous intellectual and moral training which Royer-Collard had received from the "Pères de la Doctrine Chrétienne," and which gave the name of "Doctrinaires" to himself and his followers, had armed him for his approaching struggle. To his disciples, a small but resolute band composed of Villemain, Guizot, de Barante, Victor de Broglie, Camille Jordan, he indicated two enemies for attack, the anarchy of the masses and the ignominy of a dictatorship, and one citadel to be held at all costs, the authority of the King. While Royalists of this stamp desired to see the Crown governing for the benefit of its subjects, and making all necessary concessions to their needs, their aspirations and their freedom, they would not allow its authority, based upon and recognised by law, to be curtailed by Parliamentary votes, or by the demands of courtiers. Among Royer-Collard's followers there was no more brilliant and eloquent supporter of these opinions in the Ultra-Royalist Chamber than the Comte de Serre, a native of Lorraine, a former *émigré* who had accepted Napoleon, but had always remained attached to the Bourbons at heart, and who invented in 1816 the formula, "Eschew everything that can impair the authority of the Crown."

On the advice of Decazes, on the warnings of the foreign representatives in Paris, and supported by the "Doctrinaires," Louis XVIII determined on an act of prerogative. On August 14, 1816, he requested his Ministers to dissolve the Chamber of Deputies, and to appeal in his name to the nation, wearied by the excesses of the Royalists. The order for dissolution, which was drawn up with the greatest secrecy and without the knowledge of the Comte d'Artois and his advisers, was published on Sept. 5, 1816. Fresh elections followed closely after; and, in spite of the appeals and imprecations of the Ultras, and especially of Chateaubriand, their verdict was in favour of the King, Richelieu, and Decazes. The majority, composed of moderate Royalists, elected as their president Baron Pasquier, the type of man best fitted to reconcile ancient and modern

France about the person of the King. Royer-Collard undertook the preparation of a Franchise Bill, and drew up a sketch of its general plan which was adopted by the Cabinet; Guizot, who was then a Councillor of State, drew up the detailed explanatory memorandum. Thus Decazes won with the help of his auxiliaries of the Left Centre. His new programme was expressed by the formula: "royalise the nation, nationalise the Crown."

The Franchise Bill, which passed the two Chambers after violent debates on Jan. 8, 1817, deprived the small rural nobility, the "squireens," of the right which they had claimed of nominating on the District Committees the members charged with the election of deputies. The Bill granted the franchise to every man of French birth in the department who paid 300 francs in direct taxation, while 1000 francs similarly paid were the qualification for a candidate. It directed the electors to assemble in the capital of the district, as a place in which a wealthy bourgeoisie would have a preponderating influence, and were in a position to hold their own against the nobility in the elections. With this bourgeoisie, which had borne its share in the Revolution, any relapse to the Ancien Régime became impossible. Having satisfactorily secured its own well-being, it did not challenge the authority of the Crown, which was its present guarantee for order, even as the officialdom of the Empire had been in the past. During the whole year 1817 the bourgeoisie interested itself solely in conjunction with the Ministry in restoring the equilibrium of the finances of the State by means of regular budgets, regularly audited.

With her future once more secured, France breathed again. She awaited from the Monarchy, which had given these pledges of tranquillity, the liberation of her territory and the recall of the army of occupation. On these points the Ministry of the Duc de Richelieu was engaged during the whole course of the year 1817, struggling to obtain the means of paying off the foreign claims, and anticipating the discharge of the war indemnity. The Marshal Gouvion de St Cyr, to whom the Duke had entrusted the Ministry of War, had lost no time in reconstructing a standing army of 240,000 men on the basis of conscription, a period of six years' service, and annual ballot. This scheme, which was originally devised in order to create a standing army for the Bourbons, to replace the foreign army of occupation, and which actually lasted till 1871 as the basis of the military organisation of France, was passed in 1817 in the teeth of the opposition of the Comte d'Artois and his friends. There was some irritation among the Royalists in respect of the Marshal's scarcely-concealed intention to open the ranks of the newly created army to his former companions in arms, the veterans and officers of the Empire. The blindness of the Royalists made their defeat the more complete.

When in 1818 the Duc de Richelieu induced the Allies, and Tsar Alexander in particular, to summon a special Congress at Aix-la-Chapelle to consider the liberation of French territory, the Comte d'Artois and Baron de Vitrolles committed the fatal blunder of negotiating secretly with the foreigner, with a view to maintain the subjection of France—a sorry manœuvre dictated by party spirit, which recoiled on its own authors. For "Monsieur" was shortly dismissed from the command of the National Guard, and Vitrolles from his rank of Minister of State, while both incurred in the end the severe condemnation of the people. Richelieu and de Rayneval left Paris on Sept. 20 to attend the Congress at Aix-la-Chapelle, and by Oct. 2 they had arranged a treaty for the definite evacuation of France by the Allies on Nov. 30, thus anticipating the date previously fixed, in return for a payment of 265 million francs, of which 100 millions were payable in French State Annuities. "I have lived long enough"—said Louis XVIII in a letter addressed to the Minister who was freeing his native country from foreign troops and rescuing the Monarchy from the interference and patronage of the Allied Powers—"I have lived long enough, now that, thanks to you, I have seen France once more free and the flag of France waving over every French town."

But the policy which had got rid of the Reaction and the foreign garrison at the same time, to the great profit of the restored Monarchy and through its influence, now came into collision both within and without with fresh difficulties, causing a change of Ministry. The liberty conceded by the Duc de Richelieu, though still much restricted, had the effect of restoring the courage of those leaders of opposition who did not, like the Doctrinaires, admit that the royal authority could override the national will.

After 1816 three groups had been reconstituted, in the Left of the Chamber, out of the men who had been enabled to return to France and to resume active life by the cessation of the royalist persecutions. The first consisted of the extreme Left, Republicans—or, as they were then called, Jacobins—who could nevertheless accept a monarchy if it would consent to become a mere popular magistracy. Of these were Lafayette, Voyer d'Argenson, Chauvelin, General Foy, the barrister Manuel, Dupont de l'Eure, and Benjamin Constant. Next to them, at the head of the younger men, the student world, who affected secret societies such as the *Union* and the *Amis de la Vérité* (1818–19), was a group of more decided Republicans, the successors or disciples of the leaders of the Convention, such as Rey of Grenoble, Cavaignac, and Hippolyte Carnot. A third group, again, was forming round the memories of Imperial glory celebrated by the Republican Béranger in his songs, in which the old soldiers and half-pay officers, who hated Bourbons and priests alike, found their consolation and their rallying cry. This party possessed an organ which had already become a power, the *Constitutionnel*, started by Fouché in 1815 Its editors, Jay, Tissot and Étienne, had formerly been journalists in the pay of Napoleon and were still passionate supporters of the cause of the Empire. Their best-known leader at this time was General Thiard, a former aide-de-camp to the Emperor, who had been imprisoned after the Hundred Days, and who on recovering his liberty set an example to his party by forming a close alliance with Lafayette and the Republicans. This "unnatural" alliance, for thus it was characterised by the Duc de Richelieu, was their formidable reply to the programme of the Doctrinaires, who were equally opposed to anarchy and to a dictatorship; following out the plan devised by Napoleon at St Helena for upsetting the Bourbons, it brought together Frenchmen of all classes who refused to forget either the liberty or the glory of the past twenty years. They represented the nation waking up, and asserting itself as much against the Crown and hereditary right, as against the foreigner.

The well-to-do bourgeoisie was now called upon to pronounce between the popular aspirations and the royal authority, in the electoral assemblies where the law of 1817 gave it a great influence. Its representatives were pleased to call themselves "Independents," and they formed the third group of the Left, whose boast was that they were the slaves neither of Bourbons, nor of Bonapartists. They included bankers like Laffitte and the brothers Delessert, manufacturers like Casimir Perier, merchants like Ternaux, all of course friends of order, but none the less regardful of the national interest, and enthusiastic for liberty. At the first partial elections, which took place in 1817—and particularly in Paris—the Duc de Richelieu saw with amazement this Liberal and Monarchist bourgeoisie running its candidates against those of the Ministry, and entering them on the same list as Republicans like Lafayette and Manuel and Bonapartists like Thiard. The coalition, however, turned out favourably for the Independents, who won 20 seats, and repeated their success in 1818. On May 3, 1818, all the groups of the Opposition assembled at a great banquet in Paris and agreed to form a "Society of the Friends of the Press," and to hold meetings of it in various houses, the Prince Victor de Broglie's, Lafayette's, Manuel's or General Thiard's.

When the Duc de Richelieu and his colleagues determined to refuse to the Ultra-Royalists those parliamentary and press privileges by which they hoped to coerce Louis XVIII into a policy of reaction, they had not the faintest intention of granting the same to the men of the Left, who appeared to be preparing for taking the offensive once more on behalf of revolution and the Empire. At the end of 1817, Baron Pasquier, the Minister of Justice, introduced a Bill on periodicals and publications, which, while slightly less severe on purely literary writers than the exceptional measures of 1815, still by its last clause required all journals and political prints to obtain a licence of the Crown. This Bill had been violently attacked not only by Ultras like M. de Villèle, but by all the deputies of the Left; and it finally broke down in the Chamber of Peers owing to the efforts of Chateaubriand, the most uncompromising, and the Duc de Broglie, the most liberal, of Royalists.

The Duc de Richelieu began to doubt whether the parliamentary majority, now reduced to the Doctrinaires (if their fidelity could be counted on), was still sufficient to protect the prerogative of the Crown. The news which reached him at Aix-la-Chapelle in October 1818, of the sweeping electoral victories of Manuel in La Vendée and of Lafayette in La Sarthe, victories engineered and assisted by the Moderates of the Left, completed his discouragement. "The Liberal party seemed to him to incline more and more towards revolutionary hopes." For his own part he once more had recourse to the see-saw policy, according to which it would now be the turn of the Ultras to rule. But on this point he could not persuade either the King, who bore a grudge against them, or his intimate friend Decazes, whom he would be bound to sacrifice to them.

Moreover it was not only on the course of home policy that the Prime Minister had lost touch with the King and some of his colleagues; a graver difference was about to develop as to the direction to be given to foreign policy. In calling a Congress of Sovereigns and their Ministers at Aix-la-Chapelle for the deliverance of France, the Tsar had secretly designed to carry out the objects of the Holy Alliance with the cooperation of the French King as the price of benefits received. The European Powers, France, Prussia, Austria, and even England, were to form a group as against the revolutionaries of the West, the Spanish insurgents in America; and, while they were thus occupied, Russia would be at liberty to arrange the affairs of the East to suit her own ambitions. Metternich, who was cognisant of these ambitions, and the English, who were anxious to divert the attention of Europe from American affairs, had openly shown their opposition. They declined to allow the King of Spain to send plenipotentiaries to Aix-la-Chapelle. The only hope of Alexander I lay in an understanding with Louis XVIII by the aid of which he might have forced the Great Powers into a policy of united action against the revolutionaries as a whole, and those of Spanish America in particular—"a treaty of guarantees," wrote Richelieu on October 25, "arrived at among the Five Great Powers."

To this policy Richelieu now inclined, in his desire to please the Tsar, who had been cajoled by Capo d'Istria, and was displeased with the French Liberals. Metternich put forth every effort to divert Louis XVIII from the plan. He sent the French Ambassador at Vienna, the Comte de Caraman, to Paris, and induced the Emperor, Francis II, to write to the King of France. Informed of the resistance he was meeting in the Tuileries and of the above-mentioned intrigues, Alexander I came in person to Paris on October 28; but he could obtain nothing. The Congress of Aix-la-Chapelle granted him a Declaration expressing some vague ideas as to the fraternity of sovereigns, the King of France among the number; but it declined to agree to his cherished project of an European intervention in the colonial affairs of Spain (Nov. 15, 1818). The disappointment of Alexander I was a discomfiting blow to Richelieu, who looked upon him as his benefactor. He left the Congress with a fixed determination to resign office, or at any rate, if he did not, to rescue Louis XVIII from counteracting influences, and bring him back into closer agreement with the Ultras at home and with Russia abroad.

The crisis began immediately on the return of Richelieu to Paris, on Nov. 28. He was coming back with the full intention of altering the Electoral Law once more, and restoring to the District Electoral Assemblies, in which the landed aristocracy dominated, the right of nominating electors in the second degree. Lainé, the Home Minister, Comte Corvetto, Minister of Finance, and Molé supported this policy, which was of course agreeable to the Right; while the Duc Decazes, backed by Baron Pasquier and Gouvion St Cyr, Minister of War, were opposed to it. The strife began in the Cabinet, which was divided on the question. While Richelieu tried to get rid of Gouvion St Cyr on suspicion of Bonapartism, Decazes wanted to deprive Lainé of the seals of the Home Office, because his prefects had opposed Liberal candidates.

Early in December 1818, Richelieu, who had still great influence with the King, wished to reconstitute his Ministry with entirely new men, Lainé excepted; but the latter refused his consent. Then he did his best to retain all his colleagues except Decazes; but to this neither Pasquier nor Gouvion St Cyr would agree. Hereupon Corvetto, the

Minister of Finance, resigned office (Dec. 7, 1818). As the first meeting of the Chamber was fixed for Dec. 10, his place was hastily filled by M. Roy. But, after so much dissension, the Government had lost its authority in the new Parliament. In the course of the month they resigned in a body; and it might have been thought that Richelieu, who had obtained the King's assent to the transfer of Decazes to a distant embassy, would now be able to carry out his plans. But the Right Centre, the Liberal Monarchists whose support he must have if he was to induce the nation to accept a Ministry of the Right coupled with electoral reform, refused him that support. To crown all, just at the same moment Richelieu received news from Vienna (on Dec. 13, 1818) that Tsar Alexander, annoyed at the failure of his schemes at Aix-la-Chapelle, was thinking of ordering his troops back into France, and opposing the progress of French liberation by foreign arms. Disheartened by the exorbitant demands of the Royalists and by the threats of Russia, the Duc de Richelieu finally retired on Dec. 28, 1818.

This lengthy ministerial crisis, which by suspending all administrative action weakened and paralysed the only power that the restored Monarchy possessed, ought logically to have been closed by the elevation of Decazes to the Premiership, with a Doctrinaire Cabinet. But Decazes was only 38 years of age; and neither his age, nor his antecedents as a functionary who had owed a rapid rise to the Empire, were such as to give him much weight before a House of Peers of a very Royalist type, and wedded to its own prerogative. As for the Doctrinaires, if they generally had talent on their side, they had numbers against them; hence they had been unable to secure the election of M. de Serre to the Presidency of the Chamber at the close of 1818; and the consciousness of their numerical inferiority made them hesitate, as in the case of Royer-Collard, to undertake the responsibilities of power. In these circumstances,

Louis XVIII was forced to adopt a rather shifty policy. He gave the Premiership to General Dessolles, who while a noble by birth, had seen honourable service in the armies of the Revolution, and oftener under the wing of Moreau than that of Napoleon. His colleagues were Decazes at the Home Office, de Serre as Minister of Justice, Gouvion St Cyr at the War Office, Baron Louis at the Treasury, any one of whom might very well have headed this coalition had they not been afraid of rousing the wrath of the Right by putting forward men of such marked opinions, through undue deference to the demands of the Liberals.

This Ministry lacked both the authority and the prestige required to carry out its mission. The King did his best to lessen the majority in the Second Chamber and to modify its tone by creating a batch of Peers; he called up civil functionaries and soldiers of the Empire, Baron de Barante, Comte Chaptal, Cornudet, and Daru, Baron Mounier, Mollien, and de Montalivet, Portalis and Pelet de la Lozère, Marshals Lefebvre, Davoust, Mortier, Moncey, Generals Rapp, Reille, and Rampon, and Admiral Truguet. In every critical moment the Bourbons were obliged to look for support against the claims of the Left and the reactionary demands of the Royalists to the men and institutions of the Empire. Louis XVIII moreover hoped to enable his Ministers to retain on the statute-book the new Electoral Law which deprived the rural land-owners of their exclusive influence over elections and thereby over Parliament. He permitted them to introduce a new Press Law (March 22, 1819) which was debated on April 11 and carried on May 17.

Undoubtedly the restoration of that almost-forgotten privilege, liberty of speech and thought, deserved all credit. The Press had become literally free, inasmuch as it was no longer liable to criminal prosecution save for offences against ordinary law, provocation to crime and immorality, insults to the Crown, or defamation of individuals.

The Ultras complained that this put a premium on anarchy. Liberals like Benjamin Constant, on the other hand, found great fault with it for still requiring editors to give pecuniary security, which practically involved the power to inflict a fine upon them, while the printers had been relieved of any liability. Many years had passed since so many journals were to be seen—the *Constitutionnel, Indépendant, Quotidienne, Gazette de France, Drapeau Blanc, Débats, Moniteur, Journal de Paris, Minerve,* and *Conservateur.* The discussions in the Press elicited as great a display of talent as those in Parliament. To the journals of the Right Chateaubriand and Michaud contributed, to those of the Bonapartists Fiévée, Étienne, Jay, Tissot, de Jouy; the Liberal writers make a remarkable list, Guizot, Villemain, de Rémusat, de Salvandy, Benjamin Constant, Paul-Louis Courier, de Lamennais. Nor was it long before the special value of the liberty thus given to the upholders of modern ideas began to show itself; the journals were now able to enlighten and interest the nation, to appeal to it, and to look to public opinion for the assertion and support of their rights. The Royalists, disgusted and alarmed, accused the Ministry of dissipating by this reform their cherished dream of a return to the Ancien Régime. Their wrath against the Ministers and the King himself showed itself in the summer of 1819 on the presentation of certain petitions to Parliament for the recall of the exiles of the Revolution and Empire, and even of the regicides and the Bonaparte family. It was of no use for M. de Serre to point out that these petitions were matters for the clemency of the Crown. "The Bonaparte family and the voters for the death of Louis XVI were irrevocably placed under special disabilities"; the Ultras were not satisfied. They accused Ministers of undue kindness to the Left, while the Left complained that they could not get a hearing from them. The Ultras stigmatised them as a coalition between the men of the Revolution and the servants of the Empire, which the Left called "a foolish fear."

What with demands on the one hand and threats on the other, the Cabinet very soon began to hesitate again, and, like their predecessors, to split up. Convinced Royalists like de Serre and Decazes went so far as to wonder whether they should not attempt a reconciliation with the Ultras, in order to maintain their position against the spectres of the Revolution and the Empire, which the Monarchy was unable to exorcise. But beside them sat old servants and generals of Napoleon, actual members of the Cabinet or of the Chamber, who had an indulgent feeling towards those old comrades who had not accepted the Bourbons. The disagreement in the Cabinet became more marked in the course of the year owing to sundry outside influences, to national aspirations, or to the policy of the rulers. Were they to applaud the efforts of the Germans against the tyrannical centralised system of Metternich, which inspired the decrees of Karlsbad published in August 1819 after the assassination of Kotzebue? Or were they to bow before the menaces of Alexander I, whose displeasure against Louis XVIII had reached the point of his refusing the treaty submitted to him by Baron Hulot, who was obstinately insisting on the dismissal of Decazes, and who had gone so far as to tell our ambassador M. de Ferronays that he intended to keep France "in pupilage"? On one side was risk, on the other humiliation.

The elections of September 1819 testified to the critical position of affairs. After a bare six months of existence the Dessolles Ministry could with difficulty see their way to retain office. One-fifth of the seats in Parliament were to be filled up afresh; and on these the Left scored a gain of twenty-five, won by ex-officials or deputies of the Hundred Days, Generals such as Tarayre and Sebastiani, and even by Republicans. The election of the Abbé

Grégoire, who publicly supported the execution of Louis XVI, and whom the Emperor had created a Count, had a considerable effect in Royalist circles, and in the French and other European Courts. The Ultras, who had been secretly looking forward to the elections as a way of embarrassing the Government, now shrieked at the scandal. The Tsar charged Louis XVIII and Decazes with the discredit "of this reawakening of the Terror."

A year had not elapsed before Decazes and de Serre, Richelieu's former colleagues, thought it necessary, as he had done, to modify the franchise as being too favourable to the schemes of the Republicans and the hopes of the Bonapartists. General Dessolles, the Prime Minister, and his colleagues Gouvion de St Cyr and Baron Louis, refused to follow their lead; consequently Louis XVIII, still obedient to the advice of Decazes, dismissed them (Nov. 19, 1819) and entrusted him with the duty of arranging for this reactionary move. Decazes prepared for it by proposing a revision of the Electoral Law, at the very moment when Metternich, at the Conferences of Vienna, was trying his hardest to induce the German princes to revise the charters of the German Confederation as giving too great a liberty to the masses. For Decazes the task was a delicate one, spelling reaction—almost a *coup d'état*—to the Liberals, while still insufficient to please the Royalists. The Doctrinaires who ought to have supported it, Royer-Collard and Guizot, repudiated it; C. Jordan and B. Constant condemned it from the very outset.

In this position of things a tragic event occurred, which was almost a stroke of good luck for Decazes and even for the cause of the Monarchy, in that it necessitated the resignation of the Liberal Ministry in February 1820. As the Duc de Berry, nephew to the King, was leaving the Opera House on February 13, he was assassinated in the open street by an artisan named Pierre Louvel, who plunged a dagger into his breast, in order "to set France free from the Bourbons." The crime created a profound sensation in the general public and in Parliament. The Royalists denounced it as the natural consequence of the culpable tenderness of the Government for the men of the Revolution, and charged Decazes with being a party to it. They clamoured that he should be prosecuted on the very next day, and hailed his resignation on Feb. 18 with noisy satisfaction. He was succeeded on Feb. 20 by the Duc de Richelieu as Premier; Comte Simeon took the Interior, Baron Mounier became Head of the Police, Comte Portalis Minister of Justice, M. de Serre and the other colleagues of Decazes remained in office. From these men the Royalists expected a display of energy "which should protect France from the dangers to the Crown which the crime foreshadowed only too clearly." They thought that the King, who could address the deputies in the words just quoted, ought to have selected his new Ministry from men of a temper fitted to resist the attacks of Liberals, Bonapartists and Jacobins better at any rate than Decazes.

Their demands were satisfied, but only partially, and for a very short time. Richelieu had already, in 1819, come to the conclusion that the progress of the Left could only be checked by calling into line the Right, who had been dissatisfied ever since 1817. To please them, he took up again two Bills which Decazes had brought up in Parliament on the very day when he was dismissed for weakness, two days after the crime of Feb. 13—one involving the suspension of personal liberty, by permitting the summary arrest of any one accused of plotting against the Crown or the safety of the State, the other establishing a censorship over journals and other periodicals. It was not without difficulty and after a month of discussion that Richelieu was able to obtain a final vote on these. All the speakers of the Left in both Houses, General Foy, Benjamin Constant,

Dupont de l'Eure, Marshal Jourdan, Boissy d'Anglas, Lanjuinais, Manuel, and Lafayette, as well as Chateaubriand and La Bourdonnaye of the Right, charged the Government with the violation of the Charter of their liberty, with preparing to return to the Ancien Régime by the way of a dictatorship. The more lively these attacks became, the more incumbent it was on the Government to find a basis of support in the Right, the more so as the Doctrinaires, Royer-Collard, Guizot, and de Broglie, objected to this exceptional legislation, as fatal alike to Monarchy and to liberty. The alliance between the two, which they had once contemplated, had now in their opinion become impossible. But for the Right, which approved the Bills by a narrow majority, the Richelieu Ministry would not have lasted longer than that of Decazes.

On April 17, 1820, Richelieu presented his supporters with a fresh acknowledgment of their claims in the shape of a new Electoral Law, made designedly of a complicated character for the purpose of restoring to the aristocratic land-owners the parliamentary preponderance which they had lost in the last three years. For Departmental Assemblies created in 1817 for the very purpose of breaking down this preponderance, his Bills substituted District Assemblies (*collèges d'arrondissement*) charged with the duty of electing 258 deputies, and of providing in the course of the year for the entire renewal of the Chamber every five years. It is true that, to avoid too complete a reaction, the change thus made was modified by the addition of 172 new deputies to be elected in the Departmental Assemblies, chosen by the whole body of departmental electors from among the most highly taxed of their own members, and equal in number to one-fourth of their whole body. This was a sort of compromise between the two methods of election which had served the purposes of the Right and Left alternately; but it was specially favourable to the country-squires. For the latter could now make pretty sure of success in the coming partial elections of Sept. 1820, by virtue of the double vote in the district and in the department, to which they were now entitled on their property qualification. It was in respect of these privileges that the public formed its judgment of the Act, and dubbed it with the name of the "Law of the Double Vote."

In the Chamber of Deputies the debate on the Bill was most animated. The proposed increase in the number of deputies was apparently a violation of the Charter by which the number was fixed. In certain cases it unduly favoured a very limited class in the nation, by giving the privilege of a double vote to the landed aristocracy at the expense of the great manufacturers and the commercial class, who represented interests often of a higher sort, as well as of the economic and intellectual progress of the people. The nation became excited; public manifestations of feeling in the galleries of the Chamber greeted the discourses of Lafayette, d'Argenson, Laffitte, and Ternaux. And seeing that after all the Bill was a compromise, the Ministry could scarcely count either upon the Ultras of the Extreme Right, or upon the deputies of the Left to support them or to carry their Bill. All the burden of the discussion fell on the shoulders of de Serre, the Minister of Justice, whose frail health, undermined by a mortal attack of phthisis, seemed unequal to the heroic and victorious contest that he carried on for a month. His friends the Doctrinaires abandoned him. Royer-Collard, as well as C. Jordan, Guizot, and de Broglie, twitted him with this *coup d'état,* this counter-revolution. He faced them with courage, and by dint of energy, resolution, and eloquence he obtained, on June 3, 1820, a vote of the Chamber in favour of the Bill. He displayed equal vigour in dealing with the troubles which the vote provoked in the streets of Paris (June 9), demonstrations of students ferociously and repeatedly put down by troops under the command of Macdonald, tumultuous assemblies of working-men in the suburbs, especially at the execution of Louvel in the Place de Grève on June 7, and, finally, sanguinary contests on June 10 in the very centre of Paris between soldiers and civilians. During that whole month and up to the final passing of the Bill by the Chamber of Peers on June 28, de Serre, almost single-handed, supported by the fever of the fight, and of his fatal malady, stood up against the storm, both in Parliament and in the streets.

The country seemed to be on the brink of a revolution; and the Monarchy, attacked on the right by its own dissatisfied supporters and on the left by the supporters of popular or of Bonapartist constitutions, seemed to have no protection but the skill and firmness of a few resolute defenders. "Richelieu is our last bulwark," said Royer-Collard; but he gave him no support. Resting on the army and on the centralised administration bequeathed to it by the Empire, the Government maintained the monarchic system, and forced upon the Chamber the budget which the Left refused to vote. If any Monarchists objected, de Serre did not hesitate to strike them, even though private friends. On July 17 he dismissed from the Privy Council Guizot, C. Jordan and Royer-Collard on account of their constant opposition to the measures which he adopted against the enemies of Monarchy. He offered them some compensation, which they declined; he accepted de Barante's resignation of the Customs; he dismissed prefects, military governors, and justices, and put his own men in their places. On discovering a conspiracy among the troops in favour of the King of Rome, the son of the captive Emperor, he summoned the High Chamber to its functions as a High Court of Justice and brought before it thirty officers suspected of treason. Indeed Lafayette, Manuel, and some other deputies, Martin de Gray and General Tarayre, who were fairly open to the suspicion of having favoured the plot, barely escaped from prosecution.

Any pretext was then sufficient for a conflict between a Government resolved to use its authority and an Opposition inclined to act by insurrection or mutiny. If the military revolution which broke out at Cadiz in January 1820, obliging Ferdinand VII to convoke the Cortes on July 9, was an encouragement and example to French revolutionists, it was useful to the Duc de Richelieu as an occasion for renewing with Alexander I an alliance of France and Russia against the insurgents of Spain and America. To Russia, who called for the execution of the decrees of the Holy Alliance against the insurgents, he offered the co-operation of a French force in Spain; to the French, the glory of a military expedition. Louis XVIII informed Ferdinand VII by a special envoy, M. de la Tour la Pin, that he would be glad to help him, provided he obtained a mandate from Europe; and this mandate he tried to obtain, by suggesting to Metternich that the case had arisen for one of those meetings of sovereigns provided for by the Congress of Aix-la-Chapelle. Richelieu, after obtaining the approval of the King's Council, was delighted with the prospect of a Congress, which "would enable him to see his Russian friends again"; "what an opportunity"—said his colleague Pasquier to the King—"for the house of Bourbon to get a commanding lead in Europe generally, and in the heart of the French nation in particular!" And what a victory for the policy of the Tsar as against the diplomacy of Metternich which for five years had been obstinately opposed to the Russian ideas of intervention in America and Spain!

Metternich dreaded that the contagion of insurrection which had appeared in Naples in July would spread over Italy, as had happened with the revolution in Spain; but, desiring nevertheless to retain the right of intervening in that country, he was obliged to acquiesce in Richelieu's proposal of a Congress. "The same evils call for the same remedies"—remarked Alexander I to him. It was apparently settled in Paris, Vienna, and Petrograd in August 1820 that a Congress should meet at Troppau to authorise Louis XVIII to send troops against the Spanish rebels. The Duc de Richelieu was commissioned in August to receive from Europe the mandate for the action of the French Bourbons in Spain which Russia had agreed to procure.

When, however, the Congress met at Troppau on Oct. 23, 1820, Richelieu was not there. The Tory Government of Castlereagh had up to that time favoured the Holy Alliance; but the whole of England was disturbed at the first suggestion of the possible return of a French army to the Iberian peninsula, from which they had once been driven by Wellington. The English dreaded the intimate understanding between the French and Spanish Bourbons which Russia favoured; they disapproved of the Congress about to be convoked, and declared that they could not countenance military measures against England's old allies, the Spanish Liberals. The Duc Decazes, now French Ambassador in London, in reporting to the King, whose confidence he still preserved, secretly supported the English arguments, pointing out the bad effect on public opinion in France of a military intervention concerted with the absolute rulers of Russia and Austria, while condemned by England, the only constitutional Power. By the month of September Louis XVIII had given up the idea of intervention, and substituted for Richelieu at Troppau the Comte de Caraman, the French Ambassador in Vienna, who was known to be a docile follower of the policy of Metternich, and like him opposed to the Tsar's darling and carefully concocted scheme. On the advice of Decazes, the King of France had thought it better to displease Alexander I by inflicting on him another disappointment, rather than condescend to make France the policeman of the Holy Alliance.

Louis XVIII had, indeed, been at pains to comfort Russia and Richelieu by offering, through the medium of La Ferronays, our ambassador at Petrograd, to enter into an indirect and secret understanding empowering him to intervene in Spain, and also in Naples, as "mediator" between the Bourbon Kings and their revolted subjects. But this half-measure (accepted, by the way, by Metternich on his hearing it at Troppau) had the effect of postponing indefinitely the plan of action beyond the Pyrenees as concerted by Richelieu and Russia. All that the Congress of Troppau produced was a declaration of principle of no immediate value. The Congress of Laybach, which followed and concluded it at the beginning of 1821, gave its sanction to one action only of the Holy Alliance, and that of very limited scope—the support given by the Austrians to the King of Naples. In short, the foreign policy of the Richelieu Ministry at the close of 1820 was, like his home policy and the Electoral Law, a compromise between the plan preferred by the Liberals, the friends and admirers of England, which had been gradually given up in the course of that year, and that dreamt of by the Ultras who favoured the Holy Alliance, the infatuated supporters of amity with the Tsar, never satisfied with the concessions and promises which excited the wrath of the Left and of the Doctrinaires.

Obedient prefects, supported by the district voting, had manipulated the October elections of 1820 for the benefit of the Right, whose demands grew larger and more exacting. In spite of the protests of the Left, Richelieu allowed them three posts of unattached Ministers, and bestowed them on their most influential leaders, Lainé, Corbière and de Villèle. This was a compromise, giving them the honours, without affecting the power of the Ministry; and yet it was of no avail. The intractable Royalists were able to elect the President of the Chamber by a majority of over 100, and to claim the drafting of the Address. Conscious of their power, they summoned the Ministry to resign on December 29; and the speakers of the Left, in order to force their hands, refused to vote their budget. Another criminal attack upon the Royal Palace, which was made on January 27, 1821, gave the Ultras an opportunity of repeating last year's manœuvre which had served them so well against the Decazes Cabinet. For the space of two months they kept on clamouring to the King for a Ministry more firmly determined to make the deputies of the Left, the organisers of anarchy and fosterers of assassination, pay the penalty of their crimes against public order and the Monarchy. The fall of the Richelieu Ministry, the open attacks that led up to it, and the secret intrigues in which the envoy of the Tsar took part, "form, in the opinion of a contemporary writer, the whole history of the year 1821."

The policy of the Royalists had apparently undergone no change since their return to power; it consisted of retaliation for the Revolution, and an attempt to return to the Ancien Régime. To effect this, they proposed to begin by restoring the privileges and the doctrines of the Ultramontane Catholics. In fact their hopes and their schemes, their ambitions and their political intrigues, took the shape of a moral propaganda in favour of a close alliance between Throne and Altar, and a campaign against atheism and immorality. It was at this time that they put the direction of their religious and dynastic enterprises into the hands of the "Congregation" of the Rue de Bac. This had been in existence since 1814 under the direction of Father Ronsin, a Jesuit, and served as a centre for Clergy and laity, for the nobility and the royalist judiciary, and for the legitimist youths fresh from school. By this means the *parti prêtre*, as it came to be called, though it was more royalist than religious, organised its branches in the provinces, multiplied missions at home, and pompous and well-advertised "retreats" like that conducted by the Abbé Forbin-Janson on Mont Valérien close to Paris, which might have been a crusade in a heathen country. The absolute and sovereign dominion of the Roman Church over a France purged of its revolutionary doctrines began to be boldly asserted, alike by hot-headed and strong-languaged journalists, by editors of newspapers such as the *Drapeau Blanc* and the *Bibliothèque Catholique,* and by eloquent advocates of dogmatic convictions, such as Lamennais, who wrote and published his *Essay on Indifference in religious matters* between 1817 and 1820, or Joseph le Maistre, the author of *The Pope.*

From the outset of 1821 the majority in the Chamber of Deputies kept on inviting the King "to impress the authority of religion upon the heart of the people, to purify the morals of the age by a system of education based on Christianity and Monarchism." They put forward with clearness and detail the policy which they proposed to carry out—a religious monarchy, i.e. one founded on the close alliance of politics and religion, and hostile to what they called the "materialism" of society. Thus, on the pretext of building up once more the moral condition of France, they proposed to restore the political system of their dreams, to substitute the old taxation districts for the prefectures of the Empire, to revive the old provinces, to restore the jurisdiction of the Church in civil matters, to repeal the marriage and succession laws of the Revolution, and in short to restore to the aristocracy its confiscated property, its fortunes, its influence at Court, and its power in the provinces.

At this juncture the royalist party was preparing to follow the advice of Chateaubriand, the most illustrious of its leaders, who by his speeches in the Chamber of Peers and his campaigns in the Press between 1818 and 1820 had cleared the road for its success. This brilliant writer thought he could persuade the French, a nation to whom glory was not less attractive than equality, to commit themselves to his friends, the Ultras, by offering them an active foreign policy, an armed intervention, in fact, in European affairs. It was the moment at which the people of Naples, and soon afterwards the people of Turin, were emboldened by the revolts in Spain to claim their freedom by insurrection. It was known after the Congress of Troppau that Metternich intended to obtain at the Congress of Laybach a mandate for intervention at Naples in favour of the Bourbons, with a view to the establishment of Austrian domination over all Italy. On November 30, 1820, Chateaubriand, as ambassador for Louis XVIII at Berlin, claimed a similar mandate for France and her King, alleging that he had a better claim than the Emperor of Austria to defend the royal rights of the Bourbons on the Alps and at Naples. "The white cockade," he wrote, "will take its place firmly when once it has been under fire. An act of high state-policy, which at the same time ministers to the national pride of the French, on that account alone will secure a great popularity for the dynasty."

Such were the broad lines and essential elements of the scheme of the French aristocracy in 1821. It had been brought back into power by the force of circumstances; it had been confirmed in that power by press legislation and by the late elections; and now, in its blind thirst for revenge on modern society, the spawn of the Revolution, it hoped to carry out its project. But, however much he may have desired the support of the Right and however willing to give them some satisfaction, Richelieu was not the man for a programme of this sort. "While ruling by means of the Right, he meant," said de Serre, "to rule with moderation." Was the existence of a moderate government compatible with the extravagant claims of a party burning for a counter-revolution, and therefore itself revolutionary?

When, in seeking to exist, the Richelieu Ministry had to give way to these claims, as was the case all through the year 1821, it was evident that, however moderate its intentions, it was not moderate in act.

By the pleasure of M. Corbière, who was now (December 21, 1821) at the head of the University, that august body, whose views were alike liberal and moderate, under the rude discipline of her Grand Master, found herself subjected to the control of the Bishops, who had not only the right of interfering in the Royal Colleges by inspection, but also the power of helping their competitors, the Church Colleges, out of the public purse. Professors of a too pronounced liberalism, such as Tissot and Cousin, were dismissed from the Collège de France and the Sorbonne, while a priest was nominated as a Governor of the Académie de Paris, the most important in France—all this by virtue of the Order in Council of February 27, 1821, on Public Instruction.

A little later, an Act of May 1821 gave fresh satisfaction to the Clergy, who were backed by the "Congregation" in Parliament. After reciting the insufficiency in the number of sees, and also the lack of funds at the disposal of the Minister for his own purposes and for the maintenance of places of worship, it proposed to create twelve new sees. With appetite thus whetted, the *parti prêtre* asked for more, and obtained a promise of eighteen more bishoprics. In the course of the debate, the Ministry had to carry on a desperate fight with the Liberal Monarchists, Royer-Collard and C. Jordan, who accused them of compromising the existence of the Crown and of the Church itself in party interests. And after all they lacked the support of the Right, whose demands they believed themselves to be satisfying. But how was anyone ever to satisfy the passion for reaction which carried away the leaders and the speakers of the Right, Delalot, Donnadieu, and Castelbajac, who boldly and publicly asserted that they held the ecclesiastical authority superior to that of Parliament, and that the Crown was entitled to deal with the relations between Church and State without consulting the nation, as in the good old days?

What chance was there with men like these of realising Richelieu's hope of forming a Cabinet of "reconciliation and forgiveness"? Hatred begat hatred. The Counter-Revolution woke up revolutionary passions among the Liberals and in the masses. The intrigues of the Congregation encouraged and indeed forced its opponents into similar secrecy. Officers and former soldiers of the Empire, now disgraced and persecuted, conspired together without any precise object (this especially occurred on receipt of the news of Napoleon's death at St Helena), and, watched in their wine-shops by the police, sang Béranger's popular ditties to the glory of the mighty but vanquished past. They looked to the liberal and generous youth of the bourgeoisie, whether republican or not, to Buchez, Augustin Thierry, Jouffroy, Pierre Leroux, Trélat, Guinard, to supply teachers and leaders. Thus in the first months of 1822, the so-called "sales of French charcoal" were started in Paris and the provinces on the model of Italian carbonarism and by the initiative of Bazard and Dugiez. "Seeing that might is not right, and that the Bourbons have been brought in again by the foreigners, the charcoal-burners hereby unite to restore to the French nation its right of choosing the Government it prefers." They hoped for a Republic, but would have accepted the Empire. Civil war was smouldering over the country, when the Richelieu Cabinet, unable to do anything before the secret plotting, began to show signs of disintegration.

It had but one hour of credit and authority in the Chamber, and that was when it raised the import duties and re-established a system of protection favourable to the financial schemes of the great land-owners and to the manufactures of the bourgeoisie who required the help of the Government against the vigorous English competition. But on the day that it asked for the continuance of the Censorship of the Press, it found itself defenceless before the simultaneous attacks from the Right and from the Left. Buffeted by these parliamentary storms, the ship of the Ministry was breaking up; and the crew no longer listened to the voice of their commander. The Ministers without office, Lainé and Corbière, who had been admitted as supernumeraries in 1821, demanded a greater share in the administration, and were supported openly by Chateaubriand, who returned from Berlin for that express purpose, and secretly by the Comte d'Artois; but no such share could be given them save by the sacrifice of more moderate colleagues, and these, Baron Pasquier, de Serre, and Mounier refused on their side to part with. Richelieu could no longer tell to which side to listen; Louis XVIII was his only resource in this crisis, and he began to fail him.

The sceptical old King, as unfeeling at heart as his grandfather Louis XV, had like him certain curious cravings for intimate friendship. He always had confidants, the Duc de Blacas in 1815, and Decazes in 1817. The Royalists, Vicomte Sosthène de la Rochefoucauld, the Duc de Doudeauville, and de Civrac, Cardinal de la Luzerne, all champions of the Throne and Altar, with the view of upsetting Decazes, introduced discreetly into the King's circle a young lady, who had come to the Tuileries as the bearer of a petition, and who returned there repeatedly even after the fall of Decazes, at the royal summons, to plead her cause. This lady, known as Mme de Cayla, who was the mere mouthpiece and puppet of the Ultras, had the ear and the growing favour of the King. In August 1821 she had succeeded in undermining the position of the Duc de Richelieu; and when that Minister, wearied with the demands of the Right, let Villèle and Corbière go, he himself sealed the ruin of his own authority. Perhaps it might have lasted longer, had he taken the advice of Pasquier and dissolved the Chamber. This would have put the King also to a choice between himself and his opponents; moreover he might thus have got a more obedient majority from the elections. But he dared not. The majority had him at its mercy and became still more exacting after the October elections of 1821, which increased its numbers by about fifty.

External events and influences once more came in to decide the fate of Richelieu's policy. While the crisis created by the Spanish revolution continued, another broke out in the East, where the Greeks revolted against the Sultan. Metternich had been unable to obtain from the Congress of Laybach any decision on the affairs of Spain or of the East, but had obtained a mandate to restore the King of the two Sicilies. He intervened at Turin, and at Modena dealt like a conqueror with the princes of Italy. The contrast between the activity of Austria and the inaction of France deeply offended the national pride of the French. The Liberals demanded that the Ministry should not abandon the Greeks to the tender mercies of the Turks, or the Italians to the arbitrary decrees of the Holy Alliance and the domination of Austria. The Royalists on their side were indignant at the abandonment of Ferdinand VII in Spain. Everyone called for French action abroad, each for very different reasons. If the decision had rested on Richelieu alone, it would first have taken the shape of French intervention in Spain in concert with Russia, which would have pleased the Right. But his colleagues, Pasquier, Minister of Foreign Affairs, and Rayneval, an Under-Secretary of State, had up to that time succeeded in diverting the King and his Council from an enterprise that might have embroiled us with the rest of Europe, simply to please Russia (February 1821). The disappointment had been great in Russia, as also in Paris, where the Royalists were

3—2

induced by Pozzo di Borgo, the Russian Ambassador, with the approval of the Comte d'Artois, to engage in a plot for the fall of the Ministry, Mme de Cayla being still their principal agent. Public opinion seemed to be on their side. "France," said Metternich, "is entering the path of conquest. The motives which started the former Republic and Empire upon that perilous course are once more becoming factors in the popular sentiment."

In July 1821 it looked as if an opportunity was being presented for a French intervention which might unite France and all its factions. In the month of June the Greeks asserted their independence in the now liberated Peloponnesus, and appealed for recognition to the religious sentiments of the Russians and of the Tsar. In the teeth of his own people and his religion, the Tsar could not possibly follow the Holy Alliance any longer in insisting upon the validity of the sovereign rights of the Sultan; and on June 26 he notified the fact to the Turks, to the Great Powers, and to Metternich. In France, the royalist Ultras on the one side were carried away into Philhellenism by the eloquence of Chateaubriand and docile to the influence of the Comte d'Artois and Pozzo di Borgo; the Liberals on the other, who were even more philhellenist, were irritated at the rough treatment of the Italians by Austria; thus the whole nation, breathing vengeance and war, put pressure upon the Ministers in the month of July to declare war in the East on behalf of the Greeks, in concert with Russia.

The first idea of the Ministry was to fit out a strong naval squadron; and for once all parties united in approving joint action between France and Russia. Churchmen, Royalists, Bonapartists and Liberals all acclaimed this popular war, in which France began to see a chance of wiping out the defeats of 1815, and of getting compensations in Anatolia or the Troad, or, better still, in Belgium, and on the left bank of the Rhine. When the news came of the recall of the Russian ambassador, Strogonoff, from Constantinople, on August 21, 1821, and at the same time of the massacres in Chios and Crete, the moment of recovery seemed very near. But this revival of France, skilfully handled by Metternich in the German and English Foreign Offices, was quite enough to excite the suspicions of the Powers which had combined to oppose her at Chaumont. Conferences took place at Hanover in October 1821, which were attended by the King of England, his Minister Londonderry, Metternich, and M. de Bulow, the Prussian Minister, who had taken alarm at the ambitious propositions of Chateaubriand. These resulted in the address of a sort of ultimatum to Russia from the three Powers. The Tsar, as he told our ambassador de Ferronays, could not consider without some misgiving the chances of a war "which must involve some intricate combinations, especially as he could no longer count upon the cooperation, or even the acquiescence, of his allies." He therefore left the Greeks and France to their fate. It was to no purpose that Richelieu, indignant at this desertion, put before him vividly the danger of French anger, for "the French nation is tired of its inaction." On behalf of his master, and of the whole house of Bourbon, he dreaded the effect of this disappointment. "Ministers," he wrote, "are never so near their fall as when they are despised by those whose obedience they ought to command." The Tsar would listen to nothing; and it was Richelieu (not to say Louis XVIII himself) who had to put up with the consequences of the national anger and contempt.

The debate on the Address, on the re-assembling of the Chambers, Nov. 21, 1821, gave the signal for an attack on both Right and Left from the very men who had demanded the war. All parties united against the Ministry, as they had, though only momentarily, united on behalf of the Greeks. Ultras, such as La Bourdonnaye and Castelbajac, Vaublanc, the mouthpiece of the Liberals, and General Foy, congratulated the King, with an irony which revealed their malice, upon his "friendly" relations with the Powers, and upon the existing peace, "assuming always that it is not incompatible with the honour of the country and the dignity of the Crown." The Ministers Pasquier and de Serre tried hard to insist upon the omission of the last quoted words as insulting both to themselves and to the Crown, but in vain. Of the 274 members of the Chamber, 74 only showed any inclination to satisfy their demands. All the rest, whether Liberals, Bonapartists, Republicans, Royalists, or Ultras, with scarcely an exception, were parties to the plot and had decided on the ruin of the Ministry. Louis XVIII at first indignantly declined to receive the Address. Pasquier at once resigned office as Foreign Minister, but Richelieu refused to accept his resignation, and the King was not inclined to grant his insulted Ministry the dissolution which they demanded as a right. Thenceforward the Duke did not dare to require the attendance of Baron Pasquier within the precincts of Parliament, where his very presence bred anger and abuse.

On Dec. 8, 1821, five members of the Cabinet, Pasquier, Mounier, Anglès, Simeon, and Portal, formally requested their chief either to demand of the King the dissolution of this new "incredible" Chamber, or to accept their resignations. They were naturally tired of the ceaseless struggle with the Right, in which their own friends were passing over to the enemy through their disgust at the concessions made, and made in vain, to the extreme sections. Disheartened by the desertion of Russia which had brought him to this pass, and unable to accept the task of carrying on the government without the Right and against them, the Duc de Richelieu attempted another negotiation with the Comte d'Artois, the secret abettor of the audacity and insolence of the Ultras. He reminded him that he had only accepted power on a formal promise from the Count of his steady support among his own friends. The Prince evaded the charge, "thus," asserted Richelieu, "breaking his word as a gentleman." He addressed his complaints to the King, who however, under the influence of Mme de Cayla, was disposed to resign himself very philosophically to the troubles of his Ministers, and whose only consoling word was a jest. "What can you expect? He plotted against Louis XVI, and against me: he will finish by plotting against himself."

Richelieu left to their fate these selfish princes whom he had served so well, and retired on Dec. 21, after the collapse of his loyal attempt to bring back the French nation to the monarchic faith of their fathers. His only mistake had been in reckoning too much on the wisdom of the Royalists for assistance in this difficult task, and on the Bourbons, who betrayed and deserted him. His fall prepared the ground for theirs.

CHAPTER II

MINISTRY OF VILLÈLE

The intrigue to which Richelieu succumbed was such public property that 24 hours were almost sufficient to enable his enemies to turn out a complete and homogeneous Cabinet. The Premiership, with the Ministry of Finance, was entrusted to M. de Villèle; the Vicomte de Montmorency took the Foreign Office, Victor Duc de Belluno the Ministry of War, M. Corbière the Interior, M. de Peyronnet the Ministry of Justice, the Marquis de Clermont-Tonnerre the Ministry of Marine. Besides the great ministerial departments, the secondary offices of State underwent many changes owing to the resignation of their holders. The headship of Police passed from Baron Mounier to M. Franchet; the prefecture of the Seine from Comte Anglès to M. G. Delavau, a member of the Bench of the Court of Paris; the Under-Secretaryship of Foreign Affairs from M. de Rayneval to a new and unknown man, M. Herman; the Post-Office from M. Dupleix de Mézy to the Duc de Doudeauville. Chateaubriand took the place of Decazes in the London embassy; his friend the Duc de Laval-Montmorency went to that of Rome, Baron Hyde de Neuville to Constantinople. All the great prefectures, Lyons, Bordeaux, Lille, Nantes, Macon, Toulouse, and Besançon were given to tried Royalists. The Abbé Frayssinous was given charge of the University as High Master; a gentleman of the household of the Duc d'Angoulême, a Comte de Bordesoulle, took the Polytechnic School.

These changes, by which the no-compromise members of the Right secured power, indicated clearly the method by which they proposed to keep it. After all their fulminations against Napoleonic tyranny, after the reproaches they had hurled against their Liberal opponents for the same practices, they lost no time in appropriating the machinery needed to force their designs upon France. "Centralisation," said Royer-Collard, "has made us a nation of slaves to an irresponsible bureaucracy, which is itself centralised in the hands of the Government of which it is the instrument." In Paris all decisions were taken, from Paris all orders were transmitted—a system which tended more and more to swallow up the whole life of France; and from Paris the Ultras were now preparing, on the example of Napoleon, to administer all the provinces by means of prefects, magistrates, military governors, and revenue officers. The Restoration was the golden age of officials, who took possession of France on behalf of the Royalist party, and held it for long. Prefects nominated members of the Departmental Councils and mayors, and took part in the election of deputies. Their active and ever-suspicious police kept a close eye on every movement of their opponents, and upon the report of the slightest conspiracy handed them over to an obedient magistracy whose duty was not to judge, but to oblige. Soon the officials would feel themselves to be such complete masters of the field that they would treat the country almost as conquered territory with the arrogance and carelessness attributed to them by Ymbert in his work on "Administrative Morals," published in 1825.

What mattered all this to the Royalists or M. de Villèle their leader, so long as this conquest brought them nearer the desired object, the return to the Ancien Régime? Moreover they hit upon another method (which, like Chateaubriand, they also borrowed from Napoleon) for imposing their programme upon France. "As a return for the restoration of their privileges they proposed to offer her—glory." The time seemed propitious, and the necessary elements were already there; thus their return to the "good old time" could be effected by an appeal to the revived glories of the Revolution and the Empire, with an army ready for enterprise, and a nation hungry for revenge.

Nevertheless the head of the Cabinet, the Comte de Villèle, who was taking these steps to ensure the permanence of his rule (which in fact lasted for six years, first under Louis XVIII, and afterwards under Charles X), was not one of those leaders who are inclined blindly to follow his own troops. A shrewd and practical man of business, with a firm and precise appreciation of realities, he was not one to become so intoxicated with success, like the Royalists whom he had led to victory, as to forget the lesson of 1816, the sudden defeat brought about by a premature and awkward attempt to realise profits. His plan was to proceed by well-secured stages, and not by sudden outbursts which would alarm the country. No less desirous than the Ultras of a permanent return to the Ancien Régime, he would have it little by little, and without hurry. "With a society so diseased" (and by disease he meant the plague of revolution) "much time and much circumspection is needed, if we are not to lose the fruit of many years' toil. To know where I ought to go, never to stray from the path, to take one step in the right direction whenever possible, never in any circumstances to run the risk of having to retreat—these, my friends, are the gifts God has given me, and are, I firmly believe, the needs of the time in which I have taken charge."

For similar reasons Villèle was less inclined than his followers to be deceived by the mirage of an active foreign policy. He trusted less to the effect of swaggering and costly foreign enterprises than to the results of a sound internal administration to strengthen and speed the restoration of the Ancien Régime. He hoped to make this acceptable to the French people by giving them sound finance and prosperous business. And thus from 1821 onwards the Royalists, while trying to realise their entire programme, were to do so under the guidance and by the prudent counsels of a chief who had often to restrain their ardour. And the nation, sunk by his skilful handling in slumber, enjoyed seven years of almost uninterrupted peace, well-being, and material prosperity.

Hence it was that the breach between the Cabinet which fell with such a crash in December 1821 before the coalition of the Right, and that installed in its place by the intrigues of the Comte d'Artois in 1822 at the head of an ultra-royalist majority, was less noticeable. The mischief that the breach might have caused to the Bourbon Monarchy was diminished; and the apparently impending crisis was postponed, thanks to the force that Villèle could dispose of, and the skill with which he carried out that task.

His first action was to take energetic and severe measures against the conspiracies into which the antidynastic, and even the antiministerial, parties in France had been forced by the repressive system borrowed by the Bourbons from Napoleon. Having a magistracy obedient to his commands, Villèle took ceaseless pains to present to the world isolated movements reported to him by his police, and no sooner discovered than crushed, as if they had been parcels of a vast conspiracy of the Liberals, not only against the Crown, but against society itself.

Thus it happened that some youths belonging to the military school at Saumur were arrested in December 1821 for conspiring in favour of Napoleon II, the conspiracy being nothing more than a single demonstration. At Belfort and Neubrisach the police arrested some officers on active service, and others who had retired (among them an ex-colonel of the Guard, by name Pailhès), on simple suspicion. At Marseilles documents were found in the pockets of two retired officers, Vallé and Salmon, which were supposed to be evidence of a conspiracy. There was at any rate a singular coincidence between the advent of a strong-handed Ministry and the discovery of so many conspiracies.

Three months later, General Berton, a retired officer, after trying to seduce from their duty the superior officers of certain Breton regiments, made an attempt with a handful of men on Saumur and on Thouars in Vendée (February 23 and 24, 1822). The hopeless enterprise had no consequences beyond the headlong flight of its instigator, who, after a first escape, fell into a trap set for him by the police, in 1822. In the meanwhile the lower orders in Paris, excited by a Catholic mission started in the Church of the Petits Pères, joined the students of the Quartier Latin in sundry disorderly demonstrations, which the police were able to cope with easily. At La Rochelle a line regiment, worked upon by its non-commissioned officers, was on the point of mutiny, when the colonel, a former *émigré*, arrested four sergeants, Bories, Pommier, Raoulx, and Gobin, on the charge of trafficking with secret societies, and handed them over to the police. Finally, at the moment when the revolutionists of Belfort were to be tried, another officer, a half-pay colonel of dragoons, named Caron, tried to raise a mutiny among the eastern regiments by shouts of "Vive l'Empereur," but was caught in a trap set by the military authorities.

The civil and military courts vied with one another in a pitiless shower of death-sentences throughout the year, at Tours, Poitiers, Colmar, Strasbourg, and Paris, upon such of the authors of these crimes, or their accomplices, as they had been able to catch. The four sergeants of La Rochelle were executed in Paris on September 21; Caron at

Strasbourg on September 1, Berton and two friends at Poitiers on September 6 and 7; Vallé mounted the scaffold at Toulouse on June 10. The public encouragement that Lafayette and d'Argenson with certain other deputies of the Liberal party had given to these attempts at insurrection, which after all were not very dangerous, gave the Ministers a capital pretext for taxing the whole Opposition with crime. The speech of the Public Prosecutor, General Marchangy, at the trial of the four sergeants left no room for doubt as to the capital which the Government proposed to make out of the troubles in Touraine and in the East against its opponents. Their main object was to induce a terrified France to believe in the existence "of a vast conspiracy against society, the family, and the towns, which might well plunge the country once more, as in 1793, into all the horrors of anarchy." By affecting the garb of a saviour of a society threatened by the Jacobins, Villèle obtained all the authority he required for carrying on an absolute government to please himself and his friends, the Ultras. The fear of anarchy, and of a turbulent and insurgent democracy, as handled by the judges in his pay, provided him, as they did for Bonaparte after the Revolution, with the means of organising despotism.

In January 1822 de Peyronnet, Minister of Justice, brought into Parliament a Bill on the Press, which was to place it wholly under the orders and at the discretion of Ministers. For the future no more journals were to appear without royal licence; every sheet was to be submitted to the King's proctor, who had the sole right to pronounce as to its political tendencies, and to suspend, and even entirely prohibit, its publication. Villèle had also in hand a subsidiary Bill, reviving against press offences another enactment of his predecessors, which would give the final quietus to the misdeeds of journalists; it took away the jurisdiction of the jury in press offences, and gave it once more to the royal courts, whose judges were the obedient servants of the Government. The first clause of this Draconian law inflicted sentences of five years' imprisonment and penalties varying from £12 to £240 on journals or periodical prints "which outraged or ridiculed the religion of the State, or attempted to rouse hatred or contempt of the King's Government or of any class or classes of citizens." It was obvious that this sort of legislation endowed the Ministry and the Crown with extraordinary powers in favour of the Church and the nobility. It was a weapon for the use of the Government in the warfare it was about to wage against the laicising and levelling spirit of society as constituted by the Revolution.

The two Bills very soon became law (on March 18, 1822) without amendment; and the majority of over fifty by which they were carried was an earnest of their future value as a party asset. The nation, excluded from the discussion and terrorised, gave in to the schemes of the Royalists, and put itself at the mercy of the Crown, the Cabinet, and the Hierarchy. It was useless for the champions of liberty, Benjamin Constant and Royer-Collard, to protest in magnificent language, during the often heated discussions of the Bills, against the "parliamentary Jacobinism, the legislation unsupported by argument, which recalled the system of the Revolutionary tribunals." It was useless for Sebastiani to denounce, in a direct and vigorous attack, the danger arising to the Monarchy from this step towards the complete ascendency of the party of the Ancien Régime. Villèle had taken his measures for minimising the effect of these criticisms more effectively than the authors of the "White Terror." He had succeeded in preserving the outward forms of legality; if the Acts were oppressive and obviously partisan, public opinion had been carefully prepared for their reception, and they had the approval of regular parliamentary votes.

Soon another advance was made, after the partial elections of May 1822 which left the Chambers in a condition still more favourable to the designs of Ministers. The prefects and judges had handled the electors, now fewer in number, with skill. Monarchists of acknowledged principles and zeal had been placed in the chairs of the Electoral Committees, and officials had been ordered to support the Government candidates under penalty of dismissal. Of eighty-six deputies returned, fifty-four were out-and-out supporters of the Government. And to make sure, Villèle had been careful to bring in early in January a Revenue Bill very favourable to the interests of landed proprietors and the great manufacturers, who thought it quite reasonable that by this means the cost of living for the many should be augmented for the benefit of the few. The mere announcement of this Bill, which was carried with enthusiasm in the Chambers in July 1822, had been enough to bring the whole electoral body to the side of the Government.

Sebastiani described the position of the Monarchic Right in these words: "By artificial and lying elections, that party has flooded the Chamber; through the Chamber it has captured the Ministry, and through the Ministry the administration of the country; what is left to society, or at any rate to the portion of society that does not belong to that party? The Liberty of the Press and the Jury-system are the twin pillars of the Constitution; deprive us of that security, and your party has nothing to fear; it may legislate as freely for the destruction of the new interests, as the Revolution did for the destruction of the old."

The truth of this was to be seen in the rapidity with which Villèle completed the task begun in 1821 of subjecting the schools to the Church. The President of the University Council, who was already possessed of large powers, once more, as in the reign of Napoleon, by an order of June 5, 1822, became Grand Master of the University with absolute rights of police control over the professors and their curricula. And when a priest, in the person of Abbé de Frayssinous, had been appointed Grand Master, the objects of the Clerical party were completely exposed. Their scheme of action was to keep the Napoleonic University, with its monopoly of instruction, its severities of discipline, and its well-nigh military hierarchy, so as to be able to oppose it to every form of instruction suspected of unsoundness, on the understanding of course that it served the Catholic Faith with as much zeal as it had served the Imperial Legend before its abolition. In his first circular, addressed to the Rectors of Universities, the Grand Master requested that, before all things, the youth of France should be brought up on religious and monarchic ideas, and that no teacher should be appointed who had not a certificate of religious knowledge. Guizot and Cousin were obliged to resign their chairs at the Sorbonne, the first as a Protestant, the second as a philosopher. The School of Medicine was closed in November 1822, and only reopened after the dismissal of two teachers suspected of heresy, Vauquelin and de Jussieu. Next came the turn of the Normal Schools, whose students were dismissed and scattered among the Provincial Academies. And yet there were some impatient Royalists who charged the Abbé de Frayssinous with weakness and hesitation!

These men would have in fact preferred to see the University completely ruined rather than maintain it as an adjunct to the Church; for they had been establishing rigidly Catholic schools over the whole country, and objected strongly to their being shackled in their progress by the University monopoly. They could not appreciate the more skilful tactics of the Grand Master, who was benefiting the Church by taking possession of the State schools, and who at the same time did not deny himself the pleasure of befriending the private Catholic schools. Moreover all these champions of the good cause, whether cold-blooded tacticians or hot-blooded enthusiasts, had a free hand under a Ministry which allowed Jesuits to hold the professorships in the Theological Colleges, and collect their audiences at the expense of the lay schools and the University. Indeed it looked as if the royalist party, in its zeal for a return to the past, was trying to get as far back as possible into the Middle Ages, or to the theocracy which was dear to the "priestly party."

The country, thankful after the long wars of the Revolution and the Empire for a dearly won peace, deprived of the advice of the Press and of every electoral right, without uttering a word, allowed Villèle and his friends thus to dispose of its power, and even its opinions, and to crush the few remnants of opposition, now scarcely to be found except in the Chamber of Peers. It was, with a very slight difference, a restored Imperial system manipulated for the benefit of the Bourbons and the Monarchists. At the end of 1822, after a year of this administration, the Cabinet could proudly point out to its followers the results (it is true that the concessions made by Richelieu had paved the way for them) that had been won with such ease, and above all with such tact—"the security of the individual, the complete guarantee for the execution of the law, the advancing prosperity of the finances, the diminution of taxation, and a well-filled Treasury." Without a jar and with the good-will of a consenting people, Villèle was drawing the country on towards the object of himself and his party, the gradual substitution, with the help of the Church, of the old for the modern system, which might have been deemed since 1789 to be solidly and eternally established. What seemed impossible at the fall of Napoleon seemed now to be approaching realisation. By a skilful use of the Napoleonic system, the Bourbons, who had had such difficulty in restoring themselves, were on the way to restoring the Ancien Régime. Thanks to Villèle, the impossibility of the year 1817 was being accomplished in 1822.

The Ultras then determined, against the opinion of their leader and with a view to make him move faster and farther, to compel France to forget, or possibly accept, their despotic rule, as under Napoleon, in the glory of foreign enterprise. This was the plan so dear to Chateaubriand; and he was no bad judge of the state of the French mind. His political creed was formulated in the *Conservateur*, a journal founded by him in 1819, to which Victor Hugo and his friends contributed. He scoffed at Liberals "flaunting in the glorious garb of heroes," and was resolved to fight them for the favour of the people and of the next generation, whose taste for battles, past or future, he, like the Bonapartists, would willingly indulge. The check given to this programme by the hesitation of Richelieu and Louis XVIII to interfere in Eastern affairs without the Tsar and the assent of Metternich had seriously angered the poet-statesman. In company with the Monarchists he had made Richelieu pay for it. The Duc de Montmorency, three days after he joined the Ministry, pointed out to them that, in default of Greece, "Spain was the true battle-field for the restoration of the military spirit in France and the creation of armed forces for the Bourbon." The French ambassador at Madrid, M. de Lagarde, was instructed to stir up King Ferdinand VII to resist his subjects, and he paid him subsidies to get up an absolutist *coup d'état*. He bade him look out for the appearance of a French army corps to be sent to the Pyrenees, on the pretext of forming a hygienic cordon against yellow fever, while an uncompromising Royalist, General Francisco Gesia, recruited and intrigued at Bayonne.

As it happened, Alexander I, after having with much hesitation diverted his attention from Greece and the East, had decided at the request of Louis XVIII to return to his projected intervention in favour of monarchy in Spain.

And Ferdinand, urged by French diplomacy, addressed a successful appeal to him in February 1822. In April the Tsar forwarded to Metternich the sketch of certain strong measures to which Tatischef was instructed to obtain his assent. Metternich would probably have preferred peace, now that he had diverted Russia from the East and extended the authority of Austria over all Italy; but he accepted the position with a good grace, and on June 13, 1822, expressed himself in these terms to his friend, M. de Caraman, the French Ambassador at Vienna: "We are ready to back up France by all means in our power: she has only to tell us what she wants. In this matter you take the leading rôle." His acceptance was thus complete and formal, and linked itself in a very marked way with the support which the Tsar had given to the policy of France.

France now fired the mines that she had been laying in Spain. In Navarre and Catalonia the Royalists rose at the call of General Quesada, to deliver Ferdinand from the yoke of the Liberals. At Madrid the Royal Guards, encouraged by the King, and supported by the French ambassador, tried to get up a rising against the Cortes "in favour of an absolute Monarchy"; and, with a little more courage and decision on the part of the King, it would have been successful (July 7, 1822). But Ferdinand abandoned his friends in cowardly style to the mercy of a Radical leader named Ruge, while he was secretly imploring the aid of Louis XVIII. His cause was not an easy one to defend; but for the diplomacy of the French Royalists, which was henceforth directed by Chateaubriand, any occasion was good which would give France the opportunity of displaying her strength and wiping out as an invader the ignominy of her own invasion.

They found their opportunity at the Congress which the sovereigns, on separating at Laybach in May 1821, had agreed to hold a few months later, and which met at Verona on May 1, 1822, for the settlement of the Italian question.

The English envoys scented the intrigue and the intention of the French to cross the Pyrenees, and declared both to be "reprehensible in principle"; but the Ministers of Austria, Russia, and Prussia came to an understanding with France early in August to the effect that the Spanish question should occupy almost the entire time of the Congress. The French plenipotentiaries were appointed on August 22. "This Congress is my own secret and my hope," said Chateaubriand. At first he had proposed to claim the leading part, and challenged the right of his superior officer, Montmorency, to represent France; but Montmorency refused to give way. They vied one with another to get the credit of having proposed the war in the Congress, so as to have a claim on the Royalists for services rendered to the Crown and to France. Villèle reconciled them by appointing both.

The first benefit that Villèle succeeded in extracting from the affair on his own account was the Presidency of the Council, which he took over on September 4. In the next place he made use of the rivalry between the two plenipotentiaries to neutralise both for the advantage of his own more moderate foreign policy. The war into which his party was trying to drag him gave him much anxiety. The hostility of public as well as official opinion in England, the prospect of an extension of the quarrel to America, with the possibility that the Tsar might force France to take part in it; the probability that the English might be beforehand with her there—all alarmed him. He had taken a formal promise from Montmorency, before leaving for Verona, that he would refuse to make any sort of intervention in Spain, until England, "ever skilful (he observed) in getting well out of a scrape, had engaged neither to ask for, nor to accept any further acquisitions in America."

But a man of Montmorency's birth was not going to

take orders from M. de Villèle, or to show less courage than Chateaubriand. Both of them, carried away by their high spirit, were convinced that with 50,000 French soldiers America itself might be torn from the grasp of England and of the insurgents: "France under good leadership will dictate the law." "Caution and prudence were ignored; the time for decisive action had arrived." On October 20 they requested a mandate from the Congress for the intervention of France in Spain. With confidence increased by the flattery of Alexander, and yielding to the seductions of so great a potentate, Chateaubriand negotiated on a large scale, attacking every problem, even the restoration of independence to Poland and the emancipation of Greece. On October 30 Austria, always and wholly at the service of the Royalist policy, and Russia, so marvellously obliging, declared themselves ready to support the diplomatic and military proposals of France.

The general upset that the representatives of France appeared to be proposing at Verona was by no means calculated to please either M. de Villèle or Louis XVIII. On the return of Montmorency from Italy to the duties of his Ministry, full of the glory of his initiation into the craft, he expected to make a success in the Chamber, where the new elections had added thirty votes to the royalist majority, and he expected to be able thus to force the blundering strategy of the Extreme Right upon the Cabinet. But M. de Villèle put a sudden stop to the forward action of France, which he described as "an unlucky business."

He refused to break with Spain, or to recall our ambassador, even if the Continental Powers threatened to withdraw theirs. The persistent neutrality of England led him to a constant suspicion that that commercial Power had come to a sudden understanding with the insurgents in Spain and America, which would create both scandal and damage in the French market. As between the neutrality which the

English Tory Cabinet was still asserting on November 20, 1822, and the ultimatum addressed on November 17 by the Congress of Verona to the Spanish Cortes, Villèle advised Louis XVIII to reserve his judgment. Some days later Chateaubriand also returned from Italy, bearing the formal resolutions of the expiring Congress, which finally broke up on December 14. The King had then to determine whether to repudiate his own plenipotentiaries and risk the wrath of the Tsar, or to conquer the resistance of M. de Villèle, with the danger of alienating the English, on whose behalf Wellington was then visiting Paris with menaces in one hand and the offer of combined action in the other.

Trusting to his friends in Parliament, Montmorency proposed to put the King formally to the choice. He desired to force upon him the recall of the French ambassador at Madrid, in order to please the Continental Powers, and to separate from England forthwith, as her cooperation could not be counted upon. Villèle opposed him in the Cabinet (December 24, 1822), and threatened to resign; and Louis XVIII decided in his favour in these words: "Other sovereigns may without injury to themselves and without shocking their own sense of duty abandon Spain and her King to the Revolution and to the exclusive influence of England. My duties are personal to myself; and I cannot break my relations with that country, and withdraw my ambassador from the Court of my nephew till the day when 100,000 French troops cross his frontier." Now this was just the sort of settlement which Villèle wished to postpone as long as possible. Montmorency resigned, and his resignation was accepted, December 25, 1822. The Royalists were furious; they had fully expected to realise with his assistance their dreams of an active policy, the glory of which would redound to the Legitimate Monarchy. They plotted to upset Villèle for the same reason that had operated on them the year before against Richelieu. At the same time they protested against the appointment of Chateaubriand as Minister of Foreign Affairs, in ignorance of the intrigue devised by him to satisfy their wishes.

For the ambition of Chateaubriand, who had been attentively watching the struggle between Montmorency and the Prime Minister, had suggested to him a stratagem which he would have criticised forcibly in an opponent. Concealing his secret desire to force France into action, forgetting his own attitude and language at Verona, and his dallyings with the Tsar, he had induced Villèle to believe that, having formerly been ambassador in England, he would be able as Minister for Foreign Affairs to induce France to return to an understanding with the English; and Villèle had given him the post he wanted, where Chateaubriand hoped to do "great things" in his "little Cabinet." No sooner had he accepted it than Louis XVIII, annoyed with the Spaniards for their rejection alike of his mediation and of their own King, at last declared war on January 28, 1823, and sent a message to the Chamber to that effect.

The postponement of this war had cost Villèle much of his authority among the royalist deputies, who let him feel it by electing to the Presidency of the Chamber M. de la Bourdonnaye, the most uncompromising of all the Ultras. They charged Villèle with lukewarmness towards the Spanish Royalists, while the Left blamed him for intervening against the Spanish Liberals. In vain did he try to propitiate them by making a perfect hecatomb of prefects (January 2 and 8, 1823) and replacing them by Ultras, who had been dismissed from the prefectures in 1816. Their anger was not to be abated. Chateaubriand made full use of it, and began to claim *vivâ voce,* as he did later in print, the whole credit of the affair. If the English expressed any complaint by the mouth of Canning, Chateaubriand directed his friend, the Comte de Marcellus, who had taken Chateaubriand's post in London, to make a spirited reply, knowing he could count on the support of Russia. "We are now," he wrote, "liberated from the tutelage of misfortune, and have regained our military rank in Europe." On February 25, delighted with playing the leading part, he displayed his eloquence in the tribune of the Chamber, in replying to the criticisms of Royer-Collard and General Foy. And the majority, overborne by his oratory, voted him a general licence to lead where he willed; refusing a hearing to his opponents, even to Manuel, who went so far on February 2, 1823, as to recall the memory of Louis XVI, the victim—and not without justice—of foreign intervention in the domestic affairs of his people.

The country seemed to be smitten with the same fever as the Parliament. It hailed with delight the first victories of French troops led by Generals of the Empire, the Ducs de Belluno, Reggio, and Conegliano, and Generals Molitor and Bourdessoule, under the supreme command of the Duc d'Angoulême (April 1823). On May 24 came the news of their entry into Madrid without opposition, and, after two months (July 26), of the decisive victory of Campillo d'Arenas, which gave them the whole of Spain. The Duc d'Angoulême pursued the insurgent Government to Cadiz, and dictated terms of peace to them at the Trocadero (August 31, 1823). One month later, the Cortes, who had kept the King a prisoner at Cadiz, surrendered (September 28); and Ferdinand was at liberty to return to his capital and reinstate an absolute Monarchy amid festivals in honour of the French army.

On December 2, 1823, the Duc d'Angoulême returned to Paris, surrounded by his staff of ex-Imperialists, and riding at the head of the battalions which had conquered at the Trocadero—"a force that challenged comparison with the best corps of the Grande Armée." This triumphal return was a "national festival," and the occasion of a series of banquets, illuminations, and a general flourish of trumpets.

The French forgot the object of the expedition, in which they had played the part of the Prussians in Argonne, and simply applauded the success of their arms. They congratulated themselves on having thus recovered "all their military glory and their former influence in Europe." It is needless to remark that the services rendered to France by the Bourbon Monarchy, whose restoration seemed to be at last an accomplished fact, through this barren and expensive war, were not to be compared with those which it had rendered in the past, when, under Talleyrand and Richelieu, and without a war, it had secured peace, security of frontiers, and the respect of foreigners from the year 1814 onwards. And yet the royal cause had reaped—as Chateaubriand hoped—more benefit from these easily-won victories than from its solid merits. The poet had judged better than the business man, and boasted of it. "The glory and the prosperity of my country," he writes, "date from my entrance into the Ministry."

Villèle let him have his say, and, as a practical statesman, made use of this national truce to complete the victories within his Cabinet and in his party. His first care was to increase and consolidate his authority in the Chambers. The Chamber of Peers had received no fresh blood, as had the Lower House, since 1820, and was still the asylum and trysting-place of the Liberals and of the Right Centre, who had possessed the confidence of the King up to the assassination of the Duc de Berry. In all the reactionary legislation, and in their work of counter-revolution in Spain, the Ministry had come into collision with the Chamber of Peers, with the opposition of men as frankly hostile to despotism as to anarchy, to the Ancien Régime as to the excesses of the Revolution, men such as Comte Molé, the Duc de Broglie, Baron de Barante, and their friends. In December 1823, after having secured the cooperation of the Generals who had returned as victors from Spain, M. de Villèle proposed to the

King to break down this opposition by the creation of twenty-seven peers chosen from the safest of his own friends; among them were bishops, royalist officers, Vicomtes d'Agout and de la Brunerie, the Comtes de Mesnard and de Bourbon Musset, civil servants of legitimist views, Lainé, the Comtes de Tournon and de Breteuil, deputies such as the Comtes de Vogüé, de Marcellus, de Kergorlay, de Rastignac.

At the same time, he wished to profit by the success of the Spanish expedition by giving some fixity of tenure to the majority belonging to the Extreme Right which had gradually grown up since 1821 in the Chamber of Deputies through the system of partial renewal. With a view to its duration, Villèle proposed that the old Chamber should be dissolved, and that the new Chamber should, under direction of the Ministry, declare itself to be elected for a period of seven years without any renewals, after passing the necessary fundamental amendment of the Charter of the Constitution. His calculations were realised. The Chamber elected on February 26 and March 6, 1824, under vigorous administrative pressure, proved to be all that he could desire, "a regenerate Chamber" of ardent Royalists; in a House of 434 members, 17 Liberals owned their impotence before so crushing a majority. On April 6, the Peers considered the proposal for a septennial election of deputies, and gave it their unanimous approval. The argument advanced by M. de Villèle and his party in favour of a change, whose real object was to keep them for a length of time in power, was the example of the English House of Commons. But between the practical working of parliamentary government on the two sides of the English Channel there was this grave, nay essential, difference; that in France neither public opinion, nor the liberty of the Press, nor freedom of election any longer existed. The laws against the Press passed by the preceding Chamber were severe enough; and to these the Government had thought fit to add the rigorous censorship re-established at the end of 1822. The newspapers of the Left, the *Pilote* and the *Courrier*, were prosecuted pitilessly. A royalist association was formed for the purchase of the organs of the Liberal Press, as soon as they were reduced to the last straits by overwhelming fines. The Government placed its funds and its administrative powers at the disposal of its partisans; and when the Chamber thus elected to the order of the Government had established by a Statute dated 1824 seven years as the period of its existence, it simply became one more instrument of despotism all the more dangerous for its consciousness of now possessing unlimited power, and ready—we will not say to vote—to perpetrate any and every job.

The great party triumph that Villèle expected to win from these skilfully-combined manœuvres lay in the satisfaction of the demands put forward by the supporters of the Ancien Régime. On the return of the *émigrés* from Ghent in 1815, they had applied for the restoration of the estates they had lost in the Revolution, but were met by a positive refusal. The King had formally declared in the Charter that "the rights of existing proprietors are sacred and inviolable"; and had thus laid down without qualification that the holders of property confiscated since 1789, the so-called "national property," were not to be disturbed. Nevertheless the Royalists always felt that the restored Bourbons had a special obligation towards those whose properties had been confiscated, and who had sacrificed their fortunes in the service of their exiled King. Louis XVIII, while listening to their complaints, had to consider on the other hand the promises made at his accession. He had done his best to satisfy the one without breaking the other, by giving the former *émigrés* a preference when appointing to the better-paid posts at the Court, or to offices in the military and civil services. He had thus gained time and postponed the difficulty; but now in 1824 it was more urgent than ever, owing to the commanding position that the elections had given to the Royalists. Villèle bethought him of solving the problem by means of an indemnity, without upsetting possessory rights.

He was indeed "a great man for getting out of a difficulty," as Chateaubriand had dubbed him. Thanks to the peace, which had been only slightly interrupted by the brief expedition to Spain, and thanks to the system of protection which was fostering the industries of the country, the national finances were in 1824 in a really prosperous condition. The price of 5 per cent. State Annuities rose continuously in spite of the disasters which followed the fall of Napoleon; it reached par on February 15, 1824, and stood at 5 francs premium in May. Villèle conceived that the benefits conferred by sound administration under a monarchy ought not to be confined to the purchasers of Rentes, but should reach his own party and his adherents. It was a good opportunity too for reducing the rate of interest from 5 to 4 per cent. and thus diminishing the annual charge of 140,000,000 francs on a debt of 2,800,000,000 francs to 112,000,000.

In April 1824 Villèle brought the proposition for this conversion before the Chambers. To effect it, he offered the holders of Rentes in return for 100 francs at 5 per cent., scrip for 75 francs at 3 per cent., equivalent to 100 at 4 per cent., with the advantage of bringing the whole debt to a nominal 3 per cent. basis. He enlarged on the soundness of the royal administration of finance, and on the solidity of French fortunes, as proved by the marvellous success of an operation, which "bore witness to the prosperity of the nation, and obliterated the unlucky difference between the interest on the capital absorbed by the State indebtedness, and that employed in commerce, agriculture or manufactures. "If you wish to put new life into these three mainstays of the national prosperity," he said in conclusion, "turn upon them the flood-tide of your riches." Economy for the State, increased profits to all, and especially to manufacturers—surely these were arguments sufficient to justify the conversion, the burden of which would fall solely on the Rente-holders, many of whom were not Frenchmen!

A matter that Villèle, true to his policy of judicious regard for susceptibilities, said very little about, was the use to which he intended to put the saving that he was going to realise on the State debt. Had he intended to apply it to the further development of the public wealth, nothing could have been better. But he had already destined it to a very special object, which had been at bottom the origin and essential cause of the operation. It was very soon known that Villèle had arranged with certain foreign financiers for a new loan of 1,000,000,000 francs, the interest on which was to be secured on the savings realised out of the pockets of French Rente-holders. This "milliard" was the indemnity devised for the *émigrés*, the sublime conception of the financial reign of M. de Villèle, the laurel-crown of victory for his party. When the Bill came on for discussion, the Liberals, and C. Perier in particular, had an easy task in denouncing the injustice of the operation, the wrong done to the Rente-holders and to French citizens in general in favour of a very limited class, an aristocracy that had been justly punished in former days for conspiring and fighting against their own country by the side of foreign Powers for the maintenance of their class-privileges. But the majority of the House were aristocrats; and the Bill was passed without difficulty on May 4, 1824.

By the Chamber of Peers it was thrown out on June 1. The Liberal Opposition in that House, consisting of former officers of the Empire, men of the Revolution, Comtes Roy and Mollien, Pasquier and Talleyrand, all sworn foes of the *émigrés*, had no doubt been weakened by the new creations which Villèle had induced Louis XVIII to make: and it would have been beaten, but for the help of an important fraction of the Ultras who at the call of Chateaubriand voted against the Ministry.

Since the end of 1823, the ambition and the vanity of the great writer who wished to be also the great and only Minister were disturbed by the position taken up by Villèle after the success of the Spanish war, the honour and profit of which Chateaubriand had intended to reserve for himself. He had been used by the Prime Minister to upset M. de Montmorency at the Foreign Office; and, having accepted that Ministry himself, he dreamt of turning it to account by ousting Villèle from the Premiership. While Villèle tried his hardest to put a limit on the military enterprises in which he had joined to please Russia and the Ultras, and against his own judgment, Chateaubriand was considering the possibility of extending their field even as far as America, against other nationalities which the Tsar had for a long time been begging the Holy Alliance to bring back to the yoke of Ferdinand VII. "Nobody can guess the extent of accumulated mischief which the abuse of such a policy would cause," said the Prime Minister. And he strove to anticipate that mischief by trying to establish a better understanding with Canning, the English Minister, who saw in President Monroe's message a warning of the danger of any violent intervention in America, capable of throwing the States of the South into the arms of the United States of the North (December 1823). Chateaubriand was secretly proceeding, with the help of La Ferronays at Petrograd, to carry out the opposite policy which Alexander I wanted to force upon Louis XVIII. "The burden of the whole situation," they said in Russia, "must rest on his shoulders."

With the view of giving some authority to Chateaubriand, and a lesson to Villèle at the same time, the Tsar sent the first-named the insignia of his Orders, and to him only. The King of France, angry at the slight, forbade his Minister to accept the gift; while to Villèle he said, "This is a slap in the face for me from the Emperor Alexander, although it falls on your cheek. I dub you knight of my own Orders, which are at least worth his."

The tension between the two rivals increased during the spring of 1824. They were opposed on every point. At the creation of new Peers, Villèle struck out the names of every one of his colleague's candidates. At the discussion on the proposal to dissolve the Chamber, and elect another with a seven years' life, Chateaubriand alone objected, and proposed that the term of a deputy's service should be five years. If Villèle instructed M. de Polignac, the ambassador he had recommended for London, to arrange with Canning for a policy of non-intervention and of cultivation of the Spanish colonies, Chateaubriand, obedient to the wishes of the Tsar, invited England to add her signature to a threatening note which a Congress of the Holy Alliance was preparing to despatch across the Atlantic. The crisis broke out in the French Cabinet at the moment when Chateaubriand was engaged on this ill-timed transaction in London. In the debate on the indemnity to the *émigrés* in the Chamber of Peers, Chateaubriand declined to speak in support of the Government. He kept on stealthily urging his friends to fight the Villèle Ministry, by the defeat of which he hoped to secure the triumph of his own policy of activity abroad. Villèle could not possibly put up any longer with this inconsistent combination of vanity and disloyalty.

In the beginning of June 1824 the King was called upon to arbitrate between his two Ministers; and after the failure of the proposal to indemnify the *émigrés*, which he considered a neat solution of one of the most delicate problems of his reign, he did not hesitate in his decision. He gave Chateaubriand a curt dismissal (June 6) and appointed the Prime Minister to the Foreign Office *ad interim*. The foreign policy of France, hereby restored to its pacific course, seemed to be backing away from the Holy Alliance, to prefer non-intervention to the threats and ultimata of the Congress, in short, to follow Canning rather than Metternich and Pozzo di Borgo. On the other hand there was open war within the party which Villèle had led to victory and installed in power, a war which promised to be long and merciless. The editor of the *Débats*, in whose columns Chateaubriand poured out his wrath, and attacked his foes, told M. de Villèle that they would have no difficulty in upsetting his Ministry. All the papers on that side adopted the same method of violent and passionate attack. The Premier replied by the use and abuse of the censorship, and of police prosecutions, but the judges were against him. The Opposition, whom he believed to have been silenced for a long time, noticed the breach which Chateaubriand had made in the fortress of the Monarchy.

The failure of the Bill for indemnifying the *émigrés* had as its consequence the failure of another Bill intended to satisfy Clerical and Catholic demands. The Chamber of Peers declined to empower the King to establish religious orders of women in France by a mere Order in Council, or to permit them to buy and hold property. It would have also rejected a Bill for assimilating theft in a church, i.e. in a public place, with theft in an inhabited house, so as to make it similarly punishable by death or penal servitude, and creating the crime of sacrilege, had not Villèle, doubtful as to its success, prudently withdrawn it.

It was an ill-chosen moment for the men of the Ancien Régime to fall out one with another. They were on the point of reaching their proposed goal as described in July 1824 by one of their number, M. de Bertier, amid the applause of the Chamber; viz. legislation against sacrilege and in favour of the sanctity of marriage, the distribution of indemnities to the *émigrés* and the French Clergy on account of their confiscated property, revision of the Code in accordance with the principles of religion and Monarchism, re-establishment of Commissionerships and Provincial Councils, the reservation of high military rank to a privileged class; in short, the whole of the Ancien Régime, with the Jesuits to boot. An Order in Council of April 6, 1824, confirmed a grant of the franchise to the "Frères de la Doctrine Chrétienne," and required candidates for local office, civil or educational, to obtain an authorisation from their bishop. A Ministry of Ecclesiastical Affairs was created for Monseigneur de Frayssinous, and the King's Household Service (Maison du Roi) was re-established for the Duc de Doudeauville, with a lucrative appointment for his son, Vicomte Sosthène de la Rochefoucauld, both father and son being red-hot supporters of Throne and Altar. All this work was on the eve of completion; and to see it compromised by his own friends was more than Villèle could bear.

Meanwhile Chateaubriand confronted him, ever protesting against a Prime Minister who, after seeing the enthusiasm evoked by the victories of the Trocadero and Cadiz, could not be made to understand the advantage, nay, the necessity of energetic—and glorious—foreign activity on the part of France. When his friend Hyde de Neuville attempted by the favour of the Duc de Subserza, Minister of John VI, King of Portugal, to introduce French troops into Lisbon, and thence to go on to the attack of the independent empire created by Don Pedro in Brazil, that royalist patriot was repudiated by the French Government and recalled to Paris in very sharp language, on the demand of the English, disturbed and jealous; and this again exasperated Chateaubriand and his friends.

In the very midst of this quarrel, so fatal to the royalist party, King Loüis XVIII died (August 16, 1824). In spite of his wisdom and prudence, he had not succeeded in reconciling, as he perhaps desired, the Monarchy and the French nation. He died at the moment when the partisans of Crown and Church, who had established a sort of dictatorship over France, were splitting into two equally irreconcileable parties. And the restoration of the Bourbons, the work indeed of foreign arms, but one which he would gladly have made a permanent fact, and secured by the real services of the Crown to the nation, which at any rate had lasted as long as himself, turned out on the morrow of his death far frailer than the Royalists, blinded by their success, could believe.

CHAPTER III

THE REIGN OF CHARLES X

"I cannot think without a shudder," wrote Louis XVIII to his brother and successor, "of the moment after my death." The fears of Louis XVIII were to be justified by the event. The King who ascended the throne in 1824 as Charles X, and the nation as he found it on his accession, were not made to harmonise.

This prince, who had been well known for fifty years under the name of the Comte d'Artois, was the type of those great lords of the Ancien Régime whose frivolity had compromised the Monarchy before and during the Revolution, which "had taught them nothing." A man of pleasure and of sport, a dandy and at times eccentric, amiable and superficial, he had long been incapable of conceiving of any employment for his life but in using the privileges of his birth to serve his own pleasure. When the Revolution took the liberty of questioning those privileges, he was one of the first to disappear (in July 1789), in spite of the prohibition of Louis XVI, in order to ask foreign rulers to help him to maintain them. And when Europe had conquered France after twenty years of obstinate struggle, he was again the first to be seen at Nancy in the midst of the victors, with the white cockade still pinned to his hat, and waited on by *émigrés* impatient for revenge, M. de Vitrolles, Comtes de Maillé, de Fitzjames and de Bruges, with Jules and Armand de Polignac. In 1798 this prince wrote to Mallet du Pan: "The King can only preserve the authority required for the government of a great nation if he returns to his legitimate rights by force of arms. He must not be restored to his throne by a bargain; he must not obey rules, he must make them." This was the reason why the Comte d'Artois had in 1815 accepted neither the Charter of the Constitution, which was a bargain, nor modern France, with whom that bargain had been made. It was in his palace in the Pavillon de Marsan that all those intrigues of the extreme party had been concocted, which hindered his brother's Ministers from restoring harmony between the Monarchy and the nation in the spirit of that bargain. It must be added that, as he grew older, he, the man of birth and fashion under Louis XVI, and the moving spirit of all the Court gaieties, experienced religion, but religion of the narrowest and most mystic type. He could not bear to be called the Elect of the People, but it pleased him to think himself the Chosen one of God for the re-establishment of the Faith in the country of Voltaire, and of the privileges of the Clergy among the fanatics of equality. He insisted on a solemn coronation at Reims.

After all, the French nation would have been easy enough to govern; "it did not need genius, but only good sense." To a much greater extent than at present the bulk of the people consisted of the mass of country labourers, middling farmers, and small squires, subsisting on the produce of their land. The Revolution had not disturbed the sturdy peasant character of the population, which the country owes to its climate and soil. In fact it had rather emphasised it, by increasing the number of land-holders beyond that of any European country, by the splitting-up of the great domains, and by the subdivision of estates at death. Very large towns were quite the exception. In Lyons, Marseilles, and Bordeaux the population scarcely exceeded 100,000, on a total population of 30 millions.

The agglomerations of population brought about in the nineteenth century by industry with its huge workshops, commerce, with its swift railways, began to take shape in Normandy, in the North, and in the East, at Rouen, Lille, St Quentin, Havre, Roubaix, and Mulhouse. But this was nothing more than the first dawn of a new economic and social era in which the foreigner had the larger share, bringing with him his machines, his processes, and even his working staff, English or German.

Absorbed in the working of their land, which they cultivated on a traditional system and laboriously enlarged, in order to provide themselves with food, the peasants did not covet the political rights which had been refused to them; they took no interest in the discussions of Press or Parliament. Barely able to read or cipher, their one thought was for hoarding money, and they had little fancy for spending on their children's education, or on the purchase of books, even books on agriculture or on the improvement of their dwellings, which were still poor and filthy. Their pleasures were few, the village festival, the occasional dance on Sunday, some simple games; their horizon was very limited, and their beliefs in elves, wizards, and goblins were as much a part of their traditions as their religious customs. So long as the order enforced by the Government, it mattered not which, secured them their property and the fruits of their labour, so long as nothing disturbed the even flow of their monotonous life by which they slowly gathered wealth, they asked no more. It was this readiness to accept authority, this capacity for resistance to pain, that had made them and kept them excellent soldiers; in every village there was more than one to recall the Napoleonic glories of which they had been the obscure creators. The prints hanging on their cottage walls, and the songs of Béranger, reminded them of the events of the Napoleonic wars, and of their protagonist. But they also reminded them of the foreign invasion, and set them reckoning the risks attending the pursuit of glory.

The only political life to be found in the provinces was concentrated in the small and middle-sized towns, whose interests were closely allied with those of the country-side around them, forming centres for meeting, or temporary residences of the local aristocracy and of such of the bourgeoisie as lived on the cultivation of land or on trading with the cultivators. The greater part of the towns were isolated by lack of communications, and furthermore they were split into rival and jealous classes; there were the nobles, the wealthy bourgeois, the small tradesmen, the small independent citizens. The barriers that separated one town from another, and the social conditions within the towns themselves, were so many obstacles to the circulation of ideas, to the diffusion of new ways of life, to the organisation of common interests, and common dislikes. The nobility, under the shade of the church steeple, shut itself up inside its own state-rooms and its own prejudices, brought its daughters up in convents, and entrusted the education of its sons to the Clergy, as in old days. The bourgeoisie, sprung from the peasantry, and carrying on its characteristics, aspired only to rise by dint of economy and education over the heads of the nobility who closed its doors to them; to succeed in this they adopted the principles of the Revolution, alarmed at every step backward, and at every act of excess or violence which might compromise alike their fortunes and their rights.

Under these conditions, party quarrels were always local, and generally personal; and principles were not as important as the personality of the officials who supported them. The prefects, magistrates, commandants of police, excise and customs officers, civil and military officials, linked up, by a long chain of subordinates or superiors, with the central authority which appointed and dismissed them, formed the only power in the country that made for political and social cohesion, and a power which was easy to handle. The prefects selected the members of the General Councils and the mayors, and were the means of electing more than one of the deputies; as aids to the judicial bench, they had the command of an active and suspicious police; they kept spies over the actions of individuals, robbed the Opposition Press of its weapons, and created servile party-organs of their own. They acted through the Clergy upon the conscience, through the University upon the intellect. "France," said Royer-Collard, "is a bureau-governed nation in the hands of irresponsible officials directed by the hand of a central power, whose ministers they are."

Above this mass of population, urban and rural, with small resisting power and little vitality, but discontented with its lot, another force was beginning to assert itself alongside that of officialdom, though springing from the same root. This was Paris, the political, intellectual and artistic centre of France. In a nation of thirty millions, with few towns of 100,000 inhabitants, a town of over 700,000 was a force in itself. Its material extent was not great; the city boundary and the thirty-two gates did not actually reach the line of the fortifications. The main streets were few in number; and the residences of the rich were still to be seen (though not so often as in the seventeenth century) in narrow lanes of lofty and closely-packed houses in which the lower class and the artisans lived. In all but a few distant parts, or where gardens occupied the surface, like Monceau, Grenelle, and the Faubourg St Germain, there was an intense activity; and anyone noticing the contrast with the monotony of provincial cities would think himself in another country. In Paris all was fever, either the fever of trade, such as called from a foreigner the question, "Who buys here, if everybody sells?" or the fever of pleasure, with its twenty-five theatres, its restaurants and cafés and its public balls, which attracted Frenchmen as well as numberless foreigners from afar. It was the taste alike for pleasure and for instruction which collected into the schools of the Quartier Latin so much youthful fire and intelligence. Stepping into the place of the Court, which under the Ancien Régime gave the tone, but had ceased to do so since Louis XVIII had lost his wife and grown aged and sickly, and amid the sourness and gloom of the clericalism and excessive etiquette of Charles X, Paris daily became more and more the arbiter in the world of wit, art, politics, and luxury. Since she had won back from Versailles her rank as the capital of France, she had imposed upon the country at large a supremacy analogous to that of the Court in former days.

For one thing, the whole administration of France was concentrated there in the ministerial offices and bureaux, where the fate of officials, and even of deputies and peers, was decided, and where the word of command was given which secured the tranquillity of France. Again Paris was the only spot where anyone could venture to plot, to write, or to speak freely against the omnipotent powers that be, in fact "to go in for politics," as the prudent, quiet and orderly citizen would have put it. Of newspapers competent to discuss the proceedings of the Government there were scarcely any but in Paris, the *Débats*, the *Constitutionnel*, the *Courrier Français*, the *Globe*. The only political speeches in opposition to the ruling party in France were to be heard in the Chambers, delivered by General Foy, Royer-Collard, Chateaubriand, Lafayette, Manuel, or Benjamin Constant. The only instruction in politics was to be obtained at the Sorbonne, or at the Normal Schools, where teachers of youth such as Cousin, Jouffroy, Guizot, Villemain, and Michelet found means of criticising the Government and of indicating the path to liberty by covert allusions and witty comparisons.

Paris in 1824 was still, as in the 18th century, the home of "salons," in which feasts of reason were celebrated under the direction of amiable and cultivated women, in which politicians, writers, and artists could meet, where all sorts of reputations were made—salons of the Faubourg St Germain frequented by *émigrés*, and presided over by the Duchesse de Duras, the Comtesse de Boigne, or the Princesse de la Tremoille, the "queen of the Ultras"; salons of the Faubourg St Honoré, also of royalist colour, but of more varied tints; salons of the Chaussée D'Antin, thrown open by great bankers like Laffitte and Rothschild, or great manufacturers like Ternaux, Benjamin Delessert, Davillier, Perier; salons of the great ladies of the foreign colony; literary salons, such as that of the Arsenal, where Nodier received the young royalist writers, Victor Hugo and Alfred de Vigny. There it was that intrigues began, and oppositions were organised. Despotic Ministers might fancy that they met with nothing but agreement and obedience everywhere. The metropolis combated them by every weapon at its disposal, the only weapons then at the disposal of the nation.

Paris was the home of novelties and daring, where generation after generation of youths arose, more hungry for fame than for material pleasures, for action than for order, with faces turned towards the future rather than to the past, eager to throw off the obsolete rules which their elders thought to impose on them in politics, art, religion, and literature, with spirits open to every fertilising breeze. Anyone judging of the France of that day who tried to combine in one view the Bourbon Court, with its queer old mummeries inherited from Louis XIV, and the material prosperity which it owed to the prudent and orderly administration of its officials, would find it hard to explain the Restoration, with its train of great writers, artists, orators, and journalists. Chateaubriand had the better and the sounder judgment when he "felt this land of revolutions quiver under his feet, expectant of its extraordinary destinies, this nation which M. de Villèle idly hoped to hold back and bind down earthwards."

He had himself contributed, in conjunction with Mme de Staël, to the starting of the so-called Romantic movement, created of late by lessons from abroad, by the re-discovery of the inspiration of nature, by the emotions of the lyrical poets, by the worship of beauty. In the powerful hands of Romanticism the old classic moulds had broken up. Her disciples, though at first enlisted in the service of the Faith and the Crown—witness Lamartine with his *Meditations* (1820), his *New Meditations* (1822); Victor Hugo with his *Royalist Odes* (1822); Alfred de Vigny with his *Poems* (1822) and *Ancient and Modern Poems* (1826)—very soon began to figure as revolutionists. When enamoured of freedom and fame, they threw themselves into the assault on the Bastille of Classicism; their ear was quicker for the roar of Paris than for the flaccid approbation of the Court. Their rapid and brilliant success in the capital made their names familiar to all the scholars of France, thanks to the centralisation which attracted to Paris all the intellect of the nation. Sainte-Beuve revealed the fact that the writers of the seventeenth century were being eclipsed by the new era; the brothers Antony and Emile Deschamps re-edited the *Muse Française* (1823); Beyle, better known as Stendhal, explained the policy of the Revolution in his *Criticisms on Racine and Shakespeare* (1822), in which he announced the publication of the famous preface to the drama of *Cromwell* (1827), an even louder blast from the trumpet of Victor Hugo. They were soon followed by the historians, who, tired of the France of Louis the Great, revived the whole past history of the race. Augustin Thierry published his *Letters on the History of France* in the Liberal journals between 1820 and 1827, and in his work on the *Norman Conquest of England*, like his comrade

Guizot, sought to put colour and life into history; the two were the precursors of "the romantic historian *par excellence*," Michelet.

The painters carried on the same struggle against the cold stiff school which an unintelligent admiration of the antique had imposed on preceding generations. Artists could now join the poets in worshipping the same ideal of freedom and colour. They were the *flamboyants*, the vivid colourists, for whom Géricault had opened the road by his celebrated *Wreck of the Medusa*, and whom Eugène Delacroix was to lead to victory, in spite of the resistance of Ingres, when his genius had silenced criticism with his *Bark of Dante* (1822) and *Massacre of Scio* (1824).

All this movement, which gave an enduring brilliancy to the reign of Charles X, had its centre in Paris, where it bloomed and germinated in the reunions of literary men and artists, of amateurs and professional men. A much wider popularity was given to the markedly lower but more accessible art of Béranger, the writer of songs and pamphlets, the report of whose prosecutions was a sort of halo of glory to every edition of his works. A Voltairian, the Tyrtaeus of the military glories of the Revolution and the Empire, the sworn foe of the Ancien Régime, he formed a centre for the young people of the new generation, which was then known as the "Young Guard." "Béranger has been our father," said Thiers, who often met him at the house of Manuel and Laffitte. His authority with the middle classes, and the worship paid him by the young, soon attracted the more youthful writers, who had first taken service under the Monarchy but were now returning, under Béranger's lead, to the side of the nation. "Béranger," wrote Sainte-Beuve, "was a temptation to which all yielded, Victor Hugo, Dumas, and all." "Young France" joined ranks with the "Young Guard," under the advice and direction of a group of Liberals, Royer-Collard, Guizot, and Benjamin Constant, but bolder than their directors both in their hopes and in their teaching.

"The age of these men was but little more than the age of the century," said one of them, Ch. de Rémusat, who had been trained by his mother in the worship of liberty. Odilon Barrot, the son of a member of the Convention, born in 1791, was the foe of any dictatorship, whether of Napoleon or of the Bourbons; like his friend Arthur Beugnot, the scholar, and Duvergier de Hauranne, he had deserted the royalist cause for which his father had worked. By their side stood a resolute band trained on the lectures of Royer-Collard and Cousin, young philosophers fresh from the University, anxious, like Jouffroy, Damiron, or Dubois, to base their political principles upon philosophy and forced into action by the dissolution of the Normal Schools under royalist persecution. These were soon to form the staff of the *Globe*, a journal started by one of their number in 1826. "These are the *élite* of the youth of France," said Ampère, who with Ballanche had been a constant guest in the salons of Mme Recamier and Chateaubriand since 1825. "One must hear them and see them, to find out how far their ideas have gone." Their energy was such as to fire their contemporaries with enthusiasm, and at the same time to reconcile the artists and writers of Romanticism to the Liberalism on behalf of which they were fighting in Paris, under the eyes of an interested and eventually excited nation, against a victorious counter-revolution.

Although the possibility of a struggle between the policy of M. de Villèle and the opinion of Paris and of the youth of France had by the beginning of 1825 been recognised, nobody expected it to involve a real danger. The whole nation, wearied of convulsions, and resolved to keep the blessing of a civilised industry, had greeted the accession of the King with favour, almost with enthusiasm, and was gratified to see him succeed his brother peacefully. Chateaubriand remarked, as did Mme Swetchine, on the well-nigh universal acceptance of the new ruler—"a sort of truce spontaneously agreed to by all parties." The opponents of the Government, whether Liberals or Republicans, admitted the fact, and seemed to resign themselves to some slackening in the pace; but they never doubted that, slow or fast, things would develop into a wise freedom under the rule of a prince of unchallenged title. All that was wanted to complete the reconciliation between the country and the reigning family was that the victorious side should "take up its position once for all on the side of justice and impartiality.

"There are many people"—said Mme Swetchine—"who ruin their own business." Charles X was just the man to ruin his business with the least possible delay. The breeze of popularity that swelled his sails dropped at the very outset, and by his own fault. He had scarcely been proclaimed King before he began to behave like the leader of a party, and to impose upon his Ministers a policy and a legislation which when heir to the crown he had never been able to induce Louis XVIII to accept. On December 2, 1824, he suddenly ordered 250 Generals, the veterans of the wars of the Revolution and Empire, to be put on half-pay—a piece of clumsy stupidity, all the more mischievous for having been carried out before the details of the Bill for indemnifying the *émigrés* promised by Charles X had been submitted to the House (December 22). Thus it looked like a revenge wreaked by the Ancien Régime upon the heroes of modern France. The King succeeded in turning the discussion of this law, which M. de Villèle had taken great pains to represent as a wise measure on the part of the Crown for finally healing the wounds of the Revolution, into a violent and passionate wrangle.

After a confidential enquiry into the character of the various properties confiscated during the emigration and into the income they produced, the Premier commissioned

M. de Martignac, once Secretary to Sieyès, now made Privy Councillor as a reward for his conversion to Royalism, and head of the Registration Office, to explain the cardinal points of the Bill. He insisted with great skill upon the argument that the measure would be very advantageous to the holders of "national" (confiscated) property, being in fact a guarantee against the claims of the parties dispossessed which would have been satisfied by the indemnity. Notwithstanding these precautions, the propositions of the King, with the amendments of the Ultras (who proposed to restore the actual property to the *émigrés* and give the indemnity to the present holders) seemed to constitute a violation of the new order of things. What a price, moreover, to pay for it, 1000 million francs! The figure was indeed a striking one and was never forgotten. It had been calculated upon a valuation of the income of the confiscated property in 1790. But the authors of the Bill had not for a moment dreamt of the possibility of the payment of the indemnity in a lump sum. There would be an annual payment of 30 millions to the *émigrés* as interest on account of the capital, but the capital itself was not to be repaid to them and would not therefore really increase the public debt. The annual 30 millions were to be paid out of savings due to a conversion of capital affecting rente-holders only. The Bill was none the less opposed by General Foy, Benjamin Constant, the Duc de Broglie, and Chateaubriand, by some on principle, by others for personal reasons; and the struggle was as lively as in 1824. In spite of all, it was finally carried through both Chambers by a large majority in April 1825.

For this legislation public opinion was to a certain extent prepared. But alarm was felt at the proposals of the new reign in favour of the Church; and in this matter the hand of Charles X is evident. A note from the pocket-book of M. de Villèle dated November 24, 1824, establishes that fact and also reveals the uneasiness and the objections of the Minister: "Council discussed religious laws strongly demanded by King and Clergy, but at the same time very difficult to handle at this delicate juncture." These "religious laws" were the harvest which the archbishops, and not the least of them (he of Lyons for instance), were reaping from the exaggerated churchmanship of the King and from the triumph of the Royalists.

The creation of a Ministry for Ecclesiastical Affairs for the benefit of Mgr de Frayssinous, who was already Grand Master of the University, indicated a design to place all schools once for all under the rule of the Clergy. Next came, on January 4, 1825, the resumption of the Bill in favour of female communities, rejected the year before. The Chamber of Peers only passed it with an amendment limiting the concession to the Orders already existing. The Clergy desired to mark their confidence in the King and his Ministers by depriving Parliament of the right to encourage Religious Orders and giving it to the Ministers exclusively, to be carried out by Order in Council. The Abbé de Frayssinous did not hesitate to break with modern ideas and declare himself distinctly in favour of the irrevocability of monastic vows. "For women in religion, liberty has been simply a torture." If he did not ask that the Orders should be immediately re-established, it was only from a willingness to temporise, and from a regard for Villèle whom he did not want to expose to a struggle with the laity or to their vengeance. It would be necessary to lull France to sleep and induce her to acquiesce in the restoration of the Religious Orders when required by the sole authority of a kindly-disposed King, as before 1789. Women would return first, then men; lastly perhaps the Jesuits.

The religion of the "Good Old Time" suggested to the Catholics another piece of legislation, which recalled the Inquisition, with its prohibition of all public discussion or correspondence on religious matters. A law of sacrilege was passed April 15, 1825, which appeared at first sight to be directed solely against criminals who had the audacity to steal or commit other crimes or acts of profanation in Church buildings. But, in the first place, the penalties that it imposed were outrageous, extending actually to capital punishment; in the next place, it revealed an intention of introducing into the penal code offences of a religious character and of punishing them with special penalties. "To-morrow," wrote de Broglie—who with de Barante, Pasquier, and Molé headed the opposition of the Peers—"you will be asked to drive a red-hot iron through the tongue of a blasphemer, to vacate all pulpits from which error is preached, and openly to violate the great principle of liberty of worship." The fact was that Villèle, being unable to restrain the energy of the priestly party, played into its hands, because it pleased the King.

Far from alarming the King, this "to-morrow," to which de Broglie alluded, was being actually prepared for in the Court circle. Charles X invited the Chambers on April 26, 1825, to send representatives to his coronation at Reims, where he proposed to kneel before the bishops, like his ancestors, at the foot of the altar whence Clovis had received the Holy Oil. He gave orders that the Holy Ampulla (the oil-flask used at the coronation) should be found again, though it was well known to have been destroyed at the Revolution. On May 16 it was accordingly found, and the *Moniteur* duly announced the fact to the nation. The great Ministers of State, and the representatives of foreign Powers, were invited to meet at Reims on May 28; and a Committee of official architects and upholsterers was hard at work, to give to the festival all the splendour needed to capture the fancy of the people. When the great day arrived, the bishops of France placed in the hands of the brother of Louis XVI the sword of Charlemagne, praying that he might "protect and defend the Church, repair the mischief done by the Revolution, and carry on the work of reconstruction begun ten years ago." It was in short more of a religious demonstration than a royal ceremony, though some poets such as Victor Hugo and Lamartine celebrated it as the latter; but most people either laughed or growled, while Béranger invited them to celebrate the coronation of "Charles the Simple" instead.

Charles X cared not a jot. When he was seen diligently following processions through the streets of Paris with his Court and all his Ministers behind him, the laughter increased. Caricaturists drew the King in Jesuit costume, or showed him presiding at gay banquets in 1775, and saying mass in 1825. The people of Paris are as quick to wrath as to laughter; and they were beginning to be indignant that the chief of the State should be seen abasing himself before priests. Villèle warned the King, recognising the fact that by tacking the cause of Ultramontanism to that of Monarchy, by letting it appear that he was restoring priestly rule in order to further the restoration of the Ancien Régime, Charles was running the risk of a re-awakening of the nation and putting dangerous arms into the hands of the champions of Liberalism, men of youthful audacity and intelligence, who were as likely as not to turn them against the Crown itself. The funeral of General Foy (who died in November 1825) in which more than 100,000 took part, and the subscription for his monument, which in six months reached well-nigh 1,000,000 francs, were warnings even clearer than those of M. de Villèle. "Within these walls," said Casimir Perier in the Chamber, "we Liberals are seven in number, but outside we have the whole nation behind us."

For the awakening of the nation and putting it face to face with the King, the Liberals of all shades adopted and maintained a very simple system. The nation loved order and quiet, and hated all quarrels, civil or religious; so the word was passed to the Opposition in general, and to Paris in particular, to suggest the danger of a reaction which might amount to a revolution. The youthful Mignet, after taking note of the statement in the *Quotidienne* that the task of the Royalists had then only begun, was fully justified in writing for the *Courrier Français*, "The royalist party wants a revolution; after seizing upon power, it wants to transform society. This initiates an absolutely novel political phase." "They want to put the whole past once more on its trial, to prosecute revolution," cried Dupont de l'Eure, "to indict the nation for consenting to it, and to condemn 30,000,000 souls to make humble apologies."

When Lamennais, carried away by his zeal for theocracy, started the *Catholic Memorial* in 1824, and preached furiously in favour of crushing all freedom, both in Church and in State, the French Gallicans, who were still numerous on the Bench and at the Bar, the Voltairian bourgeoisie, the young, and the artisans joined in applauding the speeches of Dupin, Mérilhou, and Portalis, and the fiery articles from the pen of that aristocrat and *émigré*, yet thorough priest-hater, M. de Montlosier. Respect, even worship, of the Charter, whose clearly expressed assurances seemed to be the palladium of society, threatened in its very essence by the reaction of priests and *émigrés*, now became the main plank in the platform of the united Opposition, which henceforth comprehended men of every age, belief and temperament. Among its members were young Republicans, who had renounced their secret societies, wealthy bourgeois faithful to the principles of Monarchy, professors such as Royer-Collard, and others like the normal scholars on the staff of the *Globe*, craving for novelty and freedom, and artisans equally hostile to Clergy and nobles.

In so critical a time, the most elementary prudence would have bidden the Ministry adopt a policy of judicious caution. But neither the majority which they had created and which they must now perforce follow, nor the King and those about him, would have been able to appreciate it. For the great gulf now on the point of being formed in France, they were responsible. At the beginning of 1826 Villèle and his colleagues, mainly to please the Chamber, brought in a Bill on Successions, to amend the law enacted in revolutionary times by the Civil Code, giving to all children equal shares in an inherited estate. This Bill empowered a testator to leave to an eldest son a larger share of the family property than was permitted in the Civil Code to stand "at the disposition of the parent," and in case of intestacy he would receive a much larger share by operation of law. Now, as the proposed law was expressly made applicable to large estates only, that is to say, to estates paying 300 francs or more in land-tax, and as the existing law by its recognition of the practice of "substituting," say, a younger son for his deceased elder brother, would practically make the new arrangement perpetual, people were warranted in seeing in these proposals a tendency to the legal restoration of primogeniture and a return to the conditions on which the nobles held their property under the Ancien Régime. All Villèle's efforts to reassure them were vain, though he pointed out that it was desirable to prevent the infinitesimal subdivision of properties, and to keep up an aristocracy of great land-owners in the country for the support of agriculture. He did not pacify all those who were beginning to notice with alarm signs of a return to the Ancien Régime under the legal forms that he was trying to force on them. The most violent opposition to the Bill was that of the Chamber of Peers, and it was successful (March 1826). Paris lit all its lamps to celebrate the defeat of the Government.

To the original reason for revolt fresh reasons were added in the religious discussions provoked by the burning rhetoric of Lamennais and the answers of Montlosier in his celebrated *Mémoire à Consulter* (Memorandum for reference), February 1826. "It will be difficult to explain the present era to our grandchildren," said a Liberal organ in 1826. "No one speaks now-a-days of any but bishops, monks, Jesuits, convents, or seminaries. Religious controversy is on the order of the day." The Government repudiated the compromising zeal of Lamennais, who called the Law of Sacrilege an "atheistic law"; they could not, and dared not, displease the Jesuits and the Congregation in order to satisfy the Gallicans and Montlosier. Mgr de Frayssinous urged "extenuating circumstances" in favour of the Company of Jesus, the Catholic Association, the Propaganda of the Faith and the Missions, and even on behalf of the Congregation itself. He praised their zeal for religion, the charity of their actions. In trying to justify them he had to admit that their very existence and growth was only due to the toleration and secret complicity of the Throne!

The beginning of the struggle in Parliament was magnificent. Casimir Perier, Royer-Collard, Pasquier, and Lainé, in accusing the Government of culpable complaisance, appealed to the nation with all the authority of their talents and character, against the theocratic principle which threatened religion and society alike, against a theocracy more political than religious, which in the words of Royer-Collard "has all the appearance of a Counter-Revolution." With greater violence Montlosier denounced before the Royal Courts of Justice the encroachments of the Clergy, and prophesied a speedy return to the tumults and bloodshed of the Ligue. He induced the Bar of the Court of Paris to pass an emphatic condemnation on the Jesuits (August 16, 1826) amid the applause of the capital and, shortly afterwards, of the great cities. The General Councils, by orders from the Government, passed resolutions in favour of the return of the Jesuits; and these were supported by several of the bishops, who were tired of giving them clandestine support. Multitudinous echoes of these quarrels were heard in the Press.

Hereupon Charles X, by way of enforcing silence, and in the true manner of Louis XV, directed Villèle to attack the liberty of the Press by a Draconian proposal, which earned the derisive name of "the law of justice and love." The Bill was submitted to the Chamber of Deputies on December 29, 1826, as a mere police regulation, on the allegation that the daily Press had reached an absolutely "unbridled" degree of licence. It proposed to return to the customs "of the old Monarchy" in which the control of all written matter was reserved as a royal prerogative. An order was to be issued to the printers, who were henceforth to be responsible, and also to the proprietors, to submit all written matter five days before publication to the deliberate examination of the authorities, and to allow nothing to appear without their "imprimatur." The severity of the proposed penalties, and the right given to magistrates to initiate official prosecutions on the slightest attack that could be construed as defamatory were a death-blow to all freedom of thought or pen. For it was not only at daily journals, but at pamphlets of every sort, even at books, that the Bill was aimed. "Why not," asked Casimir Perier, "propose at once to suppress the printing-trade of France for the benefit of the Belgians?" "A law of barbarism!" exclaimed Chateaubriand. The indignation soon extended from Parliament to the literary tribe, to the writers of the Académie, to the salons of Paris, and finally to the whole country, which understood that it was threatened with intellectual death.

At the head of this opposition Villèle once more found his deadly enemy, Chateaubriand, more impassioned and more eloquent than ever. Chateaubriand had now dubbed himself the "Lord Paramount of opinion." Since his dismissal he had not only laboured ceaselessly to bring up his friends of the Right, Bertin of the *Débats*, La Bourdonnaye, and Delalot, into the fighting rank of a party whose programme was after all the same as theirs; but he also accepted the approval of M. de Broglie and Benjamin Constant, those great Liberals, of Bonapartists like Étienne and Sebastiani, even of the Republicans Lafayette and d'Argenson. He took a positively sensuous delight in their compliments, and in his popularity with the young and with the working-man. "All were falling at my feet—friends, foes, and opponents. The youth of France had come in a body to my side, and never afterwards left me. I could not walk a yard along a street without attracting a crowd." It must indeed have been a pleasure for the defeated of 1822 to look on while their conquerors were being rent to shreds by their own men, and to see the majority which had ousted them gradually going to pieces by the action of deserters from their own camp. The moment was drawing near when the Ministry, impotent in Parliament, would be equally impotent in the country, when the country might be driven to shout "Long live the Charter" while revolting against the King himself, that blinded supporter of nobles and priests.

Villèle now began to take these matters into account, if we are to believe his private diary. He felt that his alternatives were, to join issue with the nation, or "to coerce and ignore his King, to crush the nephew of his King, the daughter of Louis XVI, and the widow of the Duc de Berry, to drive the new Gaston d'Orléans and his large family into exile out of France and to annihilate the Court pygmies whose influence over the King and the royal family and whose vexatious tricks in the Chamber of Peers made them probably more dangerous than Montmorency and Cinq Mars had ever been." But "he was not a Richelieu, nor did he pretend to be." While seeing clearly the enemy against whom he ought to employ all his energy, and in despair at having all the responsibility and all the burden of the business, he preferred to risk another arbitrary act against the threatened opposition of Paris and of the youth of France.

Paris had again illuminated and fired salvos in its delight over the rejection of the Press Laws; and shortly after, during a review of the National Guard by Charles X, cries were raised in the crowd of "Down with the Ministry! Down with the Jesuits!" On April 29 the National Guard was disbanded; and two days later, on the rising of the Chambers, a Royal Ordinance, countersigned by Villèle, Corbière, and Peyronnet, re-established the censorship over all daily and periodical papers; the censors were ordered to show no mercy to the Liberals and the Opposition journals. This deprived public opinion of every means of expressing itself. Paris was muzzled, and the despotism of Ministers triumphed.

Nevertheless the provinces seemed still indifferent. When the King visited St Omer for the manœuvres in the North, he was still received with acclamations by the troops and people. France had by no means yet caught the fever of opposition which affected Paris, and Paris alone. The general and visible prosperity, which the success of the Industrial Exhibition at the Louvre (August 1, 1827) so clearly demonstrated, was, in the view of Villèle and of the King, a sufficient justification for his attempt to keep Paris to her obedience at the expense of her liberty. For a moment it seemed possible that Villèle might have the last word in this struggle for reaction, and that, in spite of his own fears, his obstinacy might accomplish the restoration of the Ancien Régime, to which Charles X and his clique were driving him.

But for a triumph of this sort, he must of necessity retain command of Parliament. Now the Chamber of Peers had already beaten him; and their victorious resistance had given fresh strength to his enemies of the Extreme Right, while it had restored some hope to the Liberals of the Chamber, who had up to that time been lacking in numbers and power. The alliance, which was growing daily closer, between the friends of Chateaubriand, the *pointus*, who shared alike his discontent and his ambition, and the Liberals, the foes of the Ancien Régime, was cemented by the only force which could unite elements so incongruous, a new need for action, a new call to glory.

Since 1821, and ever since France had been prevented by the withdrawal of Alexander I and the machinations of Metternich from intervening in the East on behalf of Greece, she had continued to watch the development of the Hellenic crisis with passionate interest. The Catholics were indignant at the violence of the Moslems; the Liberals greeted and extolled the insurgents as the champions of Greek freedom. The cultured society of the Restoration, the writers, the educated youth (the best-educated youth of Europe in the nineteenth century), the artists, all acknowledged one over-mastering duty, which silenced political quarrels, and united hearts sundered by party prejudices, the duty of listening to the complaints and healing the wounds of Greece, the mother of civilisation and art, the native soil of beauty and literature. The Spanish successes had momentarily eclipsed the influence of these combined emotions, but had not destroyed them, as Villèle had for a moment hoped. The abominable massacres of Greeks at Patras and Chios in 1822, the heroism of the Greek sailors Canaris, Miaulis, and Botzaris, had heightened both the indignation and the enthusiasm of France. Philhellenic committees, made up of Frenchmen of all parties, sent funds, arms, and munitions to the Greeks. Volunteers joined their ranks. The Marquis de Noailles urged Louis XVIII to send a crusade against the Mussulmans, who thoroughly deserved to be called barbarians. The Liberals also demanded war in defence of national justice. And, when the Orleans family expressed its willingness to offer one of its sons, the Duc de Nemours, to the newly enfranchised nation, who needed a King for their defence, the Ministry of Charles X was not far from allowing him to accept the proposal.

But in 1825 the impulse of all political parties in France to come to the defence of a martyred and insurgent Greece became more seriously accentuated. When, to Sultan Mahmoud's appeal for aid to punish the Hellenes, Ibrahim, son of his former enemy Mehemet Ali, had replied by violent and brutal intervention, when the news came of the sack of Rhodes and Candia, the destruction of Navarino, Tripolitza, and Missolonghi by Egyptian troops, there rose from France one shout of indignation, in answer to the cry of distress from the shores of the Aegean Sea. Had they only been satisfied that the new Tsar, Nicholas I, would surely "intervene to save Greece from the disastrous effects of Egyptian intervention"! But Canning's policy did not allow this; his plan was to settle the difference between Turks and Greeks by diplomatic notes (April 4, 1826) and to meet the objections of Russia by the Treaty of Ackerman (October 7, 1826) without allowing her to take action in Greece. This left Greece exposed and defenceless to the blows of the Mussulman coalition, which was reducing it to extremities.

Villèle was determined to avoid a war in the East which would cost him his alliance with England, who had let him intervene with the warfare in Spain; and in the very midst of this conflict, so exquisitely painful to the French souls, he ordered our agents to observe neutrality. Our fleet in the Aegean was confined to the police duty of watching. It was useless for our officers to complain of acting as policemen, though Admiral Henri de Rigny, son-in-law of Baron Louis, a man of action and former servant of the Empire, claimed the post of honour and of usefulness for

France and her fleet. "Our country ought," he wrote, "to adopt a heroic attitude." His appeals to the Minister and the pressure of public opinion once very nearly decided the Minister for Foreign Affairs to agree to an intervention (July 8, 1826). Villèle once more succeeded in postponing it; he compelled his colleague, M. de Damas, to agree to neutrality. But his alliance with Canning, which he had treated since 1825 as the solid guarantee of this neutrality, was now gradually drawing him into other arrangements. The pace grew faster in 1827, as the sufferings and the heroism of the Greeks in Europe evoked a livelier sympathy and more burning desire for intervention. The Russians especially were for pushing the Tsar Nicholas into action; and the English, wishing to control and direct this movement, which they could no longer prevent, invited France to take joint action with them (July 6, 1827). By virtue of the protocol, which was Canning's last act, the French and English admirals, de Rigny and Codrington, had joined forces at the end of August with the Russian admiral, Heyden, who had arrived from Cronstadt with secret orders to treat the enemy *à la Russe*. The English admiral, Codrington, first communicated with Ibrahim Pacha with a view to avoiding an encounter; but Admiral de Rigny summoned him *à la Française*, and persuaded his colleagues to send the whole of their squadrons into the bay of Navarino. They brought with them an ultimatum, to which Ibrahim replied on October 20 by opening fire. His fleet was destroyed, and the Peloponnese was saved.

This was the doing of the French—a fact which Charles X and M. de Villèle, neither of whom had desired it, did their best to conceal. They would not admit publicly, what they said to each other privately, that "de Rigny had done the thing." In spite of them, France knew it, and was delighted on account of the Greeks, and also on her own. "The guns of Navarino," wrote Pierre Lebrun, a Liberal poet, "have marked the beginning of a new era; they herald the triumphant advance of public opinion, which is mightier than the Crown, which disposes at its will of fleets and guns, and gives her commands to admirals." The initiative given by Admiral de Rigny amid the acclamations of the nation had succeeded in uniting all parties, who, as Metternich had said, "found their point of union in the identity of their object, in the impatient yearning of both for action and glory."

While the guns of Navarino were firing, Villèle was introducing the measures which he thought it his duty to submit to the King for breaking down the opposition in Parliament, after crushing it in Paris. By the Ordinance dated November 5, 1827, seventy-six new peers were created, mostly chosen from among the stoutest supporters of the Ministry who had been elected in 1822 for a term of five years, and were now therefore liable to stand another election. In creating these peers, Charles X did not conceal his intention of setting up some defence for himself against popular power. Another Ordinance dissolved the Chamber of Deputies, and summoned the electors to hold fresh elections on November 17 and 24. In these M. de Villèle felt assured of victory, having already appointed as presidents of the election committees sundry official candidates chosen from his own disciples, and forced upon the electorate by the prefects, sub-prefects, mayors, and revenue collectors.

His Ministry could not have foreseen the coalition which was got up in a fortnight under the cloak of patriotism, between the hottest and most uncompromising of the Royalists, and the whole Liberal party from the most moderate to the most advanced. "The cynicism is equal, on whichever side you look," said the *Gazette de France* with indignation. "It is not a matter of revolution and counter-revolution; it is the same revolution in a two-fold shape, burning with two-fold rage, armed with twin daggers." During that fortnight these were neither Royalists nor Liberals, but only opponents of M. de Villèle. Thus it came about that in Paris the Royalists helped to make a majority, and a very large majority, for Dupont de l'Eure, Laffitte, Casimir Perier, Benjamin Constant, Ternaux, Royer-Collard and Baron Louis, while in the provinces, and especially in the large towns, they did the same for Lafayette, de Chauvelin, Étienne, Bignon de Kératry, Dupin the elder, Charles Dupin, and the Republican Mauguin. In return for these, the following friends of Chateaubriand were victorious at the poll—Hyde de Neuville, Bertin de Vaux, Agier, Ravez, Delalot, and Salaberry, all at the expense of the ministerial candidates, of whom only one-third were successful.

By this coalition, which destroyed in a few days the skilfully devised combinations of M. de Villèle of the previous six years, the Liberals, both moderate and extreme, recovered their influence, strong in the support of Paris and of the young generation, who celebrated their victory with riotous demonstrations. They now formed nearly one-half of the Chamber, of which Royer-Collard was shortly elected President. M. de Villèle had nothing to do but to retire; he did so with dignity on June 5, 1827. Charles X allowed him to go without any regret, being persuaded by his courtiers that the accumulated odium against the policy, and the dislike attaching to the person, of M. de Villèle constituted a danger for his own popularity, which he believed to be undiminished. "You had become too unpopular," was the Dauphin's farewell to him. "Monseigneur," replied the Minister with spirit, "God grant that the unpopularity be mine!" The Bourbons imagined that they need only throw overboard some ballast—and a Minister—to escape the necessity of marking a fresh course in the place of that laid down for them for the last eight years by the pressure of the *émigrés* and the Church, a course which led straight to destruction.

Their first difficulty was the formation of a Cabinet which should correspond to the requirements of two parties so different as those whose somewhat strange conjunction had destroyed M. de Villèle. After a month's efforts, Charles X had to recognise the fact that he could not appoint a Ministry of Ultra-Royalists in the face of a Liberal majority in Parliament, nor yet impose a really Liberal Ministry upon the Court or upon a body of royalist officials. He gave the Ministry of the Interior to M. de Martignac, a former colleague of Villèle. He did his best to conciliate the Liberals by separating Public Education, the control of which was given to M. de Vatimesnil, from the Ministry of Ecclesiastical Affairs, entrusted to Feutrier, bishop of Beauvais, and by calling Comte Portalis to the Ministry of Justice. On the other side, the reservation of the right of appointment of officers to the Duc d'Angoulême, which left to the Vicomte de Caux the bare administration of the Ministry of War, the appointment of Hyde de Neuville, the friend of Chateaubriand, to the Ministry of Marine, and of M. de la Ferronays, a royalist supporter of the alliance with Russia, to Foreign Affairs, all pointed to an intention of realising the active foreign policy so dear to the Ultras, and so warmly favoured by Chateaubriand. That statesman was shortly afterwards made ambassador in Rome.

At that moment the task of internal pacification which was laid on M. de Martignac was as troublesome as the composition of the Ministry in which he was to hold a high place. He has told us himself later of his terror on observing the "contrary courses which the Crown and the country were taking." An ardent Royalist, he had, while at Bordeaux, where he had a great reputation as a barrister, fought for the Duchesse d'Angoulême during the Hundred Days, and had refused the Legion of Honour which the

Emperor offered him. Elected deputy in 1821, he undertook his task in the same spirit as that of the royalist majority who had followed and supported M. de Villèle. He had obtained the title of Vicomte by Court favour, at the request of the Prime Minister, who had early formed a high opinion of his talents and character. Who would have believed that in 1828 de Martignac would be invited to efface the memories of the unpopular Minister to whom he owed his fortune, and whose policy he had always backed, in the matter of the laws against the Press, and the expedition to Spain? It was he who undertook in 1824 to get the Septennial Bill through the Chambers; and, as a reward, M. de Villèle had made him a Privy Councillor, and entrusted to him the duty of defending the Bill for indemnifying the *émigrés*. In the heated discussions of 1827 upon the Press Laws, he argued with equal vigour in favour of energetic preventive legislation. His antecedents differed in no way from those of M. de Villèle. But his future intentions seemed to be very different, to judge from the speech which he put in the mouth of the King, on the day of his entry into office: "Being desirous of giving better guarantees throughout my dominions for the Charter that I have sworn to maintain, I shall see that my Ministers apply wisdom and deliberation to the task of placing our legislation into harmony therewith." This constituted a formal repudiation of all those previous attempts towards a return to the Ancien Régime, which the Charter prohibited, and a final effort to dissipate the uneasiness of the people, who were as averse to the Counter-Revolution as to the Revolution.

The position which M. de Martignac tried to take up was that of a mediator between the Bourbons on one side, whose popularity was compromised by the violence of the Ultras, and the nation on the other, urged to revolt by the appeals of the Liberals, the demands of Young France, and the wrath of Paris and the popular Press. He had all the necessary qualities—a parliamentary eloquence which excelled, not in threats, but in persuasiveness in winning hearts and awakening sympathies, an easy temper, made to disarm bitterness, and an open mind devoid of all prejudice, a prudence to warn him of danger, a delicate and wise tact to guide him in difficulties, and at bottom a solid belief in Monarchy and a devotion to the public good, which ought to have given him the confidence of the Crown and of the great parliamentary parties. He was worthy of a better fate than that reserved for men who thrust themselves between two irreconcileable opposites in the hour of crisis.

His first steps towards a pacification were but ill received by Charles X or his courtiers. He thought it his duty to reinstate Guizot, Villemain, and Cousin, the teachers of the Liberal youth, in their professorships, to remove certain prefects, and especially Franchet, the head of the Police, who had joined the Clerical plot, to dismiss Mgr Frayssinous, believed to be a tool of the Jesuits, and to appoint a commission to investigate the right of that body to give instruction. Charles X growled—but behind his back—that "this was a half-way meeting between the Revolution and rank cowardice." The Duchesse d'Angoulême, and Villèle himself, considered it a sheer abdication on the King's part.

However, by frightening them with the threat of a popular rising, de Martignac was able to insist upon the necessary withdrawal, an act not of cowardice but of prudence. He bade the Opposition hope for cleaner elections, by a revision of the electoral register. He promised that "the Government and the prefects would cease to exert over the electors any but the admittedly necessary authority," and that the revision of the electoral registers should henceforth be subject to appeal to the ordinary tribunals, and to the Privy Council (March 20, July 30, 1828). At the same time, he brought up another Bill on the Press (April 10, 1888) which gave the exact measure of the extent of his Liberalism. He gave up the censorship of newspapers which he had helped to establish in 1822, which he had defended again in 1827, and which had excited the most violent opposition from both Right and Left. He also abolished the requirement of a "previous authorisation," and "offences of intention." But he did not go so far as the Liberals went on an earlier occasion, when they restored trial by jury in the matter of press offences; these were still to be brought before the ordinary tribunals, which the Government could influence. He armed these tribunals with extraordinary powers; they could suspend for three months, or inflict fines, which were secured by the previous deposit of a large sum of caution-money. "It is a new sort of Bastille," said the Liberals, "with Freedom for the watchword." Yet this law, passed in June 1828 by the skill of M. de Martignac, was looked upon by Charles X as a dangerous concession.

On June 17, 1828, the Ministry issued two Orders in Council, countersigned by the new Minister for Ecclesiastical Affairs—one, directed against the Jesuits, prohibiting any unlicensed religious body from giving instruction, and attaching to the University the eight colleges clandestinely started by the Society of Jesus; the other addressed to the small seminaries which had come into existence since the fall of the Empire, regardless of the University monopoly, and which attracted a large number of young men on the pretext of preparing them for the religious profession. The Order enjoined the students to wear the religious habit, and limited their number to 20,000. Without actually closing these institutions, it obliged them to confine themselves within the limits of the duty they professed to perform.

If the University had then been really hostile to the Church, as the Clericals noisily asserted, the steps taken by the Martignac Cabinet for reserving for the University the education of the middle classes might have been condemned as illustrations of lay violence. But the State education which their system established was then based upon essentially Catholic principles, religious through and through; and the professors, and even the Board of Management of the University, had a large number of priests in their ranks. It was true that the Crown asserted its right to settle the curriculum, but the Crown in its old character of eldest daughter of the Church. From a bigoted King like Charles X any attack on religion was highly improbable. Even the bigots who advised him, Bishop de Frayssinous, Father Ronsin, and the deputy Ravez, had been forced to recognise the expediency of these concessions.

But the satisfaction they gave to the Liberals called forth violent protests from the extreme Royalists, who had expected that the defeat of Villèle would have resulted in so much profit to their party, their tenets, and their ambition. The bishops, as the obedient servants of the Jesuits, were specially indignant. An association was formed for the "Defence of the Catholic Faith," initiated by de Bonald and Dambray. Lamennais, the eloquent champion of Ultramontanism, inveighed in angry fashion against the progress of the Revolution, and called upon the Holy See to break off, summarily, all relations with a "Sovereign who was putting himself in the hands of Jacobin Ministers"! The organs of the Ultras, the *Quotidienne* and the *Gazette de France,* declared war upon a Cabinet whose prudence was in their eyes sheer treachery. Nothing would satisfy them but that M. de Martignac should return to the policy which the Ultras had recommended to the Crown in 1816, and set up a dictatorship which the nation abhorred. "Those who give the King advice of this sort are simply madmen," replied M. de Martignac, adding, "the course which your Majesty's Ministers advise is the only practicable path to the restoration of the power and dignity of the Crown." For once, Charles X listened to him, principally because he was not prepared to allow that Royal Ordinances could be the subject of discussion. However, the pacification which the Minister hoped to bring about made but little way among the courtiers and the bigots.

And on the other side, the groups on the Left, even the most moderate of the Liberals, among whom de Martignac hoped to get some recruits for his policy of conciliation, answered but slowly to his call. They had a feeling—and a well-warranted one—that this policy was not based upon any broad principle or inspired by a real love of liberty, but was a mere armistice. Their victory at the elections of 1827, which had far exceeded their hopes, had given them more seats in Parliament than they had occupied for eight years. They expected, nay demanded, some more decided satisfaction of their claims. Incited and supported by the young journalists of the *Globe*, from whom they no longer dared to separate, they demanded that the Crown should once for all give up its intention, whether secret or avowed, of restoring the Ancien Régime and carrying on war against the laicism of modern society. They did not require of M. de Martignac a mere armistice, but a formal recognition of the victory they had just won.

It is scarcely necessary to say that they were sorely mistaken both as to the extent and as to the causes of their success. On the dissolution of the Chamber by Villèle in 1827, had the new elections been held under the then existing laws of indirect election and official candidatures, the Ministry which had been so long in power, without any national objection, would probably have continued to exist. Nothing short of the defection of the friends of Chateaubriand, the opposition of the Royalists and their alliance with the Left, would have destroyed M. de Villèle. After all, Paris, which was the scene of their main triumph, was not the nation. They would probably have been better advised, as M. de Broglie saw later on, if they had made good the ground gained by their unexpected and qualified success, by drawing nearer to the present Ministry, whose leanings were in closer conformity with their own ideals than were the demands of the Royalists, their allies of a day. However, they took the opposite course, and called upon de Martignac to amend the Electoral Law, by providing a more complete appeal to the people.

What with these demands, and the evident yearning of their antagonists for a return to absolutism, the mediation dreamt of by M. de Martignac at the end of 1828 was sorely imperilled. "In the delicate position which the new Ministry held," said M. de Broglie, "between the King who was only looking out for a good opportunity to get rid of them, and a Chamber that had no definite views on any subject, they earned much credit in this session. They had little support from the Right Centre, who considered them to lean too much to the Left, and still less from the Left who felt no confidence in them; yet they did not lose temper. Their conduct was that of a Cabinet liberal by circumstances, moderate in essence." But it needed to exist, in order to prove itself; and foreign politics were coming in, as usual, to hasten its fall.

M. de la Ferronays, who had been summoned from Petrograd to conduct the French Foreign Office after Navarino, seemed to be the right man to work in concert with Russia, who was preparing for the dismemberment of the Turkish Empire (January–April 1828), the glorious task of Revolution and Liberty. "Navarino," said M. de Martignac, "was glorious, but it was not exactly war." The Russian Government had counted rather prematurely upon the cooperation of the new French Ministry and upon the credit of the action at Navarino; but, contrary to their expectation, M. de la Ferronays' one thought was, how to avoid a general war. "Russia and Pozzo di Borgo have too long manipulated France for the benefit of their own designs," said he. The aggrandisement of Russia was in his eyes a danger equal to that of the ruin of Turkey.

La Ferronays came to an understanding in London, in the month of June, with Metternich and Wellington, to prevent Russia assuming the character of a belligerent in the Mediterranean as well as on the Danube. And he claimed, on behalf of France, the honour of sending a small army corps of 14,000 men, under General Maison, to the Morea for the purpose, not of making war on the Turks, but of compelling the Egyptians to evacuate the Morea and cease fighting the Greeks. His description of his policy to the Chambers on June 14, 1828, left no doubt as to his intention: "Between the exorbitant claims to mastery which have resulted in such disasters to our country, and the self-effacement to which she has been for some time reduced as the consequence of those disasters, there is a fair medium position from which we should not again stray, that namely of an advisory influence, whose demands are alike just and temperate, and its arguments as sound as they are strong. The wisdom of our sovereigns, the commanding influence of our habits and manners, the very situation of our country, invest us with this office, and it is right that we should undertake it. The prosperity of all countries has to-day merged into one common stock. France is in some sort the centre and bond of union of the whole."

It might have been expected that language so noble should have been gratifying to French ears, and that a Frenchman would be proud to be told that, twelve years after Waterloo, France, which had been freed from its fetters by Richelieu in 1818, and restored to its place among the Great Powers in 1820, was in 1828 entrusted with a mandate from Europe in favour of freedom and justice. And yet the contrary occurred. In the words of Bignon, a Liberal Bonapartist, who wrote the story of the great deeds of the Empire, "The action of the last Cabinet is throwing a lurid after-glow over the present." The policy of M. de la Ferronays, like that of M. de Damas, displeased all parties, because it involved peace, even though it was peace with honour. Palmerston, who was then visiting France, saw all the benefit she could derive from it: "The country is prosperous, taxation light, the people happy. She wants nothing but peace, to become powerful."

But Palmerston also noted the passionate yearnings for conquest and revenge which were awakened in the new generation by the memories of former glories. From Sebastiani he learnt that the men of the Left expected from the alliance with England her consent to the conquest of the left bank of the Rhine. It was under the influence of this hope that a triumphal reception was given to Charles X in September 1828, when that monarch, conducted by the Dauphin, visited Alsace. Chateaubriand, in opposition to the policy of his chief, wrote from Rome to his friends begging them to insist upon a policy of alliance with the Tsar and conquest. "The union of France and Russia (he said) ought to dictate laws to the world. Let us say to the Tsar, If you want Constantinople, be prepared to make an equitable partition of Turkey, and give us the Archipelago. The powers like Prussia, whose geographical position does not permit them to increase their territories, may receive compensation elsewhere. As for us, we intend to have the Rhine boundary, from Strasbourg to Cologne."

It cannot be denied that to such ambitions as these a short expedition to the Morea, limited in operation, and arrested at the very moment when the Russian forces were beginning a glorious campaign beyond the Danube, must have appeared singularly insufficient. "Instead of making an alliance with Russia, we are giving way to England, by a futile expedition only half carried out. The world is watching us!" said Lamarque and Laffitte on February 6. To the invectives of patriots the Royalists added their fiery criticisms. Chateaubriand demanded the post held by La Ferronays, who complained of fatigue and ill-health, "in order that he might give a fresh glory to France." The prize was for others, whom Charles X was already secretly preparing to nominate, in the place of his present Cabinet, which had proved powerless in the face of the coalition, and had lost his confidence owing to their demand at the beginning of 1820 for fresh concessions to disarm the Liberals. It was to Polignac that he proposed to give the Ministry of Foreign Affairs, in order to ensure a vigorous internal action against what he called the Revolution. To the Liberals, who were fretting for a new Electoral Law, de Martignac, like Necker in 1789, when the country was demanding a National Assembly, offered, in January 1829, a Bill for a freer, or at any rate wider method of electing the Communal, Cantonal, and Departmental Councils. "Look at these crowds of educated, hard-working active men," said he, "whom public life will awaken and stimulate, who by their social position, by their consciousness of capacity, and by the example of so many successful men before them, will be urged into public affairs by so many different roads. Above all, look at the generation now coming on, which is going to take our place. What means have you of satisfying their natural and legitimate demands? Open to them the doors of a new career; give them the means of satisfying their noble ambitions in the Commune or the Department; mark out for them an area in which they can gain honour. It is hard to restrain an emotion of the soul; you may by prudence direct its action, you may multiply its objects so as to diminish its ardour and insistency."

These tactics, hazardous as they were in the opinion of Charles X, were not of a sort to deceive a nation which could still recall the great days of the "Constituante," or read the story of it in the pages of Thiers and Mignet. The Opposition deputies, with the aid of the dissatisfied Royalists, forced Martignac to withdraw his Bill, April 8, 1829. His attempt at mediation between Crown and people was over; the days of his Ministry were numbered; it lasted, however, till the vote on the budget in July 1829.

Charles X had already in his own mind made his selection of their successors after the coalition which upset Villèle. He had been gradually led to make a definite choice between the two parties whose ephemeral agreement had brought to naught the six years' efforts of that Minister; he inclined more than ever towards the group of wild Royalists, who proposed, without regard to prudence or compromise, to re-establish the Ancien Régime, with its privileges and its Ultramontane Church. As to the men who, with none of the spirit of the Revolution, thought they could defend its work, he found that he had no use for them. Bigoted, and intoxicated by the flattery of his Court, he followed this dangerous path in the full belief that Providence would protect him in some mysterious way, and suffer him to carry out the divine mission which, he fancied, had been entrusted to him.

In regard to the matter then in hand, it appeared that the policy of concession, with which he would have no more to do, would have required of him even greater sacrifices than those made by Louis XVIII to appease the Opposition in 1817. What France wanted in 1815 was not so much liberty as rest. Now a new generation had arisen which, in the teeth of the will of the Bourbons on their alien-supported throne, demanded a Charter, and that not as a royal largesse, but as the expression of the will, and the guarantee of the rights, of the nation. In Paris the Opposition called with increasing insistency for the Charter, and for the recognition of principles which could not be reconciled with the ideas of Charles X as to his own rights and powers. A conflict was inevitable. "There is no way of treating with those people, and it is time that we stopped," said the King to Martignac in April 1829. When he summoned M. de Polignac from the embassy in London in August 1829 to form a Ministry, he had resolved to assert his authority and his rights against the nation.

The *Journal des Débats*, a royalist organ, but then in opposition, laid bare the intentions of the King (August 15, 1829) in an article which made an immense noise in the country, and was accordingly prosecuted by the Ministers. In alluding to the three principal members of the new Cabinet—Polignac, the *émigré* who had conspired with foreign Powers, the accomplice of Georges Cadoudal, Bourmont, the hero of the war in Vendée, who had deserted during the Hundred Days, La Bourdonnaye, the inspirer of the "White Terror"—the writer said, "Coblentz—Waterloo—1815! These are the three fundamental principles of this Ministry! Put it under rack and press! Nothing will distil from it but humiliation, misfortune, and danger!" In Paris all the organs of the Liberal Press replied to the royal challenge by a shout of wrath; in Lyons people were already saluting the Republic in the person of Lafayette; in Brittany and elsewhere associations were formed to defend the Charter, and support a refusal to pay taxes. "An adventurous policy," said the Duchesse d'Angoulême, who could recall the days of the Revolution, "has never brought us luck."

Although Polignac appeared to have made up his mind, on taking office, to carry out the scheme desired by Charles X, nevertheless he showed some signs of hesitation. He announced the intention "of reorganising society, of restoring to the Clergy their influence in matters of State, of creating an aristocracy and fencing it round with privilege," but he did not pass on at once to action. It was perhaps the fault of his colleague La Bourdonnaye, the

Minister of the Interior, who, after threatening modern society for ten years with war to the knife, now showed himself incapable of carrying out or even of conceiving of any plan of action. He retired on November 17, 1829, in disgust at the influence which the King allowed to Polignac. It seems probable, however, that La Bourdonnaye was responsible for the indecision of that period. "Polignac is not wanting," said a Liberal journal, "in faith in his cause, or in courage. Personally he is a man of resolution, but he has not made up his mind as to its object. He is always looking to see what is to be done." The mischief of it was that in his search he left everything to Providence with the tender confidence of a mystic, and waited for it to fix the hour and give the signal. The only way to carry out the act of violent absolutism for the purpose of which Charles X had created this Cabinet would have been to be quick, and to surprise and intimidate the Opposition by a rapid exhibition of sheer force. "Our position is ridiculous and therefore criminal," said M. de Montbel, the new Minister of the Interior.

As Minister for Foreign Affairs, Polignac had perhaps calculated that he might induce France to accept his programme of reaction and counter-revolution, by offering her the glory of conquest, according to the usual practice of his party. When he took the reins, on August 9, 1829, Russia had just planted her victorious forces at the gates of Constantinople, and the occasion seemed favourable for foreign policy on a large scale. If Charles X was prepared frankly to abandon the Turkish Empire to the Tsar Nicholas, might he not recoup himself on the left bank of the Rhine and in Belgium? Scarcely had Polignac attained to power when he commissioned our ambassador at Petrograd, the Duc de Mortemart, to settle a scheme of division with Nesselrode; but his offer, which arrived in September, was too late. Nicholas I had found at Berlin, and particularly from his brother-in-law, Prince William, the support he required to complete his victories, and a mediation so powerful as to induce the Turks to admit his success in the Treaty of Adrianople. By this peace Greece was set free, under the Presidency of Capo d'Istria, a tool of Russia (September 1829); Servia was erected into an autonomous state (though subject to the same influence) under Milosch Obrenovitch; the Danubian principalities were placed under the direction of the Russian General Kisselef; and last of all, the Porte was left "in a position in which life was impossible except by the protection of Russia."

Down to the end of 1829, Polignac flattered himself that the advantages realised by the Tsar in the East would give him an appetite for more at the expense of Turkey, "who had received her death-blow," said Wellington. He asked M. de Boislecomte, who acted as political director in his administration, to prepare a scheme for the revision of the Treaties of Vienna on the basis of the Treaty of Adrianople. What a success would it not be for the Bourbons, if they succeeded by this arrangement in effacing the defeats which ended the struggle between united Europe and the Revolution and Empire! While thus furthering the glory and grandeur of France, would they not also recover the right to govern their own country as absolute masters, like Napoleon, whose memory they would efface? These were the combinations on which the Prince de Polignac was working, towards the end of 1829, with the view of preparing for his expected act of absolutism. But in the month of January 1830 they crumbled to pieces under the weight of the overwhelming influence now established by Prussia at Petrograd. On January 3, 1830, Frederick William IV issued a curt *non possumus.* "At no price would he give up the left bank of the Rhine to France"; and all had been said.

When the Chamber met again in March 1830, Polignac

had not decided upon the programme of reaction which he proposed to force on them. The fair and seductive scheme of conquest which he intended to barter for it had had its day. But the Opposition had prepared its plan of campaign for the decisive struggle between Parliament and the Ministry. Prudence had now become a rule among all Liberals, even among those who were not afraid of a revolution or a change of dynasty, and even the younger generation, who were secretly conspiring in the *National* and the *Globe*, along with Thiers and Mignet, to get rid of the Bourbons. They knew that, as between themselves and the King, between Paris and the Court, it was the people who would have the last word, a people weary of revolutions, held with a tight hand by the Government and the officials, yet a foe to disorder. Skilful in making the best use of the fear with which the threat of a return to the Ancien Régime was beginning to inspire the French people, and delighted with the provocations given by the Court, they studied how to avoid frightening the people on their side, so as to reap the whole benefit of their opponents' threats. Being further convinced that for them union was strength, the most hot-headed remained calm, the wildest Republicans kept silence, standing in defensive array behind the bourgeoisie, the great writers, and the school-teachers, Liberals though Royalists, who represented order and legality in conflict with violence and arbitrary rule. And these men did not decline the duty which devolved upon them by common consent. On the contrary, Royer-Collard himself said that they must strike, quickly and strongly. "Probably nothing can save the Monarchy; but, if it can be saved, it will be by dragging it with all speed out of the path which leads to the abyss." In leaving to men of this type the care of organising the defence of liberty and of modern society, the Opposition gained the advantage, in the eyes of the nation, of appearing as the champions of order and public tranquillity.

On March 18, 1830, Royer-Collard, at the head of a deputation of the Chamber, presented to Charles X an address voted by 221 deputies, charging him, though still in respectful language, with having called to his counsels a Ministry bent upon governing against the wishes of the people and the country. This protest did not surprise the King, who had taken steps to meet it and had called to the Ministry of the Interior a fighting man, M. de Peyronnet, whom he soon afterwards ordered to dissolve the rebellious Chamber and to summon the electors to meet in the following May. He fancied that France would approve this act of authority.

For lack of a conquest on the Rhine, M. de Polignac had started with all speed a grand expedition against the Dey of Algiers. Huzzein Dey, an energetic and clever adventurer who had established himself at Algiers in 1818, had insulted the French consul in 1827, destroyed the buildings of the French agency at La Calle, and refused all reparation; and he had then obliged a French squadron to spend two months in a laborious and useless blockade. When Admiral de La Bretonnière visited him in July 1829 with renewed demands for satisfaction, he replied by opening fire on him. At the end of January 1830, M. de Polignac, finding that he must give up his more brilliant schemes, set to work with M. de Haussez, his Minister of Marine, to organise an expedition against Algiers. Forty thousand men in three brigades, and a strong fleet, were placed under the orders of Marshal Bourmont, and sailed from Toulon on May 25.

"If this expedition is intended to facilitate a *coup d'état* within our frontiers," said Talleyrand, "it is a grave mistake." For the nation had no attention to spare then except for the conflict between Crown and Parliament. Paris declared itself from the first moment in favour of the Opposition; in the provinces, banquets were given to the

221 deputies, the re-election of whom was now the watchword of the party; and the country was so undisturbed in its certainty of victory, that the price of the public funds actually went up. "It was to order and peace," said M. Guizot, "that every member of the Opposition looked to make his fortune." The nation which was supporting the Liberals in their resistance to the King was composed, according to Armand Carrel, "of the readers of the newspapers, who are interested in the discussions of the Chamber, the capitalists, the leaders of industry, the possessors of the soil, the whole of Paris, the artisans, tradesmen, and merchants of the great towns, the owners of country-houses." This nation, which had so long submitted to the commands of the royal officials, now, on June 23, and July 19, formally recorded its condemnation of the policy of the King, and M. de Polignac, his Minister. Charles X dissolved the Chambers; they sent him back the same majority increased by 53 new members, making 274 Liberals against 100 who were still loyal to the Court party.

This lesson, which might have enlightened another prince, only exasperated Charles X. He had just received news that the army sent to Africa had occupied Algiers on July 9; and this success encouraged him to treat the opposition in France as he had treated the Dey. After all it was only by a miracle that he had succeeded in Algiers. About the time when the French fleet was leaving Toulon, the English Government, disliking the enterprise, had induced the Sultan (on April 25) to appoint another Dey, one Tahir Pacha, who was sent with all speed to Algiers on board a Turkish vessel with orders to give the French the required satisfaction, and so stay the expedition. The naval officer in charge of the blockade stopped the Turkish ship, and sent it to Toulon where it was kept in quarantine; but for which, the expedition would have come to an end before it had well started, and Polignac would have had another disappointment to add to that of the triumphant re-election of the 221 Opposition deputies.

The most serious trouble for himself and his master was to come, when he induced Charles X to strike an arbitrary blow, directed not only at the Chambers, but at his rebellious people, the blow that was to cost him his crown. At some time between July 20 and 25, 1830, in order finally to overcome the Opposition in the Press and in Parliament, the King determined to promulgate, by virtue of his sovereign power, two laws, one dealing with the Press, the other with elections—matters which the Charter he had sworn to obey forbade the Crown to touch without the concurrence of the Chamber (§§ 8, 15, and 35). The first of these suspended or, to speak plainly, totally destroyed the freedom of the Press. The second enacted that the number of deputies should be reduced to 250, to be elected at the chief town of the departments under the control of the prefects, from a list of candidates or of men of local mark drawn up by the district committees; and once more he dissolved the Chamber. In the Royal Council, de Peyronnet, Minister of the Interior, Guernon-Ranville, Minister for Ecclesiastical Affairs, and de Montbel, Minister of Finance, loudly asserted the illegality of these measures as opposed to the text of the Charter and to the spirit of the Constitution. They were met by a reference to § 14 of the Charter, which gave the Crown the right of making "regulations and ordinances for the administration of the laws, and the security of the State." This was the argument by which Charles X and his Ministers tried to induce the country to adopt the "Four Ordinances" published on July 25—the first on the Press, the second on the new mode of election, the third dissolving the Chamber, the last summoning the electoral committees on Sept. 6 and 18.

Neither the King nor his advisers were under any illusion as to the import of their decision. "I count on you," said the King, "as you may count on me. Our cause interests us both alike; and, be it for life or for death, we are pledged to one another." But they had not taken into account the reception that public opinion in Paris would give to their challenge. On the day on which the Ordinances appeared in the *Moniteur*, Charles X left the palace of St Cloud to hunt at Rambouillet. Polignac had not even thought it necessary to notify Champagny, the Minister of War, nor Marmont, the military governor of Paris, to be ready in case of disturbance. The Funds were going down, but the prefect of police, when summoned to advise the Council, reported that Paris was not moving.

On that same evening, while the journalists were collecting at the offices of the *National* to sign a protest drawn up by Thiers, shouts were raised in the streets of "Up with the Charter! Down with the Ministry!" Crowds were now swarming in front of the Ministers' offices, and the deputies arranged to meet on the following day at the house of Casimir Perier, being still minded to avoid any recourse to violence. The actual rioting arose in the afternoon of the 27th, on the news that the Government were seizing the printing-presses of the Liberal papers. It was caused by artisans and school-boys who had raised the tricolour flag and were taking up arms against the Bourbons, to avenge the defeats of 1815 to which the Restoration was due. "This is a national revolution!" said one of these young Republicans. "The sight of the tricolour has roused the population of Paris; and it would now be far easier to lead them to the Rhine than to St Cloud!"

Like his brother in 1789, Charles X believed that he had only to deal with a city riot; and his Ministers expected to be able to get the better of it with ease. Polignac moreover had full confidence in the Divine protection; he related to Berryer that the Virgin had appeared to him, and his confidence gave heart to the King. Marshal Marmont had taken steps to defend the Tuileries, but, by the 28th and 29th, he discovered that he was cut off there by the rioters around him who held all the centre of Paris, and enfiladed him from the left bank of the Seine. His troops offered a poor resistance to the popular attack. During these blood-stained days, the deputies and journalists whose opposition to the Crown had unwittingly let loose the forces of the people, were really more alarmed than the King, who went on playing chess quietly at St Cloud while his throne was at stake. "You are ruining us," said Casimir Perier, "by deviating from the law; you are making us give up a splendid position." Sebastiani, Guizot, and Dupin refused to march under the tricolour flag, which the rioters were flying; Thiers fled into the country; A. Carrel and Rémusat expressed their disapproval of the popular violence. Their hopes returned for a moment, when the Liberal Peers on July 29 deputed M. de Semonville and M. d'Argout to St Cloud to implore the King to stay the disturbance by dismissing his Ministers, and revoking the Ordinances. But it was too late; the mob had captured the Tuileries; and a Provisional Government resolved on the expulsion of the Bourbons was being formed at the Hôtel de Ville at the summons of Lafayette. It was no longer with Charles X, powerless now as he had been blind before, and cowering before a street riot, that the Liberals of the Chamber were to deal, but with the great democracy of Paris, whose excesses they dreaded no less than those of the Counter-Revolution.

Thanks to Lafayette, whose popularity was then such that he might have been the President of a glorious democratic Republic, they succeeded. Casimir Perier, with the help of Laffitte and Thiers, hastened to meet Lafayette on July 29, for the purpose of combating the influences which prompted the wayward hero of the American War and the French Revolution to prefer a republic. They offered him the part of Monk, with the leading rôle to the Duc d'Orléans, whose candidature for the throne Thiers was beginning, during the night of July 29, to set afloat on the public mind; they urged with vehemence on the General, and on the populace who idolised him, that the best sort of Republic would be "a popular Monarchy under a prince who had fought for the Revolution of 1793 against the *émigrés*." This solution satisfied everybody, Guizot, Aug. Thierry, Thiers, and the young Liberals, who were always drawing a parallel between Charles X and James II, "having their minds full of the Revolution of 1688, its success, and its results in the foundation of a strong and free constitution." Louis Philippe at first evaded the offer, but afterwards, on the advice of his sister, Madame Adelaide, and of Talleyrand, accepted it in the shape of the "Lieutenancy General of the Kingdom." This took place on July 30, at the very moment when Charles X, in order to protect his children, submitted to the dismissal of his Ministers and the revocation of the Ordinances. Too late!

On July 31 Charles X, who had first retreated to Trianon, left St Cloud, not feeling himself safe there, since the Duc d'Angoulême had been deserted by his troops while trying to close the Pont de Sèvres to the Parisians. He hoped to get to Rambouillet, and thence, with the support of France, "to fight with one hand, and treat with the other." On August 2 the Duc d'Orléans, after issuing a proclamation stating that henceforth the Charter would be a reality, went to the Hôtel de Ville to receive from Lafayette the investiture from the People. It was the People of Paris, and no foreign armies, that had created this new dynasty. On August 4 Charles took the road into exile, carrying with him to Holyrood in Scotland the dream that he and his purblind and clumsy-handed followers had tried in vain to realise, the Restoration by the help of Providence of the Ancien Régime.

CHAPTER IV

THE EARLY YEARS OF LOUIS PHILIPPE

For the revolution which sent the Comte d'Artois and his family back into exile after fifteen years of power the signal had been given by the leaders of a party that was not, in any sense of the word, a popular party, being composed of Peers nominated by the Crown, of deputies elected by a very small minority of the nation, of an aristocracy of property, and indeed largely of landed property. When the 221 deputies who presented the address of March 30, 1830, had thereby tempted Polignac and Charles X to the double dissolution of the Chamber, to the promulgation of the Ordinances, and to the experiment of a *coup d'état,* they had no notion that they were creating a revolution involving the overthrow of a dynasty. They were anti-revolutionists and Monarchists; their efforts had been directed against the Ministry whose absolutist and reactionary proposals they deemed to portend destruction to the Bourbons. Their sole desire was for the maintenance of the Charter and the reconciliation of the Legitimate Monarchy with modern France, imperilled by the Polignac Ministry, and they did not notice that in the game then being played Charles X and his Ministers were partners for weal or woe, and that the defeat of the Ministers involved assured ruin to the King and to Legitimate Monarchy.

The riot in Paris, the revolt of the youths in the schools which had been brought on by memories of the Republic and by the work of Bonapartist agents, in obedience to the summons of the Paris Press, had suddenly, in three days, overturned the throne of Charles X. These three days, during which Paris had been able to coerce the Government, had sufficed to deprive that Government, whose power was centralised in Paris, of its control over the nation, which was either indifferent or hostile to the Bourbons. "It is the Capital that has beaten the Bourbons and secured our liberties," said Salverte, a Liberal deputy, on July 31. The Government that Paris had created for herself, the Municipal Committee sitting at the Hôtel de Ville "in the place of an authority imposed on us by foreign arms," spoke up "in the name of an upstanding nation," pronounced the fall of Charles X, and proclaimed that France demanded democratic institutions based on popular sovereignty, "in which all classes should have the same rights." A Committee of Parisians, which called itself the nation, relying on the help of the National Guard restored on July 29, had forthwith taken possession of the administration of France, which had collapsed with the fall of Charles X, just as Louis XVIII had done after the ruin of Napoleon.

With no right beyond what the necessity of the case conferred, the Hôtel de Ville appointed as "Provisional Commissaries" Dupont de l'Eure to Justice, Baron Louis to Finance, Comte Gérard to War, Admiral de Rigny to the Marine, Guizot to Education, the Duc de Broglie to Home Affairs, M. Bignon to Foreign Affairs. The Comte de Laborde took the Prefecture of the Seine, Bavoux the Police, and Chardel the Post-Office. Some of these selections, and especially those of Guizot and de Broglie, indicated an attempt on the part of the Liberal bourgeoisie to regain hold of the direction of affairs which it appeared to have lost by the riot of July 29. They had hurriedly returned from their constituencies on the summons of Casimir Perier, and felt that their numbers warranted them in vindicating the authority of the provinces which had elected them against the will of Paris alone. On July 28 they drew up with the help of Guizot an address expressing their continued loyalty to the King and the Charter. They negotiated with Marmont and the Chamber of Peers for the defence of the monarchical system against the riots of Paris, as well as of the Charter against the Ministry. But the decisive victory won on that day by the insurgents had speedily determined them to seize the opportunity offered them on July 29 by the partisans of the Duc d'Orléans, Thiers, Laffitte and Talleyrand, to save the principle of Monarchy by changing the dynasty, on the analogy of the Revolution of 1688.

This resolution, which made the fortune of Louis Philippe, also made the fortune of this group. When the deputies who had been sent about their business by Charles X re-assembled on July 30 in their Chamber, they had a better right to represent France, even in the absence of the members who remained loyal to the Bourbons, than the people of Paris had. Of course Laffitte, their President, moved an address to the combatants of July; but the wording of it was not entrusted to Republicans like Labbey de Pompières and Salverte, but to Guizot, Villemain and Benj. Constant, all confirmed Royalists, and it was carried by acclamation. The last-named deputies were preparing to maintain the Monarchy so as to "obtain, under the Duc d'Orléans, the constitutional developments that were called for by the Charter." They declared it their intention to pass laws to settle the Constitution, and, although they represented only a minority of the nation, they spoke, in their discussions with Paris, in the name and on behalf of the whole of France. Before this assertive attitude, and helped by the compliments which the Duc d'Orléans was wise enough to pay on July 31 to Lafayette and the victors of the Hôtel de Ville, in order to gain them over to his side, the

Provisional Commissaries, and the revolutionary Government of Paris drew back, and shortly afterwards abdicated. Of the contest fought during those three days the advantages fell to the Chamber which Charles X had dissolved, and to the Duc d'Orléans, its elected sovereign; otherwise no trace of it was left but the National Guard in arms for freedom. Lafayette took command of this body, and was confirmed in the office by Louis Philippe on August 1, 1830.

On that day a new Government took up its abode in the Palais Royal. It was still only provisional, but of the sort wanted by the Liberal bourgeoisie, having been constructed to "secure guarantees for social order and for the security of person, property, and law," as announced by the Lieutenant-General. Louis Philippe laid stress on his intention of "allowing himself to be guided in this noble task by the Chambers." He called (August 1) for the cooperation of men who had the confidence of the bourgeoisie, selecting Dupont de l'Eure as Minister of Justice, Comte Gérard for the Department of War, Baron Louis for that of Finance, Guizot for the Home Office, M. Bignon as Minister of Education, Marshal Jourdan as Minister of Foreign Affairs, Sebastiani as Minister of Marine, Girod de l'Ain as Prefect of Police, and Odilon Barrot as Prefect of the Seine.

Thanks to the Duke and to the courage he showed in the streets of Paris when faced by a populace still hot from battle, thanks to his skilful handling of Lafayette and the Republicans at the Hôtel de Ville, the deputies reaped the benefit of a revolution which they had not made, or even desired. At the beginning of August 1830 they found themselves as completely masters of France as the senators and deputies of the Empire were after the fall of Napoleon; and like them they straightway created a Monarchy and a Constitution in the name of the French people.

After electing to its Presidency Casimir Perier, a name which represented the combination of order and monarchy, and after the ratification of the election by Louis Philippe, the Chamber proceeded at once "to consolidate the powers of the nation in the hands of the Prince-citizen," to use the language of that same President. On August 6, Bérard, one of its members, speaking from the tribune, said that the supreme law of necessity, which laid upon the Parisians the duty of repelling oppression, and upon the Chambers that of securing the tranquillity of the country, had now caused a vacancy on the throne, which must be provided for; and that, in conformity with that necessity, the elected of the people, whose interests they were bound by their office to defend, and whose wishes they were charged to express, should proceed without delay to determine the conditions under which Monarchy should be restored.

The discussion of this Constitution lasted for two days only, August 6 and 7. It was not exactly a Constitution such as those which the Assemblies of the Revolution had elaborately concocted; it was rather a revision of the Charter granted by the Bourbons and then withdrawn by them. There were many in that Constituent Assembly, notably Royer-Collard and Guizot, who were satisfied with their triumph alike over the Ministers of Charles X and over the populace, over reaction and revolution, and who would have preferred to make no new and fundamental alterations, and not to change the Charter in any way. They would have been glad to escape the reproaches of the defenders of monarchical power, Hyde de Neuville, and Chateaubriand; the latter saying with supreme eloquence, "The law is of your making; it is you who are proclaiming the sovereignty of brute force." At any rate they succeeded in attenuating, by all the draughtsman's artifices that they could command, the extent of the very substantial and fundamental alteration which they were enacting in substituting the sovereignty of the people for that of the Crown. They omitted some matters, and they added others. They made no declarations of rights like those of 1789, though they were called for by the Republicans, Demarsay and Mauguin, and actually moved for in the Chamber by M. Persil as "indispensable." They simply struck out the preamble of the Charter of 1814, which had been in a sense an assertion of the royal prerogative "purporting to grant to Frenchmen as a favour the rights that belonged to them by nature," as the member in charge of the Bill, Dupin the elder, said with the assent of the Chamber (August 7). Nowhere, not even in the arguments of M. Dupin or in the decisions of the Chamber, was a word said about the will of the nation; only an assertion of "the hopes and common and urgent interests of Frenchmen," whose sovereign was to be henceforth styled the King, not of France, but of the French.

In the same way and with the same intentions the deputies struck out § 14 of the Charter, by an abuse of which Charles X had usurped the power refused to him by the Charter of legislating by Ordinance without the cooperation of the Chambers as provided for in the next clause. On the other hand, clause 16 of the Charter, which reserved to the Crown the right to propose legislation, was enlarged by extending that right to the two Chambers equally. However much the new builders of the Constitution might try to conceal the fact, they were practically returning to the distinction established by their predecessors in 1789 between the executive power delegated to the King and the legislative power delegated to Parliament by the people, from whom, and from whom alone, they knew, if they did not then say, that all power must be derived.

In the next place, with a view of putting an end to the alliance between the Throne and the Altar, and doing away with the intrigues of the priestly party, and "their impudent pretensions to exclusive domination, as contrary to the spirit of religion as to freedom of conscience, pretensions which have caused the fall of the reigning branch of the Royal Family, and brought the country to the verge of ruin," the deputies decided that the Catholic religion was no longer the religion of the State, but the religion of the majority of the French people. The words no longer conferred a right; they were a mere statement of fact; and the only reason for their unexpected appearance in the middle of an Act of Parliament was to explain the maintenance of the Concordat, and prevent a formal separation between Church and State.

On the other hand, when the deputies laid down that the rights of the nation had precedence of all others, and that the nation was an independent entity, as against the claims of the Crown and the Church, they should logically, and as a matter of course, have abolished the privileges of the Chamber of Peers, as a body existing outside and in possible opposition to the nation by virtue of birth or of royal favour towards the nobility. But they preferred to "reserve for future discussion the questions connected with the Peerage, on which the best intellects and the most ardent friends of liberty might find themselves divided." The problem of the existence of a House of Lords in a democratic country, which worshipped equality, was harder than that of the establishment of a Monarchy elected nominally by the people, but actually by the deputies, harder than that of the maintenance of a Concordat with a Church which had lost all its claims upon the State; and nearly two years were spent in finding a solution. A law passed on December 29, 1831, in substitution for clause 23 of the Charter, abolished the monarchic and hereditary Chamber of Peers, while retaining its name, and set up in the place of it a sort of Senate recruited by the Crown out of certain limited classes of citizens distinguished by their services to the nation; each appointment was to be separately made and for life only. Meanwhile the old Chamber of Peers continued to exist, but in a mutilated form. The Peers nominated by Charles X were excluded; a hundred Legitimist members withdrew. With these changes, the Chamber survived, pending the nomination by Louis Philippe of the new Peers whom the Constitution empowered him to choose and nominate. It survived indeed for some months, distrusted or despised by the democracy, and only preserved in despite of consistency by the deputies, who were pleased to see their Constitution and their King receiving approval and investiture from another body, the Upper House.

The next step was that, after completing their labours by the abolition of the censorship over periodicals and books on behalf of the journalists, and by the promise of a law as to juries in press prosecutions, the deputies drew up, in concert with the Peers, a declaration for submission to the Lieutenant-General, setting forth the conditions upon which the Crown was to be offered to him. "Here is a nation," said the deputy who submitted it to the Chamber, "in full possession of its rights, which says with equal dignity and independence to the illustrious prince to whom it is proposed to offer the Crown on the terms laid down in the Law, 'Will you reign over us?'" And just as if they had actually been the nation, the deputies made their way to the Palais Royal bearing the new Constitution to the Duc d'Orléans. "I regard it," said the prince, "as the expression of the will of the nation." On August 9 he convoked the Chambers, and informed them that he accepted all the clauses and pledges without reservation or restriction, and swore to observe them. He was then presented by the Marshals of France with the insignia of the Monarchy, thus restored after a short interregnum for the benefit of himself and his family.

Here, then, the representatives elected under the Constitution of the Restoration stood face to face with the people whose efforts had destroyed the Monarchy hostile to these representatives on the one hand, and the new Monarchy by means of which they proposed to deprive the people of the benefit of those efforts on the other; and, mediating between the two with skill and good fortune, they succeeded in establishing a system which for the next eighteen years was to shackle the strength of both Crown and people. It is true that they announced a long programme of proposed legislation, on electoral rights, on the right to trial by jury, liberty of conscience, public education, liberty of instruction, and the organisation of the National Guard; to the last-named had been entrusted the care of the revised Charter and of the rights which it recognised, and as a symbol thereof it wore the tricolour cockade. But they reserved to themselves the right of choosing the time and fixing the conditions under which these promises and concessions to the democracy should be realised. And in the meantime, by virtue of the law, and with the support of their new-made King, they were able to establish themselves in power. From the metropolis which had apparently laid down its arms before them, they were at once able to control France, by means of the administrative centralisation which had so well served Napoleon and the Bourbons.

The greater part of the Ministers appointed by the Lieutenant-General remained in their posts, only in the Ministry of Foreign Affairs M. Molé was appointed in the place of Marshal Jourdan, and the Duc de Broglie in that of M. Bignon as Minister of Education. Nearly all of them, with the exception of the Duc de Broglie, belonged to the upper bourgeoisie of a Liberal tone, and had made their reputations in the army or the civil service of the Empire (as had Guizot, Baron Louis, Sebastiani, General Gérard, Dupont de l'Eure) or their fortunes in business, like Laffitte and Casimir Perier. Either from caprice, or necessity, they changed the whole administrative machinery, judicial and military, by which France could be made to accept their laws and their government—the high officers first, prefects of the Seine and of police, prefects of departments, members of the Council of State, government representatives in the principal provincial Courts of Justice, military governors, commanders of army corps, and admirals. They were thus enabled to give the principal posts in the State to men of their own class, Liberals either old or young, whose fortunes, depending on their own, ensured the execution of their wishes and guaranteed the permanence of their power, such men as Benjamin Constant, the elder Dupin, Bernard de Rennes, Barthe, Odilon Barrot, Daunou, Villemain, Generals Soult, Lamarque, Clauzel, Marbot; Thiers, Mignet, and Baude from the staffs of the *National* and the *Temps*. "There are 40,000 place-hunters in Paris," said one observer; and all of them were intriguing and back-biting. A poet, Auguste Barbier, stigmatised the "pot-hunting" of the day. Under a King, who whether by choice or policy was inclined to act the part of a middle-class, popular monarch, the French bourgeoisie spread themselves out in France as if in a conquered country. And shortly afterwards, the Electoral Law of April 13, 1831, which doubled the number of electors by lowering the electoral qualification by 100 francs, merged the landed aristocracy in the general mass of commercial men, tradesmen, and manufacturers who from this date make up the legally recognised nation.

Behind this façade, hastily put together out of the materials and by the workmen left behind them by all the successive political builders from Napoleon onwards, "lay France with its 30,000,000 souls, France, that wanted no disturbance," said Dupin, "France, that only asked to be strongly governed." Alarmed for a moment, on the close of the reign of Charles X, at the mere thought of a return to feudalism, this nation of peasant proprietors, of agricultural traders, was glad to accept the Constitution manufactured for them by the bourgeoisie of Paris and the officials whom they sent into the provinces to secure peace and all the benefits of modern life. There were some districts so backward that they could scarcely understand what it was all about. "What is this Charter that people are talking about?" asked a peasant woman of the Cevennes in her *patois*. "Why," replied a neighbour, "she's the wife of Louis Philippe." Taken as a whole, the country was ready to provide the "Monarchy of July" and its statesmen with a body of easy-going electors, not difficult to bring into line, ever ready, now as heretofore, to vote in favour of any existing government, indifferent indeed to every political question, and incapable of sacrificing themselves for the general interest. All the nation asked was to be allowed to carry on in silence its task of labouring and saving, and to take its political direction from the officials and deputies sent down from Paris by the bourgeoisie which had come into power with the new King, to guarantee public order and the rights of property.

Though they had so easily made themselves masters of the Government and of the country, the leaders of the higher bourgeoisie were yet unable to induce the world to forget with equal ease that, in the interval between the fall of Charles X and their own appearance, Paris had for an hour been the mistress of France, and that Paris here meant the population of the suburbs, the operatives, the soldiers of liberty, in one word, the Democracy. The courage that had given victory to the People, the moderation and good conduct they had exhibited in success, had suddenly engendered in this mob a moral tone; and those who expected to find them such as they were pictured amid the bloodshed and disorder of the Terror had reason to be surprised at their own mistake. Their rights had been allowed public recognition—even their right to insurrection, which had turned out to be the safeguard of France against the powers of reaction. Pity and justice joined to attract attention to the social conditions of these working classes. Although Armand Carrel had been the bitter foe of all popular movements before the days of July, no one felt more strongly than he, or described more truly, the effect of the insurrection in Paris. "It emancipated the lower classes, as that of 1789 had set free the middle class; it summoned them to take their share in governing, a share ever growing with the growth of civilisation." The progress of industry and commerce, so marked during previous years, had not only given the heads of factories and of banks an authority which the Revolution now recognised; it had also and by the same act increased the numbers and enlarged the functions of the rank and file of the operatives in Paris, in Lyons, and in the great industrial centres of Alsace. As the population of Paris increased, it became conscious alike of its power, its authority, and its future.

There were divers small but zealous and active centres in which the younger Republicans were brought into contact with the survivors of the Great Revolution; and in these men they found not only counsellors to instruct but also leaders to encourage them. Such counsel was found in the school of St Simon, who had died in 1825, leaving his ideas to act upon the age like a new social and economic religion, through the mouths of Bazard, Enfantin, Olinde Rodriguez, Michel Chevalier, Laurent de l'Ardèche, Hippolyte Carnot, Charton, and Pierre Leroux from the publishing offices of the *Globe*; such again were the disciples of Babouvisme, among whom Buonarotti, who had been picked up in 1830 by Voyer d'Argenson, was discussing the conditions of the working class with Cabet, Blanqui, Raspail, and Louis Blanc; such finally were Cormenin, Garnier-Pagès, Achille Roche, Auguste Fabre, Cavaignac, Trélat, Bastide, Thomas, in their various societies—the "Aide-toi, le Ciel t'aidera," "L'association de la Presse," "Les amis du peuple." All had but one object for their militant propaganda, the material and intellectual advancement of the working classes, by the conquest, more or less speedy, of their political rights. Their popularity in the suburbs may be imagined.

This popularity was enhanced by their ardour in claiming for the French people the right to intervene against foreign sovereigns on behalf of oppressed nationalities. From the Revolution onwards it had been a tradition that the idea of a democratic republic was closely linked with that of propaganda. The satisfaction of the victors of July was based mainly on the hope of "a national war which should once more rouse the echoes of the bugles of the Convention and Empire!"—a singular mixture of vanity and altruism, of crusade and conquest. "If I had refused the Crown," said Louis Philippe later, "we should have had anarchy, and with anarchy, war." Thus the efforts of the statesmen who had called him to the throne for the purpose of reassuring France and Europe were thwarted in Paris and in Lyons by the circumstances of the time and by the democratic leaders, who were craving for "action." In the opinion of Augustin Thierry the good sense of the provinces should have been called in to deal faithfully with the turbulent metropolis.

It was clear from the outset that the prevention of an immediate conflict between the bourgeoisie and the people was the precise task for which the new King was wanted. He may have wished to undertake this delicate duty; at any rate he accepted it, and he was perhaps the only man competent to cope with it at that moment. He had qualities and capacities which are rarely united. A Liberal by family tradition, as well as by education and temperament, he was recognised as the citizen-king who had fought at Jemmappes on the side of the Revolution; none the less was he a lineal descendant of Henri IV and Louis XIV. His simplicity and good-humour gave him the air of a democratic official, while his birth warranted his assuming the deportment of a king. He was courageous, and could be familiar. Lafayette in the ceremony of his investiture had represented his accession as creating "the best of all republics"; the choice of Parliament marked him as the true head of a bourgeois Monarchy.

In the first months of his reign, Louis Philippe felt that he was more popular than the bourgeoisie that had elected him; and he did not fail to cultivate that popularity, believing that a "democracy needed to be flattered and made friends with." He used to saunter on foot about the capital in a white hat with an umbrella. He welcomed the workmen who offered him a drink, the National Guards who shook hands with him at their reviews. From his balcony in the Palais Royal he would join with the people in singing the Marseillaise. His special predilections were for the men who had the command of popular favour—for Lafayette, the idol of the Parisians, whom he called "his friend and protector," for the banker Laffitte, Odilon Barrot, and Dupont de l'Eure. The democrats on their side liked the King better than the deputies, whom they nicknamed "Guizotins," and whose fights with Charles X had soon been forgotten, while their conservative policy was disliked. But for the skill of Louis Philippe, a conflict might have broken out between the people of Paris, in their full fever of revolution, and the heads of the bourgeoisie, which Casimir Perier called upon (on September 29) "to assure itself as quickly and forcibly as possible of the power requisite against the threatened return of rioting." The Clubs continued to be agitated, urging the operatives to pass the most violent resolutions against Ministers, and against the Chamber of Deputies, the dissolution of which they demanded; it had been already dubbed "a decrepit, illegitimate Chamber" by their backers in the daily press, such as the *National*. And yet the Chamber had, at the people's demand, permitted the impeachment of the Ministers of Charles X, though at the same time they petitioned the King for the abolition of the death penalty. On October 17 a furious mob marched to the Palais Royal, and thence to Vincennes, for the purpose of seizing and summarily executing M. de Polignac and his colleagues; and it was with difficulty that Lafayette, commander of the National Guard, and Odilon Barrot, Prefect of the Seine, could be induced to assist the Ministry, who had accordingly to capitulate to the rioters on October 19. "Between the France of 1830 and the Ministry," said the *National*, "there is some incompatibility of temper." In order to save the unpopular Chamber and to avoid compromising himself, Louis Philippe allowed de Broglie, Guizot, Casimir Perier, Baron Louis, Dupin, and Molé to resign; and put the reins into the hands of his friend Laffitte, assisted by Marshal Maison, Marshal Gérard, General Sebastiani, de Mérilhou, and a young deputy who owed him his good fortune, the Comte de Montalivet (November 2, 1830).

The King played this part of mediator with the same skill and upon still more delicate ground, on the frontiers between France and Europe. On the first news of the events of July, foreign governments had adopted an attitude of unfavourable reserve. On August 4 Metternich had already advised his sovereign to call a Cabinet meeting forthwith. "Italy (he said) will be affected by these revolutionary practices." He suggested to the Emperor Francis to come to an understanding with the other sovereigns which would have revived against France the Treaty of Chaumont, "a difficult, but absolutely necessary task." Two days afterwards, at Carlsbad, the Chancellor of Austria and Nesselrode, the Chancellor of Russia, drew up and signed a scheme of alliance, known as the "chiffon de Carlsbad," for the consideration of Prussia.

After all, this tendency to concerted action among the absolute monarchs was not perhaps entirely determined by the fear caused by the Revolution in Paris. The King of Prussia had plainly stated his willingness to remain neutral, if France did not threaten the Rhine; Metternich did not conceal his wish to utilise any French intervention in Italy as a pretext for occupying the principalities of that peninsula; and the Tsar Nicholas, whose ambition had been first excited and then arrested by the peace of Adrianople, was urging the German States into conflict with the French, so as to get by this means a free hand in the East, like his grandmother, Catherine II. Whatever were the interested motives of the politicians who met at Carlsbad, the public exhibition of them was calculated to irritate the French, who were tempted, after defeating Charles X, to try their hand on the overthrow of the Holy Alliance which had supported and restored him. And these menaces supplied the precise opportunity they wanted for denouncing the treaties of 1815, which they had always abominated.

In the months of August and September 1830 Belgium rose against the domination of the Dutch. Of course it was not solely the Revolution in Paris that had given the signal for this outburst, which had been in preparation for some years, and owed its being to the opposition of Catholic Belgium to the Protestant house of Nassau. But the champions of Belgian liberty came at once to an understanding with the conquerors of Charles X, dictated alike by interest and by sympathy; de Celles, Gendebien, de Merode, and de Brouckère at once took advantage of this feeling, for the French rather yearned to cross swords with the Holy Alliance in Belgium, and to see Louis Philippe once more at Jemmappes.

For this, however, Louis Philippe had not the faintest inclination. When he accepted the crown on August 31, he knew that the one condition on which he could establish his sovereignty in the place of a republic, was that he should resist the propagandist tendencies of the nation on the one hand, and the provocations of absolute monarchs on the other. One of his first cares was the careful selection of envoys to foreign Courts to carry the assurances of his pacific intentions; indeed he did not even wait for their departure before acquainting Europe with these intentions in the course of August, either directly by letter, or in conversations with the foreign representatives in Paris. He wished it to be understood as soon as possible that he had accepted the gallant and delicate task of protecting the future of France and the repose of Europe from "terrible calamities." If the insurrection in Brussels had not come to rouse the party of action in Paris, and if the sovereigns of Europe had not demanded better guarantees than pacific assurances to induce them to suspend their threatened measures, this first attempt at mediation on the part of the King of the French, the first effort and starting-point of his rule, might have had a good and speedy result.

But the Tsar did not answer the letters of Louis Philippe until September 19, and then very coldly; and he deferred his complete recognition of the new Monarchy to January 8, 1831. While the French were urging their King to declare himself in favour of the Belgians, Nicholas I did not conceal his desire to form a coalition at the Hague against them, simply to subserve his ambitious designs, and at the risk of a general conflagration in Europe.

Louis Philippe then turned to England. He had found her well-disposed towards him from the outset, and quite ready to recognise him from September 1. To conduct negotiations with her which should secure a peace, he selected

Talleyrand, the man who at the Congress of Vienna had succeeded in checking the allied ambitions of Prussia and Russia by a secret accord with England. In spite of his age, the Prince de Benevento established himself at the French Embassy in London on September 9, whence he carried on a frequent and secret correspondence with Louis Philippe, his sister Madame Adelaide, and the Cabinet, and thus became practically the principal Minister of the new régime; so distinctly did the mission of peace entrusted to him stand out as the main interest of that régime. With Wellington and Aberdeen, the Tory Ministers whom William IV had retained on his accession, he established a close understanding, which for the next three years was the principal factor in the pacific policy of Louis Philippe, the main-spring of the mediation between France and Europe which he induced both parties to accept. Not that the English Conservatives, who were often accused by the Whigs of sympathising with Charles X, were particularly fond of the Revolution; they disliked its propaganda, and were rather afraid of its infection. But they appreciated the fact that it was to the interest of Louis Philippe to preserve peace. And peace had always, since 1815, been the main object of the prayers of England, as it was now the essential principle of the Tory Cabinet.

The actions of Russia in the East, just now connected with the rising in Greece, whose future had been lately settled with great difficulty by the Conference of London, had been disturbing England for nearly ten years. If the Tsar, on his side, preferred upheavals in Europe which might give him an opportunity of advancing into the Balkans and perhaps of partitioning Turkey, the object of England, *per contra*, was bound to be to anticipate or stop all causes of quarrel among the Powers; and of these none could be more dangerous than a revolt of the Belgians, and the consequent menace of a French invasion of the Low

Countries, the danger against which England had invariably during the last century taken up arms.

Hence it was that at this moment the English Cabinet and the Orleans King had very strong reasons for combining against the policy of Russia and the propagandism of France. The understanding suggested by Talleyrand was more than the mere mutual attraction of two Liberal Administrations; it was a necessary alliance, founded on community of interests. It was consequently concluded without difficulty. Talleyrand yielded to the English the credit of settling the Belgian question in London. He recognised gracefully that England owed some support to the King of Holland, as she had acquiesced in the Dutch annexation of Belgium in 1815 as a compensation for sundry Dutch colonies ceded to herself. He was very careful not to formulate explicitly in London the doctrine of non-intervention with which Louis Philippe had at once met the threats of the Continental Powers. In return for his politeness he obtained on October 15, 1830, a secret treaty from Lord Aberdeen, the first pledge of peace and cooperation, invaluable to the new and scarcely yet accepted dynasty, the first benefit of that dynasty to France and to the Belgians. This treaty laid down that no armed intervention in the quarrel between the Belgians and the King of Holland would be tolerated, and that no mediation, except of a pacific character, should be attempted between them. On October 20 Austria and Prussia agreed to this arrangement, tendered to them by the Duke of Wellington; and Russia, being now in the isolation that it had intended for France, was obliged to disarm. Of course it did not at all suit the designs of the party of action, or the propagandists of Paris. But Talleyrand let them grumble. He had the pleasure of hearing the Conference which had assembled in London on November 4, 1830, for the settlement of the Greek question, appoint a Committee of Arbitration as to the Belgian matter with instructions to maintain peace.

The first decisions of this Committee, which owed its existence to French diplomacy, were issued on December 20, 1830. They called upon the King of Holland to give up his Catholic provinces and forced the absolutist sovereigns to recognise the freedom of a nation that had won it for itself; on the other hand they imposed on that nation an obligation never to apply for French aid for the acquisition even of territory to which it believed itself to be entitled, Breda, Maestricht, and Luxemburg. This was an instance of the mediation, favouring alike national rights and European peace, which Louis Philippe, with the support of the English alliance, was then carrying out. The Papal Nuncio had good reason to congratulate him, on January 1, 1831, on having "ever more and more confirmed tranquillity in France, and by that very fact secured the peace and harmony of the whole of Europe."

Yet at that date the difficult task he had undertaken on the morrow of the days of July was far from being completed. The struggle between the democratic party and the deputies representing the bourgeoisie, strengthened by 150 new members in October 1830, had not been concluded by the retreat of the leaders of the bourgeoisie. The Laffitte Cabinet gave pledges to the people, whom Lafayette, the darling of the Parisian mob, and Odilon Barrot, Prefect of the Seine, a "Republican without knowing it," were flattering with all their art. Thereby they immediately became objects of suspicion to the Chamber of Deputies, who at once asserted their opposition to the policy of action, by re-electing Casimir Perier to the Presidency of the Chamber by a majority of 120.

The trial of the Ministers of Charles X, which had begun in the Chamber of Peers on December 15, 1830, seemed a favourable opportunity for a final rupture. The populace was beginning to be agitated and demanded death sentences, standing in deep masses at the doors of the Court during the six days of the trial, to intimidate the Judges. The Ministers whose duty it was to maintain order, Lafayette and Odilon Barrot, anxious only not to offend the irritated mob, called off the troops who might have kept them down, and delivered Paris over to the National Guard, who in their turn proposed on December 20 to deliver the prisoners over to the rioters. But for the vigorous intervention of the Minister of the Interior, the King's private friend, Montalivet, who ordered the ex-Ministers of Charles X to be removed from the Luxembourg to Vincennes, the rioters would have had the better of the law; and the accused might have died a violent death on the same day that the Chamber of Peers condemned them to imprisonment for life. The news spread on the following day, and further excited the anger of the mob. The students made a demonstration before the King, demanding republican institutions.

The Chamber, being satisfied that the country was tired of this disorder, and that the business and industry of the nation were suffering from the agitation in Paris, determined to give a lesson to Lafayette, and a warning to the Cabinet. When the discussion on the organic law as to the National Guard came on, on December 24, 1830, the Chamber abolished the office of Commandant General of National Guards, on the understanding however that the decision was not to be retrospective, and that Lafayette was to retain the office for life. But the old General showed spirit, and tendered his resignation, being persuaded that neither Louis Philippe nor his Ministers would dare to accept it. Furthermore he demanded the abolition of the Chamber of Peers, the dissolution of the Chamber of Deputies, and universal suffrage. Combined with his dictatorship, this would mean the abdication of the King, and the accession of democracy. Louis Philippe forbade his Ministers to accept the conditions demanded by Lafayette, though it cost him the services of Dupont de l'Eure; the General retired with the contempt even of the friends whom he had disappointed, and was succeeded by Comte Lobau (December 27, 1830). Thanks to the King, the Chamber came out of this crisis victorious; and, regardless of the Ministry which did not possess its confidence, passed the laws relating to the National Guard, to Juries, elections of Mayors and Municipal Councils, and to direct taxation as promised to the Liberal bourgeoisie.

The conflict was all the more acute because complicated by the profound dissension of the various parties on matters of foreign policy. Louis Philippe had barely escaped the first danger, the possible conflagration in Belgium, when he had to face a general European crisis. Between December 1 and 15, 1830, news was brought to France of the insurrection of the Poles against the Tsar. "An event of real joy to us as a nation!" said the young Republican, Louis Blanc. The heroism of the Poles was extolled in all the theatres of Paris, as "another Revolution of July." For the Orleans dynasty it was of essential importance at this moment to muzzle Lafayette, who held obstinately to the memories of the Revolution of America, and was publicly preaching the "propaganda" to the nation in arms. The Belgians, dissatisfied with the decisions of the Conference of London, and encouraged by the diversion created by the Poles in the East of Europe against the sovereigns of Russia and Prussia, were appealing for aid to the Republicans of France, and inveighing against Louis Philippe and Talleyrand. Lastly, the Italians were preparing in Modena and the Romagna for a revolt organised by the Bonapartes and favoured by the Carbonari, by Mazzini, and Menotti. Metternich of course was prepared to seize Italy by force of arms; but the Italians found lively sympathy, if nothing more, in the ranks of the party of action in Paris, and even in the family of Louis Philippe in the person of the Duc d'Orléans, his eldest son.

No sooner then had the King of the French succeeded in stopping a fresh outbreak in Paris, and keeping the mob off the bourgeoisie which had called him to the throne, than he found himself involved in this general European crisis. His Ministers were somewhat loth to turn a deaf ear to the appeals which the insurgent nations addressed to the French nation. Talleyrand wondered for a moment whether the better policy for the new Monarchy would not be to swim with the current rather than against it, and annex a part of Belgium. One disturbance followed another in the capital, as the news arrived from that country and Poland. The most serious was that which broke out on February 14, 1831, at St Germain l'Auxerrois; the students and the mob sacked the church, where the Legitimists were assembled to celebrate an anniversary mass for the death of the Duc de Berry. Louis Philippe was thus in an embarrassing position, and the supporters of the old Bourbons wondered whether this did not give a chance of retaliation. The nation was in a state of unrest, dissatisfied at the lack of a governing hand. "Everybody," wrote the *National*, "is dissatisfied with everybody." Madame Adelaide had to admit the uneasiness of the King; she said to Talleyrand, "Our dear prince does not know what road to travel now!"

Louis Philippe extricated himself from these difficulties, the most serious that he had yet met with, by the method that he had adopted from the beginning of his reign, making himself a sort of personal arbitrator between the parties at issue both in France and in Europe. The easy-going levity of Laffitte allowed him to take the direction of Foreign Affairs into his own hands and thus to consolidate the alliance with England, by which he set great store. On January 20, 1831, without consulting his Ministers, he accepted Palmerston's proposal for the neutralisation of

Belgium, which would arrest the French propaganda and deprive the Belgians of its expected assistance in resisting the Conference of London. The Belgians tried to put him into difficulties by offering their crown to his son, the Duc de Nemours, but the King refused the offer very decidedly February 17, 1831. On the same date he selected as ambassador to the Tsar the Duc de Mortemart, who was sure of a welcome at Petrograd, with instructions to explain clearly the attitude of the French Foreign Office in the matter of Poland. Lastly, when revolution broke out at Bologna (February 1831), he enjoined upon his Ministers a policy of absolute neutrality. The Republicans twitted him with indifference, and with the abandonment of oppressed nations, which in their view reduced France to the position of a secondary Power; "the policy of France," said Mauguin, "ought to correspond to her power." Louis Philippe let them talk, being convinced that peace abroad was the sheet-anchor of his authority, which had suffered from the never-ceasing conflict between the People and Republicans of Paris on one side and the bourgeoisie on the other. When, in May 1831, he had secured himself abroad, he restored to office the leaders of the bourgeoisie whom from prudence and good tactics he had allowed to resign in November 1830.

Since the sacking of St Germain l'Auxerrois, rioting had been so to speak permanently established in Paris. Well-disciplined and organised, it would break out, first in one quarter, then in another, on the slightest pretext. On March 2, 1831, a party given at the Palais Royal was broken in upon by a crowd of working-men who insisted upon planting a Tree of Liberty in the garden. The public treasury was almost empty through stagnation of business. Then the King stepped in, in person, as he had done in the foreign question. He described his method, which he defined as a "happy medium between freedom and necessary order, between *action* and *resistance*." M. de Montalivet, the Minister of the Interior, was intriguing for the dissolution of the Laffitte Ministry; and Thiers, under-secretary to Laffitte, was instructed to invite him to resign. Laffitte had an audience with the King, and tried to take a strong line; but the dread of another riot, which all but broke out on March 10, called forth protests from the Chamber of Deputies. On the following day Louis Philippe summoned the President of the Chamber, Casimir Perier, and forced Laffitte to give way to him. On March 13, Perier, Baron Louis, and Admiral de Rigny returned to office. It was the victory of the "Happy Medium."

The Ministry of Casimir Perier

These few critical months had not after all done any harm to the bourgeoisie; and Louis Philippe had been of great use to them, first in giving office to the party of action, and then in dismissing them when the experiment had gone far enough, and a continuance of it would have wearied the nation. Casimir Perier now returned to office strengthened by the general desire of the country for rest at home, and for freedom to work in peace. "Order," said one of the journals, "is the present pressing need of France. Credit is shaken; commerce is dying. Order alone can restore us to security." If on the morrow of the Revolution the leaders of the bourgeoisie had tried to impose by force upon the Parisians, the victors of July, the programme which six months later France was imploring them to carry out without delay, they would have had a dangerous task, and would probably have risked not only the destruction of the Monarchy, but the loss of the very power that the deputies had usurped. The Laffitte Ministry had been one of transition skilfully handled by the King. Louis Blanc, one of the boldest of the republican leaders, stated afterwards with regret: "The conflict would have broken out, if the dissatisfied party had not been put on a false scent by the presence of men like Lafayette, Dupont de l'Eure, and Laffitte in the Ministry, whereby public opinion was misled." The tactics of Louis Philippe, more successful than those of the parliamentary party, who had been inclined at the outset to a policy of resistance, had secured his crown and assured the victorious return to power and activity of the men who had offered it to him. By forbidding the "propaganda" to cross the French frontier, by dissolving the impending coalition of the Continental Powers by means of the alliance with England, he had been no less useful to the cause of European peace. In fact, he had discharged every obligation that he might have contracted with the men of the middle class on the day when he accepted the crown of Charles X at their request, in order to avert the disturbances which they had determined to master; and in the meanwhile by his dexterity at home and his diplomacy abroad he had avoided the rocks on which the new fortunes of the bourgeoisie together with his own had risked shipwreck.

In this fashion, after only seven months of uncertainty, the authority of the parliamentary party had been securely established; it had been contending alike against democracy, the "tyranny from below," and against the Ministers of Charles X, and their "tyranny from above," and it claimed to occupy the "happy medium" between Republicanism and Legitimism. Under the rule of Casimir Perier, who had twice been elected to the Presidency of the Chamber by large majorities, there could be no doubt that the chief power would be in the hands of the Assembly; and the Electoral Law lately passed (April 8, 1831) had finally decided that point after long discussions. It is true that M. de Montalivet, Minister of the Interior, when bringing in a Bill on that subject at the end of 1830 had stated that it would be one worthy of the nation, and "not merely one of those laws by which the best Charter in the world could be stultified in the interests of any power, any party, any theory"; and he had not hesitated to add that the Bill would confirm and keep intact the right of the middle-class proprietor to political existence. But the Chamber had rejected the Bill "for fear of foul play on the part of the Administration"; they thought that the Government, when doubling the number of electors as fixed by previous legislation, had reserved to itself the power of selecting them exclusively from the more highly taxed citizens; for their part, they would have given the suffrage to all citizens paying a tax of 200 francs, whatever their number, believing that class to be the true bourgeoisie, and the friend of the Revolution. But the troubles in Paris and other towns supervened, at the beginning of 1831; and it occurred to the deputies that the Government were perhaps right in wanting to restrict at any price the number of electors, for the present at any rate. "Party pressure was less likely to act upon a limited and enlightened body than upon the Mayors." In order however not to give themselves away, they finally decided to adopt the 200 francs limit for their qualifying tax, but they rejected the extension of the suffrage to the classes suggested by the Government, the members of the liberal professions and of Councils General, magistrates, university professors, barristers, and solicitors. Members of the Institute and retired field-officers alone got any mercy from them, and that with great difficulty.

This aristocracy of wealth that had now come into possession of power allowed its views to be known as soon as the question of the minimum qualification for deputies came on for discussion. The Government, desiring to reach the landed nobility who had been the main-stay of the Bourbons, had proposed to reduce the sum fixed by the Charter by one-half. It was thought for a moment that the majority, desiring to recruit its numbers from the wealthy classes, whatever the origin of their wealth, would insist on keeping the figure up to 750–800 francs. "The characteristic of the last revolution," said one orator, "is the victory of democracy. The Chamber has gained everything that the other powers of the State have lost." It was impossible to put it more clearly. "If the Chamber does not include some elements of aristocracy, and also some of those who do not object to a sudden incursion of democratic ideas, no one can answer for the future." When the time came for voting, however, the Chamber took no action, fearing unpopularity; they diverted their precautionary zeal to another sort of safeguard, and tried to diminish the ratio between the number of deputies and electors in large towns.

This aristocracy had now secured power, owing to the complicity of the King's Ministers (April 15); having received some new blood in the elections of July, it now proposed to make use of that power through the agency of the Ministry, a body appointed by the King, but responsible in all matters to the Chamber, able to resist the King, but unable to resist the Chamber. "The confidence of the Chamber alone," said the new Prime Minister, "has earned me the confidence of the Crown." His statement on March 17, 1831, of the principle of government that he proposed to adopt was not less precise. "The principle of the Revolution of July is not insurrection, but resistance to any aggression by the sovereign power." Words could not more clearly indicate that popular disturbances might avail against the Bourbons, but would not be tolerated against institutions settled by the Charter of 1830. "It is to the Chamber, and to that alone, that we must henceforth look for the reforms so impatiently demanded. What then should France require of its Ministers, pending the meeting of the Chambers? Simply to act. Order within Law, and capacity to enforce it—that is what society needs. Order must be maintained; laws must be carried out; power must be respected."

This spirited language was a direct challenge to both the popular and the legitimist parties, whose weakness Casimir Perier did not hesitate to expose; but it was also a curious echo of the speeches of the First Consul to the nation in 1802, when wearied and sick of revolution. It corresponded to the desire which the country at large, and the bourgeoisie in particular, had felt during the past year—a desire for order and peaceful industry. We may imagine, then, the welcome with which it was received by a country which, though seduced for a moment into accepting the revolution in Paris, was always more interested in its private concerns than in politics, and was easy to govern through a government of any colour, if only it were strong.

For lack of the masterful and methodical hand, which at the beginning of the century had manipulated the constitution of France to this end and in behoof of his own authority, the Cabinet of Casimir Perier declared its intention of ruling on the same system as the Bourbons had adopted on their return from exile—they were to act as one man on the principle of the joint and several responsibility of Ministers. "This common responsibility which unites us will give us a right to require of our subordinate officers the same bond of union that we have accepted for ourselves. Harmony must prevail in every branch of the Administration. The Government must be obeyed and served in the true spirit of its proposals; it expects to receive the cooperation of its agents without reservation on any point." He was not speaking of the King, whose name in fact Casimir Perier scarcely mentioned in his first official statement; he was thinking of the leaders of the bourgeoisie, as the men who were collectively going to make use of the centralised system of Napoleon. The Prime Minister is quite willing that the King should reign, and even occupy the Tuileries, at the Premier's invitation. But he intends to govern for himself, like a First Consul, for and by means of the bourgeoisie, to dismiss the highest officers of the State, if they join any "Patriotic" or "National" Association against his wishes, and to intervene in the elections, in which he will not hear of "the neutrality of the Administration." To prevent the revival of the past which the Revolution of 1830 had made impossible, though the Legitimists would have restored it to life, to protect the country in the future from the onrush of a democracy which in Paris threatened mischief, Casimir Perier created in the name of Louis Philippe a sort of bourgeois and conservative republic which all through the nineteenth century proved itself to be the most stable government for France. A journalist of the day called it "a doctrinaire throne surrounded by cast-offs of the republican party."

And so it turned out. From the beginning of April, 1831, Casimir Perier set his battle in array against the revolutionary party, "denying them the right to force Ministers into precipitate action on political reforms." He prosecuted sixteen Republicans on the charge of conspiring against the Monarchy in the month of December (July 6, 1831). One of these was Godefroy Cavaignac, a son of the member of the Convention, who proclaimed his republican faith before the jury amid the applause of a crowded audience. Lafayette appeared, to give the prisoner the support of his popularity; his advocates, Marie, Bethmont, Dupont, Michel de Bourges, Republicans like himself, were unsparing in their attacks on the bourgeoisie. Their clients were acquitted amid the acclamations of the Parisians. Their acquittal all but gave the signal for an insurrection, and served at any rate as a pretext for a democratic banquet, followed by a popular procession to the Vendôme Column to the strains of the Marseillaise.

Casimir Perier, in no way alarmed, directed the law officers to keep up incessant prosecutions against the republican journals—the *Tribune,* in which Armand Marrast was preaching permanent riot; the *Figaro,* edited by Alphonse Karr, Félix Pyat, and Gozlan; the *Caricature,* in which Daumier used his talents for the advancement of his republican convictions. Next came prosecutions of Republican Associations, the *Amis du Peuple,* under the direction of Raspail, Trelat, and Blanqui, the *Société des Droits de l'Homme,* which took its inspiration from memories of the Convention. In spite of the sympathy of the Parisians for the victims, this energetic action of the Ministry maintained order, and clogged the wheels of the propaganda. Little by little the riots became less frequent; those arranged for July 14 and 28 came to nothing. The news of the capture of Warsaw on September 16 and 17, 1831, kindled fresh disorder, but Casimir Perier met it with energy and success. The result of the general elections of July 1831, when even in Paris the Ministry were successful in the case of eight candidates out of twelve, encouraged him to go on. Armand Carrel had to confess that he was increasing his unpopularity by the frequency and ineffectiveness of the democratic attacks; he had to contend against "the power of panic in the word Republic." By virtue of his struggles with the Republicans, Casimir Perier came to be looked upon as a saviour.

He was, moreover, the resolute defender of the modern system against any aggressive return of the Ancien Régime and of the Bourbons. If the Carlists, as they were then called, had only been Conservatives attached to the principles of order and stability represented by the Orleanist bourgeoisie, they would have recognised it as to their advantage to acknowledge the mistakes made by Polignac and the Ultras, which by allowing the democracy of Paris to get the upper hand, though only for a moment, had cost

Charles X his crown. But either from loyalty, like Chateaubriand, or from a spirit of revenge, like Genoude of the *Gazette de France*, they obstinately insisted on pursuing the phantasm of a restoration of the Ancien Régime, even by means the most abhorrent to their own principles. Since August 10, 1830, they had gone beyond even the Republicans in their demands, asking for the liberty of the Press, liberty of Associations, the free elections of Mayors, and universal suffrage. Any weapon was good in their hands against a victorious democracy. These Ultras, who in 1819 were insulted by the notion of sitting in the same Chamber as the regicide Grégoire, who in 1822 persecuted Manuel with their abuse, now did not show the slightest objection to an understanding with the admirers and apologists of the Convention—a temporary alliance no doubt, but still a singularly risky one for champions of Divine Right, and one which in the eyes of the nation transformed them, yes, even them, into revolutionists. They forgot that La Vendée had left behind it as bitter memories as the Convention, when they joined the republican conspirators in Paris in getting up a rising in that district. The Duchesse de Berry (representing the Duc de Bordeaux), assisted by her friends the Duc de Cars, the Duc de St Priest, and Marshal Bourmont, was doing her best, first in London, and afterwards in Italy to organise another Vendean war. To prevent this, Casimir Perier despatched a lieutenant-general into the West on March 16, 1831. The Duchess' ridiculous undertaking broke down completely, and, in the words of Metternich, "was bound to have a result contrary to her wishes. It did not shake the throne of Louis Philippe; it only made his seat more secure."

In six months Casimir Perier had thoroughly established his own authority in the Chamber, and the authority of the Chamber and of the bourgeoisie over the country and the King himself. He had realised the policy conceived fifteen years earlier under the Restoration by a Liberal bourgeoisie, that of a continuation of the Imperial system without the Empire, fighting the battle of the bourgeoisie against both democracy and absolutism. The democracy of Lyons revolted once more at the end of 1831, and carried with it the National Guard; but the Ministry met it victoriously with a force under the command of a son of Louis Philippe, and bearing the authority of the King in whose name it fought. Against the partisans of the Ancien Régime, the irreconcileables, and the Ultramontanes, he had recourse to the abolition of the hereditary peerage and to the principles of Liberalism. Physically and morally endowed with all the qualities that make a leader, tall of stature, of commanding mien, "having the gift of making his friends obey and his foes give way," Casimir Perier wielded a sort of dictatorship, but a dictatorship with a tendency to Liberalism. This Napoleon of the bourgeoisie was surrounded by a group consisting of Dupin, the "Voltairian bourgeois who loved order and hated Jesuits," Guizot, the disciple of Royer-Collard, who held the love of revolution to be the principal obstacle to freedom, and Thiers, whose ambition was at times embarrassed, in this alliance with older men and Conservatives, by the memories of his own revolutionary youth. These were the conditions under which the laws were passed whereon the Constitution of July henceforth worked. On October 24, 1831, Montalivet brought in a Bill on Primary Education, which eventually served as the draft for the great work carried out by Guizot in 1833. In March 1832 the Minister of War proposed a measure for organising the recruiting service of the army by a new law on Conscription.

The fact was that Casimir Perier understood that to induce the nation to acknowledge the authority of the middle class and of himself he must provide it, if not with some tangible glories and victories, at any rate with some gratifications to its vanity. As he had once said, "I am counting on the help of those who desire a France calm and free; I call on them in the name of the strength, the armaments, the pride of our common country." In loyalty to the policy pursued by Talleyrand and Louis Philippe in London, he determined to put a final stop to a propaganda which would end in embroiling France with the whole of Europe. "We need peace; and when this warlike effervescence has subsided, my work will have been done, and I may retire." It was he who signed the two Conventions of June 26 and October 14, 1831, drafted by Talleyrand, by which the liberty and neutrality of Belgium were assured. The strength of his conservatism was as marked in foreign as in home policy. He said, "The Revolution of 1830 has not created either France or Europe afresh; and we cannot ignore the necessity of adapting ourselves to these entities as they exist." In spite of the sympathy of France for Poland, that unfortunate nation was abandoned to the vengeance of Russia, who was congratulated on her victory by Austria and Prussia (September 7, 1831). Nor were the French allowed to go to the assistance of the Italians in their insurrection against their princes.

This policy of abstention however, which General Lamarque and Marshal Clauzel characterised as a regrettable abandonment of the interest and honour of France, was not, either in the intention of the Minister, or in fact, a policy of eclipse. This was clearly seen when the King of Holland, counting on the aid of Prussia, invaded Belgium, and occupied Antwerp (August 1–12, 1831). Casimir Perier forthwith asked and obtained of England liberty to send an army into Belgium, and obliged the invader to retreat. No doubt the almost immediate recall of this force was not welcome to the pride of the French, who would have preferred a longer chance for activity and consequent renown. Yet it was difficult to deny that it had fulfilled its object, more so perhaps than a longer war for securing the liberty of the people. Similarly in Italy, when Pope Gregory XVI called for the assistance of Austrian regiments in the Romagna, the despatch of a French regiment to Ancona on February 22, 1832, was a return thrust, as vigorous as it was prompt, to the crafty tactics of Metternich, who was preparing to lay hands on the Italian States, in spite of his promises to the contrary to Louis Philippe in July.

Alike in the Italian peninsula and in Belgium, Casimir Perier boldly claimed on behalf of France a right of arbitration which was as disinterested as the protection of Austria and Prussia respectively was selfish. If we may estimate his intervention by the anger it provoked in the European chanceries, it did not give the impression of being a timid policy, and scarcely looked like a surrender. The Prussian Government compared it to the "brutality of Bonaparte"; while Austria and the Holy See expressed their indignation at this "violation of the Law of Nations." To the criticisms of the ambassadors Casimir Perier replied in a speech of feverish wrath, which may well have recalled to them the violent scenes with Napoleon. He almost trampled upon them in his rage. "It is I who am defending the Law of Nations, not you; what I have done was demanded by the honour of France. I am entitled to the confidence of Europe, and I fully count upon having it." Metternich was bound to admit that Casimir Perier's object had been to flatter the pride of the nation, and that he had succeeded in so doing, without provoking a rupture between France and Europe. He had been looking for some way to maintain peace—a necessary condition—and at the same time to afford to France the satisfaction of figuring as the *grande nation*, the protectress of peoples, for which she was so anxious. And Europe forgave him; his remedy was a "little pill," as the Duc de Broglie called it, less formidable than the earthquake from which Casimir Perier saved the world, by wresting

France from the grip of the insurrectionists through his firmness at home and his spirited demeanour abroad.

The material and moral authority of the bourgeoisie never again advanced so quickly or reached so high a pitch as in the days when Casimir Perier was making good his position in the way described. Thiers compared the work it did to that of the Consulate after the Directory; and it was in fact, like that, the wind-up of a revolution. Louis Philippe was at first annoyed at the ways of his Prime Minister, who held meetings of the Council without him, refused the Crown Prince admission to them, and insisted on seeing despatches before the King. But he had too much good sense not to appreciate the value of his services, too much shrewdness not to discover some means of getting in his voice: "Perier" —he used to say—"gave me some trouble, but I managed to break him in at last." He had reason thereafter to regret the loss of so good a servant, who died in harness, on May 16, 1832, carried off by cholera. When the Premiership was offered to Casimir Perier, by M. de Segur and Montalivet, he said to them: "You are asking me for my life. You don't know what I suffer; I shall be dead before the year is out." His death, at the time when the epidemic appeared to be weakening, after claiming so many victims during two months, was not so much the result of the disease as of exhaustion of an already shaken constitution; for the last month of his life he watched himself die. His Ministry had lasted barely more than a year; but he had worked so energetically for the maintenance of peace at home and abroad that the nation, consoled by the revival of commerce and industry, and by the re-establishment of her finances and her credit, declared itself in favour of the Ministry which he had created—"the system of March 13th."

CHAPTER V

LOUIS PHILIPPE AND THE PARLIAMENTARY BOURGEOISIE

The opinion of the French nation was clearly expressed in the following months. Immediately after the death of Perier, on May 28, 1832, the Opposition whom he had beaten published a manifesto, a report signed by Laffitte, Odilon Barrot, and Garnier-Pagès, which, while asserting its loyalty to the dynasty, declared that "France was being humiliated and the Revolution stultified by the Conservative bourgeoisie." The nation treated it with indifference; in Paris alone an attempt was made by the republican clubs to get up disturbances among the working-men and foreign revolutionists, who assembled on June 9, 1832, for the funeral of General Lamarque, the Liberal orator, another victim of cholera. A riot broke out on the bridge of Austerlitz, started by the display of a red flag amid shouts of "Vive la République!"; barricades were raised on the left bank of the Seine, round the Pantheon, in the neighbourhood of the Hôtel de Ville, and as far as the Place des Victoires. But they were driven to retreat on the evening of the same day by General Lobau, supported by the King who had hastened to the spot from St Cloud with his loyal troops and the citizen force of the National Guard. On the following day the victory was complete; and the King appeared in person, with courage and resolution, surrounded by applauding crowds, while the republican leaders did not show their faces. This revolt of Paris, the most serious that had taken place since 1830, was crushed. One month earlier, on May 21, the Duchesse de Berry, who with the help of certain royalists had tried to raise La Vendée, was compelled by the royal forces to take flight and go into hiding at Nantes. Lastly, news arrived that the son of Napoleon, the Duc de Reichstadt, the hope of the Bonapartists, had died in Vienna on July 22, 1832. When Casimir Perier assumed the reins of government, he bade his friends take courage, and profit by the weakness of their opponents; much more might he have done so now, when by the working of his policy and the accidents of the time all these opponents had been reduced to impotence.

Indeed it was not from the democracy of Paris nor from the exiled Bourbons that the bourgeois party in the Chamber, whose authority had been secured by Casimir Perier, had most to fear in the way of retaliation after the death of their all-powerful chief, but from the King, who had acquiesced in the tutelage of his Ministers without accepting it. The crown may have come to him as the gift of the Chamber in August 1830; Louis Philippe now claimed that he had also won it, and certainly kept it, by his own courage and skill; it was odd, he thought, that anyone should now want to prevent him from governing or to give him a "vice-king" to do his work. The practice that he adopted in June 1832, on his own initiative, of showing himself once more boldly in the midst of a Parisian crowd, seemed to conceal a calculated purpose, and a wish to restore the dignity of his position at the head of France which had been compromised by the leaders of the bourgeoisie, by coming to the front at a critical moment under the eyes of all men. His remarks in 1832 to Odilon Barrot and Laffitte, when they came to assure him of their loyalty, indicated some intention of the sort. "In the Council of Ministers, outside which it appears that I am to be kept, I have my own system of government."

Certain acts of his pointed in the same direction. Louis Philippe seemed to treat the death of Casimir Perier as a deliverance from a personal rival, so deliberate was he in filling up his place. He seemed to intend to take upon himself the Presidency of the Council, though Casimir Perier had often designated Guizot as his successor. With his youthful Minister of the Interior, M. de Montalivet, whom he transferred from Public Education to that office, he took the administration into his own hands, and proposed not to reign only, but to govern. With Sebastiani still at the War Office, he could use the army against any troublesome people at home, or beyond the frontiers defend the result of his labours in Belgium (where his daughter Louise was now queen, having married Leopold of Saxe-Coburg on August 9), or check Metternich in Italy. He laid himself out to be seen and to be doing, and did not conceal his regret that he had so few opportunities of addressing the Assembly or the Nation.

The parliamentary leaders were disturbed and disappointed; they did not conceal their annoyance at seeing themselves ousted or threatened with that fate. They took their revenge all through the summer by charging the Ministers, who furnished the King with his administrative staff, with weakness and incapacity. This was the starting-point of a latent struggle between Crown and Parliament which was eventually to be mischievous to both. Louis Philippe was irritated by the Doctrinaires, who feeling secure in their seats claimed the right to speak in the name of the Nation. The Doctrinaires on their side recalled to memory the services of Casimir Perier, and sneered at the efforts of the "Pygmies" (the adherents of the King) against both Legitimists and Revolutionists; the latter seemed to be unable to check the Duchesse de Berry, to obtain a conviction against Berryer, the most famous of her defending counsel, or to stay the progress of socialistic teaching and

Saint-Simonianism. The hottest foe of the King's policy was Dupin, who was skilfully selecting for himself a leading rôle in the conflict which was now approaching.

Louis Philippe was wise enough to settle that quarrel, which was as dangerous for the Doctrinaires as for himself, by making concessions. He had applied to Dupin, who had tried to dictate conditions, and was dropped. Marshal Soult, to whom Louis Philippe next applied, was more accommodating, as was also M. Guizot, who was willing to accept the Ministry of Public Instruction instead of a first-class post. The Duc de Broglie took Foreign Affairs, Thiers the Ministry of the Interior (October 11, 1832). The King brought the friends and colleagues of Casimir Perier back to office. He allowed Marshal Soult, speaking in their name, to say that his policy would be that of his illustrious predecessors, "A national policy, such as the two Chambers had formulated"; but he fully expected to be able to command the President of the Council owing to the docility of Marshal Soult, Duc de Dalmatie, and also the Ministry of the Interior, the youthful holder of which was not in the least a Doctrinaire, and in fact owed his fortune to the King. He had an opportunity a little later to explain his actions: "If these three gentlemen, Thiers, Guizot, and de Broglie, agree, I am neutralised, and cannot make my opinion prevail. They are just Casimir Perier in three persons." For the moment he seemed to acquiesce in the doctrine of the sovereignty of the majority, on the necessity of which Thiers insisted; and this was so much to the good for these successors of the parliamentary dictator. The King was satisfied for the moment with having got rid of Guizot, whom Casimir Perier had designated as his successor in the Presidency of the Council.

The system of that great Minister survived him for four years, through a number of ministerial changes; and during these years the French bourgeoisie succeeded in establishing themselves in power, on the methods taught by him, which required sufficient energy and spirit in the conduct of foreign affairs to satisfy the national pride without arousing a real conflict with Europe, sufficient authority and resistance to anti-constitutional factions to ensure order and the new social system, and to negative any return to the doctrines or practices of the Ancien Régime. They declared themselves to be, in the words of Soult, "as devoted to the glory as to the security of France."

The first act of the Ministry was a summons to the King of Holland to withdraw his troops from Belgium on November 12, 1832, at the latest. A Convention made with England on October 22 authorised France, in case Antwerp was not evacuated by November 15, to send an army corps into Belgium, on condition that it returned to France immediately and did not occupy any fortified place. Marshal Soult was dexterously silent as to this condition, and only gave the French the pleasure of seeing (on November 20, 1832) a brilliant array of troops and among them the King's sons. Part of these, under Marshal Gérard, laid siege to Antwerp; part, under Sebastiani, marched on the Scheldt. By the success of this expedition, which ended on December 23, 1832, in the capitulation of Antwerp, Soult was able to induce the nation, proud of its feats of arms, to overlook his severity against his enemies at home.

On November 7, 1832, Thiers determined to arrest the Duchesse de Berry, who was still buoying up the hopes of the royalists from her hiding-place at Nantes, her sole protector being Queen Amelie. "We want to capture the Duc d'Enghien, not to shoot him. We are not rich enough in glory for that." A spy in the pay of Thiers discovered the secret harbour of the princess, who was taken along with some of her friends and lodged in prison at Blaye. This accomplished, Thiers was transferred to the Ministry of Public Works (December 11, 1832), leaving M. d'Argout, a Legitimist, the task of being what he called the Fouché of the new régime. Against impenitent Legitimists, the Ministry now held a hostage; and they held her up to the day when the secret marriage of the Duchess to a Sicilian named Lucchesi Palli came to light, followed by her confinement on June 10, 1833. This was a decisive blow and a cruel mortification to the Loyalists. "The Queen begged and prayed me," said Louis Philippe later on, "but I was bound to let my Minister have his way. No personal considerations could be put into the scale against the imperious necessity for crushing a great political faction." The eloquence and devotion of Berryer were henceforth to be the sole supports of a lost cause. Public opinion was ebbing away from it; the Catholics abandoned it at the call of Lamennais and Montalembert, and set up, in *L'Avenir*, an organ wholly and solely Catholic.

The Soult Ministry was now in a position to turn upon the Republicans, who had not laid down their arms in spite of the repressive measures in June. M. Guizot had been rather premature in telling the Chamber on February 16, 1833, "The riots are dead, the clubs are dead, the revolutionary propaganda is dead." Under the ashes of the conflagration, only half extinguished in 1832, lurked a spark, which the chiefs of the democratic party fanned into flame. The effect of the vigorous repression had been to give the propaganda a more secret character, and to increase the influence of the more advanced groups of the party.

One lately founded club of pronounced republican views, the Club of the Rights of Man (*Société des Droits de l'Homme*) had begun during the past year to absorb all the others; its president, Godefroy Cavaignac, wanted to return to the Constitution of 1793 "for the moral and political enfranchisement of the proletariat." Now and again, members of this club who had also seats in the Chamber, such as Puyraveau, d'Argenson, de Ludre, Garnier-Pagès, and journalists or barristers who appeared in defence of Republicans (twenty-seven of whom were thus prosecuted in 1833) proclaimed their democratic tendencies pretty loudly in Court; but the subterranean work of the associates was far more dangerous. It now spread over the whole of France. In Lyons, Petetin, Baune, and Lagrange were organising the "mutualist" groups; at St Étienne, Caussidière and Bastide described Republicanism as "advancing with giant steps"; at Grenoble, the National Guard had been gained over; at Dijon, Cabet had been elected to the Chamber; at Strasbourg, the committee was formed of Lichtenberg, a leader of the bar, and Anstell, a brewer; Dornès was organising at Metz; the Comte de Ludre, a deputy and a man of high birth, was inspiring the democrats at Nancy. "From Metz to Montpellier," said the *Tribune* on August 22, 1833, "the map of the Republic is ready for issue." Besides these, there were republican centres and republican journals, carried on at Arras by Frédéric Degeorge, a Republican from the first, at Clermont by Trelat and Achille Roche, at Nantes by Victor Mauguin and Dr Guépin, at Toulouse by the advocate Joly, at Montpellier by the family of Renouvier. In 1833 the club had nearly 5000 members, divided into Parisian and provincial sections, each with some audaciously revolutionary name which foreshadowed coming troubles. "The revolt," wrote Louis Blanc, "possessed, in the very midst of the State, its own government, and administration, its own geographical divisions, its own army." In 1833 its executive committee was no longer discussing the legality of a political and social insurrection; it was calculating the most opportune moment to give the signal.

During that summer Thiers' proposal for the fortification of Paris, and the anniversaries of the month of July, the "days" of democracy, combined with sundry strikes, gave excuses for some attempts at revolt. They acted as a warning to the Ministry, who woke up from their sense of security, and prosecuted Raspail, Kersausie, and d'Argenson in the Assize Courts. Their acquittal gave new zeal to the democrats, while it stiffened the resistance of their adversaries. On the one side, Marrast, editor of the *Tribune*, and Cabet of the *Populaire*, published and spread far and wide a manifesto from the Committee of the "Rights of Man" appealing to the memories of the Convention and setting forth the hopes and demands of the democratic party. The Ministry, on the other, passed a law on public announcements, and was preparing another still more drastic upon Associations; by the latter it asked the Chamber to grant it power to dissolve any association, literary or political, to inflict fines and even imprisonment on their members, and to indict the conspirators belonging to secret societies before the Courts of Paris. It was all but a "Law of Public Safety." It was passed by a majority, on March 25, 1834, in spite of the protests of the Liberals.

It was at this point that Thiers resumed the office of Minister of the Interior in the place of M. d'Argout, who was made President of the Audit Committee (*Cour des Comptes*); on the same day, April 4, he appointed M. Persil, an energetic colleague, to the Ministry of Justice. The bourgeoisie were evidently arming and organising for the work of repression, as the Republicans were doing for their decisive effort. The struggle broke out first at Lyons, on the occasion of some proceedings brought by the Government on April 9, 1834, against the leaders of a general strike in the factories. It lasted for five days of bitterness and bloodshed. For the first three days, from April 9–12, the rioters seemed to be masters of the town and had driven back the royal troops. This encouraged the Republicans of St Étienne, Vienne, Perpignan, and Marseilles to try to follow their example on April 11. In Paris on April 12, and more decidedly on the 13th, the mob, to which a military formation had been given by the democratic clubs, took up arms in the Faubourg St Antoine and St Jacques, and raised barricades in the narrow streets of the central districts, St Denis, St Martin, St Merry, the Central Market, and the neighbourhood of the Hôtel de Ville. At the head of the troops were placed the Ducs d'Orléans and de Nemours, to keep up the zeal of the National Guard and the regulars against the insurgents. Thiers directed the operations in person. No quarter was given. A house inhabited by the working class in the Rue Transnonain was destroyed by artillery fire. The bourgeoisie put their trust in Thiers and in Guizot, and were determined to get the better of the republican party, its clubs and its revolts, at any price. This was what they termed their "Resistance."

The attitude of the Chambers proved their intention. The two Chambers began by sending deputations to the Tuileries, as at the beginning of the reign, to assure the King of their "patriotism and sense of social duty." On April 15, 1834, the Chamber of Peers resolved itself into a Court of Justice for the trial of the supporters of the insurrection. The Chamber of Deputies passed votes of thanks to the army and the National Guard; they passed a Bill introduced by the Keeper of the Seals prohibiting the reception and storage of warlike weapons, and voted a sum of 14,000,000 francs for the increase of the army. The general elections held in June further strengthened the majority, and expressed the public verdict against the Republicans then on their trial before the Chamber of Peers.

Thus beaten in its last appeal to popular force, disorganised by the laws against Associations, and deprived of its leaders by their incarceration on charges of conspiracy and attempted violence, the democratic party was not destined to raise its head again for a long time. The lieutenants of Casimir Perier had crushed it, even as they had crushed the Legitimists and driven them to give up the brigand scheme of La Vendée. It was due to their leading that the bourgeoisie had triumphed over the mob by which it had won power in 1830; owing to their energy, it remained mistress of the government of France, and showed itself the only authority, since the days of Napoleon, which had been able to protect public order against both anarchy and despotism.

Next to that, the principal claim that it could put forward to justify its rule lay in the evident material prosperity of the country. The Ministry, aided by financiers like Baron Louis and Humann, had earned the credit of restoring equilibrium to the Treasury so fatally menaced in 1832, without sacrificing anything absolutely necessary in the economic machinery of the country. The creation of a separate Ministry of Public Works, the post to which Thiers was appointed in December 1832, had been a new and most successful departure. The completion of four canals begun during the Restoration, and more especially the law as to parish roads passed in 1836, were steps towards the provision of means of circulation hitherto lacking to the products of agriculture. Although the peasantry were still closely imprisoned within the walls of their routine, they were being gradually influenced by the superior intelligence of large proprietors, whether Legitimists who had been restored to their property, or Liberals educated in the school of Mathieu de Dombasle, the agriculturist of Lorraine, or retired officers of the Empire to whom peace had brought leisure, like General Morand near Pontarlier, or Colonel Bugeaud in Périgord. The State established model farms, provided sires for the stud and pedigree cows, and encouraged agricultural societies. Slow but sure progress was being made, especially in the north, in Flanders, and in Alsace, so that it was possible to record in 1835 a production of wine doubled in twenty years, a surplus of cereals for export, and an increased acreage of new crops, such as potato and beetroot.

But it was specially towards industrial development that the efforts of the bourgeoisie were directed. They were devoted above all things to the policy of "material interests," the link between the deputies and the electors whose wealth gave them the vote, manufacturers, great and small, bankers and merchants. On the suggestion of enlightened men, like Benjamin Delessert and Lasteyrie, the "Society for the Encouragement of Industry" advised Frenchmen to realise their capital, and invest it in the Shareholders' Companies which were required by manufactures on a large scale. The progress of these could be estimated by the consumption of coals, which rose in twenty years from 11 to 40 million cwt., by the number of machines which could be supplied at home, and lastly by the growth of the industrial towns, Roubaix, Lille, and St Étienne. It was at this time too that the brothers Séguin d'Annonay opened the first important railway, from Lyons to St Étienne (1832), and the banker Pereire exhibited for the amusement of Paris a railway from Paris to St Germain. On developments of this sort the Government exercised a large influence. So long as they showed no interest in railways, their progress was slow; on the other hand they were bringing their mail-coach service to perfection.

As the whole administration was centralised in Paris, it was principally to the improvement of Paris that the Government devoted the funds at their disposal. When Thiers, on April 19, 1833, submitted to the Chambers a proposal for a loan of 100,000,000 francs for public works, he assigned one-quarter of that sum to the monuments of the capital. He foresaw the union of the Louvre and the Tuileries, the enlargement of the Royal Library, the completion of the Arc de Triomphe, the Madeleine, the Pantheon, the Museum of Natural History, the School of Fine Arts, the

Palais Bourbon, and the Collège de France, the decoration of the Place de la Concorde, where the obelisk was erected, the opening of many streets and numerous bridges across the Seine. Having become the masters of France, the bourgeois of Paris spent their money in thus changing the face of their city, which attracted within its circuit the whole foreign and provincial world for pleasure and for business. Paris was attacked by a perfect fever of speculation and work, which bore witness alike to the pride and the wealth of the citizens. Their efforts were seconded by active and intelligent prefects, M. de Bondy and M. de Rambuteau.

The King himself spent five hours on May 1, 1834, with the whole royal family, in inaugurating the Exhibition of Industry, and on July 14 came to congratulate the exhibitors in person, and distribute amongst them Crosses of the Legion of Honour. The great names of French industry—Erard the pianoforte maker, Fouquet-Lemaître, cotton-spinner, Hartmann and Koechlin, makers of oiled-cloth, Sallandrouze and Thomire, makers of carpets and of bronze, Guimet and Grange, whose trade-marks were world-known—had the honours of that day, on which the wealth and the labour of the middle class received its official recognition. "You, Sir, have earned our thanks," said Baron Thénard to the King on their behalf; "in preserving peace with honour, you have done more for France than by winning battles, or conquering provinces. Our factories have multiplied; our machines have been brought nearer perfection; our manufactures have improved, and their cost has diminished. Our connexions have been enlarged, new arts have actually been created." In thus thanking the King, the bourgeois were really honouring the success of the Government of order, peace, and commerce, assured by Casimir Perier and followed up by his successors—a success in whose final establishment they rejoiced, as the outcome of the Charter which they were proud to have bestowed on France.

In order to justify its tenure of power from another point of view (and again in the style of the First Consul), the bourgeoisie proceeded to frame a scheme of legislation corresponding to the wants of modern society as it understood them, and as they actually continued to be through many successive changes of government. They passed a law, after very long consideration, on General and District Councils, which enabled, as the Republican Mauguin said, "some elected members to sit by the side of those nominated by the Government." This was an act of Liberalism, in that it lessened the Napoleonic centripetal pressure, while in other respects it maintained the power of election in the hands of the middle class.

The same spirit inspired the law passed in 1833 on the expropriation of owners of land required for public works. In 1807 Napoleon had reserved to the State, acting through the Courts of Justice, the sovereign right to settle the amount of compensation. On the proposal of Thiers the Chamber entrusted the duty to a jury, who though proprietors, would also be citizens.

Ever since 1830 the bourgeoisie, while claiming to guide the destiny of the nation, had been specially anxious to furnish it with the means of instruction, and of self-government on some future day. This was a formal promise recorded in the revised Charter—"public education, and freedom of instruction." Louis Philippe had begun to fulfil the promise by an Ordinance dated October 16, 1830, and was pressing forward measures to "hasten the progress and improvement of elementary instruction in all the communes of France, the introduction of better methods, and the creation of Training Schools." To carry this out fully, his Minister Barthe had brought in a Bill for public education and a scheme of law, which was submitted to a commission of primary inspectors charged with the duty of making a general enquiry into the schools throughout

France. In the fulfilment of this liberal and patriotic promise, Guizot took the final step, when he brought in his Education Bill in 1832.

It is only right to say that, in presenting this Bill, Guizot never disguised from the very first that it was brought forward mainly in the interest of the middle class. The school which he proposed to establish in every commune was intended "to calm and quench the people's thirst for action, as dangerous for itself as for society, to restore in their minds the inner sense of moral peace without which social peace would never return." And in order to succeed the better, while appealing to the light, he also appealed to religious beliefs, "whose dominion we ought to enlarge." With the Catholic Church, the only power which could be regarded as competent, along with the State, to direct education, he made a positive scholastic Concordat. For, while granting to the Church freedom of instruction in elementary schools, he retained for the University, on behalf of the State in its capacity as teacher, the monopoly of the education of the middle classes, "which include representatives of every grade in society, and form the essential element therein." In using the words just quoted in his speech in support of that beneficent measure, the Education Law of 1833, Louis Philippe's Minister expressed without reserve or circumlocution the precise character and principle of the task which the Cabinet intended to impose upon the nation, on the lines and after the example of Casimir Perier.

Social and religious peace, untroubled by the anathemas launched by Lamennais against modern society—and twice condemned, by the way, by Pope Gregory XVI! Peace and industry! Surely this, and neither more nor less, was the programme put forth by Bonaparte for his Consulate; from him came its main support, the administration he created, the tradition of which the bourgeoisie largely trained on his methods, were reviving, in order once for all to secure themselves in power, with the successors of Casimir Perier. To the heirs of the First Consulship one thing indeed was lacking—Marengo and Hohenlinden; nor were they likely to forget it, considering how Press, journals, and theatres resounded with the echoes of past triumphs.

Poets of the first rank were the leaders in this choir—Victor Hugo with his "Feuilles d'Automne," and more especially his "Chants du Crépuscule," and the "Ode à la Colonne"; and Alfred de Vigny, with a poem "Paris et Napoléon." Sainte-Beuve gave them his blessing, and praised them for doing patriotic work and reviving memories of an "Era of Glory." Balzac, sitting in his study with a bust of Napoleon facing him, determined to do with his pen "as much as the great conqueror with his sword, and more!" Jules Janin recommended his countrymen to read works devoted to the glory of Bonaparte. With less talent, but greater influence, Béranger spread the legend far and wide through all classes in France: "He is more than the poet of the people, he is the people turned poet!" His songs were soon to be illustrated by Charlet, whose pencil shows us the obscure, light-hearted, hot-blooded heroes of that epic; or by Raffet, who, even better than Charlet, recorded in his lithographs the poetic vision of those masses and of their leader, mutually attracting each other on along the road to glory. On every wall might be seen the advertisement of the work of the poet Barthélemy, *Le Fils de l'Homme,* which Raffet illustrated. There was the beautiful, pale, pensive face of the Martyr of St Helena, at the moment of victory, in the glorious dawn of his immortality. The people of Paris went in crowds to the Diorama, Daguerre's new invention, to do honour to the heroes of the Grand Army, as so excellently depicted by General Langlois. The artist-general did more to excite the enthusiasm of the spectators than any historian or journalist. Since 1830, and during the two first years of the Monarchy of July, all the theatres of the Boulevard, the Vaudeville, Nouveautés, Variétés, Ambigu, Porte St Martin, even the Odéon and the Opéra Comique, in comedies, dramas, verses, and pantomimes, reproduced the various phases of the heroic life of Napoleon from his youth at Brienne, through his military career, to his agony at St Helena, the episodes of his obstinate struggle with Europe, the doughty deeds of his old soldiers and officers, so loyal to their Emperor, the symbol and supreme architect of the national glory.

In correspondence with this feeling on the part of the public, a party began to grow up within the majority in the Chamber, composed of men who would not have dared to start an aggressive policy in act or word under the Republic or under the Empire, but who claimed to be a necessary factor in a more Liberal, more National, policy. It was not an avowed opposition, but a sort of conspiracy. The leader was Charles Dupin, who was dissatisfied with having been left out in the distribution of offices; the most active members were Liberals such as Sauzet and Passy, or converted Bonapartists like Étienne, the editor of the *Constitutionnel*. This "tiers parti," as it was called, worked for popularity, but did not in the least want to fall out with the Monarchy, especially as the Duc d'Orléans, the heir to the throne, was in some sympathy with them, and Louis Philippe himself, although his motives differed from his son's, gave them secret encouragement. Thus the Ministry which had authoritatively imposed itself on the nation on October 11, 1832, as the successor of Casimir Perier, appeared to be weakening in the spring of 1834, owing to divisions in the majority, on whose blind obedience it could no longer count.

The first sign of this crisis was the retirement of the Duc de Broglie, who had to leave the Ministry of Foreign

Affairs on April 1, 1834. His conduct of these, since 1832, had been condemned as wanting in spirit and in patriotism, both in the East and in Spain. In the East he had found himself opposed to the whole of Europe in the quarrel between Mehemet Ali, Pacha of Egypt, and the Sultan Mahmoud II. Mehemet Ali, dissatisfied with the payment he had received for assistance given to Turkey against the Greeks, had sent his son Ibrahim, on October 31, 1831, to effect the conquest of Syria; and Ibrahim had been victorious, at Homs and Beilan in July 1832, and at Konieh in December. The French, who had been furious at the intervention of Mehemet Ali against the Greeks, were now delighted with these successes over the Turks, saluting the Pacha of Egypt as an heir of Napoleon, "an elect hero of modern revolution." "The sound of cannon awoke their warlike ardour, their appetite for glory and action." M. de Broglie and Louis Philippe took no part in this enthusiasm. They had done their best in November 1832 to reconcile the two adversaries; their agents at Constantinople and Alexandria, M. de Varennes and M. Mimault, had worked hard to induce the Pacha of Egypt to disarm, by suggesting cessions of territory, but these did not satisfy the Pacha, and were objectionable to the Sultan.

The victory of Konieh seemed to open the door to Ibrahim in a more important direction, to wit, Constantinople; and it increased the exigency of his father's demands. Thereupon, Sultan Mahmoud II, seeing himself threatened in his capital, placed himself under the protection of the Tsar Nicholas, and invited the Russian land and sea forces to occupy the Straits. The former sympathy of France for Egypt was now turned into anger against Nicholas, for trying to stay the hand of Mehemet Ali and make himself master of Constantinople, and she heard with satisfaction of the mission entrusted to Admiral Roussin. That officer had boldly entered Turkey (January 18 to February 13,

1833), with instructions to require the Sultan to dismiss the Muscovite troops, and to call upon the Russian admiral to depart "with his tail between his legs." But this energetic action of the Duc de Broglie was not followed up. The Sultan yielded to the French ultimatum only on her guarantee that Ibrahim would offer peace on reasonable terms. Admiral Roussin, to save time, had omitted to secure the previous assent of Ibrahim, who now refused it. On March 20, 1833, the Sultan recalled the Russians, and posted the troops of Nicholas at Buyukderé, to cover his capital. This was a fresh challenge to France.

Possibly she would have picked up the gauntlet thrown down by Russia, if she could have obtained the cooperation of England, which she had been seeking for six months. Since the Peace of Adrianople (1829) and during the two first years of the reign of Louis Philippe, France and England had followed a common policy in regulating the affairs of the Near East, as they had done with regard to Belgium at the Conference of London, at which the Liberal Powers had held in check the absolutist Courts, especially that of Russia. But the English were quite as nervous as the Russians about the growth of Egyptian influence, especially if it was to assist French ambitions, as about the Tsar's progress at Constantinople. They took action without consulting France, and in concert with Metternich brought Mehemet Ali to reason, by threatening Alexandria with their fleet. Ibrahim's troops were recalled, and peace was signed between the Sultan and his rebel vassal, who obtained as a reward for his enforced good behaviour the government of Syria and Caramania (May 1833). England had thus succeeded in getting rid of the Russians, who left Constantinople on July 10. The advantage was most certainly not on the side of the diplomacy of the Duc de Broglie, who, after seeming to threaten Russia, had only been able to induce her to retreat by abandoning Mehemet Ali to the menaces of others.

If indeed it could be called a retreat! For news soon came that Count Orloff, Minister of Nicholas I, had secured, on the eve of his departure (July 6), the Convention of Unkiar Skelessi. Turkey thereby consented to place herself for eight years under the protection of the Tsar, not to apply in any quarter but Russia for aid against any new danger, and in return therefor to permit Russia to fortify the Dardanelles so as to close them entirely to the rest of Europe whenever desirable, and convert the Black Sea into a Russian lake. Fearing "to let loose another Eastern Question," M. de Broglie bowed before this diplomatic success of Nicholas I, which was approved and recognised shortly afterwards at Münchengrätz (September 1833) by Metternich, who hoped to secure the hegemony in Germany. The first article of this Münchengrätz arrangement laid down that, whereas every independent sovereign, be he Turkish Sultan or German Prince, is entitled to appeal for assistance to any other sovereign, be he Tsar or Emperor of Austria, "it shall not henceforth be permissible to any Power, not so appealed to, to intervene for the purpose of hindering such assistance." "This was the bargain," to adopt an expression of M. de Broglie, "by which Russia and Austria agreed reciprocally to abandon their respective claims in one part of Europe or another, on a basis of mutual compensation."

This was a serious moral, and even material, check to French policy; and it also constituted a danger for England, inasmuch as Palmerston had thus induced her to depart from the understanding with France established in 1830 (pp. 131–2). But Palmerston had reserved to his country another field of influence and action in which he was about to inflict another check on French diplomacy. In the Iberian peninsula, torn asunder by the conflict of the Carlists with

Queen Isabella in Spain, of the Miguelists with Doña Maria in Portugal, he had reserved for England a leading part and a strong following, by means of negotiations skilfully concealed from the French. He had upset the Spanish Minister Lea Bermudez, and obtained from his successor a promise of intervention in Portugal in favour of Doña Maria, a lady of whom France by no means approved. He had secretly arranged a Triple Alliance of the Liberal sovereigns of Spain, Portugal, and England, the essential and secret conditions of which forbade any French forces to cross the Pyrenees, and involved the presence of an English fleet at Lisbon (April 15, 1834).

Ever since January 1834 the French Opposition had been complaining of the inefficiency of French action abroad and the excessiveness of the concessions made. On these points the Opposition met with some sympathy, even in the royal circle, and notably from the Duc d'Orléans, young and lusting for glory. They took as a test case the treaty that M. de Broglie had negotiated with the United States as to the payment of certain damages or compensation for injuries inflicted on America by Napoleon's government between 1806 and 1810, during the economic war with England, which damages had been assessed at 25,000,000 francs. The Opposition declined to accept the treaty, and took the opportunity to record that "the Government were discrediting French diplomacy, and humiliating the nation, by its cowardice towards foreign powers."

Louis Philippe, in his secret heart, was not sorry to get rid of a Minister of Foreign Affairs who would not listen to his advice or submit to his influence, and he had perhaps contributed secretly to his fall; at any rate he accepted his resignation and appointed in his place Admiral de Rigny, the conqueror of Navarino, whose very name seemed to suggest energetic action in the Levant. "We shall not allow England," said the new Minister in May 1835, "to move alone, and keep for herself all the honour and profit of intervention in Spain." But these were jejune and formal satisfactions to the Opposition, and gave them no real power in the Cabinet; the King kept his most important Ministers, and refused to admit for a moment that France should renounce its policy of observation, conservation, and expectancy. When his Ministers tried in August 1834 to draw him into action against the Spanish Carlists, he refused, and he carried on secret negotiations with the Austrian representative in Paris, Prince Esterhazy, to postpone the execution of the articles in the Treaty of Quadruple Alliance; his object being to find an alliance in Vienna which might gradually take the place of the English alliance, which "only involved him in revolutions."

Thus the Cabinet which had attempted to follow up the policy of the great master of the bourgeoisie, Casimir Perier, with the aid of his successors, incapable now of satisfying the demands of the Opposition either in the Chamber or in the country, weakened by the amputations it had suffered, thwarted by the secret inclinations of the King himself, kept on throughout 1834 losing more and more of its authority and prestige.

Algerian affairs gave the signal for another ministerial crisis (July 18, 1834). The Monarchy of July, having succeeded to the conquest of Algiers as part of the inheritance from the Ministers of Charles X accruing to their estate, at the last moment, had carried on war on African territory, with apparently no very clear notion of its object on the part of the nation, their parliamentary representatives or their elected King. There had been at one time some idea of reducing the numbers of the army in Africa; but General Clauzel, who was appointed to the chief command of it on September 2, 1830, had received practically no instructions. On being threatened by Arabs and Kabyles instigated by the Bey of Didjeri, he had occupied and again evacuated Blidah and Medeah, leaving only a small garrison at Oran. His retreat had given heart to the natives, who were blockading in Algiers the French division in occupation, now reduced to 10,000 men. General Clauzel's previous experience had been in the West Indies, where he had succeeded General Leclerc in St Domingo, and had there initiated a colonial policy; but he had subsequently retired to take up a large ranch in Louisiana. It may be that he now had some idea of presenting France with an African colony.

General Berthezène, who succeeded him in Algiers on February 21, 1831, was reduced to an unlucky and humiliating defensive during the whole year. The Casimir Perier Administration then sent the Duc de Rovigo in his place, but solely to carry out the defensive action which now appeared to be required for the honour of France. He had effected but little, when he returned to Algiers in bad health and died on March 4, 1833. And, even then, the Government only appointed General Voirol to be his successor *ad interim*, as if they wished to reserve the power of evacuating even Algiers. Nevertheless, during such leisure as was allowed them by the attacks of the natives, the officers and soldiers of the army of Africa had done good colonising work; they had transformed the face of the towns they occupied, had created roads, carried out drainage-works, brought in traders, established native markets, set on foot courts of justice, and a police; and a Commission of Enquiry composed of peers, deputies, and officers, on their visit to the nascent colony in July 1833, had been able to report in a sense very favourable to a permanent establishment there.

The question of Algiers had thus been brought, in the spring of 1834, before the Chambers, where the problem of the colonisation of Northern Africa by France was for the first time submitted to discussion, and investigated in all its bearings. On one side were deputies who wanted to stop colonial enterprise and utilise the troops brought back from Africa on European fields where more glory was to be won—Republicans, men of the "tiers parti," de Sade, Dupin, Pelet de la Lozère; they dwelt on the incapacity of the French for colonisation, the uselessness of colonies, and the certainty of failure in the present case. But a large body had already been formed among the deputies ready to answer them, men who had been convinced by the report of the Commission of the preceding year, or by the arguments of General Clauzel, the official advocate of the colony, and who foresaw the future of French Africa. M. de la Pinsonnière declared that it would eventually be the India of France; Baude, Delaborde, Piscatory pointed out its importance for French commerce and the general influence of France in the Mediterranean. The one point however upon which objectors and supporters were in agreement was that this African experiment must not be allowed to retain the character of a military enterprise. "If Algiers," said Piscatory, "was to remain under military authority or administration, it were better abandoned at once."

In this great debate, which was to decide on the existence of the colony, the Government had not taken a side, and its chief, Soult, Duc de Dalmatie, declared himself unable to suggest any general or definite scheme; but they felt that they must say, or at any rate do, something. They spent the months of June and July in considering a constitution for the new colony. But this consideration brought out a strong conflict of opinion among the principal members of the Cabinet; for Guizot and Thiers desired to satisfy Parliament by abolishing the military government, while Marshal Soult was naturally determined to maintain it. Soult resigned on July 18, 1834, thus producing another crisis, all the more dangerous to the Ministry in that the general elections of June 1834 had introduced some new members who felt less respect for the ideas of the Doctrinaire party than the members of the old majority. The King appeared to have avoided the difficulty by accepting the resignation of Soult, and appointing in his stead the hero of the French intervention in Belgium, Marshal Gérard, the heir of the popularity of Lafayette. But on the other hand he insisted on his Ministers retaining the military administration established by the Ordinance of July 21, 1834, entitled the "Government of the French Possessions in North Africa," whereby all its institutions, as to police, justice, finance, and education, requisite to a colony, were placed under the control of an old General of the Empire, Count Drouet d'Erlon.

Towards the end of 1834 the Ministry was visibly weakening. It had been through several crises, insecure of its majority and belittled by the King, who was delighted to see the authority of his Ministers diminishing, while his own increased. The bourgeois party in Parliament, who had forced themselves upon the King and the nation by the methods and on the example of Casimir Perier, felt that power was slipping from their hands. To recover their hold on it, Thiers, Guizot, and their friends took advantage of a difference of opinion between the King and Marshal Gérard on the question of a general amnesty to Republicans, to compel the King and the mutineers of the majority to declare their option between the Ministry and the leaders of the mutiny. On November 8, 1834, they resigned office. Possibly they might have retained power, had the King been willing to call the Duc de Broglie to the Presidency of the Council again. But the King was obstinate in his refusal to take back a Minister of Foreign Affairs who would not allow him to conduct these affairs as he liked; and he was therefore forced to try the experiment of a Cabinet formed from the dissident members of the majority, Dupin the younger, Sauzet, and Teste, with another ex-official of the Empire, Maret, Duc de Bassano, as President. This Ministry lasted three days (November 11–14, 1834), being unable to command a majority, and forced to admit the fact. It was greatly regretted by the Duc d'Orléans, who considered that a Ministry like this, of more Liberal and more national tendencies, was emphatically *his* Ministry, and the only one capable of satisfactorily restoring to the Monarchy the public favour which had been alienated by the Conservative bourgeoisie.

The miscarriage of this three-day Ministry was a lesson to the "tiers parti," and looked like a decided return of good luck to the heirs of Casimir Perier, and a pledge of permanency and success to their policy. On November 18, 1834, Thiers, Guizot, Comte de Rigny, Humann, Duchâtel, and Admiral Duperré, made their appearance once more before Parliament, grouped round their President, Marshal Mortier, Duc de Trevise, and seemed to have recovered the authority which they had lost since the year began. On December 3, 1834, to the appeals of Thiers and Guizot, whose united eloquence seemed once more triumphant, the majority replied by a categorical vote of confidence. To all appearance the Doctrinaire Cabinet, after a year of hesitation and uncertainty, had once more found the needful parliamentary fulcrum for its operations. But there was no reality in it all. At the beginning of 1835, the Chamber, when applied to by the Ministers to take the necessary steps for the erection of the Chamber of Peers into a High Court of Justice for the trial of the Republicans implicated in the riots of April 1834, came very near rejecting the application. It was the merest chance that they did not vote for an amnesty instead of the adverse verdict asked for by the Ministry. And, while they were running a risk of losing their majority, the difficulties between themselves and the King continued. Thiers was very angry at the claim of Louis Philippe to the exclusive direction of Foreign Affairs. He contended that he was entitled to conduct them himself, and thus become the chief man in the Cabinet; and he made Cuvillier Fleury, tutor to the Duc d'Orléans, the confidant both of his anger and his desires. Guizot was inclined to favour the return of the Duc de Broglie to office, whether the King liked it or not, hoping thus to restrain at once the ambition of his young colleague, and the authority of the King; while the King encouraged the attacks of the "tiers parti" by way of bringing his Ministers to reason. Irritation was accumulating on both sides.

At last the Ministry fell by its own act, through the resignation of Marshal Mortier on February 20, 1835; and France remained without a Government for three weeks of delays, negotiations, and intrigues. The Ministers expected by their resignation to impose conditions on the King, as they had imposed them on the majority in November. "They forced me," said Louis Philippe, "to take M. de Broglie." He accepted the situation; and Thiers, whose secret desire was to become leader, accepted it also. On March 12, 1835, the Duc de Broglie resumed the charge of Foreign Affairs and the Presidency, with the colleagues who the year before had helped him to keep the Conservative bourgeoisie in power. The old Ministry of October 11, 1832, returned to duty much the same as before, with a programme of resistance at home and action abroad, still inspired by the lessons of Casimir Perier and the example of the Consulate.

Taught by this year of crisis, the Duc de Broglie showed great consideration for the King and for Thiers, while he adopted a very firm tone with the Chambers. On May 5, 1835, he indicted before the Chamber 120 Republicans, among them Cavaignac, Marass, Guinard, Baune, de Kersausie, and de Ludre; he was in no way alarmed by the line of defence adopted by their counsel, d'Argenson, André de Puyraveau, Garnier-Pagès, Bastide, Carnot,

Ledru-Rollin, and Jules Favre, as advocates of the whole inculpated Liberal party, who proposed to take advantage of this monster trial to hold "a solemn assize on the republican conspiracy" in the face of the triumphant bourgeoisie. This state trial lasted for three months; it was conducted by Baron Pasquier, the President of the Court, and supported by the Ministry with untiring determination and coolness. Judgment was given on August 13, 1835, when the leaders of the defeated and shattered republican army were sentenced to imprisonment or exile. The severity of the Peers and the firmness of the Ministry were justified by the crime of Fieschi committed on July 28, when in an attempt on the life of Louis Philippe forty victims were sacrificed, including generals, officers, national guards, and bourgeois. "Uneasy for the safety of her King and her institutions, France demands of her rulers the protection she has a right to expect." With these words the Duc de Broglie introduced to the Chamber on August 4 three Bills on the Jury, the Press, and acts of rebellion, which were passed on August 29, 1835, and were afterwards known as the "Laws of September." All opposition was crushed by these exceptional measures, whether in the Press or from the platform or in the clubs. Royer-Collard, in his anxiety for liberty, likened them to the tyranny of the First Consulate; other Radicals compared them to the Terror. The Orleanist bourgeoisie thus conferred on the Duc de Broglie and the successors of Casimir Perier, by an enormous majority of over 100 in a house of 220, the means of annihilating what he called "revolt, and the spirit of revolt" against the institutions which he had established since 1830.

Throughout France, throughout all Europe, the energy of the Ministry, the support it received in Parliament, and the renewed popularity of the King among his subjects owing to the attempt of Fieschi, appeared to give a final sanction to the political system founded by the parliamentary bourgeoisie. "Everything prospers surprisingly," said Tocqueville in 1835. "The possibility of permanency has penetrated into men's minds for the first time for five years, and with it the taste for enterprise. Activity has deserted politics to busy itself about material welfare." The political crisis of 1834–5 had been a long one, but it seemed to be at last settled, and on such terms as to realise the programme of order and prosperity at home, which was that of the middle classes, the masters of power. But from the end of 1835, throughout the whole of 1836, a profound discord between the monarchy and the bourgeoisie, and one decisive of the future of both, was in the course of development, on the question of the part to be taken by France in outside politics. "In my opinion," said M. de Remusat a little later, "all questions that might divide us are of secondary importance compared to the questions of foreign policy." The nation wanted the peace and order conducive to the progress of its well-being and its business; but the order must be combined, as in the days of Bonaparte, with some glory-earning part on the European stage. The whole world of Paris had rushed to the reception of Thiers at the French Academy, simply because they would there be able to applaud the memories of the Consulate; they flocked to the sale of pictures by Gros, the painter of the glories of the Empire, and to the formal completion of the Arch of Napoleon's Triumph. "France," in the words of Carrel, "proposed to hand on the tradition of the great man."

The statesmen who had assumed charge of the destinies of France, Louis Philippe, his counsellors and his son, were alive to the fact that whoever aspired to govern it must satisfy its national aspirations. But they differed diametrically as to the means of doing so. The King was fully determined to avoid all complications abroad, having secretly agreed with Austria to oppose the ambition of the

Tsar in the East, and the turbulent policy of Palmerston, who "offered me nothing but revolutions." He thought it would be enough to give the French a few platonic satisfactions, to build at Versailles a museum of military glory, and to keep as festivals the victories of the Revolution and the Empire. The Ministers and the "tiers parti" looked forward to more real and less distant satisfactions. Thiers talked about an intervention in Spain in aid of the Liberals and against the Carlists, either with England or in spite of her, which would have embroiled France with Austria. Louis Philippe opposed this scheme, and only permitted the creation of a Foreign Legion, which was afterwards sent to Algeria. M. de Broglie had quite another policy in his mind. He was displeased with the encouragement given by the Continental Powers since 1833 to the advance of Russia in the East, and he desired to secure an alliance with England, whom this advance disturbed. With that before him, he considered the possibility of French action in the Eastern Mediterranean, and did not hesitate to face the risk of war, perhaps immediate, but anyway inevitable, if Nicholas I was to be forced to abandon Constantinople. "The more solid the situation of France becomes, the greater will be the part she will play in this war." And towards the close of 1835, in view of this eventuality, he considered attentively a proposal for an alliance with England sent to him by Sebastiani from London.

Although the Duke reserved for himself exclusively the direction of foreign policy, Louis Philippe kept an eye on this development of it with the decided intention of stopping it. On January 29, 1836, he told the Sardinian envoy, "Rather than yield on this point, I would smash the whole Cabinet." Since January 18, 1836, a new ministerial crisis had opened, owing to the independent action of M. Humann, Minister of Finance. Without consulting M. de Broglie, he had proposed to convert the French Rentes; and on February 4 the

Chamber, taking the opportunity of putting the Ministry, solid as it seemed, in a minority, forced M. de Broglie to resign on this question.

It was the belief of many that the opposition in Parliament, which had been concerted under the roof of a M. Ganneron, an obscure and ambitious deputy, had been brought about by a Court intrigue. M. de Remusat records his opinion to that effect: and M. de Segur heard as much from M. de Broglie himself, who described his retirement as due to his inability to get the King to accept his policy. Talleyrand contributed to it, and advised the King to consult Thiers, whose youthful ambition seemed to promise greater tractability; but Talleyrand was always urging Louis Philippe to withdraw from his connexion with England, and get into better touch with Austria and the Continental Powers. Louis Philippe had always chafed under the authority of the leaders of the parliamentary bourgeoisie, Casimir Perier and his successors. He was tired of their resistance to his will, and was secretly undermining their power in Parliament. He now thought that by calling M. Thiers to power after the fall of M. de Broglie he had won his case.

CHAPTER VI

LOUIS PHILIPPE AND THE PARLIAMENTARY OPPOSITION

Thiers formed his Ministry on February 22, 1836. Three of the number were former colleagues who remained in office, Marshal Maison, Admiral Duperré, and Comte d'Argout; three were members of the "tiers parti," Passy, Sauzet, and Pelet de la Lozère; another was the King's confidant, M. de Montalivet. It looked as if the chief of the new Cabinet had planned a réconciliation between the former Ministry and the Opposition, between the King and the colleagues of M. de Broglie. The Cabinet declared its firm determination to remain loyal to the spirit of its predecessor, and to continue the policy of resistance to disorder, but expressed a wish that members of the "tiers parti" who had deserted this policy during the two past years might be induced to return to it for "love of conciliation." By the satisfaction he proposed to give in the matter of activity abroad, M. Thiers hoped to compass the solution of this delicate problem. He sought his opportunity first in Algeria.

Abd-el-Kader had been allowed by some weakness in French policy to inflict a rebuff upon the army in Africa at La Macta and to establish himself at Mascara. To punish this, Marshal Clauzel had on July 8 resumed the command of that army; and Algeria was now becoming the theatre of a real war waged to please the French. The Duc d'Orléans, the King's son, asked for leave to serve under

Marshal Clauzel. Thiers, who had but just then been installed in office, waxed enthusiastic over the Marshal's task, over the army of Africa, and over the glory that it seemed to promise. He sent reinforcements under General Bugeaud, whose victory on the banks of the Shichak in July seemed to give the finishing touch to the Marshal's operations. He then determined, though unfortunately with too restricted means, to carry out the conquest of the whole Regency from Oran to Constantine (August 2, 1836).

Already recalling the memories of the Egyptian expedition, Thiers hoped to win the favour of the French people for his Ministry by vigorous action; and the fever of activity began gradually to dominate him. As hoped by Talleyrand and Louis Philippe, he had at the start entirely broken away from Palmerston, whose conquering airs offended the Continental Courts. He had paid his addresses to Metternich and to Prussia, in the hope (not afterwards realised) of obtaining their assent to the marriage of the Duc d'Orléans. On the eve of the journey of the Duc d'Orléans to Vienna and Italy to ask for the hand of an archduchess in marriage, he had given a pledge of his pacific intentions by totally refusing, on March 18, 1836, the request of England for French intervention in Spain. On hearing that Metternich had met the advances of the Orleans family with a negative, Thiers considered that he was released from any obligation; and in the month of July he set on foot an expedition to deprive the English of the glory of defending Queen Isabella and Austria of the hope of seeing the triumph of Don Carlos, the champion of the absolutist system. He doubled the strength of the Foreign Legion on the Pyrenean frontier, and proposed to give the command of it either to Marshal Clauzel or to Bugeaud. "I am going to set myself up again in Spain," he said publicly. Like Chateaubriand, he saw his Spanish war in his dreams; and he had every intention of forcing a war upon the King, much as the King disliked that or any other military enterprise which might let loose the revolutionary and chauvinist passions of France, and excite the anger of Europe.

"I am very proud," said Thiers to Louis Philippe. "I," replied the King, "am prouder still, for I am too proud to say so." Louis Philippe in fact was watching his young Minister, prepared to take strong measures to stop him, at the council-board first, and afterwards, if necessary, elsewhere. A revolt against Queen Isabella took place in Madrid on August 12, 1836, and forced her to submit to the dictatorship of the most revolutionary elements in the country, in order to break down the Carlists; and this hastened the ministerial crisis in Paris. Thiers declared himself ready to give immediate assistance to the Queen of Spain, to enable her to beat Don Carlos and to relieve her of the necessity of taking her instructions from rebels. General Lebeau, who had taken command of the Foreign Legion at Pampeluna, made an announcement to that effect on August 15; but Louis Philippe repudiated the General and his promises by a note in the *Moniteur* of August 24, 1836. This was tantamount to repudiating Thiers, who had informed Austria of his intention of "annihilating Don Carlos." On the following day the King insisted on the disbandment of the recruits whom his Minister had raised in order to increase the numbers of the Foreign Legion. The two policies—of the King and of his Minister—came into collision at the Council held at the Tuileries at the end of August. "The King's will was law," as the Prussian Ambassador said. "We must take a decided step," said Thiers annoyed. "The King will not have an intervention. We insist on it. I retire." Some days later, Louis Philippe entrusted the government to a Ministry of his own choice, under the lead of Molé, to the delight of the Continental Powers who favoured Don Carlos (September 6, 1836).

Thus ended the secret conflict which had really lasted

for four years since October 11, 1832, between the men of the parliamentary bourgeoisie on one side, who, claiming to act in the name of the nation, had tried to force a government upon the democracy and the King, and Louis Philippe on the other side. It was true that the King was one of their own choice and their fellow-worker against the democracy; but he was none the less persuaded that that task was essentially his own and resolved neither to abdicate nor even to lower his authority before theirs.

The feature in the affair which afforded so much pleasure to the Prussian representative, viz., that "M. Thiers had been overturned by the King alone, and not by the Chamber," gave it its special significance. This act of royal authority, being inconsistent with the principles of parliamentary government, threw a sudden light for all Frenchmen upon the yearly growing misunderstanding between the Monarchy and the Conservative majority. The alliance formed against the Revolution of 1830 in the days immediately following it, between the Duc d'Orléans, the leaders of the Doctrinaires, the *National* and Thiers, though gradually relaxing, continued to exist so long as the power it procured them seemed still insecure. The destruction of the republican party in September 1835, and the ruin of the Legitimists, hastened the break-up of the alliance, now that their victory was assured, and that they were confronted by new problems which their very victory made inevitable. The parliamentary party claimed to have made both King and law; but they were too prone to forget that without the King they could hardly have escaped a Republic or subjugated the democracy; their views were expressed in the formula "the King should reign, but not govern." The King, on his side, was convinced that without his diplomatic skill the Republic would have been victorious; and, turning upon his own Ministers the skill of fence which had stood him in so good stead in dealing with the people of

Paris, he claimed the right to govern, and to exercise power while he left them its responsibility. The Doctrinaires and Thiers, once their ally, then their enemy, like the Ultras under the Restoration, now in their turn found fault with the Government. They required the King's help in resisting the republican propaganda only; in the matter of action abroad, they proposed to make him their instrument. In order to make his own authority prevail, Louis Philippe was now almost prepared to get rid, by intrigue or force, of the men who had upset Charles X to place him upon the throne.

In this contest the dismissal of Thiers in 1836 was the critical point at which the possibility of the leaders of the bourgeoisie being defeated on the morrow of their triumph over Republicans and Legitimists first came into view. Their defeat was neither immediate nor complete; Louis Philippe did not wish to push his act of prerogative to an extreme. While insisting on the appointment to the combined Presidency of Council and Ministry of Foreign Affairs of Count Molé, an entire stranger to the policy of the Doctrinaires and a devoted servant of the King, he made some advances to M. Guizot, who was by no means pleased with the resignation forced on him through the ambition of Thiers, and full of resentment against the colleague who had played him false. The King allowed him to return to the Ministry of Public Education, but with an escort of friends devoted to his own views and his person—Count Duchâtel as Minister of Finance, Comte de Gasparin at the Interior, and M. de Remusat; the last-named now began public life as Under-Secretary of State for Public Works. It is very likely that the King did not dismiss Thiers till he had satisfied himself of the certainty of the cooperation promised him in sundry quarters through M. de Montalivet. Louis Philippe felt that without this cooperation he would be unable to render palatable the dismissal of a Ministry which had so far appeared to enjoy his confidence, and which he only got rid of because their foreign policy was too energetic.

To this work M. Molé set himself with all speed, and without ignoring the delicacy of the task. "We have inherited a tough job," he wrote on September 7, "in Spain, Switzerland, and Algeria. It does not matter, I keep up my spirits, and we shall get along." On the Pyrenees, the auxiliary army corps was disbanded; and, not long afterwards, the Foreign Legion left Spain for Algeria, the conquest of which it was gradually to effect. In Algeria, orders had been given to Marshal Clauzel to slacken his pace, and to restrict his efforts to the occupation of Constantine. In connexion with Spanish affairs the course approved by the Chamber was what Molé called "the policy of Cardinal Fleury."

The repulse inflicted on Marshal Clauzel before Constantine on November 24, 1836, was a severe humiliation, well-nigh a disaster, for the army of Africa, and served to condemn more completely the venturesome policy of conquest adopted by the preceding Ministry. Clauzel was recalled, and his post taken by General Danrémont, who was instructed to effect a "limited and pacific occupation," and to bring the Algerian venture back to the proportion of a colonial and commercial affair, "above all, without war." While Danrémont, with a view to make an end of it, prepared for the occupation and siege of Constantine, where he gained glory but lost his life, Bugeaud on May 30, 1837, concluded with Abd-el-Kader the Treaty of La Tafna, which was in fact a treaty of partition of the two provinces of Algiers and Oran between France and that chieftain. During two years, the work of restoring peace went on in Algeria.

In Spain also peace was made possible through the successes of Espartero over the Carlists, and the dictatorship of that rough soldier, who dealt as he would with Queen and kingdom. The Peninsula ceased to be the battle-ground of the Powers struggling, one for the liberal, another for the absolutist cause; and France, who by abstaining from action had brought about this solution, now reaped the benefit of it, being freed from the risk of being caught between the calculated violence of Palmerston and the self-interested tempers of the Continental Courts.

Finally, Louis Philippe obtained the assent of Prussia, and even of Metternich, to the marriage of his son with Helena of Mecklenburg-Schwerin. All the sovereigns of Europe recognised his merit and applauded his skill and readiness, well served as they were by the prudence of the Ministry which he had succeeded in imposing on the nation and the Chamber. The premature attempt which Prince Louis Napoleon, relying on the growth of the "Napoleonic Legend" (cf. p. 164), had made at Strasbourg on October 30 of the previous year (1836), only served to demonstrate the indifference of the masses and the stability of the Orleans government. Guizot and his friends the Doctrinaires had given their adhesion to Louis Philippe's policy; and it was doubtless due to them that it had triumphed in Parliament. But their agreement with the King was not of a sort to last.

From the very first, Guizot had been dissatisfied with his subordinate position in the Cabinet; and his friends encouraged him to remonstrate. "Is it reasonable," wrote M. de Broglie, "that the most prominent man, the very heart and main-spring of the Cabinet, should occupy the lowest post in it?" The Doctrinaires could not help treating Molé as an upstart, who had had better luck than he deserved in his clever court intrigues; and he was thus obliged to take up the defence of his personal dignity and of his legitimate authority. Molé, on his side, had always kept himself aloof from those upper-middle-class Conservatives, whom Louis

Philippe, without really liking them, had brought into power; and the ideas and policy that he brought with him widely differed from theirs, at any rate in outward appearance.

Molé had begun his career under Napoleon, and since the fall of the Empire had succeeded in improving his position under all the successive systems of government. Circumspect, full of tact and adaptability, courteous and agreeable, he had always governed his conduct and his politics by circumstances, and like the King had a greater belief in practical expedients than in theories. Now that he had reached the highest post, he was mistrustful of those colleagues of his, who were always talking of "resistance," and who, by gratifying the national desire for active measures abroad, were obstinately keeping a fighting government in power. "The true idea of government," said Molé, "consists in meeting facts just such as they actually present themselves, with a mind free from prejudices borrowed from the past." Between this Minister, the agreeable and insinuating man of expedients, and the Doctrinaires, lofty of principle and proud of their superiority, there was almost as much difference as there was in 1823 between M. de Villèle and the Ultra-Royalists, with their obstinate dreams of foreign activity and a return to the past. Their agreement could not last. Molé was tired of the contempt, and vexed at the unpopularity that Guizot brought on him; Guizot was only awaiting an opportunity of recapturing the power which he claimed for himself and his friends.

The opportunity came on March 7, 1837, when a vote of want of confidence was moved in connexion with certain exceptional measures against ringleaders of plots, which the Doctrinaires had forced Molé to introduce against his own judgment. The vote involved the resignation of the Minister of the Interior. Guizot asked for the post, was refused by Molé, and resigned in his turn. He hoped by retiring to oblige the King to recall M. de Broglie and Thiers (whom he invited to forget their former quarrels) and reconstruct the great Ministry of October 11, 1832. Louis Philippe encouraged him for a moment in the hope. "I am the King's favourite statesman," he assured his friends. But then the King said, "You are too unpopular"; and his final decision was in favour of Molé. After the first hours of the crisis, the King made up his mind to throw off the protection of these princes of debates, these tenants *in capite* of representative government, who thought they had a "vested right to direct the affairs of the country"; while he believed he was capable of doing it better himself with more tractable Ministers. The breach between Louis Philippe and the conservative bourgeoisie was completed by the constitution of a Molé Ministry, April 15, 1837. The country learnt the fact of the breach, but knew nothing as to the preliminaries. It was not long before it had to act as arbitrator.

The task of M. Molé, confronted by a Parliament the majority in which was accustomed to another leader, was not an easy one. The elections held in October 1837 no doubt diminished the authority of the Doctrinaires in the Chamber by introducing more than 100 new members; but it was only by force of will, an unexpected skill of tongue, and the support of the King, given this time with vigour, that Molé succeeded in getting the deputies to accept his programme. Looked at through the vista of years, the work accomplished by this Minister may be appreciated at its proper value, when seen apart from the almost daily scuffles in the midst of which it was carried on. He describes it in a letter to his friend, M. de Barante, thus: "I have always been a strong supporter of any form of truce or reconciliation between parties, the moment the hour for it has struck. On September 6, and still more on April 15, it had become necessary to lay a new course, to try another tack, whatever it might cost us, under penalty of losing our way altogether. This is what those inflexible souls who evolve everything out of their own consciousness, instead of looking round them, can never be got to understand." After repression, reconciliation. Of what use were the decisive victories of the "new system" over Republicans and Legitimists in 1835, if the victors were not to reap the profit in the shape of internal tranquillity? Molé's programme had at least the merit of being opportune. His first act was the proclamation of an amnesty to the Republicans on June 10, 1837, the wedding-day of the Prince Royal.

The effect was almost immediate. The defeated parties began to forget their grievances, and to postpone the threatened struggle, once more directing their hopes to the future. The Republicans who, in exile or in prison, had been meditating on the causes of their disaster, and on the violence which had justified the use of force and exceptional legislation against them, determined to substitute "the force of argument for the argument of force." Ever since 1834, Dupont, a barrister, and founder of the *Revue Républicaine,* had gone so far as to advocate, in lieu of a servile imitation of Jacobinism and the Terror, a course of democratic instruction which would "restore confidence to the country by enlightening it." He described the democratic ideal as "government by the people for the welfare of the people," and recommended men to study the duties of the State in social matters, the question of salaries, and the conditions of labour. This appeared to him to be the true programme of his party, and not violent action. His views were approved by Raspail and Kersausie, who wrote in the *Réformateur*: "Let us have done with personal quarrels, done with social struggle." When the insurrection of April and the Laws of September 1835 had justified the warnings and strengthened the conclusion at which these Republicans had arrived, the development of the idea became daily more marked. Armand Carrel, and after him Charles Thomas in the *National,* devoted themselves to the investigation of social and democratic questions. On the *Nouvelle Minerva,* a literary organ, were collected the Republicans, young and old, who had resolved henceforth to carry on their propaganda solely by the strength of their ideas. Louis Blanc in the *Bon Sens* and the *Tribune des Prolétaires,* Victor Considérant in the *Phalange,* the journal started by Fourier in 1836, popularised the principles of this republican and social school in that same year. In full opposition to the middle class whose power had been consolidated by Napoleon, these men asserted the victorious force of an ideal of social and political progress, and their determination to make it prevail, relying no longer upon conspiracy and violence.

No one did more for this ideal than Lamennais, when in 1836, in the preface to his *Third Miscellanies,* he declared his agreement with the democratic party. His book, *The People,* written in 1837, showed a talent and a generous spirit which gave it considerable influence, spreading even into the lower strata. "I address myself," he said, "to cold reason and to philosophy. It seems to me that there exists a whole universe of truths to be revealed. I believe that Social Science is as yet far from possessing any complete theory, and that this theory, when completed, will be of great assistance for hastening on our future development. We are advancing towards a magnificent unity." The future of modern society, to which Lamennais looked forward, was to be realised in peace and concord. "The polemical spirit," he said again, "has shaken many a truth, but has never established one. We are beginning to understand that violence persuades no one. Talk to people in the language of union; preach to them the gospel of peace."

It looked as if, in giving liberty to Trelat, the friend of

Lamennais, in opening the prison-gates of Clairvaux and Doullens, in recalling to their native country the exiled Republicans in Switzerland and England, Molé had wished to put into action the advice of Lamennais. His programme of hopefulness and pacific progress had in 1836 received the approval of Victor Hugo, who supplied the *Presse* with a column on social questions. Georges Sand brought to the cause all the ardour of her enthusiasm, in alliance with Michel de Bourges, Lamennais, and Pierre Leroux. From this time forth, the more the Republicans got of this invaluable assistance, the less need they had to appeal to war. Instead of memories of the "Mountain," nothing was to be heard at their meetings but words of hope and pity for the lowly, of counsels of prudence and good sense. Fewer of them now called themselves Republicans, more were "Democrats" and "Radicals"—men like Arago, Dupont de l'Eure, and Lamartine, who would willingly come to terms with the Government, if they would consent to restore to the "pacific propagandists" their right to use the platform and the Press.

At this time also a similar and decisive change was going on in the Legitimist party, which had been crushed by the defeat of the Duchesse de Berry, disgraced by her adventures, and finally deprived of its head by the death of the exiled King in 1837. It was now re-shaping itself as a great party with its own principles and its own propaganda, which left the *émigrés* to their quarrels and intrigues, while they collected a band of younger and more active disciples, devotees of a loftier ideal than the mere restoration of an abolished system. In this re-shaping, the influence of Lamennais made itself felt, at least as a lesson to the Catholics, from whom he separated amid some noise. The support that he took away with him to the democrats was only the result of the bad reception given to his views by the adherents of the Ancien Régime, by Roman priests and French bigots. He might have bidden them "Strike, but hear!" But he had been struck first, and not heard, when he prophesied the mischief that would accrue to the Church from the alliance of Catholics, the true conservatives, the defenders of divinely established order, with the huckstering ways of the returned *émigrés*, the blind or interested defenders of a dynasty which a breath could extinguish. Without breaking, like him, with Rome, his disciples Montalembert and Lacordaire were soon calling on the younger Legitimists, attracted by their talent and their zeal, "to let be the turmoil of politicians, and busy themselves thenceforth with the things of God." Under their influence, this group of young men, led by Ozanam and the founders of the *Société de St Vincent de Paul*, with the principal contributors to the *Correspondant* and the *Univers*—de Carné, de Champagny, de Meaux, and Foisset—denounced "the fatal alliance between Throne and Altar" as one denounces a treaty which is no longer useful and has become pernicious, in order that "hand-in-hand with Jesus they might move towards the people."

In 1835 Lacordaire, preaching in Notre Dame, put their aspirations into words. "I have the greatest possible respect (he said) for the old royalist party, the respect one feels for a veteran covered with glory. But I cannot rely upon a veteran whose wooden leg prevents him from scaling the heights up which the new generation is pressing." The Archbishop of Paris and the Legitimists silenced Lacordaire, "this tribune, this Republican." But, when Montalembert was taking his place in the Chamber of Peers, where he was distinguishing himself by his eloquence, the royalist youth, recognising his power, approved his conduct in refusing to isolate himself any longer from the new régime in a useless retirement and mingling in the movement of ideas and men, where he could assert their common hopes, and prelude the triumph of their religious and social creeds.

In dealing with these men, who by their youth and their high hopes were equally averse from the fatal spirit of the *émigrés* and the Ultras of the Right, and from the ways of the Carbonieri and the violence of the Terrorists on the Left, no well-advised Government could be content to act on a mere policy of resistance. Against revolutionists of the Right who proposed by intrigue or force to restore the Ancien Régime, or those of the Left who were incessantly appealing to riot, resistance was intelligible. It meant the defence of public order, the only possible way to avert civil war. But both sides had now laid down their arms; and from this time forth it was not by compulsion and exceptional laws that the peaceful dissemination of ideas in a free country was to be restrained. Circumstances had changed, and demanded a change of policy. It was Molé's merit that he grasped the fact.

At the same time that he set the Republicans at liberty, he reopened to Catholics the Church of St Germain l'Auxerrois, which had remained closed during the Legitimist demonstrations; and the crucifix appeared once more on the walls of the courts of justice. Montalembert, addressing the Peers on May 19, 1837, congratulated the Ministry on these two conciliatory steps, not less fair to Catholics than to Republicans. He asked his friends (whom he called Catholics thenceforth rather than Royalists) to recognise that these measures were the starting-point of a new policy. For his own part he would give up his old Legitimist regrets and hopes, and transfer his fealty and sympathy to the Monarchy of July, if it was prepared to give the Catholics enlightened protection and impartial toleration.

By a method which was not that of Casimir Perier, but equally well adapted to the changed circumstances of the time and equally successful, Molé was securing order and peace and establishing the dynasty. Between 1837 and 1839 there was no anarchist crime, and only one republican conspiracy, got up by a working-man of Alsace, Aloys Huber by name, a dreamer and a mystic, and his friend Steuble. "The Legitimist party," wrote the Duc d'Orléans, while visiting the south of France, "has crumbled away to nothing in every direction, ever since the clergy deserted it." The Government, now free from all anxiety, was ready to undertake its proper duty of governing.

With the support of Parliament and especially of the Chamber of Peers, they carried further the work of legislation, the foundations of which the bourgeoisie had been wise enough to lay in 1830 for the benefit of modern society. They decided to increase the number of Justices of the Peace, kept an eye over lunatics, passed regulations as to bankruptcy and insolvency, and by a law of April 1838 extended the principle of Councils General in the departments, and of local political life, so as to accustom the French to the use of liberty.

In the same fashion they proposed to advance the well-being and prosperity of the nation, which had never before been so well established. In 1836 M. de Barante remarked that the lower classes for the last fifty years had not looked better off, or more contented with their growing prosperity. The French budget, which in the first years of the new régime had to bear an extra burden of 100,000,000 francs, was now finally relieved of it. In spite of the cost of education and the expenses of the army and of Algeria, which were met out of the ordinary revenue, it now showed a surplus of 80,000,000, brought about by the increase of manufactures. All over the country there was a fever for enterprise of all sorts; savings-bank deposits increased; the growth of indirect taxation indicated the abundance of capital. The Five per cent. Funds were at 20 francs premium, the Three per cents. almost at par. The Ministry applied all their available funds in further developing the economic machinery of the country. By a Law on Public Works, passed in 1837, some 800,000,000 francs were devoted to ports, bridges, canals, and roads, and to the encouragement of commerce and manufactures, which brought wealth to the middle classes and work to the lower. Modern France, the France of the nineteenth century, was growing into shape. All that it now lacked was a net-work of railways; and Molé has the credit of putting a scheme for the purpose before Parliament. As alive to the needs of the hour in industrial as in political questions, this "little minister," as he was contemptuously called by the Doctrinaires, proved himself of clearer sight and prompter initiative than his opponents. Molé proposed to create a great State railway for the whole of France with a capital of 100,000,000 francs; but Parliament threw out the scheme.

The Frenchman of that day asked no more of a Ministry to ensure his approval and obedience. He was after all much the same as at the Restoration, indifferent to politics so long as they did not interrupt him in his daily business of gaining and saving, accepting every order emanating from Paris so long as it secured tranquillity in the provinces, silently absorbed in his own particular interest, his own well-being, his own family. "The public," wrote M. de Barante from Auvergne, "is absolutely indifferent; and its rooted indifference applies equally to all governments. It would seem that the country has only the one desire—peace, that every man may attend to his own affairs." "France is fast asleep," wrote Royer-Collard, "and does not even dream. The truth is that there is no such thing now as politics and we get on very well without them."

This general silence was accepted by Louis Philippe, delighted at the good service of his Ministers, as an approval of his action in calling Molé to office. With Molé by his side, he could at last govern to please himself. General Bernard, the Minister of War, permitted his son, the Duc d'Orléans, to take an active and intelligent part in the direction of military matters; and, being a glutton for work, the King did his own diplomacy, his favourite pursuit, receiving the ambassadors in person, and settling with them the peace of Europe.

In this year he completed the liberation of Belgium for the benefit of his son-in-law and with his cooperation. Since the King of Holland had been forced by the Anglo-French alliance in 1832 to give up the booty won at the Treaty of Vienna, that monarch had been constantly waiting, sword in hand, for the moment to give the return blow. He thought it had come in 1838 through the misunderstanding that had existed since 1834 between France and England. Suddenly, as if desirous of testifying to the pacific intentions of his people, he offered to recognise the independence of Belgium, which hitherto he had always refused; but he put forward one condition, the immediate abandonment of Luxemburg and Limburg. Now the Belgians had kept these duchies in defiance of the Treaty of 1815, though with the consent of the Powers. Hereupon these Powers, suddenly regardless of the interest that the Belgians naturally felt in these provinces, which had been associated with them from the first in their struggle for liberty, and of their wish to keep a territory which for six years they had hoped to own, at the risk of insurrections in Brussels and of another war, gave their support to the obstinate demands of the King of Holland. Luxemburg was occupied by Prussian troops; and at the Conference which met in London in June 1838, Palmerston roundly insisted on the immediate submission of the Belgians.

France was then able to step in very efficaciously as a mediator, not with England, who was inclined to open up the whole question again, but with the King of the Belgians, whose new-born monarchy was seriously threatened. At the beginning of 1839 Leopold, assisted by the diplomacy of Louis Philippe, succeeded in getting the Conference to sanction a reduction of the debt imposed upon Belgium by the Treaty of 1832, in exchange for the provinces in question which he induced his subjects to evacuate. The King of Holland was, however, still in hopes of reducing Belgium to obedience when the settlement of April 19, 1839, made her an independent State. As soon therefore as he talked of insisting on a cession of territory, Leopold took him at his word, accepted his terms, and forced him then to recognise the work of emancipation which had been accomplished at his expense. France, by assisting in the work, gave permanency to her victory on behalf of the rights of nations, against threats of counter-aggression.

In Italy the diplomacy of Louis Philippe was equally successful. With the object of compelling France to withdraw her troops from Ancona, where they had remained from the time of the Perier Ministry, Metternich had conceived the notion of withdrawing from the Romagna the Austrian regiments who had occupied it at the same date. Molé quietly observed in Parliament that "the only purpose of the occupation of Ancona was to show the fixed determination of France not to allow any Power to have an excessive preponderance in Italy." Since Austria was now retiring behind the frontiers assigned to her by the Treaty of Vienna, the object of French action had been gained, and the presence of French troops was no longer required. The sentry which the Monarchy of July had thought it necessary to post at the frontiers of the Papal State could now be taken off. Belgium was free; Italy was at least saved, and its freedom would come in good time.

Finally in Greece, while Russia and England struggled for the supremacy, and stirred up the rival factions of Metaxas and Mavrocordato, Louis Philippe aided in establishing the authority of the new king, Otho of Bavaria, with no design but that of consolidating the liberty of

Greece. His action gave valuable assistance to the patriotic middle-class supporters of Colettis' Ministry, a Ministry of truly national views, anxious to develop in this young nation, once more free, its proper resources and its own life, through agriculture, trade, and education, and to obtain for it a moral and material position corresponding to its independent status among the nations of Europe.

Thus, from one end of Europe to the other, the beneficent policy of Louis Philippe in 1839 was successful in imposing upon individuals and upon States, without recourse to force, settlements which did more to maintain the equilibrium required for the development of national energies than more brilliant enterprises, either social or military. It consolidated all gains which might otherwise have been wasted. Molé, speaking on behalf of the King, was able to say on January 14, 1837, "We hate absolutism; and we pity the people which knows its own power so little as to put up with it." These words might be taken by the absolutist Courts as a "universal summons to rebellion," but it was not in fact incendiary language. It was only the formulation of a policy, of which the liberties of Europe were alike the object and the prize.

Little by little, the Courts of Vienna, Berlin, and Petrograd recognised the fact and bowed to it; Metternich intimated that Louis Philippe "had not had a better Minister for the past seven years." His sympathy for liberty was forgiven for the sake of the peace and protection which with his master's aid he gave against revolutions. Clear-sighted and impartial Frenchmen, and the nation at large, quiet and happy, were grateful to him for having consolidated the liberties of Europe and the peace of France.

And yet it was precisely on this point that the Opposition, consisting of the Doctrinaires and the great party chiefs who had been ousted from power by the resolution of Louis Philippe, directed their attack. The main grievance of the

Opposition, the only one in fact that they could make good against Molé, was that at the time when he was summoned to office by the King, Thiers, though in disagreement with Louis Philippe, had not suffered any defeat in Parliament; a second grievance was that Molé had been selected in the place of Guizot, who was, in the eyes of all, the true leader of the majority. At the decisive moment, when the King formally undertook to fight the parliamentary bourgeoisie, Molé was considered by politicians as the blindly obedient humble servant, the lackey, one might almost say, of Louis Philippe. The absolute agreement between the two on all points of external and internal politics, the invariable approval of Molé's conduct expressed in the Court of the Tuileries, seemed more and more to justify this description of the Minister. The result was that the war declared against him in the Chambers turned out to be aimed at the King himself and his "personal government." The struggle which had been going on for a long time out of sight between the King and his bourgeois allies was now patent to all. The youthful Doctrinaire, Duvergier de Hauranne, with more vigour and force than his elders, or even than his leaders, Thiers and Guizot, who were keeping dark for the time, did not hesitate to write a book accusing the King of violating the constitution, and summoning him to return to the "principles of representative government." It looked like a return to the days when 221 deputies (and this was now about the number of the Opposition) were once more to attack the Crown, and upset the Monarchy of July as they had overthrown the Bourbons.

But Louis Philippe was not Charles X, nor was Molé Polignac. The personal government of Louis Philippe at home and his refusal of power to the leaders of the bourgeoisie bore a very faint resemblance to the absolutism of the Bourbons. And at bottom, the work of Molé, in calling a truce and offering amnesties to both sides, was rather favourable than not to liberty. He was to be attacked by a coalition between the Doctrinaires, who blamed him for pardoning the Republicans, and the men of the Left, from Dupin to Thiers, who objected to his toleration of the Catholics. The inability of his opponents to unite in their criticisms was the best proof that neither the King nor his Minister had really jeopardised the rights of Parliament. The only object of the coalition was by a formal defeat to give a lesson to this obstinate King, who, for the sake of establishing the authority of Molé, had allowed him to dissolve Parliament on October 3, 1837, and thereby secure a majority.

The coalition had been got up by the efforts of the younger Doctrinaires, Remusat, Duvergier de Hauranne, Jaubert, and Piscatory, who had mediated between Thiers and Guizot, and induced them to forget their quarrels and combine their grievances against the King and his Minister. The first step towards an understanding had been taken early in 1838. Duvergier de Hauranne invited the more advanced men of the dynastic Left, the "tiers parti," Odilon Barrot and Dupin, to join; and the treaty was sealed on January 18, 1839, upon the discussion on the Address. This coalition of unbridled and disappointed ambitions, with no common basis, and practically directed against the King himself, could not possibly have any plan of action other than criticism of the work that the King had made specially his own—a foreign policy firm without aggressiveness, pacific without weakness. As between the two parliamentary parties united against Louis Philippe, one demanding order, and the other liberty, there was only one common watchword possible, the defence of the national honour. They had to prove that the King pushed his dread of war to the point of forgetting the national dignity, and that the servility of his Ministers had sacrificed that dignity at the dictation of the sovereigns of Europe. From the beginning of 1838 the attack was unceasing, in the Press and in Parliament, Thiers, Guizot, even the Duc de Broglie, Villemain, Duchâtel and the whole staff of the Conservatives, Mauguin and his Republicans, and finally Berryer, the eloquent orator of the Legitimists, all vying with one another in their zeal to demonstrate and stigmatise the supposed treachery of the Monarchy.

If France had induced the Belgians to give up Luxemburg, in order to avoid a conflict which would have threatened their independence, and for which their enemies were watching; if she had given in Greece an example of unselfishness, to put a stop to the intrigues which prevented that country from developing freely; if she had evacuated Ancona in order to make sure that Austria should never again be able to occupy the Legations; if she had broken with England rather than be an accomplice of the policy of Palmerston, who "had nothing to offer her but revolutions"—these were but so many transactions for the Opposition to distort into accusations against the King. The only step that could have disarmed them would have been one of those exhibitions of force which had been demanded with such persistency under the Restoration. The wonder was that the severe critics of the party of action in 1830 and 1831 should now be supporting a policy of practically the same nature, in order to get the better of Louis Philippe. The proceeding was singularly dangerous not only for the monarch, but for monarchy. Bertin de Vaux, the editor of the *Débats,* was careful to warn his friends, the Doctrinaires, thus: "I am as friendly with you as I was with Chateaubriand; but I am not going to begin once more undermining the present form of government, which I want to see established. Once is enough." In destroying the royal authority, they ran a great risk of destroying royalty itself.

Ever since the Consulate the French nation had, along with its love of order and of a government favourable to the hard worker, only one burning and persistent passion, the desire to occupy a great military position in Europe, worthy of its part under the Convention and the Empire. When Thiers—who in his enforced retirement was now beginning the *History of the Consulate*—visited Italy to consult the heirs of Napoleon, whose hopes he was encouraging, when in company with Guizot he negotiated alliances in the Bonapartist salon of the Duchesse de Massa, —surely Lamartine was justified in warning the Royalists against Bonapartist perils? Again, what are we to think of the astounding audacity that induced Berryer, out of opposition and party spirit, to pronounce an eulogium on the government of the Convention? And what a pleasure must it have been for a Republican like Béranger to note attacks of this sort. "This coalition is dealing mortal blows at the Throne; and the most singular thing is that the men who are bringing it to this pitiable condition are Monarchists." To ask France to forget the blessings bestowed on her by this government to which she was now becoming accustomed, in order to awaken her pride and the memory of her past glory, was not only unfair but tactically clumsy. Lamartine long afterwards expressed his belief that it was the origin of the revolution which ten years later destroyed the work of its present authors.

To counteract it, Louis Philippe did his best to find for the country some compensations which might flatter its vanity. He sent his sons, d'Orléans first, and Nemours later, to fight in Algeria at the head of the army of Africa, and to win victories at least as striking as those of the Egyptian expedition. The nation cared nothing for colonies, and, led astray by the envenomed criticism of the Opposition, failed to grasp the greatness of the "gift now made to it." The pension to the widow of General Danrémont, the hero of Constantine, was made the subject of minute discussion, while that to the widow of General Daumesnil, the defender of Vincennes in 1814, was at once carried, and by acclamation. Louis Philippe tried in vain to stay by a homoeopathic treatment this fever of martial memories with which the bourgeoisie had infected the nation. He founded at his own expense the Museum at Versailles, opened in 1838 and dedicated "to all the Glories of France," especially to military glories, hoping that the homage thus done to the national heroes would calm the impatience of a people who were always on the look-out for slights. The remedy had its dangers too; at any rate it was not of the kind suited to disarm the Opposition.

The struggle, ostensibly waged between the Opposition and the Molé Cabinet, but really directed against the King, lasted from December 26, 1838, to January 19, 1839, and was one of the longest and fiercest parliamentary battles that had hitherto taken place. The Ministers were attacked by the leading speakers of the Right, Left, and the Centre. Thiers spoke thirty times, Guizot twelve. Alone against all these, Molé took his stand, determined and cool; the anger excited by his tenacious resistance became daily more lively and bitter. At the end of it all, when Molé, exhausted with the effort, pleaded fatigue, cries arose from the Opposition of "Die then, dog!" He was treated almost as a criminal. However, he won the victory on that day, though by a majority of eighteen only; but he failed to establish his authority in that Parliament, where both parties were at the mercy of a few deserters.

Thereupon he persuaded the King to dissolve the Chamber (February 2, 1839) and appeal to the electors (March 2). The obvious line for the Opposition to take was to call the proceeding a *coup d'état*, and to compare Louis Philippe to Charles X. An appeal from the heads of all the parties combined against the King, signed by Thiers, Guizot, Odilon Barrot, Garnier-Pagès, and Berryer, called the attention of the nation to the unconstitutional character of the measures and proposals of the Cabinet. It soon became clear that the efforts of the parliamentary bourgeoisie, for the sake of a victory over the King, to arouse the suspicions and alarm of the French nation against him, had been successful; the country, so calm in 1837, so contented, so indifferent to parliamentary quarrels, was now in a state of fever and anxiety such as had not been seen since 1830. After all, how could it be expected that France would not be alarmed when she heard these deputies, who, after the "days of July," had shown their marked hostility to an active foreign policy, who had actually created for themselves a new dynasty to stop this activity, now publicly recant their errors, and charge the King of their choice with arbitrary conduct for declining to follow them on the path that led back to the spirit of propagandism and the worship of military glory? There could be no doubt as to the verdict of the electors. Cajoled and disquieted, they voted by a large majority in favour of the parliamentary bourgeoisie against the King, against Molé, against these dictators, these "Napoleons of peace," and that not so much on account of their dictatorial policy, as of their pacific tendencies. The parliamentary chiefs now got their revenge for the slights put upon them by Louis Philippe in dismissing M. de Broglie in 1834 and 1836, Thiers in 1836, and Guizot in 1837.

But it was a two-edged blade that they wielded against Molé and Louis Philippe. The call upon the country to arbitrate between the King and the Chambers was a fatal admission of the unconstitutional conduct of these same deputies in 1830 when with the aid of Louis Philippe they laid violent hands on the rights of the people, and, without consulting the nation, legislated in its name. Were they not teaching France that the Monarchy of July was not after all the best of Republics? At any rate the nation acted on the lesson ten years later.

Moreover, as they had only combined to destroy what Thiers called "the King's absolute plenipotentiary power," they could not possibly remain combined long enough to form a compact government majority like that of Casimir Perier. The differences of principle, the incompatible ambitions, which separated the various elements of the Coalition—the Doctrinaires, the Royalists who had reluctantly abandoned Charles X, the Legitimists, and Liberals of the shade of Thiers, Dupin, and Odilon Barrot—were evident from the day (March 8) when Molé placed his resignation in the hands of the King; and they also accounted for the long ministerial interregnum (to May 19, 1839). Marshal Soult, to whom Louis Philippe had entrusted the duty of forming a National Ministry, was unable to do it for two months, in the face of the division of opinions and ambitions among the parliamentary chieftains. Guizot was heard to say, on the day after the struggle with Louis Philippe, "I should prefer the rule of the King to that of M. Thiers"; while Thiers claimed to be designated as successor to Molé, because he was actually in office and master of Parliament at the moment when the King had forced him to resign. Dupin and the "tiers parti" were no less certain that their hour of success had come.

This was the moment chosen by the impenitent Republicans, socialists brought up in the school of Buonarotti, who met at the Club of the *Saisons*, to organise an attack upon the dynasty which had been compromised by its own partisans. Barbès, a Creole from Guadaloupe, with the spirit of an apostle of Christian Socialism and a passion for martyrdom, Blanqui, who had fought in July and was a strong believer in the war of classes, Martin Bernard, a logician and a fanatical admirer of Robespierre, setting at naught the advice that the Republicans had been giving to the democracy for the last four years, determined to take advantage of the difficulties of the Crown and Parliament, to retaliate on the part of the democracy of Paris. The ministerial crisis had hindered general business, and the mob having nothing to do seemed ready for a street riot.

On April 4, 1839, when the Chamber elected on March 8 assembled without Ministers or a speech from the Throne, a riotous crowd accosted these deputies thus abandoned to themselves with yells and cat-calls. A month later, on May 12, the uneasiness continuing, the ring-leaders, specially Blanqui, thought that success was possible. He summoned the members of the *Saisons* to meet in the Rue St Martin, in the heart of working Paris, gave them arms taken from the gunsmiths' shops, and tried to seize the Prefecture of Police and the Hôtel de Ville. People had given up believing in the possibility of disturbance, and the consequent surprise at its appearance alone gave it at first some success; but the action of a small body of troops in the Rue Greneta sufficed to put an end to this premature attempt in a few hours. Barbès was taken prisoner: Blanqui and Martin Bernard escaped into hiding, but were eventually captured. The democracy of Paris had remained a stranger and almost indifferent to these miscalculated efforts.

Now the news had already reached the Courts of Vienna, Petrograd, and Munich, that the devil of revolution was once more unchained in France, and that Louis Philippe had gone the way of Charles X. Seen from afar, this was the appearance presented by what Béranger lightheartedly called "the quarrel between bourgeoisie and Crown." And this fact was bound to awaken certain salutary reflections in the bourgeoisie who, after wresting the governing power from the democracy, now refused to yield it up to the King. They saw that their own divisions, and the bad feeling of their own leaders towards the King, were more dangerous to themselves than the insurrections which they fomented. Fear and selfishness combined to bring them back to reason and loyalty. Doctrinaire deputies like

Duchâtel and Villemain, followers of Molé like Cunin-Gridaine, members of the Left Centre and of the "tiers parti" like Passy and Dufaure; left their own leaders Molé, Thiers, and Guizot, absorbed in fighting each other, to form a new group around Marshal Soult. They offered their services to the King unconditionally, terrified by the mere sound of rioting. They allowed him without discussion to resume the conduct of foreign affairs, which their friends had made the principal grievance against him. In this manner there arose a new contract between Crown and Parliament, which, when carefully looked at, was less favourable to Parliament than that of 1831. The influence of the Crown, far from being reduced and controlled as they proposed, was to be a still more important factor in this "neutral" head-less Ministry. Casimir Perier, and after him M. de Broglie and Guizot, had been able to keep the authority of the Crown under eclipse; but after the conflict of 1839 it shone out more brilliantly in its relations with Parliament and its opposition to the bourgeoisie than in 1832.

But neither King nor Ministers, much less the parliamentary majority, were able at once to silence the passions which the Coalition had aroused in the country by its strictures on the pacificism of Molé, and its appeals to the dignity of the nation. The fever of vanity that it had created, the yearning for action, the "desire for activity abroad which reminded men of the propaganda of 1830"—these all were fed from the springs of the Napoleonic legend, which was more vigorous than ever. "The events of the four last months," wrote M. de Barante in May 1839, "the appeals to the touchiness of the nation and the bad feeling excited against foreign Powers for the purpose of getting or keeping popularity, and the growing habit in France of fancying insults and threats everywhere—all this has created a feeling of alarm which it will take long to dissipate."

CHAPTER VII

LOUIS PHILIPPE AND THE EASTERN QUESTION

It was precisely in this year 1839 that the Eastern crisis, the widest and most serious international dispute since 1830, began. Nothing could have been better devised for inflaming passions in France and distrust in Europe, for exciting suspicions of the good faith of Louis Philippe among his subjects, and stirring up the European Powers against the Cabinet of the Tuileries. The coincidence of the internal with the external crisis greatly increased the difficulties of the French monarch.

This crisis, as might have been foreseen, was provoked by the policy of Palmerston, who could not bring himself to accept the victory won by the Tsar Nicholas at Unkiar Skelessi (1833). Since the Russians had shown themselves strong enough to establish an exclusive influence at Constantinople and in the Levant, that statesman had done everything in his power to rival their success. Once established in the Ionian Isles and in Greece, English merchants were encouraged to extend their operations to Constantinople, Trebizond, Galatz, the mouths of the Danube, and the Black Sea. "As soon as English commerce is established in the East," wrote de Barante from Petrograd, where these proceedings were being closely watched, "its interests and even its opinions may do much to decide the action of the Cabinet of London; and the moment will come when peace or war will depend on them." Palmerston had already obtained the agreement of the French ambassador in London, Sebastiani, who knew his way about Eastern matters, to a plan of aggressive campaign against Russia to which M. de Broglie had taken no objection. On August 16, 1838, the English Minister Urquhart, a vigorous opponent of Muscovite influence, obtained from the Sultan a treaty of commerce very favourable to his fellow-countrymen, inasmuch as it exempted them from all import duties in Turkey. And on the refusal of Mehemet Ali, the Pacha of Egypt, to permit its application within his territories, the Sultan invited the English to establish themselves at Aden, and authorised their ships to cruise along the coast of Syria and Egypt. He flattered himself on securing a striking revenge upon his recalcitrant Viceroy, by handing him over to England.

Queen Victoria had scarcely ascended the throne in 1837 with a Whig Government, when Palmerston had a long conversation with her about Russia and the Turks, in order to instruct her in the duty of an English sovereign when faced by such a position as that taken up in the East by the Tsar Nicholas. And at the end of 1838, he remarked in an unguarded moment to Ponsonby, then charged with the protection of English interests in Constantinople, "Here is an excellent opportunity coming for getting rid of the treaty of Unkiar Skelessi."

The opportunity was a frontier quarrel between the Turks, who wanted to reduce the Kurds to submission, and Ibrahim, the Egyptian commander, who was annoyed at being unable to make forced levies of recruits in the Lebanon. The Turkish and Egyptian forces were face to face in April 1839. In June Mahmoud declared the Viceroy in rebellion, and began operations for the recovery of Syria. "It is to our interest," said Palmerston and Ponsonby together, "that the Turks should conquer Syria and threaten Egypt." But, on their first encounter, the Turkish army was routed and captured at Nezib; while Admiral Achmet surrendered to Mehemet Ali the Turkish fleet cruising off Alexandria. Sultan Mahmoud died in despair, leaving a disordered empire to a child, Abdul Medjid. The advisers of the new sovereign had reached such a pitch of desperation that in July 1839 they offered to invest Mehemet Ali with hereditary power, transmissible to his son, the victor of Nezib, which meant practical independence. This was the most visible result of what Metternich called the "Turkish frolic," of the service which Palmerston proposed to render to the Porte, as compensation for the war into which he had driven the Turkish Government. To escape the reproach of having deceived the Turks at the time, Palmerston dissuaded the Divan from making peace with the Viceroy too quickly. In fact he was more earnest than ever in advising war, intending to profit by their weakness, as he had before meant to profit by their victory; for he hoped this time to force the youthful Sultan to look to London for the help which in 1833 his father had sought in Petrograd.

At this point France came on the stage. Instead of winding up the crisis by a speedy peace, which was perhaps most to her interest, the Soult Ministry prolonged it for the pleasure of dictating to Russia. What glory for this commonplace Ministry to be able to prevent the Turks from running for help to the Tsar Nicholas for the second time, to utter in the name of Europe those words of menace which would stay the intervention of Russia! "For England, as for France, and also for Austria, the main object is to keep Russia in check. She must be trained to deal with Eastern affairs in association with other Powers." The initiative taken by France, and her marked intention of forcing upon Nicholas I a European convention of her own drafting, as a substitute for the stipulations of Unkiar Skelessi, fulfilled Palmerston's every desire and plan. "Soult is a jewel," he wrote on June 19, 1839.

Threatened by the diplomacy of France, the Tsar took immediate steps to meet it and to maintain his influence at Constantinople, by arranging a peace as quickly as possible between the Divan and Mehemet Ali. The firman for its ratification was signed before the end of July. "It would be a pity," said Soult, "if the crisis should be solved by some precipitate arrangement in which the Powers have had no time to intervene." Events justified his remark. Austria intervened, in time to prevent the Turks from making the concessions advised by Russia; and on July 27 the French Ambassador, Admiral Roussin, had the honour of speaking in the name of the five Powers whose agreement had been secured, and presenting a note on their behalf. France and Europe called upon the Sultan to "suspend any premature settlement." Louis Philippe's Ministers were very much gratified at the receipt of this mandate, imagining themselves already at the head of the European Concert for the preservation of Turkey from ruin and from the influence of Russia. With their advice and under the protection of Europe, now substituted for the protectorate of the Tsars, the Ottoman Empire was to recover stability and life; and the moment was approaching when, by the Charter of Gulyané (published November 3, 1839), the reconciliation between the Sultan and his Christian subjects, due to the Liberalism and initiative of France, would open new destinies to it. "This Empire," said Soult with pride, "is now returning into the community of European states; every Power is called upon to protect it, and the whole body of them to guarantee its independence. And thus too all the disturbing influences which have during these latter years created an Eastern Question are now reduced to order. Russia is broken!" Palmerston could not restrain his satisfaction. "Soult and I," he said, "treat one another like members of the same Cabinet."

It must be admitted however that, to obtain this result,

France had been obliged by the pressure of England to mobilise its fleet and send it to the mouth of the Dardanelles. So absorbed was she in these measures of attack or defence against Russia, that she had neglected, and even prevented the re-establishment of peace in the East, and allowed a crisis to continue which in former days Louis Philippe would have taken the precaution to avoid. Though a friend to peace, the King of the French did not dare this time, after the internal crisis of 1839, to refuse some satisfaction to the national love of glory in the flattering shape of a leading part on the Eastern stage. He had been so seriously blamed for his favour to Molé that he thought it well to support the policy of Soult's Cabinet, "the most glorious," said Jouffroy in the Chamber, "that has had charge of affairs since 1830."

It soon became possible to appraise the value of this empty glory. Irritated by French rhodomontade, the Great Powers, including even those apparent enemies England and Russia, combined in the month of August to oblige France to sacrifice the Pacha of Egypt, Mehemet Ali, and his conquests, for the sake of the integrity of the Ottoman Empire which she had so proudly proclaimed. "All for France, and by France!" said Metternich. "These are brave words for French ears, but ugly for all others." With the ill-temper of all Europe at his back, Palmerston carried on his plans; after having used France to get rid of the Russians at Constantinople, he now proposed to go counter to the will of France by snubbing the Viceroy of Egypt to please the Turks. We need only remember what an enthusiasm the victories and the greatness of Mehemet Ali had awakened among the French to understand their opposition in 1839 to the schemes of Palmerston and the decisions of Europe. The Soult Ministry and Louis Philippe found that they were more and more implicated in this quarrel; and this time they had all the Powers against them. They tried to make the Cabinets of London and Petrograd give way somewhat, by warning the Whig Ministry that, if they allowed a Russian fleet sailing for Egypt to pass the Bosphorus, a French fleet would at once enter the Dardanelles; and the threat had some effect. The Powers sent a note to Mehemet Ali dated October 3, 1839, offering milder conditions, including the right of succession in Egypt to his son and the pachalik of Acre, in lieu of Syria. A peace at this price would have relieved France of some embarrassment, but, unluckily for her, Mehemet Ali, having beaten the Turks, was not in a humour to accept orders from Europe, and obstinately insisted on the same terms as the Sultan had been ready to offer him after his defeat at Nezib. So the crisis continued (October 1839) in a shape favourable to Palmerston's fixed plan of restoring the credit of England at Constantinople by reducing the power of Egypt.

At the beginning of 1840 the debates in the French Parliament, in which Thiers took a leading part, indicated the existence of a feverish desire for action, which the Ministry encouraged by word and deed. A quarrel having arisen in 1838 between Bustamente, the President of Mexico, and the French established there, Admiral Baudin was instructed to blockade the Mexican ports. He occupied Vera Cruz, shelled St Jean d'Ulloa, and on August 6, 1839, compelled the President Santa Anna to sign a peace for which France took much credit. Similarly Louis Philippe did not hesitate to declare a warlike blockade at the end of 1839 against Rosas, the President of the Argentine Republic, whose occasionally severe measures had not spared Frenchmen. Finally, when Abd-el-Kader in Algiers tore up the Treaty of La Tafna, and called out the Arabs to a Holy War, Louis Philippe immediately raised the number of the army of Africa to 60,000 men. General Valé, who had made good use of the last twelve months of peace to organise his conquests methodically, now undertook their defence, with the support of the Duc d'Orléans and sundry officers—Duvivier, Changarnier, Lamoricière, and Cavaignac—who devoted themselves thenceforth exclusively to this task.

At every point where French interests were injured or threatened, France showed a firm front with her sea and land forces. So great a country, easily persuaded of its right by these striking proofs of its might, was not disposed to abandon Egypt to the, perhaps interested, resentment of England. "Whatever happens," said Soult, "we will maintain our principles, and decline to sacrifice to anyone our rights, our interests, or our honour." On January 26, 1840, he informed the English Cabinet that "in his opinion the proposal to inflict humiliating conditions upon Mehemet Ali was impracticable." And as a last step, in order to counteract the apparent inclination of the English Cabinet to defer to Russia and her ambassador, M. de Brunow, he sent one of the most prominent men in Parliament, M. Guizot, as ambassador to London (February 19, 1840).

All these concessions to the feeling of the people, however, did not allay the anger of France at the English proceedings against Mehemet Ali; and Parliament intimated as much to the King by refusing the application of the Ministry for a grant on the marriage of the Duc de Nemours, June 20, 1840. "The lesson is intended," said an opposition journal, "not so much for the Ministers as for the Power that selects them." The Soult Ministry resigned. Once more we see a conservative and pro-dynastic bourgeoisie endangering the Monarchy it had itself created by first frightening the nation into demanding an aggressive and militant foreign policy and then backing up the demand. Thiers, who had led the attack in the dark, returned to power on March 1, 1840; and the humiliated King had to resign himself "to the situation." No one can doubt that the authority of

Thiers, as against the King, came from his being the Minister of the Nation. "The opinion of Paris on the Egyptian question," wrote M. de St Aulaire, "has acquired greater force than I could have believed possible." The formula that Thiers devised to express the essential principle of his policy was: "The maintenance of the Turkish Empire; a benevolent and effective interest in the Pacha of Egypt."

Being however a man of great prudence, and of skill equal to his vigour, the new President of the Council could not conceal from himself that the application of these principles might well lead to a breach with Russia and England at the same time. In Parliament he was all for Egypt; but he tried hard to provide the country with matter to divert its attention elsewhere. He requested England to restore the ashes of Napoleon to France; and they were brought back with great pomp by the Prince de Joinville to the Invalides. He pressed upon Parliament the need of putting down Abd-el-Kader, and of giving liberal support to the Algerian business. "Let us go to Algeria; let France get herself talked about, earn some reputation, produce some soldiers. Europe has been at peace for twenty-five years; and the blood is hot in our veins." He hoped to be able gradually to accustom the French to forget Mehemet Ali, to take their own time over the settlement of the Eastern question, without either following the lead of England in every detail, or thwarting her by a curt refusal.

Guizot too did his best to carry out this temporising policy in London. Being a Protestant, and quite at home in English history and English society, he was just the man wanted to get the ear of the colleagues of Palmerston, Lord Holland, Clarendon, Lansdowne, and Melbourne himself, all Liberals, who objected to an abandonment of the alliance with France and to the cajoleries of the Tsar. The young

Queen was entirely absorbed in the delights of her marriage, which took place in the spring of 1840, while her cousin of Saxe-Coburg had married the Duc de Nemours; and she did not dream of favouring any policy that could cut her off from France. The delay thus caused in issuing to Egypt the ultimatum of Europe (practically Palmerston's) was used by Thiers to start direct negotiations between the Sultan and the Viceroy for a peace which would have ended this dangerous crisis outside the frontiers of Europe. He directed his agents at Constantinople and Alexandria, M. Pontois and M. Cochelet, "to repair the broken links between these two cities." In the month of June 1840 the dismissal of Chosrew Pacha, the Grand Vizier, a mortal enemy of Mehemet Ali, and the mission of Sami Bey, a confidential man of the Viceroy's, as envoy to the Sultan, seemed to point to an approaching solution.

But Palmerston had received due notice of the calculations of Thiers on assuming power, and of their interference with his designs. With perhaps simulated anger he complained to his colleagues and to Europe that France had determined upon a personal and separate line of policy, and was in fact playing fast and loose with them. Ponsonby, his confidant at Constantinople, who had given him the information, did not wait for instructions, but acted at once. He hastily sent his first Dragoman, Wood, to Syria to raise the tribes of the Lebanon against Egypt; the incident occurred at exactly the right moment for the separation of Syria from Egypt, as the Syrians were demanding their independence. Palmerston, determined to give a lesson to Louis Philippe and his Ministers, called a European Conference in London July 15, 1840, to which France was not invited. It was there decided to impose terms upon the Viceroy of Egypt. The Treaty of London put these terms into shape; they were Palmerston's revenge and triumph; and they were at the same time the revenge of the Tsar

Nicholas, who was delighted to address this ultimatum to France, after her pride in presenting the ultimatum of July 27, 1839, to Russia. Mehemet Ali was invited to evacuate Syria, with permission however to retain Acre, if he bowed to the will of the Powers within ten days; Admiral Stopford was in the meantime to patrol the coast of Syria with the English fleet.

These measures, well adapted as they were to earn for England the gratitude of Turkey, thus saved by a miracle, were no less effective as a lesson in modesty and humility to France, who found herself face to face with a new Compact of Chaumont. The isolation in which she had been placed in order to strike her protégés a rude blow, "was a lesson," said Metternich, which "her fussy and ambitious policy, her boasts, and her exorbitant demands had fairly deserved." She accepted it as an insult demanding satisfaction. The wound "inflicted on the feelings and interests of the nation," said H. Heine, "is bringing about an armistice in the belligerent camps. The people are all flocking round the Tricolour, not so much in consternation, as with a joyous enthusiasm. The watchword of the day is 'War with perfidious Albion.'" Even the most moderate of the journals in August 1840 took up the glove so unexpectedly flung down by the English statesmen who had been the prime movers in the insult, and threatened England with a revolution in Ireland. The diplomatic action of the Powers had completed in those critical days the warlike awakening of the French nation up to which for the past two years the policy of both political parties had been working. "We must make an end of it," said even the most pacific.

King Leopold, who was in Paris at the time, writing to his niece, Queen Victoria on July 26, said, "The secrecy with which the Turco-Egyptian affair has been concluded, the way in which France has been thrust aside in a matter so near her and affecting so many of her interests has had a disastrous effect here. I cannot conceal from you that the consequences may be serious, especially as the Thiers Ministry is supported by the popular party, and is as careless of consequences as your own Foreign Minister, and more so. Thiers indeed would not be sorry to see everything upside down. He is strongly imbued with those ideas of renown and glory which were so marked a characteristic of the Age of the Republic and Empire. In fact, the reappearance of a Convention in France would not disturb him much, for he believes himself to be the man to lead the Assembly; and last year he told me that it was perhaps the strongest form of government for France. France has been simply *kicked* out."

Had Thiers called the Chambers into Session in August, nobody could have said what might not have been done by the deputies and the Government in the intensity of their excitement. But he at once perceived the danger that might result from an immediate and curt reply to the challenge of Europe. "To involve France in a struggle in which she would stand alone against the whole of Europe," he said to M. de St Aulaire, "would be to incur a terrible responsibility. Neither wounded vanity nor a deliberate infatuation for Mehemet Ali would be a sufficient excuse for such recklessness." If he did not entirely dismiss the idea of finding in this crisis a favourable opportunity for French activity, at any rate he did not consider that the defence of Mehemet Ali was a reason of sufficient weight. "Whatever happens," he said, "France will not fire a gun in the East." He believed moreover that Mehemet Ali would be strong enough to withstand the threats of Europe, and perhaps even without help to monopolise the attention of England and Russia. He awaited patiently the moment for impressing upon Austria and Prussia that there was some danger in arousing the resentment of France.

The conduct adopted by Thiers, immediately after the receipt of the insult, undoubtedly pointed to war, but to a war on the Rhine; nevertheless it served well enough the designs of Louis Philippe, which were essentially and at bottom pacific. The King's first feeling on receipt of the news of the Treaty of London was one of anger, especially against Austria. "For ten years I have been building up a dam against the Revolution, at the expense of my popularity, my ease, and it may yet be of my life. It is to me that they owe the peace of Europe, and the security of their thrones; and this is their gratitude! Will they not be satisfied till they have seen me put on the Cap of Liberty?" But he recovered himself very soon, hoping with Thiers that the Pacha of Egypt would be able to make head against the coalition alone and without other help. With Thiers too he thought he could avoid a conflict with England. Through Guizot, who clung strongly to the *entente* with England, he tried to act upon Palmerston's colleagues, Melbourne, Lord Holland, and Lord Granville, and through the King of the Belgians upon his disciple, Queen Victoria, to whom the King was in the habit of showing the letters he received from Louis Philippe. In order to mask his proceedings from the French, who would infallibly have accused him of treachery, he pretended to favour the energetic measures adopted by Thiers in August in view of a possible continental war, measures which sorely disturbed the Courts of Vienna and Berlin—the call to the colours of the classes of 1836–9, and the extraordinary credits for the purchase of war-material published by the *Moniteur* on July 29. "I am pleased with Thiers; he is as prudent as I am; and I am as *national* as he." But he watched him nevertheless, having guessed his plan and recognised that on ultimate analysis it differed from his own. He confided as much to M. de St Aulaire before his departure for Vienna. "I do not mean to let myself be drawn on too far by my little minister. At bottom, he wants war, and I do not. And if he leaves me no other way out, I shall smash him rather than break with Europe."

In this crisis, which was even more dangerous for his dynasty than the parliamentary crisis from which it arose, Louis Philippe showed equal skill and coolness. Standing alone, faced by a public opinion that had got past control, with Ministers inclined to accept its lead in order to make a reputation for "glory," he managed to "muzzle the tiger." "Having to face serious and difficult problems," wrote Leopold, "he puts up with unbearable annoyances and all the troubles of his delicate position with a firmness and courage which ought to earn him a kinder treatment from the Great Powers." On August 6, 1840, Louis Napoleon Bonaparte made a second attempt to upset the Orleanist throne; but the landing at Boulogne, though a more serious attempt than the Strasbourg affair (see p. 186), ended no less ignominiously. The pretender appealed to popular passions excited to danger-point by the legend of his uncle and by the insults of Europe. He was speedily captured and imprisoned; and the public, to all appearance, remained indifferent to his fate. The transfer of the ashes of the great Emperor from St Helena to the Invalides, which took place at the end of the year, was calculated to show the world that the Government had no dread of a revived Napoleonism. The King's sons, however, became anxious about their own future, and were more inclined to drag their father into strife than to restrain him. But to threats and to suggestions Louis Philippe opposed a firm resistance. At no previous moment, at no graver moment in all his reign, did he rely more completely on his personal, but industriously dissimulated policy, though something like it had occurred in his two first years of rule.

If all Europe, and especially if the English Government had listened to Palmerston, Louis Philippe would then have suffered final shipwreck; indeed the attitude of that Minister continued to complicate the business for six more months. With frigid obstinacy and an absolute disregard for everybody, Palmerston on the morrow of August 15 urged England forward along the path which Ponsonby had opened to her in the East so much to his satisfaction. Metternich compared his method to that of the gambler who on getting a run of luck tries to break the Bank. In the presence of the French squadron, which had been taken off its war footing through the conciliatory policy of Thiers and Louis Philippe, the English squadron received orders to attack Ibrahim at Beyrout on August 14; a month later, on September 11, Sir Charles Napier bombarded the town and destroyed it. On the same day another squadron, reinforced by some Austrian vessels, landed a small force of 8000 Turks and 1500 English in Syria. On September 14 Ponsonby won from the Porte the decisive victory for which hand in hand with Palmerston he had been working for more than a year, for the aggrandisement of his country, and his own influence in the East. The Sultan, on his advice, formally proclaimed the deposition of the Viceroy of Egypt and his son. After having been humiliated and conquered for ten years by his rebellious vassals, he now obtained, by the help of the English, a striking revenge for his flouted authority.

In Paris on the contrary, on the news of the decree of Europe and of the Sultan against Mehemet Ali, all was consternation and rage. As soon as it was known, on October 20, 1840, Heinrich Heine records "an agitation passing all belief. The recruiting offices were crowded like the entrances to a theatre; and in all the theatres the Marseillaise was sung," as in the revolutionary days of the universal levies. Funds dropped 4 francs, business came to a standstill. Most of the journals, even on the ministerial side, were doing more to further than to check the outburst. Even the English Ambassador was alarmed, and wrote, "I think war is not improbable." In Louis Philippe's own circle the same fears were expressed in a letter written by one of the King's daughters to the Prince de Joinville. "We are passing through a critical moment, the most critical for the last ten years. Within the country opinion is in a nervous state, and some incitement to revolution; at our gates a foreign war, with all Europe against us. God alone can save us." The gravest feature in the whole affair was that at this moment, in spite of the judgment of many of his colleagues and of his own sincere anxiety, Thiers should have taken the risk of active measures, rather than risk his popularity by opposing them. After ten years of pacific effort, Louis Philippe had been brought round the full circle, by the parliamentary bourgeoisie, by the Ministers, and by public opinion, back to his starting-point, with a nation on one side hungry to avenge Waterloo, and on the other side Europe, given up to the schemes and enterprises of ambitious Powers capable of forcing their subjects into a new coalition against France. This was the great danger for France at that moment.

Lord Palmerston felt that against the French he had the support of a portion of the public opinion and of the English Press, flattered by the important part that he was making England play in the East, and pleased, though surprised, at the unexpected cooperation of the Tsar. As to Austria and Metternich, even if they had wanted to avoid a conflict with France, they would have felt bound to accede to the patriotic call of the new King of Prussia. In Germany the whole nation—princes, professors, private citizens, and students—united by that common belief in the grandeur and unity of their country due to the scientific education which had awakened the appetite and stimulated the pride of the Germanic race, were prepared to accept the war, "and to wage it between people and people." Thus, while France was wasting time over dreams of a revolutionary force triumphing over crowned heads and supported by popular sympathy, it looked as if a new league was ready to be formed, as in 1813, to parcel her out among its members. Palmerston talked of punishing French folly by depriving them of their colonies and their trade, while the Germans cast covetous eyes on the "German Rhine." "If Germany ever becomes a nation again," said Heinrich Heine, "M. Thiers may fairly claim a hand in it; and the history of Germany should give him credit for the fact."

Louis Philippe was not in a humour to let him get that credit. "I know well," he said sadly, "that he is to be the national Minister, while I am the foreigner's King." The past three years' struggle of the parliamentary bourgeoisie against the pacific policy of the sovereign had familiarised him with this comparison between their respective positions; but, while he recognised the danger to his authority, his conviction was unshaken that the interests of the country and those of his own dynasty did not lie in a war with Europe, which might let revolution and invasion loose on them. It may have been the conviction of an aged man threatened with the return of a past of terrible memory; but it was one which harmonised at bottom with the wishes of the country. Palmerston was not mistaken when he wrote to the Queen at that time, "There are in France a vast number of proprietors and industrialists who object decidedly to a useless war, and are determined opponents of the revolution. These people have not put themselves forward so far, but, if the question of peace or war came to be discussed, they would demand a hearing. The French nation is no longer what it was in 1792. It is now as much interested in avoiding a revolution as it was then in getting rid of the enormous and intolerable abuses that existed. The French then thought that they had everything to gain by foreign war. They now know that they have everything to lose by it."

The clamour of the Press and the invectives of the Opposition, which alarmed Thiers, did not prevent Louis Philippe from discerning accurately the true interests and the unexpressed desires of the nation. "You think I am too pacific," he said one day to his Ministers; "I tell you, I am not nearly so pacific as the country. You do not know how far the yearning for peace can carry this country." When, on October 5, Thiers had to decide whether to yield or resign, the King argued with him thus: "I do not want a war which in Europe would mean a struggle of one against four, and in France would let loose revolution. I do not believe that France is bound in honour to throw herself into a war in which she would be alone against the whole world, solely to keep Ibrahim in Syria." If in the face of a clear statement of this sort Thiers had resigned, as for a moment he thought of doing, his retirement would have obliged the King once more to disclose himself as the author of the policy objected to, while his Ministers appeared still to possess the support of Parliament. It was a continual struggle—and the fact came out more strongly at every stage of it—between the King and the leaders of the majority, which threatened to upset the order of things established with such difficulty in 1830, for the benefit of the mob who would decide between them. The journals friendly to the Cabinet, the *Courrier Français* and the *Constitutionnel,* insinuated that it was useless for Thiers to attempt to defend the interests and honour of the nation against the system of peace at any price advocated by the Crown. "A revolution at the same time democratic and warlike," seemed to the King of the Belgians to be on the cards.

The fear of this result now opened the eyes of the principal leaders of the parliamentary bourgeoisie very decidedly to the mistake they had been making for six years in contesting, and thereby weakening, the power of the Crown. All the Doctrinaire party, M. de Broglie, Guizot, Duchâtel, Villemain, etc., all of them Conservatives before everything, alarmed at the threatened riots and at the feverish excitement which they had themselves created, combined on October 6 to prevent Thiers from provoking the King and at the same time the English by a resignation. "Do you really propose to play the part of Espartero, and to be carried back into office by rioters?" wrote de Broglie to Thiers. Villemain declared that the name of the King and his personal action were needed to maintain peace and order. Guizot worked without ceasing on similar lines. Yielding to their arguments, Thiers withdrew his resignation on October 6; and on the 7th he assented to a compromise which the King required him to propose to England.

Shutting his eyes to the slight put upon him by the destruction of Egypt without consulting him, the King of the French suggested to England an arrangement on which they might meet. He would agree that Syria should be taken from Mehemet Ali, but insisted that the Sultan should leave him Egypt. "It was a great effort," said Guizot, when presenting the note to Lord Palmerston on October 9, 1840, "made by the peace party." Melbourne told the Queen that the success of the proposal would depend upon the amount of amiability with which England received it. A Cabinet Council was sitting at the time the note arrived; and the Queen had been duly prepared for it by the advice and influence of the King of the Belgians. Lord John Russell and his colleagues, with Melbourne and the Queen, had all agreed to insist upon a prompt and friendly answer from Palmerston, who had perhaps not entirely given up the hope of ruining Mehemet Ali. On October 15, 1840, the English Cabinet announced that they had invited the Sultan to grant the investiture of Egypt to Mehemet Ali, even with hereditary succession, if he now submitted.

On the same day a man, crouching beneath a lamp on the Tuileries Embankment, fired a rifle-shot at Louis Philippe. His name was Darmès, a floor-polisher by trade, and a member of communistic societies. Surely, now that peace was re-established, it was high time that these ever-recurring threats of revolution in Paris should be restrained! As Thiers insisted on masking his compulsory retreat by constantly talking of armaments and the national strength, Louis Philippe thought the time had come for an appeal to the Conservatives. He could give them what they desired, order and peace within the nation, while they could obtain for him the peace abroad which he considered essential. On October 18, he said to Duchâtel that "the first time that his Ministers tried to force his hand, he should take them at their word." He spoke of M. Guizot as his "hope," and said there was only one possible Cabinet, Soult, Guizot, Villemain, and himself. The opportunity soon came. The Chambers were summoned to meet on October 28 after a long holiday. The King and Thiers could not agree as to the exact language of the Speech from the Throne, Thiers wishing it to be firm, rather haughty, almost threatening, while Louis Philippe would have it conciliatory, calm but dignified, firm but moderate. "I feel that I am keeping," he said, "my royal oath, in devoting my life for the preservation of France from a war devoid of cause or object, and consequently without justification before God or man. I will not yield, either to factitious clamour or to the bullet of the assassin."

On October 20 the Thiers Cabinet resigned; and when, on the following day, the Duc de Broglie tried to patch up matters, the King replied with a decided refusal, and called in Soult and Guizot. This act of prerogative once more revealed the extent of his personal intromission and put his dynasty at the mercy of the Doctrinaires. "The state of opinion is very alarming," wrote the King's daughter; "a worse riot than any we have yet seen, and even a revolution, are possible." It was precisely this fear of disorder and anarchy that decided the Conservatives at last, and for eight years to come, to support a King whose personal interference and whose exaggerated love of peace they had so long denounced to the democracy.

CHAPTER VIII

LOUIS PHILIPPE AND GUIZOT

When, at the close of 1840, in the midst of an internal crisis aggravated by dangerous foreign complications, King Louis Philippe called upon Guizot to form a Ministry, the two men had decided that they were reciprocally necessary to one another, and also necessary to the maintenance of the institution which was the foundation-stone both of the parliamentary bourgeoisie and of the Orleans dynasty. "Louis Philippe," said Guizot, "had once more done his country a service, as the Crown had done it several times before." "Guizot," said Louis Philippe, "is my hope."

At the sight of this reconciliation, the public and the Press were reminded of the accession of Casimir Perier to power, and of the occasion when the great bourgeois Conservatives had combined with the King in a firm stand against the spirit of conquest and against insurrection. Since that time they had fallen asunder, and even fought. Now they were coming together again, with Guizot and Soult at their head. Duchâtel at the Interior, Humann as Finance Minister, Villemain as Minister of Education, Martin du Nord at the Ministry of Justice, Admiral Duperré as Minister of Marine—these men had looked into what Molé used to call "the abyss," and Guizot described as the "contact of the revolutionary spirit with Gallic enthusiasm."

In order to understand one another and to avoid future quarrels, each side had to sacrifice something. Guizot and his friends, repairing the mischief they had made gave up their nationalistic policy, their hopes for revenge and their patriotic pride, to support the reasonable and pacific projects of the King. Louis Philippe, in return, acquiesced in what four years before he had called the unpopularity of Guizot, gave up the little courtesies which, while in the company of Molé, he allowed himself to pay to liberal ideas, and resigned himself to the support of the conservative policy of the Doctrinaires. Each being very proud of his own contribution of skill and experience to the political partnership, the King and his First Minister felt no doubt of their capability to deal, when united, with the difficulties that brought them together. "I know," said Louis Philippe to M. de Montalivet, "that I have improved greatly in the last ten years." The Minister on the other hand was heard to say with a confident air, "My taste is for enterprise, however difficult, so long as it is reasonable." For the next eight years these two were to abide closely by the programme that they now drew up in concert, which provided for the defence of the dynasty and the maintenance of the power of the bourgeoisie with peace at home and abroad.

With rare frankness and without the slightest embarrassment, Guizot, as Minister for Foreign Affairs, announced to Parliament in the month of November his views on foreign policy, now identical with those of Louis Philippe which he used to criticise. "Revolution and war, as methods of action, are obsolete for France. She would do herself a great wrong, if she persisted in making use of them. Her methods of influence to-day are, peace, the spectacle of a sound government reposing on a broad liberty. Let us not talk to our fellow-citizens of lands to conquer, or of great wars of revenge. Rather let France prosper, and live free, intelligent, full of spirit, and tranquil."

Guizot proceeded at once to apply this pacific programme to the European crisis, which the Eastern business had provoked. Owing to the numerous friends Guizot had left in London who disliked Palmerston's concert with Russia, and also to his intimacy with Clarendon, Lord John Russell, and Melbourne, combined with the influence of the King of the Belgians over Queen Victoria, he was able to make a great point of the renewal of the understanding with England for which the note of October 8 had already prepared the way. "I am only taking the Premiership," he said to Prince Albert when leaving London, "in order to patch up matters between the two countries." Perhaps he expected at first that the English Minister would facilitate his task by some further concession. Like Louis Philippe, who was corresponding secretly with Leopold and even with Metternich, he was in hopes even on November 6, 1840, that an indulgent Europe would allow Mehemet Ali to hold, besides Egypt, the pachalik of Acre and even Crete for his life. "It is not the extent of the sacrifice, but the fact of it that matters"—this was the way he put it in London, in Vienna, and elsewhere, when trying to extract from the Courts of Europe some balm for the wounded pride of France. If he could have come before the then-opening Parliament with such a pledge of peace from Europe, he would have found it more easy to silence opposition.

Palmerston, who cared as little for the politeness of Guizot as for the anger of Thiers, refused to allow it. "If we yielded," he said, "the French nation would think that we were yielding to her threats, and not to the prayers of Louis Philippe...the only way to keep straight with such people is to make them understand that you are ready to repel force by force." He might possibly have met with some opposition among his colleagues and from the Queen, had not the military situation furnished him with an opportune and decisive argument. The army of Ibrahim, surrounded on all sides, and in the midst of a hostile population, had to evacuate Syria; and St Jean d'Acre, following the fate of Beyrout, was lost to the Viceroy on November 3. Napier's ships were now threatening the Pacha actually within the harbour of Alexandria; and this was not the moment for discussing the advisability of leaving him the smallest foothold in Syria. The chance of finally crushing him was too good to let slip; and both England and Palmerston desired that the Sultan should give the credit of the catastrophe to England. "Palmerston dreams of completely ruining Mehemet Ali"—this was the news forwarded by the King of the Belgians to Soult on November 7. "We must act quickly, so that the whole business should stop at Syria"—such was the advice given on the other side by Metternich to Guizot.

Confronted by the enmity of the general public, of the friends of Thiers, and of Liberals irritated by the news from the East and the demands of Europe, Guizot found himself in a difficult situation, when the discussion on the foreign policy of France opened in the Chamber of Deputies. On November 25 the Ministry had to meet a fierce combined attack by Thiers and Berryer, who severely blamed Louis Philippe and his Ministers for having humiliated by their cowardice and lack of confidence in the people a great nation that was still capable of wiping out the disgrace of 1815. By dint of eloquence and coolness, like that of Molé in former days under his own attacks, Guizot succeeded in repelling the assault. "The battle is won," he said, "but it is only the beginning of a long and severe campaign." He could not indeed feel secure of having reached harbour, but at any rate he had weathered the most dangerous point.

In the midst of Guizot's manœuvres in Paris, an invaluable supporter turned up for him in London. On November 15, 1840, Queen Victoria wrote Palmerston a decisive though courteously worded letter, which brought her impetuous Minister to reason. "My one ardent desire is for peace; I attach a high, nay, extreme importance to our coming to some conciliatory arrangement with our neighbours." The advice was practically a command, to which Palmerston could only bow. When Commodore Napier appeared before Alexandria, it was not to destroy the power of Mehemet Ali, but to offer him an honourable peace, which the Viceroy, yielding to the representations of Walewski, the French agent in Cairo, had the good sense to accept, with the certainty of finally securing Egypt for himself and his son. The crisis created by the Treaty of London and the threatened war between Europe and the King were at last settled. The protégé of France came out a smaller and a weaker man; but he was not annihilated. And everything warranted the hope that, in Egypt at least, his dynasty was safe.

The time had now arrived for the re-entry of France into the European Concert, from which she had been excluded six months before, that she might secure this concession for her client, this sole surviving result of the victories of Ibrahim which Palmerston and Europe had been able to neutralise. "I still keep in view the restoration of the European Concert," wrote Guizot to M. de St Aulaire on December 10. In resolute language he gave England to understand that the offer of hereditary succession in Egypt to the Viceroy must be made "as a concession to France," so that she might once more take her place with honour and dignity at the council-board of Europe. At the same time, "for the safety of the country and the satisfaction of men's minds," he kept up her armaments for such time as she remained isolated, and passed the law as to the fortification of Paris which had been initiated by the preceding Ministry. Even this cost him some trouble; although his majority had supported him for two months, he was still uncertain of it under the constant attacks of Thiers and Molé.

Once more Guizot was all but wrecked at the harbour-mouth; for Lord Ponsonby, perhaps on the secret advice of Palmerston, was urging the Sultan at Constantinople to refuse the Viceroy of Egypt the right of succession which the Convention of Alexandria had promised him, and to decline to ratify that Convention. But on the opening of the English Parliament on January 26, 1841, the Tories under Wellington and Peel criticised the demands of Palmerston and the intrigues of Ponsonby with such vigour that Palmerston had to yield. He admitted that a power wielding such a naval and military force as France could not be excluded from the Councils of Europe, and that "no arrangement could be treated as definitively settled in which she had not taken part in one way or another." On February 1, 1841, Palmerston announced to the Queen that the Turkish business was settled. On the previous evening, the Sultan had been formally requested by a collective European note to grant to Mehemet Ali the right of succession in Egypt; on the following day the Conference of London confirmed the language of Lord Palmerston, and approached France with a view to her return into the European family.

As a tribute to French feelings of dignity, morbidly excited by the Opposition, Guizot with some craft pretended to be in no hurry to respond to these advances, thereby at the same time putting himself in a position to make his own conditions. If he had had his own way, he would have invited Europe, in answer to her appeal, to go back to the terms of the note of July 27, 1839, inspired, not to say dictated, by France, whereby the Turkish policy of the Tsar had been checkmated, the Turkish Empire rescued from the hands of its Russian protectors, and its integrity loudly proclaimed as an article of the international law of Europe. The policy of the King and his Minister aimed at being national, without being bellicose; and its present object was, without hectoring or provocation, to blot out the Treaty of London and its humiliating exclusion of

France, and take up again the note of July 27. The only danger was that Russia, who was specially aimed at, might still have influence enough in London to induce the English to withdraw their suggestions, should France want to discuss them in excessive detail. The French Ambassador in London, M. de Bourqueney, pointed out the danger. "Of the four Powers, three at least believe that they are offering France a handsome and honourable door of re-entry into the European Concert. It lies on us to decide whether we consider it adequate to our dignity, at the risk of closing it definitively."

On March 5, 1841, the European Conference by a final minute annulled the Convention of July 15. On this essential point France received due satisfaction. If, owing to the resistance of Russia, she failed in obtaining her desire in the shape of a new treaty confirming the note of 1839, and proclaiming the integrity of the Ottoman Empire under the protection of Europe, she could watch at any rate the preparation of a treaty which was to close the Dardanelles and the Bosphorus to all European fleets, and especially to Russian men-of-war. Indeed she had the pleasure of inserting among its articles the statement that the Straits were thus closed "for the better security of the Ottoman Empire." Lastly she received the official invitation of the European Cabinets who had excluded her, to resume with them her rôle in the East by their side. "Our honour is absolutely intact, and the advantage of taking our place once more in the Councils of Europe vastly outweighs the slight meagreness of the treaty," wrote Guizot, with the support and approval of the King, whose policy was endorsed by this dignified and yet pacific conclusion.

Still, all was not yet over. On March 15, 1841, the signatures of the plenipotentiaries were to be affixed to the international treaty which settled the crisis created by the attack of the Turks on the Viceroy. But the Sultan, still under the pressure of Lord Ponsonby and quite prepared to take an unfair advantage of his unlooked-for success, had by a Hatti Sherif dated February 13, 1841, once more raised the question of the independence of Mehemet Ali and his right of succession. Three months of further discussion, the dismissal of a Grand Vizier, Reschid Pacha, who was compromised by his subservience to Lord Ponsonby, and an energetic intervention on the part of Austria, were needed before the Sultan could be brought to sign another Act (June 1) in better conformity with the will of Europe. France had to bring her influence to bear on Mehemet Ali, before he would accept the conditions of his suzerain. And finally Palmerston's ill-will, which manifested itself by his obstinacy in delaying the final signatures in hope of another Eastern crisis, was rendered harmless by the attacks of the Tories, who in the summer of 1841 put their antagonists in a minority and forced the Whigs to appeal to the country. On July 13, 1841, the Treaty of Peace between the Sultan and Mehemet Ali, and the Convention as to the Straits, were simultaneously signed.

It is clear that the principal gainer by this long-delayed conclusion was Palmerston; and yet he too probably wanted more. "Our four-fold guardianship in the East," said the French Ambassador in London, M. de Bourqueney, "means simply Palmerston." With the cooperation of France in 1839 and 1841 he had succeeded in destroying all the elaborate preparations of Russia at Unkiar Skelessi, and in substituting for Russia, as the dominating influence in Constantinople, Europe or, in fact, England, whose representative, Lord Ponsonby, was more powerful than the Grand Vizier. In opposition to France, or without her aid, he had broken the fortunes of Mehemet Ali, which in his opinion constituted a danger for England in the Levant, and, without any fear of risking a war, he had made the French feel the superiority of British strength.

Guizot and the Doctrinaires, who agreed with M. de

Broglie, were very indifferent to the enthusiasm of the Liberals for Mehemet Ali, "the elect one of modern revolutions"; but they felt the substantial advantage of the maintenance of the English alliance, and of the part that France had been enabled to take in the European successes over Russia at Constantinople, while avoiding a revolutionary war on the Rhine or in Italy. But in France the principal success fell to Louis Philippe. After five years of hard work his pacific policy had finally triumphed over the provocations of Palmerston, the impulsiveness of the French character, the menaces of the Tsar, and the appetites of the German races which had been for a moment displayed. One day when Apponyi, the Austrian Ambassador in Paris, had been extolling the merits of Guizot, the King replied, "The praise of Prince Metternich is very well deserved, I agree. But one must never let these gentlemen believe that they ever succeed in anything, unless the King has had a word in it."

Desiring nevertheless to give the military spirit of France some encouragement, the King determined to complete the conquest of Algeria. To the Opposition, who as usual made him personally responsible, and who were charging him with a secret compact with England for the evacuation of the new-born colony, he replied by raising the numbers of the African army to 100,000 men, and giving the command of it to General Bugeaud who was known to be determined to wrest the country from Abd-el-Kader and the Arabs. In the spring of 1841 he sent to Africa his third son, the Duc d'Aumale, who was intended for the army, as Joinville was for the navy, and was proud to show himself by the side of Bugeaud and his African officers, whose campaigns were beginning to earn renown. The Opposition grumbled over the expenses of the war, to which they would have preferred one on the continent of Europe; but the funds were duly voted.

Like the King, who had committed himself to this course,

the majority approved, after some hesitation, of the distinctly conservative internal policy which the Minister was persistently carrying out. On November 6, 1840, he had announced his intention of repressing anarchy. The law-officers were entrusted to curb the violence of the Press, and keep a hand on assemblies and discussions tending to disorder. At the beginning of 1841, Jouffroy speaking officially on behalf of the majority in support of the same policy, approved of the Ministry abiding by the laws of September 1835, and shelving all electoral reform. "We are scarcely," he said, "up to the level of the institutions which we already possess." Their programme clearly manifested the intention of the Conservative party to refuse every additional liberty to their countrymen. "The Ministry," cried Thiers, "is locating itself in the extreme Right; its majority is all in the rear." Guizot took no notice of his criticisms. He prosecuted all newspapers and books that attacked the dynasty, in Paris or in the provinces. At Le Mans he obtained a verdict against Ledru-Rollin, who, in canvassing for the seat left vacant by the death of Garnier-Pagès in June 1841, had publicly arraigned the institutions of the country and the Crown. On the outbreak of troubles at Toulouse on a question of revenues, he put them down with vigour. His manners, rather rough and haughty, and suggesting an imitation of Casimir Perier, were a source of annoyance even to the Conservatives, who dubbed him "pedagogue." His unpopularity had never been greater. But, as Metternich acutely remarked, the system of "centralisation which was the essence of French political life," enabled Guizot in spite of his unpopularity to carry out his designs and to secure their acceptance. He had, like Metternich, made up his mind to put "an absolute veto upon all innovations in public life"; and henceforth Louis Philippe, willing to work with this Ministry, so long as he secured peace abroad, did not trouble himself about the possible demands of the Left and the Liberal party, as he had done in Molé's time.

But a matter which had escaped the observation of the King and his Ministers, when founding, as they hoped, representative government and a new dynasty, was the change going on unknown to them in the feelings and aspirations of the French bourgeoisie, and of the urban and rural democracy.

From the day when the French bourgeoisie established itself in power by the aid of Louis Philippe, and by the same impulse forced the country to recognise its political and social privileges, it began to split up into segments and to obey varying influences. As new generations succeeded those which had grown up in the spirit of the eighteenth century, and had witnessed the throes of the Revolution, generations younger than Louis Philippe or Guizot (born, the one in 1763, the other in 1787), this French bourgeoisie underwent an insensible transformation under the influences, religious, social, or economic, which had developed in so many different directions since the beginning of the nineteenth century. One section of it had worked itself loose from the critical and sceptical spirit with which Voltaire had inspired its fathers in the previous century, but without indicating as yet in their conduct any real awakening of a religious faith. These men sent their children to the Catholic Colleges, which continued to exist or had been revived, alongside of the State institutions where eclectic philosophy ruled, a sort of modernist State Catholicism, constructed, evolved and enacted by Victor Cousin. It was they who made the success of the pamphlets and publications in which the Clergy tried to destroy the monopoly of the University and the philosophic religion above described. They applauded Lacordaire in 1841 on the day when he took the Dominican habit; they encouraged the Jesuits to show themselves again with heads erect, in the teeth of the law;

finally they favoured the spread of "Congregations" over the length and breadth of the land. Little by little the French bourgeoisie was giving up the conception that, religion being merely a necessity for the common people, the Clergy might be required to obey the rules of a Concordat and assimilated to other State functionaries. A hot-headed bishop at Chartres, Mgr de Montals, declared that the coming struggle on these points would last for ten years. On this part of the opposition field, the section of French citizens which had fought Charles X and the priestly party in 1830 was now preparing to support the religious demands of the young Catholic party which had been reconstructed on the ruins of the Legitimist party at the call of Montalembert, Lacordaire, and Ozanam, for the spread of the Faith, by the example of their charity. The *Univers Religieux* was the organ and standard-bearer of this branch of the bourgeoisie; Veuillot, whose name was eventually so closely connected with it, was then still in the Government service.

Among the middle-class French who took no interest in religious questions or who still dreaded Ultramontanism and the Jesuits, another evolution was taking place which also had its dangers. Careless about political questions, even about those disputes on foreign policy in which they had taken a passionate interest during the last twenty years, the men in question had got so far as not to attach the slightest importance to them. Business, money, manufacture, commerce and the Stock Exchange absorbed them almost exclusively. In this lust to enrich themselves by every means that the progress of modern invention, steam, and railroad placed at their service, they were ever on the hunt for wealth and for the luxury and pleasure it can procure. If a bourgeois of this sort continued to adhere to an order of things which would guarantee the future well-being of their schemes, he was not prepared to sacrifice anything in its defence; this was a business to be left to Government, its prefects, and its functionaries. And gradually the habit of business on a large scale, the sense of affluence, the need for progress and the taste for it, disposed them to look with favour, even in politics, upon novelties which they would not have demanded, but which they were ready to accept. The strength of these new tendencies might be measured by the success of the journal *La Presse,* which was founded about that time by Emile de Girardin, a man of business, a journalist, and a deputy, for the discussion of public rights. The editor, who declared himself a Conservative, but indifferent to the form of government and favourable to any experiments, so long as they were really novel, and productive of comfort and pleasure, interpreted accurately the ideal of this new bourgeoisie, which, in the words of Lamartine, "demanded above all things not to be bored." The zeal of Thiers, the furious attacks of his friends Jaubert and Duvergier de Hauranne, the eloquence of Lamartine, pleased them; the puritanism and austere self-sufficiency of Guizot disgusted them.

Insensibly the effect of these attractions and repulsions had brought together this conservative and dynastic bourgeoisie and the Republicans whose younger generations had on their side also diverged from the Revolution, forsworn violence, and found new recruits in the bourgeoisie. The first reference in Parliament to an extension of the right of voting to a larger class of electors, which was the nearest approach that the Republican party could make to their ideal of universal suffrage, was the act of a bourgeois, a Progressive Conservative, by name Rémilly, deputy for Versailles, who mentioned electoral reform but only indirectly. All the men of the dynastic Left, from Odilon Barrot to Laffitte, during 1840 recommended political reform. Their journals, the *Courrier Français, Siècle,* and *National* made this theme their own, to the delight of the

Republicans Arago and Garnier-Pagès, whose banquet-speeches were full of demands of the suffrage for the people at large. Guizot had scarcely come to power before a closer intimacy was set on foot between the partisans of the democracy, and these dissentient bourgeois who sought for popularity and novelty, among whom might now be reckoned, by the side of Thiers, Moderates like Dufaure and Passy, and above all Lamartine. It seemed as if the last-named statesman had heard the appeal addressed to them by Louis Blanc in winding up his *History of Ten Years*, when he exhorted them "to bind themselves to the people by some indissoluble bond, to re-temper and strengthen themselves in the people." The question to be resolved was a serious one for a Ministry which ran the risk of losing its supporters by a mistake. It was a sagacious observer, M. de Carné, who said, in 1835, that, "after all, the Republic might perhaps owe its existence to the bourgeoisie."

The most serious matter was that for the last ten years the democracy, especially the urban democracy, had been growing daily stronger and more conscious of its strength. The development of manufactures and commerce caused the working class to collect in the towns where business and luxury reigned. Between 1831 and 1846, the population of Paris increased by 300,000; and at Lyons, Marseilles, Lille, and Roubaix the rate of growth was the same. It was certainly not for their pleasure that the inhabitants of the French country-sides flocked into districts destitute of light and air to earn a wretched wage in cramped workshops by long days' work, from which neither women nor the tenderest children were spared. But their number and their miserable condition aroused in themselves, and in the public, a sense of their needs, and of their value in the world. The singularly painful picture which Dr Villermé drew in 1840, at the request of the Academy of Moral Sciences, of the physical and moral condition of the workers in certain manufactures marked the starting-point for the first working-class legislation ever passed in a French Parliament.

To the cause of these masses of workers, whose lives it was alike their duty and their wish to ameliorate, many a writer devoted his labours and his talent—Pierre Leroux, with his noble work *Humanité*, by which he won Georges Sand as a disciple; Buchez, with his review *L'Atelier*, started in 1840, in which he exhorted working-men to start workshops for themselves; Cabet, whose *Voyage en Icarie* of the same date opened to the working class new vistas of hope and well-being; Louis Blanc, who at the age of thirty (1841) demanded the "organisation of labour," the corner-stone of State-Socialism, which was spreading rapidly and gaining numerous disciples; lastly Proudhon, who by his *Mémoire sur la Propriété* (Treatise on Property) tried to work up the proletariat to the defence of its class-interests. All this literary matter appeared simultaneously, while, owing to the spread of primary instruction and the frequentation of political and social clubs, the working-man was enabled to read and educate himself, especially in Paris, and would soon be ready to make himself heard on his own behalf and that of democracy.

On the other hand, the masses of the rural population remained much as they had been since the beginning of the century, closely attached to the land and to their patient and humble toil, frugal and orderly, and uninterested in the Government, which on its side did not dream of asking their opinion. Yet the memories of the past worked in them, very much as the yearning for better things to come acted on the artisan. It was mainly in this class that the Napoleonic legend was preserved, the legend of the heroic days when France took her crop off Europe on a regular system, when the small French peasant was destined to become a marshal of France, rich, and renowned, or to die before the enemy. The French people had forgotten the Cossacks and the invasion, and only remembered the stages of that pleasant and profitable European tour on which they were conducted by Napoleon. Their imagination was fed entirely upon these epic dramas, the plots of which they read in their books, or were taught through the medium of the Government. When Louis Philippe and his Ministers deposited the ashes of Napoleon with great pomp in the Invalides in 1841, Lamartine was heard to remark, "For my part I am not a disciple of the Napoleonic cult, nor do I hold with that worship of force which has been for some time past taking the place of the true religion of liberty in the mind of the nation."

For a Government that wished to be permanent, it was undoubtedly no easy task to find, among the various currents of opinion and of feeling which drove French society in various directions, the one to which it could best trust itself to escape shipwreck, to avoid collision with the middle classes on the one hand and the common folk, urban and rural, on the other. The situation being such, Guizot, while supported and approved by the King, could devise nothing better than to remain in port, out of the way of the inconstant and capricious waves of public opinion raised by aspirations which he was determined to ignore. He called upon the bourgeoisie not to let themselves be carried away by surface movements made to order by the action of newspapers and committees, but to follow his lead and stay safe in harbour, according to the prudent advice of Lucretius: "Suave mari magno, turbantibus aequora ventis, etc."

This harbour, in the shelter of which he hoped to preserve safely the institutions created by the Orleans Monarchy, consisted of the "country" as constituted by law, with electors paying 200 francs in taxes, and deputies chosen from those who payed 500 francs on their revenue. What they most wanted, in order to avoid the squalls that might still reach them from the ocean, was the solid break-water of a good stout majority. In Parliament Guizot was a success during the whole year 1841, with his haughty air of authority and the lustre of his talent. In the electorate Comte Duchâtel worked by his side incessantly, with all his characteristic qualities and method. He was a big man, of a sceptical turn of mind, and apparently indolent, who thoroughly understood how to manipulate men through their vanity or ambition, an excellent administrator, who kept his staff in good order. And, thanks to the centralised system, by a careful distribution of government favours, and by taking advantage of the right of functionaries to sit in Parliament, he had no difficulty in manipulating the 200,000 electors, and the still smaller number of qualified candidates, to which France was now reduced, so as to get the right to speak and govern in their name.

"The bourgeoisie has got the crown of the causeway," said Cuvillier Fleury, "and means to keep it." Nor was this all, for, as he further remarked, there was the National Guard, "a devoted and well-tested body." The bourgeois electors, whose votes were being thus organised, also supplied the officers, commissioned and non-commissioned, of this Civic Guard, whose duty it was to repress crime and to protect the national institutions. "I make you a present," said the hosier Paturot to his nephew, "of my retail business; the day after receiving it you will become an elector, as you pay 310 francs for your licence. Now give a fair field to your ambition; you can elect Members of Parliament; you can be a candidate at municipal and departmental elections; you are a National Guard, and on the Jury list. Next you may launch out a little, and become a leader; you may work your district, and get yourself appointed Captain of your Company. More than one 'White-cotton Night-cap' has become a Minister." No doubt the privates of the Guard, being recruited from the class of citizens paying direct taxes, however small, were but humble folk, not far removed from the proletariat class; still they were above the rank of artisans, who could not afford to pay for the required uniform. But all the officers were devoted to the King, who flattered them, invited them to the Court, gave them decorations, and appointed them commandants of battalions. In Paris and in the provinces they formed the armed protectors of established order as understood by the bourgeois, prepared to enforce respect for law in conjunction with the functionaries who knew the value of their support. On this force rested the hope that Louis Philippe had formed of handing on to his sons the authority with which the bourgeoisie had invested him in 1830.

But in 1842 the work done by the King in concert with his Conservative Ministry was still in a very unstable condition. Guizot was by no means sure of his majority; it had evidently given him only doubtful support on February 22, 1842, when the whole of the Opposition, both Right and Left—Berryer, Thiers, Odilon Barrot, Billault, and some of Guizot's own friends—voted against the Treaty on the Right of Search. This treaty, which had been lately concluded with England, raised no question of political interest, being inspired only by concern for a "noble and holy cause"—the pursuit of slavers, who were still carrying on their trade after its formal abolition by the Congress of Vienna. It was hoped that by a general agreement among civilised Powers it might be put down. But it was understood in Europe, and particularly in France, that this "cause"—since the Treaty of Paris (1814) had, by the will of England and the right of victory, forced France to recognise the abolition of the Slave Trade—might furnish England with a pretext for exercising a superior right of police at sea.

In the treaties which Talleyrand had negotiated in London in 1830 and 1831, Louis Philippe had tried to reconcile the principles of humanity with the dignity and interests of the French navy. The Right of Search on merchant ships had been limited to certain zones; and the relative numbers of English and French men-of-war who were to exercise it had been settled. But in 1833 Palmerston, always on the look-out for more, tried to extend the limits of these zones, and to ignore the conditions prescribed as to the number of vessels to be employed. The French Government had declined to agree; but Guizot, being desirous of giving the new Tory Ministry a pledge of goodwill as a step towards a good understanding with England, thought he might find his opportunity in non-political humanitarian conventions of this sort. When the French Parliament was informed of the signature of the treaty, the indignation was universal, not so much on the score of the treaty, as to emphasise the general objection to any concession to England. "Palmerston," said one who was a friend both of Guizot and of England, "has made the word English hateful and 'an object of suspicion in France.'" The Ministry were unable to obtain the ratification of the treaty from the Chamber. If the Whigs had been still in power and had taken up the challenge, war might very easily have resulted, although the incident had no political bearing. In June 1842 English visitors to France still talked freely and with composure of a coming war. Aberdeen tried to calm public opinion in London, but there were men like Peel even among his colleagues, who did not conceal their annoyance at the "hostile peace" which the French Parliament seemed to be demanding from Louis Philippe and his Ministers.

The elections were now drawing nigh. Louis Philippe had determined to provide his fellow-workers with the necessary majority; and for that purpose he dissolved the Chamber on June 13, 1842, fixing the new elections for July 9. This appeal to the (so-called) "country" seemed to him to be all the more likely to be effective because, in order to gain the support of manufacturers and commercial men, the Minister of Public Works, aided by Comte Duchâtel, had succeeded in passing the great and long-expected law establishing a net-work of national railways. Ministers confidently looked for the gratitude of financiers and business men, to whom the proposals opened out great possibilities of profit.

The first election results published were those of Paris. There, out of twelve deputies elected, ten were of the Opposition, two of these being republican lawyers, Marie and Bethmont. The bourgeoisie of Paris had deserted Guizot because of their Liberalism, and voted for Ganneron, Carnot, de Lasteyrie, etc., emphasising thereby their wish for progress, and giving a striking importance to the vote of the democratic capital which, to use the phrase of the *National*, "could condemn and execute Ministries." When we remember that Paris then returned only 14 deputies out of 450, it is hard to understand the consternation produced by these elections at the Court and among the Ministers. "Villemain looked abject," said Cuvillier Fleury, the Princes' tutor, "and Duchâtel was dismayed." The fact is that, when the nation at large is indifferent or silent, the capital is the only place where the Government has no power, the only place therefore which can force it to listen to its call to progress, the only home of an independent Press, the great centre and nucleus of attraction, in the midst of a centralised civilisation, for wealth and talent of all kinds. "What is going on in Paris will go on throughout all France," said Duchâtel on July 10, 1842.

He was wrong, however. The Ministerialists returned from the provinces more numerous than was expected, sufficient at any rate to make a parliamentary majority equal to, perhaps a trifle larger than, its predecessors. So the disappointment was not so important, although it was still serious for Guizot and his fellows, who had counted upon a more decisive answer from the "country." "Not to win," said they, "means to lose everything." They had taken formal note of the desertion of the bourgeoisie, especially in Paris. They attributed it to the pessimism of Paris and to the stupidity of the electorate, but never for a moment to the defects of their own policy. And under the influence of Duchâtel in particular, rather than bow to the demands of the Opposition, they did their best to detach from it, by every means in their power, a sufficient number of deputies to enable them to beat it. A functionary working under Duchâtel's orders is said to have remarked a day or two later, "We won you some twenty votes, but they cost us dear." In Louis Reybaud's sketch of the parliamentary methods of that day and their bargainings and corruptions, we hear a Minister saying to one of his supporters, Jerome Paturot, "No doubt you are our friend, but So-and-so is just on the dividing line of parties; his vote may go one way or the other. We have to set ourselves exclusively to satisfying these delicate shades of opinion; they are the odd coppers on which the Cabinet balance is built up."

At the time when the Guizot Ministry began to carry on these illegitimate practices to neutralise the Opposition, its principal asset was the authority which the dynasty had once more acquired among the people. Perhaps they were at last recognising the merits of Louis Philippe and his services to his country in maintaining peace abroad and at home; it is clear at any rate that the inclinations of the electorate, though very slightly ministerial, were very strongly monarchic. "The fiercest members of the Opposition never dared insinuate a word against the King, as they had done in 1839." The sudden death of the Duc d'Orléans by a carriage accident which occurred at Neuilly on July 14, 1842, just after the elections, while it struck a heavy blow at the affections and the dearest hopes of the royal house, at the same time showed the extent of the national sympathy for the King and his family and even helped to increase it. The Prince was beloved for his uprightness and his generosity, and was the idol of the army. "The nation and the dynasty drank of the same cup of profoundest sorrow." When the Chambers were called upon to settle the order of succession disturbed by this sudden death, they were ready to agree to any proposal made by the King, or by the Duc d'Orléans (who did in fact mention it in his will), as to the Regency of the Duc de Nemours during the minority of the Comte de Paris; and the country was ready to ratify their decision. Thiers, always on the look-out for popularity, conceived that the most popular line at the moment would be to move the Chamber to give a unanimous vote in favour of the wishes of Louis Philippe and his son. The Opposition, fearing the conservatism of the Duc de Nemours, tried to get the Regency conferred on the Duchesse d'Orléans, a lady from whom rather more docility might be expected; but Thiers backed up the Ministry energetically in support of the King's wishes, which received the assent of the Chamber in August by a majority of over 200.

If we compare this vote with those which during the whole previous year had threatened the existence of the Guizot Ministry, we shall be able to gauge the difference between the attitude of the Opposition towards the King, and that which they adopted towards the Conservatives with whom he had joined hands. If Louis Philippe had then and there abandoned the Doctrinaires and their leader, as he was asked to do, his popularity would have been greater than at any time in the last ten years. But he did not even dream of it. He thanked Thiers for his support in words which must have caused him a cruel disappointment: "Now, you must support my Cabinet!"

If the King remained true to this alliance, which was bound in the long run to exhaust his credit, it was due to his clear appreciation of the advantage which accrued to the country from Guizot's maintenance of peace abroad, largely by the help of the Tory Ministry in England. He saw that France was quiet, assured of the future, immersed in its own affairs, and in the economic activities from which it drew its riches. The returns of indirect taxation, and the figures of the Customs and Navigation, bore witness to a material advance, equally beneficial to the individual as to the whole body politic; and their testimony is corroborated by every writer of that prosperous age. The Algerian affair, after long discussion, was at last taking shape through the military energy of General Bugeaud. An old soldier of the Empire, with the muscles and temperament of a fighter, Bugeaud had landed in Algeria with a burning desire to take terrible vengeance on Abd-el-Kader, and a plan of campaign well adapted to a country where the enemy seemed always to slip out of reach. With mobile columns, and strategic bases of supply and of defence organised along the shore, first extending through the whole of the Tell, then carried to the borders of the desert, he pushed forward, compelling the tribes to submit by harrying the tribal property, and gradually isolating them from the influence of the Emir within the confines of the three provinces. Followed by Changarnier, Lamoricière, and younger men who devoted their whole lives to the business, Daumas, de Martinprey, Pélissier, Bosquet, Charras, Trochu, de Montagnac, and Ducrot, he had by the end of 1842 conquered the province of Algiers as far as Blidah, and forced the pass of the Chelif in order to effect a junction with the province of Oran, now the assumed prey of France in spite of a fresh raid by Abd-el-Kader. "If we succeed, as I firmly hope," wrote Bugeaud to Lamoricière at the beginning of 1843, "in establishing the authority of France in this fine country between the sea and the desert, we shall have done a great thing."

How was it that the Sovereign, who was equally aware of the greatness of this enterprise, did not do everything, concede everything, to secure the peace of Europe which was the *sine quâ non* of its success? "We must do some Cardinal Fleury work!", he was fond of saying, carrying back his mind to that remarkable understanding with the England of Walpole, to the truce called in the midst of the great wars of the seventeenth and eighteenth centuries which had enabled France to develop her power in America and Asia. In order to restore to her in Africa and in the world at large the place that she had lost since those days, the help of Guizot seemed indispensable. Again, it was just at this time that, by treaties made with native kings, France was establishing herself in Guinea, at Grand Bassam and Assinie, on the Gaboon where the town of Libreville was shortly afterwards built, and where she held Nossi-Bé; in Mayotta and the protectorates of the Sakalavas and Antankaras in Madagascar. On September 7, 1843, Admiral Dupetit-Thouars entered into an agreement with Queen Pomaré for placing Tahiti similarly under the protection of France. By its activity in distant lands the French navy was completing the work begun by the army of Africa in Algeria. It was an overflow of national life in every direction, the affirmation of the future of the race. Not for a century had a similar effort been witnessed; and it took place at the moment when Europe in general was preparing to extend herself over the globe. In the opinion of the King of the French, the Crown was justified in allowing the Guizot Ministry to make sure of the future by calling this halt between two orders of things, this pacific and fruitful truce.

Relying on the King's support, Guizot continued to realise his programme. In foreign affairs he carried out his pacific design of an understanding with the English, while not forgetting Austria, who was prodigal of praise and politeness. In this he was encouraged by the eloquent language used in the English Parliament by the illustrious Liberal, Lord Brougham: "I do not hesitate to declare," he said, "that the peace of Europe may be summarised in three words—'peace with France.' I offer the olive-branch of peace to the two countries." In the House of Commons Peel used the same language, imploring the two nations to lay aside their national jealousies. Louis Philippe and his Minister were ready to establish a cordial and sincere understanding, which would be—wrote the King—"alike to the interest of both nations, and a real security for the peace of Europe." At every point at which the policies of the two countries came into contact, wherever a possibility arose of a conflict with English influence, they were eager to make concessions.

They did not give up all hope of getting the French to accept the convention as to the Right of Search, the abandonment of which had earned the reproaches of the Tories. When England put its veto on the scheme for a Customs-Union offered to the manufactures and commerce of France by Belgium at the end of 1842, Louis Philippe gave it up without a complaint, or a reproach. When Christine, Queen-Regent of Spain, had resumed at Madrid the place that Espartero had taken from her before his own fall in July 1843, and the possibility was discussed of the marriage of the Duc d'Aumale to her daughter, who was to be declared to have attained her majority, Louis Philippe firmly declined the Spanish proposal, so as not to irritate England or Queen Victoria, who were already accusing him of bringing about the fall of Espartero. Queen Victoria appeared to be grateful; she lavished expressions of friendship upon the Orleans family, and even took the initiative, on the advice of the King of the Belgians, in inviting herself and her husband to Eu, where she received an enthusiastic reception from Louis Philippe and the French nation on September 2, 1843.

But the hostility of the Whigs in England to the policy of the *Entente Cordiale* was as strong as ever, and received some encouragement among the officials and the lower classes. In Greece the English envoy, Lyons, was plotting to upset the Colettis Ministry, as too favourable to the French, using for the purpose a constitution that had been forced upon King Otho on September 15, 1843. The French envoy, Piscatory, although he had been instructed to "retire from any contest rather than sacrifice the Entente," did not conceal his anger, and watched for a chance of revenge. The Druses of Syria, being Mussulmans, had been stirred up by the Turks to attack the Christian population of the Lebanon, the Maronites, who were protégés of France; and they were secretly supported by the English officials, Wood and Col. Rose, who were trying there, as in Egypt, to restore the authority of the Sultan to the detriment of French influence. Finally, on the occasion of the Queen's acceptance of the hospitality of Louis Philippe at Dieppe, Lord Melbourne, who still acted as her tutor behind the backs of the Tories, wrote to her on September 6, 1843, that "he would be shocked, if her visit to Eu resulted in the signature of a treaty favourable to France on any European question whatever."

Now the Queen had not come to Eu to sign any treaty; having ascertained that the King would not try to put a son of his on the throne of Spain, she hoped to get him to go farther and consent to a plan conceived two years before by Prince Albert for securing that crown for his cousin Leopold, the brother of the King of Portugal. The English Ambassadors in Spain, Sir G. Villiers, and after him Sir Henry Bulwer, then received instructions to prepare the ground for a proposal of marriage between Leopold and the young Queen, which had been the dream of the Queen and the Prince—a dream, however, which was but a poor return for the disinterested conduct of Louis Philippe.

"Why should the Tory Cabinet and the Queen," so Guizot asked with justice, "insist on following the old rut of rivalry with France in Spain, when Louis Philippe and his Ministers had left it for good?" Lord Aberdeen appreciated this at once, and so completely, that in his conversations with Guizot at Eu, he gave up the candidature of the Prince of Coburg. But neither Prince Albert nor the Queen had given it up, and it remained, a germ of future misunderstandings which weighed heavily on the amicable relations of the sovereigns.

"The passions of the people are sometimes very troublesome for administrations," Leopold wrote to Queen Victoria shortly after her visit to Eu. But, however little interest the French nation at large might appear to take in the Ministerial policy towards England, the Opposition was always ready to make use of it to alarm or to irritate. It was the weapon that it kept always to hand in the Parisian Press and in Parliament. When in 1843 Guizot announced "agreement without intimacy," and in 1844 "friendship and a cordial understanding" with England, he was invoking, as Metternich neatly remarked, "reasons of sentiment, which lend themselves most easily to excited and malevolent criticism, and to the evolution of opposite sentiments."

Thiers, who had kept out of sight since the death of the Duc d'Orléans, and had retired into a sort of learned solitude to continue his *History of the Consulate*, came out of it in the beginning of 1844 to begin fresh attacks on this favourable ground. At first Parliament would not listen to him. But when, a month later, the news came that out of regard to English susceptibility the Ministers had repudiated Admiral Dupetit-Thouars' action in deposing Queen Pomaré at Tahiti for resisting the French protectorate and insulting the tricolour under the influence of the English Consul, Pritchard, there was an explosion of wrath throughout France. The Admiral was pitied as a victim, and commended in the Press of both Right and Left. There was even some talk of going to war for this trifle. But it was much worse some months later; before England had had time to recall Pritchard, he was arrested by one d'Aubigny, a lieutenant in Admiral Dupetit-Thouars' squadron, and his property confiscated. The English Cabinet demanded satisfaction. "We are not going to tear each others' hair," wrote Guizot to Lord Aberdeen, "for the sake of Pritchard, Pomaré, and d'Aubigny." He agreed to pay an indemnity, on the understanding that Pritchard did not return to the Society Islands (September 2, 1844). "The stamp of shame is on you," was the Opposition cry against the Ministry; and the majority were opprobriously dubbed Pritchardists.

It was evident, then, that the one thing wanting to this *Entente Cordiale* between English and French was cordiality. Affairs in Algeria, as well as those in Oceania, gave rise to hatred and jealousy between the two nations. A brilliant feat of arms on the part of the Duc d'Aumale in 1843 seemed to have completed the work of General Bugeaud; by a sudden movement he seized the Smala of Abd-el-Kader, and forced the Emir to fly to Morocco. But the flight had been arranged with Muley Abd-er-Rahman, the Sultan of Morocco, and was the prelude to a counter-attack by the Moslems on the acquisitions of France. The repeated attacks of the Moorish cavalry without any declaration of war upon the French post of La Moulaiah decided Marshal Bugeaud in June 1844 to declare war against Morocco. The French fleet was at once sent to Tangier and Mogador, under the orders of the Prince de Joinville, and shelled both towns. At the same time the Marshal inflicted on the army of Morocco a decisive defeat at L'Isly (August 14, 1844). These demonstrations of the might of France were met by loud protests in London. If England had acquiesced, not without regret, in the establishment of the French in Algeria, this did not mean permission to conquer Morocco, or to occupy Tangier in the very face of Gibraltar. Such a conquest would have been premature and very risky, and neither Louis Philippe nor Guizot nor the victor of L'Isly ever dreamed of it. They had not the smallest wish to plunge France into the "wasps' nest"; and would be satisfied if the Sherif of Fez, having received his lesson, withdrew his assistance from Abd-el-Kader. As soon as he showed himself disposed to that course, negotiations began; they resulted in the Treaty of Tangier, September 18, 1844, concluded by General Delarue.

The Treaty of Tangier, supplemented by the Convention of March 18, 1845, for the settlement of the frontiers of France—very badly drawn withal—and the Sherifian Empire in a little-known country, guaranteed the integrity of Morocco, and restored to her the cities of Mogador and Ouldja without asking any war indemnity; the only condition was that Muley Abd-er-Rahman should disband his army, declare Abd-el-Kader an outlaw, and expel him from his dominions. For two more years Abd-el-Kader remained obstinately within his "disra," engaged in disturbing the frontier. But, when at length the Sherif of Morocco, after much hesitation, had made up his mind to carry out the last-mentioned article against him, the Treaty of Tangier became, and for fifty years remained, the basis of the relations between France and Morocco, and was respected by both. "Good sense advises us, nay, demands of us," wrote Guizot shortly afterwards to Marshal Bugeaud, "to maintain between ourselves and the Emperor of Morocco the existing situation of general peace and good understanding, with a half-alliance against Abd-el-Kader." In view of English mistrust, which might easily have been converted by a war with Morocco into a dangerous attack on the rights of France in Algiers, the cautious and prudent diplomacy of Louis Philippe was undoubtedly the surest means of giving permanency to the French occupation of Algeria.

But the Opposition, already annoyed at the Pritchard indemnity, now found in this new concession to England fresh reason for condemning the whole policy of Guizot, which Duvergier de Hauranne described as "a policy of 'thorough' even in its weakness." At the end of 1844 the majority in the Chamber, worked upon by the leaders of the parliamentary bourgeoisie, as well as by the Republicans, by Molé, Montalivet, and Thiers, as much as by Lamartine and Ledru-Rollin, seemed disposed to condemn Guizot and his so-called work of "peace," meaning, as Lamartine remarked, the English variety of it. It was in vain that the King gave a vigorous support to his Ministers, and marked his agreement with them by going to London to return the visit which Queen Victoria had paid him in the previous year. His authority seemed no longer sufficient to dispel the storm that was brewing among the deputies, who, however much attached to his dynasty, were daily more opposed to the continuance of the Guizot Ministry. On the discussion of the Address in reply to the royal speech, the Government majority was but small (January 27, 1845).

In his internal policy, too, Guizot met with quite as many obstacles. The Conservative bourgeoisie, to which he looked for support, like his allies of the *Entente Cordiale*, made demands that he had difficulty in satisfying. To the Catholics who petitioned through Montalembert for liberty of instruction, to enable them to compete with the University in educating the youth of the bourgeoisie, he had offered in 1841 through Villemain a proposal for a Bill for abolishing the University monopoly. The obligation to send children of the middle class to the State Colleges, and to hold a certificate of University study in order to qualify for the degree of Bachelor, was repealed. But it was not proposed to repeal the licence duty levied on secondary schools, except in the case of 20,000 children on the rolls of the smaller religious seminaries; and above all it subjected the professors of all the Free Colleges, even those appointed by the Clergy and the bishops, to examinations as to literary capacity and enquiries into moral character. Confronted by the violent opposition of the bishops and of the Catholic Press, who raved at the notion of the State intervening in any education given by the Church, seeing moreover that the Catholics treated these concessions as unacceptable, while the Liberals, the champions of the University, objected to them as far too wide, Guizot gave way; and Villemain withdrew his Bill.

If either of them thought that the anger provoked by this experiment would calm down, he was mistaken. The Catholics, worked up by the violent campaign that Veuillot was carrying on in the *Univers*, by the pamphlets inspired by hot-tempered bishops, and by the appeals of de Carné and Montalembert, were readier than ever to take up arms and do battle against the University. Its supporters defended it as the necessary bulwark of the laity against the Ultramontanes, and retorted upon the calumnies by which it was attacked, by denouncing the laxity of moral tone among the Jesuits, and their political greed. In the Collège de France, Michelet and Quinet devoted their lectures in 1843 to a violent criticism of the Jesuits, which excited enthusiasm on one side and fury on the other. De Lacretelle did the same at the Sorbonne, Dufaure at Bordeaux, Libri and Lerminier in the *Revue des Deux Mondes*. At the beginning of 1844, the Chamber of Deputies, obedient to the ideas which the enemies of Ultramontanism were victoriously spreading in Paris and the great cities, called upon the Crown to "maintain the authority and activity of the State in the matter of public education."

The violence of the dispute and the attitude of Parliament troubled Guizot, who was now required by both parties to come to a decision. He then thought he might satisfy the Catholics by the abolition of the University monopoly, if they on their side would satisfy and reassure their opponents by allowing France to be closed against the Jesuits. "We must hold the place," he said, "but keep the gate open." This *entente cordiale* with the Catholics was the foundation-stone of his home policy. His Minister of Religion, Martin du Nord, a pious and timid person, desired it as much as he. Duchâtel, who had protected and employed Veuillot, gave the Clergy decorations for their persons, and subsidies for their churches. Villemain took in hand once more, in February 1844, his former Bill on liberty of instruction and enlarged its scope. This time he cut out all payment of duties, and gave every Frenchman full and complete liberty to open secondary boarding-schools and institutions, imposing no conditions on the staff but those of supplying evidence of morality, of a University degree, and of moral and intellectual sufficiency to the civil and academic authorities, and of submitting the schools to inspection. On objections raised by the bishops, however, ecclesiastical houses and seminaries were exempted from the necessity of showing University degrees and testimonials of moral character, the only reservation being that the number of pupils should not exceed that already laid down by the law of 1828. On the other hand, the Bill insisted very precisely that no French citizen should enjoy these rights, who could not make a statement in writing that he did not belong to any "religious congregation not legally recognised in France"; in other words, the burden of proof lay on the claimant, that he did not belong to an unrecognised society, like the Jesuits.

This second attempt, from which Guizot had anticipated

some benefit, met with no better reception than the first. The Liberal journals, the *Constitutionnel* and the *Siècle,* charged Villemain with betraying the University of which he was Grand Master; while the whole Catholic Press, the *Univers,* the *Correspondant,* the *Courrier de France,* called upon the Catholic bourgeoisie to petition in a body against the fraud and trickery of this proposal. On its discussion in the Chamber of Peers in June 1844, Thiers would have none of it, while Montalembert and Berryer put forth all their eloquence against its injustice; and Guizot was compelled to withdraw it once more. Indeed he was obliged to take a new Minister of Public Instruction better liked by the Catholics, M. de Salvandy, and to appease his exacting allies by the promise of "a more generous Bill and one more conformable to liberty of conscience."

The moment Salvandy took office, he suspended the lectures of Mikiévicz at the Collège de France, and compelled Quinet to resign his professorship. This blow was directed against the enemies of the Jesuits. By an Ordinance of December 7, 1844, the supporters of the University were deprived of their influence in the Royal Council on Public Education, by the addition of twenty extraordinary members selected by the Minister. This was intended to prepare the way for the concessions, larger than either of those offered by Villemain, which he was now considering, and which could be so drawn as to favour the teaching Congregations, including the Jesuits, with whom the Catholic clergy and laity were evidently making common cause.

Going thus from concession to concession in order to preserve his alliance with the Catholic bourgeoisie, Guizot was running the risk of a collision, on the most dangerous ground, with Villemain, Cousin, and the writers on the *Journal des Débats* and the *Constitutionnel,* the men who, supported by the University, had been carrying on a ceaseless war for thirty years with the priestly party. In May 1845,

Thiers as their spokesman gave a detailed account of the advances made by the Society of Jesus, their twenty-seven houses divided into two provinces, and the illicit toleration accorded to them, invoking against them the "immediate and strict application of the law." Dupin, an indefatigable Gallican, who had lately published a *Manual of Law* which had been placed on the Roman Index, came to the rescue; but the Chamber called on the Government by an enormous majority "to see that the laws of the country were carried out." Even behind the moderate language of this first challenge, a threat was visible; and Guizot recognised it so clearly that he opened confidential negotiations with the Papal Court through Rossi, in order to induce Gregory XVI to recall the Jesuits to more prudent courses; on July 6, 1845, he announced in the *Moniteur* that the Pope had persuaded the Society to dissolve itself in France. "Seemingly beaten, we are in reality victorious!" wrote Lacordaire, who was very well informed as to the meaning of this dissolution. Some houses were closed, but their members were allowed to join one of the others, of which by far the greater number were preserved. "God gives only the shadow to our enemies," said Lacordaire again. "I think that in religious matters success without triumph is the best that can happen." By this skilful handling Guizot acquired one more title to the gratitude of the Catholics; by his own avowal he had delayed the blows intended for the Jesuits, and so managed that the French public and the Opposition, though deceived, acquiesced, and forbore to insist on the application of the laws against them.

One thing is certain, that Thiers was not the dupe of these manœuvres for long; the year had not closed before he had arranged for an offensive alliance with Odilon Barrot to revenge himself and to make an end of the Conservative majority. This alliance was a serious matter, for it created an indirect connexion, through Odilon Barrot, between Thiers, whose fidelity to the dynasty was never in doubt, and the moderate Republicans who called themselves Parliamentary Radicals. Under cover of a demand for a change in the franchise, reducing the qualifying tax to 100 francs and doubling the number of electors, Thiers was joining a coalition which, in order to upset Guizot, would not hesitate, if necessary, to strike at the King.

The greatest service that Guizot could then have done to the cause of Monarchy, after having compromised himself in his alliances with England and with the Catholics, after seeing his majority reduced almost to zero, would have been to resign. What with the demands of England, and the paroxysms of rage of the patriots of Paris, what with the Conservatives dragging him towards Ultramontanism, and the monarchists playing into the hands of the democrats, the situation of his ministry both at home and abroad was unstable and precarious. For a moment Guizot and Duchâtel considered the idea of retiring, on the advice of their friends, the Princesse de Lieven and the Duc de Broglie (January 1846). The opportunity was a good one. Nobody could dispute the fact that it was to them that the country owed its prosperity, its Algerian conquests, its tranquillity and its wealth, and that it might well regret their loss. They gave way, however, rather too readily to the request of the King, whose political acuteness was becoming blunted by age, and to the entreaties of their most trusty followers—Delessert, Salvandy, Generals Jacqueminot, Bugeaud, and Sebastiani—and generally of the rank and file of the party. Being now resolved to go on at any price, after having done so much to remain in power, they did not hesitate to make regular and almost open use of the means of corruption, which were first to give them a majority, and next to bind that majority to the fortunes of the Ministry. This was what Guizot called "influence," and defended as legitimate. The King, by way of helping them, dissolved the Chamber, July 6, 1846. The attacks of Thiers on his personal exercise of power, renewed again in the month of March with no small stir both in Parliament and in the Press, did not alarm him, so important did he consider the preservation of this Ministry which left him free to work and govern the country.

Duchâtel did not wait for the issue of the royal order for a dissolution before preparing for the new Chamber. Since the month of May 1846 he had made it his business to ensure the success of his own candidates in every electoral district. Intimately acquainted with their individual circumstances, though they were more than 400 in number, he applied his personal stimulus to each; he was prodigal of advice; above all, he lent them the support of his functionaries, prefects, sub-prefects, judges, revenue officers, police, and the small fry of the ministerial bureaus. Through the candidates and the functionaries at their service, he proposed to obtain a permanent disposing power over the whole of the existing electorate. The method was not a novel one; it has been testified to and described by writers of the day, Stendhal, de Bernard, de Balzac, and Louis Reybaud. It has not yet disappeared in France, where parliamentary life and the working of a centralised administration are closely interwoven. The only fault of Comte Duchâtel and Guizot was that they overdid their part to such a point that its defects were too obvious. "The nation was led to believe," said Tocqueville, "that the representative system was a mere political machine for maintaining the preponderance of certain private interests, and for giving the monopoly of offices to a certain number of families."

Again, the greater number of these ministerial candidates were functionaries, state-councillors, law-officers, councillors of the Supreme Court, general officers, high university officials, heads of great administrative departments of the

State, who depended on the Government for their position, career, promotion, and recognition. One half of the Chamber, more probably a majority of it, would, if the efforts of Comte Duchâtel were successful, be formed of these elements, and, so far as could be seen, would be absolutely docile.

The private honesty of the men who had recourse to these ugly tricks to ensure their ministerial existence, who in fact practised parliamentary and electoral corruption, was above any suspicion. But they yielded to the temptation of utilising the resources of administrative centralisation which had enabled the united bourgeoisie in 1830, and the Royalists at the Restoration, to usurp the power created by the Napoleonic institutions, for the benefit of their own party in their need. They reckoned on the indifference of the country, of the mass of the peasantry who were far more interested in potatoes than in politics, and even (as matters then stood) on the indifference of the whole middle class, who were suffering from a positive fever of financial enterprise due to the introduction of railways, and who read the Stock Exchange Gazette with more interest than the parliamentary debates. Tocqueville has given a vivid picture of this middle class. "Its triumph in 1830 had been so final and complete that all political power, all electoral rights, all special privileges, in fact the whole administrative machine, had been absorbed bodily into one small class, all below being ignored in law, all above it in fact. It not only monopolised all influences on society; it even farmed it out, so to speak, for its own advantage. It found its way into all offices, the number of which it increased enormously; it soon learnt to live almost as much on public moneys as on its own industry." No sooner had this great result been accomplished than a calm fell over political passion, while the public wealth began to increase rapidly. "Politics are dead," said the writers in the *Revue des Deux*

Mondes, M. de Barante and Guizot himself. The Government of Louis Philippe took this general silence, not as a warning, but as an encouragement to deal with their countrymen as they pleased.

These pretensions of theirs however were still resisted in Paris. In the provinces Comte Duchâtel might manipulate the elections, but in the capital the Opposition was preparing a formal indictment of his misdeeds to lay before the nation. The Central Committee of the Electors of the Seine, of which Thiers was spokesman and Republicans were the most active agents, adopted as their battle-cry, war to the knife against all ministerial candidates whatever, without regard to subtle distinctions. On one side the Association for *liberty of instruction*, of which Montalembert was the soul, brought together the Catholics and Legitimists in favour of the candidate offering the largest amount of religious liberty. "It is true that in the existing electorate the capital has only fourteen electoral districts, but its influence goes far beyond its walls." All the first-class journals of France—the *National*, whose policy Armand Marrast, assisted by Carnot, was directing towards an understanding with the dynastic Left, the *Réforme*, in which Ledru-Rollin and Flocon demanded universal suffrage and labour legislation, the *Presse*, which under Emile Girardin was lapsing from Conservatism, the *Temps*, the *Siècle*, which Dutacq had worked up to great prosperity as the organ of anticlerical republicanism, the *Univers* under Veuillot, the *Correspondant* under Carné and Falloux—took their orders from Paris and passed them on to the provincial Press. Against this propaganda the Government had nothing to oppose in Paris but the *Journal des Débats*; and even that was more devoted to the King than to Guizot.

Moreover Paris was still, and more than ever before, the centre of the intellectual life of the nation. And there was a dangerous coincidence between the loss of political ideals by the bourgeoisie of Paris, and the growing importance which it gained in literature. If Guizot considered his system wholesome and efficient, all the great French writers of established or rising repute were of a contrary opinion. While romantic poetry was declining, exhausted by the efforts which had excited the enthusiasm of the last generation, Lamartine was carrying on a passionate warfare in favour of democracy. Victor Hugo, though a peer of France, had a leaning towards social reforms. Béranger, whose songs were still popular, ecstatically predicted the fall of the Monarchy, and obtained the help of Pierre Dupont of Lyons to write *Les Ouvriers*. Novel-writing, which attracted the talent of the day more than poetry in France, in the hands of Balzac, that St Simon of the bourgeoisie, became a satire, and an immortal satire, of the manners which he described. Of equal importance and similar effect were the works of Charles Bernard, such as the *Nœud Gordien*, and those of Louis Reybaud, such as *Jérome Paturot* the hosier, the type of the elector and the deputy of the day. Georges Sand deserted lyrical romance for social stories, such as *Le Compagnon du Tour de France* (1840), *Consuelo* (1842), *Le Meunier d'Angibault* (1845). From Eugène Sue, again, the author of *Les Mystères de Paris*, a work of extraordinary popularity, the public heard passionate appeals for a future better than the present. It had been prepared for this by the democratic propaganda of Lamennais, who was now closing in retirement a life which had been as fruitful as that of Chateaubriand.

History had taken a new departure in the earlier years of the reign. In the hands of Augustin Thierry it had passed into the service of the Tiers État, and with Guizot it had studied in the school of England. Historians had pried into the distant past to discover some authority for the claim of the bourgeoisie to monopolise the power of Parliament in France, but had now given up all allusion to the crisis of 1840; the subjection of the Chambers resembled too closely that of the nation at large to the nation "as by law established," with its limited electorate. The historians of this second period, who were even greater than their predecessors, deeper thinkers, more brilliant writers, devoted themselves to the study of democracy. Michelet, in his *Tableau de la Révolution*, published in 1847, evoked the holy form of the People, "terrible, fruitful, generous as Nature itself"; Tocqueville depicted its triumph in America as due to its good morals. Quinet, in his "Essay on Christianity and the Revolution" (1845), dwelt on the sovereignty of democracy, and the worship of it, as contrasted with the claim of the Roman Church to govern France on behalf of the bourgeoisie. Lamartine dreamt of a return to the Republic of the Girondins, whose story he wrote. Henri Martin, a lay Benedictine, formed in the school of Augustin Thierry, tried in his historical works to set forth the mission of France as defined by him in *La France, son Génie et ses Destinées* (1847), a pamphlet breathing the true republican ideal. Lastly there was Thiers, who published the first volumes of his *Histoire du Consulat* in 1845.

It was surely a remarkable fact that all these writers, historians, poets, novelists, and politicians, whose reputation Paris had made and the nation and foreigners also had been quick to endorse, should now be insisting so strongly upon the breach between themselves and the middle classes, who had once honoured their teachers and encouraged their first efforts. To the journals that were fighting the Conservatives in Paris they brought the aid of their talents and the support of their ideas. Victor Hugo, Alexandre Dumas, Eugène Sue contributed to the *National* and to the *Presse*; Alphonse Karr, Félix Pyat, Georges Sand, Henri Martin to the *Siècle* and the *Réforme*. They set an example and supplied copy for their brethren in the provinces, for Rybeirolles at Toulouse, Claude Tillier at Nevers, Dufour at St Quentin, Hégésippe Moreau at Provins, Frédéric Degeorge at Arras. In 1846 war was declared between the "Joseph Prudhommes" whose type Mounier has preserved to us in his satires and drawings, worthies whom nothing would have induced to give their daughters to "scribblers," and the men of culture who were more interested in the common folk with all their roughness and ignorance—"roughness (said Louis Blanc) which meant energy, force of virile instinct, love of what is great, readiness of devotion"—between the provincial electors and deputies of Guizot's party, and their Parisian adversaries, turbulent, acute, active, and generous.

In art a similar conflict was going on, between the stubborn champions of the cut-and-dried in school and institute, and all that was young and ardent in the life of Paris, artists hungry for the new and the beautiful, and sick to death of the hide-bound formulae which had sufficed for the bourgeois world since 1830. In the comic papers, especially in the *Charivari*, Daumier, with a fecundity and a vigour which spared no one, and a talent to which the greatest had to do homage, branded and exposed the middle class, its types, its oddities, its prejudices of all sorts. A Republican from the first, the advocate of every kind of liberty, in art as in politics, the foe of every restriction behind which private interest and satisfied selfishness could shelter themselves, he was all for Michelet and Quinet and against Guizot. From his modest dwelling on the Île St Louis he urged on to the struggle with the Institute these young masters, the coming glories of the French school—Théodore Rousseau, who had been refused exhibition by the Institute, Jules Dupré, Daubigny, Corot, and later on, Millet, the master landscape-painter of the Barbizon school.

Then there were the sculptors, a less combated, and also

less combative class. There was Rude, the son of a working-man to whom the Institute offered no temptation, but whose combined vigour and science perplexed the good bourgeois accustomed to admire Ingres and Pradier; there was Barye, the animal-sculptor, exclusively occupied in the study of nature far from the noise and strife of the world. These formed a school of French sculpture still indeed banned by the prejudices of that day, but with a triumph before it, like that of Carpeaux, the mason's son, the sculptor of *The Holy Alliances of Nations,* which was to regenerate French art. Finally it was in this same year 1846 that Berlioz, the unrelenting foe and fierce critic of Italian music and of the French comic opera of Herold, Halévy, and Auber, so dear to the bourgeoisie, with its lack of lyrical and symphonic qualities, performed *La Damnation de Faust* to an empty concert-room.

Over all this energy of idea, talent, youth, and aspiration, which gave Paris its ever-growing influence in France as well as in Europe, neither Guizot nor Duchâtel had any command any more than M. de Villèle twenty years before, when like them he tried to stem the advance of Liberal and modern ideas. In carrying out the policy of resistance and conservation on which Louis Philippe and his Ministers were bent, the July Monarchy found itself, like the Restoration, under the necessity of combating the Parisian Press and Parisian ideas which in 1830 had carried it to victory. Its blunder was in failing to see therein either a danger or a menace.

And yet the elections of August 1846 were an absolute success for Ministers. The electorate had been carefully worked by Comte Duchâtel and his agents, and gave Guizot a good majority of nearly 100. The battle-call of the Opposition in Paris had failed to make itself heard in the provinces, except at a very few points. Proud of his victory, Guizot announced his policy more loudly than ever, treating his section of the bourgeoisie as if they were the whole of France, and insisting on the privilege of wealth in all its crudity. At that time he was at the full ripeness of his talent. Never had his oratory been finer, his reasoning closer, or his language more decisive and vivid, than when he stepped forth full of confidence, in the teeth of justice and necessity, to keep up the iniquity of a tottering social system at the risk of a cataclysm. To that period belonged one of his finest speeches, that which he delivered at the beginning of 1847 against the admission to the electorate of the so-called "Capacities"—in other words, "Intellectuals," i.e. persons, who, while deficient in taxable quality, were wealthy in intellect—the lawyers, doctors, professors, in fact all the bourgeoisie who had nothing to their credit but enlightenment, who had the work, but not the pay.

It was to no purpose that he was warned by long-sighted Conservatives like de Barante, that he ought to "change his point of view." His success, his certainty of an obedient majority, his extreme and often asserted contempt for the violent and malevolent criticism which as a Puritan he spurned and as a statesman he ignored, all prevented him from making any concessions. "Give nothing, nothing!" said one member of his majority; and he seemed to have adopted the maxim for his own, as the men they had given him as colleagues, "the satisfied Conservatives," had certainly done. Of these new arrivals we have a clever sketch by an eye-witness, M. de Remusat, who describes them as young men, audacious, resembling Balzac's heroes, using politics simply as a field to be cultivated, an opportunity for speculation and fortune-making, sceptics and sensualists. In the opinion of Tocqueville, the country was then divided into two unequal zones, an upper which ought to have embraced all the political life of the nation, but in which languor, impotence, and immobility reigned, and a lower, in which political life was beginning to manifest itself in feverish symptoms.

Just at the moment when Guizot was winning his triumph over the Opposition, in June 1846, destiny willed that the Tory Ministry of Peel and Aberdeen should have to give way to a Whig Ministry in which Lord Palmerston resumed the direction of Foreign Affairs. The English Government had anticipated the effect on Louis Philippe of the return to power of this violent, rough-handed and still more rough-tongued Minister. Prince Albert had manœuvred to avoid it; in fact the Whig Ministry of Lord John Russell, which might have taken the place of the Tories six months earlier, had only then failed to be constituted owing to the refusal of Lord Grey to be associated with the provocations that were to be expected from Lord Palmerston. If Palmerston had not been stubbornly determined to return to Foreign Affairs, and had not promised to behave properly, the Whig Ministry would have gladly passed him over. Queen Victoria was obliged to put up with him and to accept his promises. No sooner was the deed done, than Guizot thought it advisable to make a move against him. "I am expecting his hostility," he wrote to M. Bresson, French Ambassador at Madrid, "and I shall behave accordingly. It shall not be I," he added, "who will give up Spain to Lord Palmerston."

Forthwith he plunged resolutely into a struggle with the English Minister, speedily accepted by the latter, which was to occupy the whole of his attention, and prevent his giving the necessary care to his internal difficulties. The opportunity which he wanted was given him by the still unsettled question of the marriage of Queen Isabella. Guizot had in his hands one weapon which he believed to be effective, in Lord Aberdeen's promise given at Eu to withdraw definitely the proposal of Prince Leopold of Saxe-Coburg for the hand of the young Queen, and to allow

Louis Philippe, after the interval required for the marriage of the Queen and the birth of an heir to the Spanish throne, to arrange the marriage of his son the Duc de Montpensier to the second daughter of Queen Christine.

At the beginning of 1846 Sir Henry Bulwer, the English Ambassador at Madrid, faithful to the policy of Palmerston, and anxious perhaps to please Prince Albert, had tried to revive the candidature of Prince Leopold, and had made secret attempts to influence Queen Christine; but his action was repudiated by Aberdeen, Queen Victoria, and Prince Albert himself, all of whom were obliged, much as they disliked it, to disown him. Without waiting to see another intrigue set on foot, which might possibly hand Spain over to Palmerston, Guizot instructed Bresson to arrange for the marriage of Queen Isabella to her cousin, the Duc de Cadiz, forthwith. And to this instruction he added another of greater gravity; "put the Duc de Montpensier by his side." On July 11 the French envoy announced to Queen Christine boldly that his Government would be pleased to see a double and simultaneous marriage of her two daughters with the Ducs de Cadiz and Montpensier respectively. On September 4 a note in the *Débats* announced the marriages to England and to Europe as a victory of French diplomacy.

In London, among the Whigs, who took their note from Lord Palmerston, and on the most moderate of his colleagues, the effect was immediate. "The *entente cordiale* is at an end; our news shows only too clearly that in Paris they want neither cordiality nor *entente*. It is the most glaring act of political ambition and self-aggrandisement perpetrated in Europe since the Empire." The terms of the indictment, like the ill-temper on which it was based, went beyond reasonable bounds. If Louis Philippe had, like Louis XIV, made his son King of Spain, the indignation could not have been greater. To understand it, we must remember the scandalous story repeated currently in English and Spanish circles as to the supposed incapacity of the Duc de Cadiz to continue the royal line, and judge from that the extent of the ambition with which the King of the French was credited on behalf of his son. "My only answer to this interested credulity," said Louis Philippe, "is contempt."

Always contempt! whether for opposition criticism in Paris, or for English irritability! He would have done better to call attention to the article to which he had attached his signature, providing that the Montpensier marriage should not take place until the scandal as to the Duc de Cadiz had been disproved. His first comment on the matter had been the right one, when on being informed of the demand made of the Queen of Spain without his approval as to the simultaneity of the marriages, he wrote to Guizot: "A formal disavowal must be made. I have never yet played false to anyone." Unwilling to disavow Bresson, desiring also to give Palmerston a lesson, and hoping that the Queen of England and her Ministers would not, like Palmerston, want to break the *entente* for so small a matter, Guizot had gradually worked upon the King not to keep the promise (to defer Montpensier's marriage) given at Eu, alleging the necessity of anticipating the intrigues by which Palmerston and Bulwer were once more trying at Madrid to bring in the English candidate and displace French influence.

Neither of them knew anything of the letter written on August 17, 1846, by Queen Victoria to Lord John Russell, in which she had in firm language expressed her wish to discontinue "a policy which involved quarrels between France and England, and condemned Spain to constant agitation." This honourable desire to prevent the renewal of intrigues that had embroiled her with France contrasted painfully with the weakness of the King of the French in yielding to his Ministers. The Queen of England was keenly alive to the difference. On September 7, 1846, she expressed to the King of the Belgians her indignation in these words: "When they decided that the marriages of the Queen of Spain and of Montpensier should be simultaneous, they did a disgraceful thing. The King should be informed that we are thoroughly indignant, and that it is not by actions of this sort that he will preserve the *entente* which he desires." The anger of the young sovereign was kept up by the vexation of Prince Albert, who had never quite despaired of getting the Spanish crown for his cousin, and had had the trouble of paying visits and civilities to the Orleans family for nothing. "They duped us first, and now they boast of it." "As for Guizot," they said, "he cheated Palmerston, from the mere wish to beat him; the suspicion always attaching to Lord Palmerston has been the cause of the *unjustifiable* conduct of the French Government."

In later years Guizot himself acknowledged that the advantage gained by the Spanish marriages was probably not worth the risk. "He had been caught (he said) in the flagrant anachronism of giving certain matters an importance, as objects of dread or of desire, which they did not really possess." Was it prudent or beneficial to excite throughout England, and actually in the English Court, angry feelings which went so far as to threaten war in February 1847, and, by rallying the whole of the country, including the sovereign, round Palmerston, to restore him the authority he had lost among reasonable people? Queen Victoria one day made a remark to the King of the Belgians, as profound as it was just: "To think that the King should have done this in his seventy-fourth year, and left such a legacy to his successor, his grandson, a child! Friendship with us was of the greatest importance to Nemours and the Comte de Paris; yet he prefers the trouble of governing Spain, which will always be a source of worry and anxiety, to the cordial understanding which used to exist so happily between the two countries." It was clearly not to the interest of the dynasty, or of the Ministry, to provoke Palmerston. "The Queen is very angry with me about it," said Louis Philippe to Tocqueville, "but after all, scolding will not stop me driving my coach as I choose." "I doubt," adds Tocqueville, "whether Louis XIV would have used such an expression in speaking of his acceptance of the Spanish succession; at any rate, to use his own metaphor, the Spanish marriages did in fact a good deal to upset his coach."

While however the breach was widening between Guizot and the Whigs, Thiers, who was in the heat of his battle with the Ministry and the King, was drawing nearer to his old adversary, Palmerston, and entering into very friendly relations with him. As was neatly said by de Barante, "they had their *entente cordiale* together after 1846." To Palmerston, with whom he had some connexion through Panizzi, an Italian exile who had become Librarian of the British Museum (1837), Thiers wrote, "I am a revolutionist in the good sense of the word, and I desire the success of my brethren in the faith in every country." A regular correspondence on this basis was carried on between the Opposition in Paris and the Whigs in London, with the object of ruining Guizot, and forcing the hand of the "faint-hearted Louis Philippe."

Palmerston's policy had remained the same since 1836, but it had been invigorated by his dislike of the French Conservatives, and was now in fact the same as the National and Liberal programme which the followers of Thiers desired to impose on the King. Ambitious, insolent, anxious to secure to his country a leading position, Palmerston had created for himself in every country of Europe a connexion, formed of malcontents and impatient men; and using the spirit of opposition and love of change both as fulcrum and lever, was with the assistance of Thiers plunging every country into revolution. By his advice his envoy in Paris, Lord Normanby, openly supported the Opposition. To maintain the peace of Europe, Louis Philippe and Guizot had now no resource but the help of Metternich, who, like themselves, had grown old and feared the prospect of revolution. Their task was a very hard one, and unfortunately engaged all their attention, just at the moment when in France itself the attacks of the Opposition, and the danger of the as yet unseen revolution ought to have had all their care. "Keep your mind on this," wrote M. de Barante to Guizot on September 8, 1847, "however important may be the foreign affairs you have in hand."

In Spain Palmerston, by way of revenge for the Spanish marriages, pushed Serrano into office, in March 1847. This man was playing the part of dictator, but all in favour of the Radicals, who, like Espartero on his return from exile, had been won over to the English side. Narvaez was upset; the Queen's husband was got out of the way by some feminine intrigues, of which Bulwer held the threads. It is right to say that in the month of October Isabella, alarmed at the progress of the revolution, returned within the sphere of French influence, and took back Narvaez (whom she made Duke of Valencia), together with her own mother and her husband. The English envoy, Bulwer, annoyed at his failure, set to work, like Normanby in Paris, to try to restore his friends to power by encouraging conspiracies and risings; so much so that in 1848 he was dismissed from Madrid. Guizot had not spared trouble or pains "to secure thus much solid ground for French influence in Spain."

In Portugal, Palmerston had incited the Radicals under their leader, the Duc d'Antas, another Espartero, against the Queen Doña Maria, although her husband was a Coburg; and here also France was on the watch lest this princess should be overthrown by a revolution. France took part in the naval demonstration of July 1847, which Prince

Albert had insisted on from the Whigs to overawe the Portuguese Radicals, and for the benefit of his cousin. Palmerston did not get the revolution that he wanted, which would have cut off the French from Lisbon. All he obtained was the admission of some of the rebels into the Cabinet which the Queen had been called upon to accept.

In Greece there was also a succession of what Thouvenel elegantly called *Palmerstonades*, which he reported and opposed, following the example of Piscatory, who preceded him at the Athens Legation. One question involved the dismissal of Colettis on charges of breach of trust and electoral and parliamentary corruption, in favour of Mavrocordato, the leader of the English party. Next was the matter of the support given by "his very impetuous Lordship" to a plot against the Bavarian dynasty, organised at Malta and Corfu by Louis Napoleon Bonaparte. Finally in the month of April 1847, Palmerston ordered an English squadron to the Piraeus to demand payment of the interest on a debt which this pauper infant kingdom had contracted with England, a menace which might have produced a riot, or even a revolution. The death of Colettis in September 1847 was not followed, as he had hoped, by the appointment of Mavrocordato to office; and riots broke out at Patras, in Acarnania, and even in Elis, which were openly favoured by the English envoy, Lyons. King Otho, whose independence Guizot was resolutely supporting, had to be persuaded at any price, either by advice or by threats, to govern in the "English fashion."

In Switzerland an opportunity for intervention occurred, of which Palmerston gladly availed himself, in the quarrel between the Radical Unionists and the Catholic Democrats who upheld the sovereign rights of the Cantons and had formed the *Sonderbund*, or separate Confederacy. Out of respect for the neutrality of Switzerland, the Guizot

Ministry had been careful not to mix themselves up in this quarrel. Their abstention favoured the formation of an understanding, in July 1847, between the English Ministry and Ochsenbein, the leader of the Radicals. By offering their mediation between the two belligerents, they succeeded in protracting the negotiations, and giving time to the Swiss Diet and the Unionist party to subdue the Catholic Cantons of Lucerne and Fribourg (November 14–24). There was undoubtedly a good deal of feeling in Europe at the thinly-disguised intervention of England in Swiss affairs. Metternich wanted Guizot to call for an European Congress; the Opposition in Paris on the other hand charged him with sacrificing the influence of France and betraying the cause of liberty. The Swiss revolution was one of the most difficult matters that Guizot had to settle at the time. The Collective Note addressed by the Powers, in default of a Congress, on January 18, 1848, to the Swiss Government had no effect but to strengthen the agreement between the Unionists and England, now represented by her impetuous envoy Sir Stratford Canning, and to hasten the Radical triumph, which was already assured by the new constitution of Switzerland (July 1848).

Throughout all these schemes, which were everywhere directed by Palmerston's agents, Normanby, Bulwer, Lyons, and Stratford Canning, and which seemed more adapted to increase English influence than to further the cause of liberty, the Whig Minister found trusty and ardent allies in Paris, with Thiers as their chief. In the debate on the Address, in January 1847, he had spoken bitterly of Louis Philippe's—and Guizot's—hostility to the claims of the Progressist party at Madrid and Lisbon and to the Liberals generally; of their support to every sort of reaction, whether that of Metternich in Austria, of Narvaez in Spain, or of the Jesuits in Switzerland. "It is plain," wrote the Duc de Broglie from London, where he had accepted the post of ambassador for the purpose of patching-up the *entente cordiale* again, "that, if the Guizot Cabinet went out, the new Ministry would have to accept the yoke of Palmerston, and that France would take rank next to England at the head of the Radical nations of Europe" (December 1847). Palmerston and Thiers combined again to greet the Liberal initiative of Frederick William IV, King of Prussia, who had lately presented his subjects with a constitution, in the teeth of Metternich. Guizot was more clear-sighted when he pointed out the advantages that Prussia was likely to get out of the two dogmas which she seems to have made peculiarly her own, "the Unity of Germany, and the Liberal Ideal."

But it was mainly in regard to Italian affairs that the community of action between Palmerston and the Paris Opposition made itself felt. "On the day that France and England speak with one voice," said Thiers in the same Chamber as that in which ten years later he was to be heard inveighing against Italian unity, "on that day, Italians, your salvation will have come!" In September 1847, Lord Minto went to Italy to preach liberty to Charles Albert and his subjects in Savoy, to check the outrages of Ferdinand II at Naples, to protest in Rome against the employment of Austrian troops at Ferrara, to ensure the combined action of the English agents in all the Italian courts against Austria and in favour of Italian independence; and the Liberals in Paris were very severe upon Louis Philippe for his supposed dislike of Italian unity, and his refusal "to place at the service of this cause, which was not the cause of liberty solely, the wealth and the strength of France."

French opinion was irritated by the obstinate resistance of the sovereign and his Ministers to all reform at home, and concluded, though wrongly, that they allowed the same principles to govern their relations abroad. The country found fault with the Ministry for separating from England, the friend of revolution, going to Vienna to look for counsels of reaction and absolutism, and betraying the hopes and aspirations of free nations by accepting a new form of Holy Alliance. Their caution and prudence in these matters, in which France ran the risk of enhancing the prestige of England at her own expense, and of favouring the progress of races and people who might (and did) turn against her later, did not deserve such passionate and unwarranted condemnation. It was their misfortune that Palmerston should have returned to office, their blunder that they encouraged him in his aggressive and turbulent policy by a sort of defiance, their mistake that in this year 1847 they thought more about Europe than about France which some concessions might possibly have pacified.

The decisive moment arrived when the opponents of the dynasty, led by the veteran Odilon Barrot and a young Conservative, Duvergier de Hauranne, determined to develop a temporary alliance, made for the purpose of the elections of 1846 with the Radical Republicans under Pagnerre, Marrast, and Marie, into a permanent league extending over the whole country for the suppression of parliamentary and electoral corruption. "Constitutionalists and Republicans," said Duvergier de Hauranne, "have for the moment the same interest; and they ought to have the same object." The object of both was to wrest the country from the domination of the Guizot Ministry, by awakening in it a political spirit; but it involved for Monarchists the risk, for Republicans the hope, of attacking the person and the dynasty of Louis Philippe. It was resolved that with that object in view both parties should organise petitions and political banquets by common arrangement. The first banquet of 1600 guests was fixed to take place in Paris on July 9, 1847; and it was agreed that "the republican speeches should be very moderate in tone, and those of the Left Centre very violent."

Perhaps the assistance given by the royalist Opposition to the antidynastic hopes of the Radicals would not have produced an immediate effect on opinion, which was still very indifferent, had not the demonstration coincided with a scandalous affair which seemed to justify the action of the authors of this reform campaign. It appeared that on May 2, 1842, a mining company of the Haute Saône had been solicited by General Despans Cubière, peer of France and ex-Minister of War, whose letters were read in court and admitted as evidence, to pay a large sum to a Minister of Public Works, a colleague of Guizot, who had since become chief of the highest judicial court in the kingdom, the Court of Appeal, one M. Teste. The Government immediately summoned the General to appear before the Chamber of Peers, and directed an enquiry to be held. Teste, the ex-Minister, also a peer of France, was formally indicted, and, after resigning all his offices and titles, took his place in the dock to be duly tried and sentenced by his peers.

On July 5 the royal equipage passing through the Faubourg St Antoine, on its return from a fête given by the Duc de Montpensier at Vincennes, was met by cries of "Down with thieves"; and Dr Recurt, a Republican, remarked to Duvergier de Hauranne: "If we had chosen, we could easily have turned the indignation of the people into a riot, or even a revolution." What a magnificent field for the accusations brought by the speakers at the first reform banquet against the Government, held responsible for all these scandals and misfortunes, "the inevitable consequences of a crooked policy which, lacking the strength to enslave France, is doing its best to corrupt her"! The very words were an echo of the republican language of Lamartine to his constituents at Mâcon on July 18: "Government has become a trade; the régime of the bourgeoisie is as foul with stock-jobbery, bribery, and scandalousness as the régime of the Palais Royal." In short, the summons had gone forth for a new revolution, "the revolution of contempt!"

The Chambers were prorogued in August 1847, and both Ministry and King hoped that, during the silence of Parliament, criticism would once more be lulled to sleep. But the luck was all against them. A new scandal broke out on August 18 in the peerage, in the shape of the murder of the Duchesse de Choiseul-Praslin, daughter of Marshal Sebastiani, by her husband. at the instigation of his mistress, and the confession of the murderer, before taking poison in the Luxembourg prison. "Society was thoroughly upset," wrote a journalist, Léon Faucher. The same feeling now spread into the remotest corners of the provinces, and even into Algeria, where Cavaignac wrote, "A society that can breed robbery and murder in its highest classes stands condemned." "The Duc de Praslin's deed," said Sainte-Beuve some months later, "had as much to do with the revolution as the conduct of M. Guizot." There were dull rumbles in the political air, warnings of a coming storm, recorded by witnesses on all sides, Doudan, the Duchesse d'Orléans, Tocqueville, Molé, and Mme de Girardin. "This is the way," wrote Tocqueville on August 27, 1847, "that revolutions are bred."

This restless uneasiness could not but tempt the Opposition. The District Councils, on meeting, asked that measures should be adopted against corruption. Corruption was the chief theme of the crowds of reformist speakers who addressed the rural population at the banquets which in September and October 1847 were being very generally organised. Odilon Barrot spoke or was present at more than twenty of these. At Le Neubourg on the Eure, Dupont de l'Eure and Picard demanded electoral reform for the regeneration of France; at Meaux, Odilon Barrot and Drouyn de Lhuys attacked the personal power of the Crown, the main-stay of the Conservatives who preserve nothing, "neither the welfare of the State, nor the integrity of the Administration, nor the dignity of France, nor her alliances, nothing but the abuses by which they live." Crémieux at Orleans, Garnier-Pagès at Montpellier, Duvergier de Hauranne at Nevers denounced the blunders and humiliations of the ministerial policy which had been carried on under the aegis of the King "for seventeen years." And the like happened at Melun, Rouen, Strasbourg, Valenciennes, Chartres, St Quentin, and in every part of France. The alliance of the Monarchists with the Radicals gradually provided for Republicans what they had hitherto lacked, a larger stage than that of Parliament, and an audience daily growing more sympathetic. "The question," as Guizot confessed in the debate in January 1848, "has passed out of the Chamber, into that vague, obscure, turbulent outside world which blunderers and idlers call the people." "I know," replied M. de Morny, the future Minister of Napoleon III; "and it is on that account that I am uneasy. If the movement continues, if we go as far as it would drive us, we shall arrive—Heaven knows where—but at some catastrophe."

Finally, upon this nation which was being moved by fair words or invective to flout its own institutions and its own sovereign, another force was brought to bear, mightier than speech-making at banquets, in the shape of hunger. The bad harvests of 1845 and, still more, of 1846, and the floods in the centre of France reduced the inhabitants of the country, of the towns, and of Paris to ruin and starvation. The bourgeoisie had compelled its leaders to adopt a strict Protectionist system. As there was no regular organisation for the importation of wheat, and as the means of transport were still so slow as to spoil the efficiency of the distribution, the supply of it began to fail. Scarcity once more appeared in Paris and its suburbs, with the other troubles of the Ancien Régime, the consequent anger of the populace, and the suspicion that the market had been forestalled. It was necessary to regulate the price of bread by ordinance, to open charitable workshops and to find the funds to meet a general run on the savings-banks. The mob that shouted "Stop thief!" before the Courts of Justice, now added "the people have no bread, while these scoundrels are taking their ease!"

On the eve of the session of Parliament which was to be the last under that constitution, threatened as it was by convulsions at home and abroad, the Ministry had nothing to do but to resign—unless they chose to make concessions. "Tell M. Guizot that it is time for him to go," wrote Rossi, the French Ambassador in Rome. The same desire was expressed in Louis Philippe's own circle by Montalivet, Rambuteau, Prefect of the Seine, Marshals Sebastiani and Gérard, and even Dupin. Nothing would have served better to split the coalition between Royalists and Radicals than the triumph of the party that wanted reform, but did not want revolution; and nothing would have so entirely embarrassed Thiers, who had invented these banquets, but was too much afraid of compromising his political future to attend one. But, at that moment, Guizot had no eyes for any but foreign affairs. "Look," said he, "at my last despatches from London, Berne, Vienna, Berlin; you will see that I simply cannot go." The principal influence, however, exerted upon him was the will of the sovereign, the obstinate will of an aged man fixed on one single idea, and unable to take in another, in his overweening confidence in his own experience. "Thiers means war, and I do not want to see my peace policy ruined. No, no, a thousand times no! I have a great mission to fulfil, not only in France, but in Europe. It is my destiny, my hope of glory. You cannot make me give it up."

Guizot, while refusing to resign office, was considering a small measure of reform, on the advice of the Duc de Broglie, and perhaps of a majority of his own majority, as tending "to calm public opinion, which had been much disturbed by the banquets and the bad season." Having been pressed by his opponents in the debate on the Address, and tired of an unequal and troublesome struggle which had lasted more than a month from January 1 to February 12, 1848, the Prime Minister announced his intention of moving two resolutions, one for the prohibition of street agitation and banquets, the other for a project of electoral reform. On the same evening Louis Philippe declared his approval of the prohibitions, but repudiated once more all concessions. "There is not to be any reform; I will not have it. If the Chamber of Deputies carries it, I have my Chamber of Peers to throw it out. And even if the Chamber of Peers passed it, my veto remains." Unmistakeably the language of a King as determined as Charles X to go to extremities.

A curious document found among the papers of the Duc de Nemours at the Revolution is a letter addressed to him by his brother, the Prince de Joinville, from Italy, off which he was lying with his squadron in November 1847. It throws a light on the conduct of Louis Philippe, at this moment so critical for his dynasty, and in the previous years. "Forgive me for what I have to say about my father, but we ought to have some quiet talk over him; you are the only person I have spoken to. We are bound to look into the future, and it alarms me. The King is inflexible, and will listen to no one: his will must have its way everywhere. Some notice is sure to be taken of what appears to me to be a danger, the pressure that my father exercises on every point. It will be difficult to prevent a discussion in the Chamber this year on the present abnormal situation which has taken the place of the constitutional fiction. Ministers no longer exist; their responsibility is gone; all centres in the King. He has arrived at an age at which a man no longer accepts criticism. He is accustomed to govern, and likes to show that he governs. With his immense experience, his courage, and his fine qualities, he knows how to face danger boldly; but the danger exists all the same."

These were the conditions in which Louis Philippe, in the month of February 1848, determined to defy the Opposition, to reject the advice of his friends and his family, and brave the opinion of the world. Thereupon Paris, with its "leaning towards a revolt that might become a revolution," began to raise its head. On the return of the deputies who had employed themselves during the parliamentary vacation in awakening the anger and exciting the passions of the provinces, the various classes of the population of Paris thought it was their turn to make a demonstration. The success of the Republicans in the elections of 1842, repeated in 1846, had been, or ought to have been, a warning to Louis Philippe.

Careful note should here be made of the constituent elements of this Parisian opposition, whose motive force was dislike of the Guizot Ministry which had long been unpopular, and whose object was a measure of reform which would destroy his majority. They consisted of (1) the young people of the schools, enamoured, as ever, of novelty and progress, and indignant at the punishments inflicted on their beloved teachers, Michelet and Quinet; (2) the working classes of the slums, whom the distress of two hard winters was inciting to formulate their demands in violent fashion; (3) the members of socialist societies, such as the *Société Nationaliste* and the *Société Communiste,* both republican; these were few in number, but very active;

(4) socialists proper, or democrats; (5) lastly, journalists, especially those of the *Réforme*, Flocon, Louis Blanc, Ledru-Rollin, Pascal Duprat, and Arago, those of the *National*, directed by Armand Marrast, and, notably, the young editors of the *Avant Garde* and the *Lanterne* in the Quartier Latin.

In the city of Paris, as it then existed, outside the districts inhabited by the proletariat and even to a certain extent within them, there lived a lesser bourgeoisie of small employers, with their employés, engaged in retail business, in the manufacture of the luxuries that form part of the life of a capital, in the lower walks of law and of the civil service, men of intelligence, ultra-critical, and—since the day that they had been embodied into a National Guard—bearing arms. Very proud of having at the beginning of the reign established a constitution and a King of its own choosing, it had continued to support them for ten years with its sympathies—and its muskets. Then, little by little, disaffection had crept in, especially since Louis Philippe, either tired of constantly flattering them, or too old for it, had given up the practice of calling them out for an annual review. Being excluded from the franchise by the high figure of the qualifying tax, this portion of the middle class had been daily more and more irritated by the opposition of the higher and conservative bourgeoisie to any lowering of the qualification. They hated Guizot as the personification of their grievances, and turned a willing ear to the complaints of the lawyers, authors, and others who suffered like themselves from his opposition to reform. Their dissatisfaction found expression in the elections of the National Guards, and in their selection of officers, both commissioned and non-commissioned, of the same republican or reformist views as those of the deputies. On December 13, 1847, the officers of the 12th Legion, belonging to the District of the Schools, assembled under the roof of a painter of the name of Delestre, to advocate legal reform or, in default thereof, revolution, and determined to start a banquet in Paris as a demonstration against the bourgeois aristocracy and the Ministry. On the refusal of the prefect to allow them to hold a banquet in Paris in favour of electoral reform, similar to those sanctioned in 1830 against Polignac, the lesser bourgeoisie determined to solicit the help of the deputies of Paris. This being granted them, they determined to abide by the date of January 24, 1848, for their demonstration, and to lose no time in instituting an attack on the state and departmental authorities.

"The bourgeoisie is working up for a riot," wrote Pierre Leroux on February 16, 1848. "If we mix ourselves up in it, it will be a revolution." Indeed that an insurrection should be fomented in Paris by the officers of the National Guard, which for the last seventeen years had been inculcating upon them reverence for the Crown and the dynasty, simply meant that Paris was rising as one man for reform and perhaps for something more. Circumstances had changed since 1830, when the higher Liberal bourgeoisie called for the assistance of the industrial population of the capital against the threatened return of the Ancien Régime under Charles X and Polignac. That bourgeoisie was now, under Guizot and Louis Philippe, taking the shape of a legalised tyranny; and their opponents were the lesser bourgeoisie, the more numerous of the two sections and the more modest, with leanings towards democracy and supported by the whole young generation, the men of letters, the industrials, all of whom, like itself, were excluded from political power. Now as on previous occasions it was the capital that was taking up the glove thrown down by the King and his advisers. "If they push me too far," said Louis Philippe, "I shall abdicate." They took him at his word.

CHAPTER IX

THE REPUBLIC AND THE DEMOCRACY

On January 27, 1848, the day after Guizot had firmly refused to the people of Paris both their banquet and their measure of reform, M. de Tocqueville warned Louis Philippe and the bourgeoisie that a revolution was at hand. "Do you not feel a breath of revolution in the air? Have you at the present moment any certainty of reaching to-morrow? Do you know what may happen a year hence, a month hence, perhaps to-morrow? You do not know; all you know is that there is a storm on the horizon, and that it is advancing towards you. Let us unite to meet the common danger."

It seemed as if this despairing and prophetic appeal had at length reached the ears of the parliamentary bourgeoisie, whose discordant leaders had been at such deadly strife for five years. Just at the moment when the controversy about the banquets was passing into an actual revolt, Guizot let it be understood that a proposal of reform would no longer meet his absolute opposition. On the other side, Odilon Barrot, Remusat, de Lasteyrie, and Vavin, when solicited by the democrats of the 12th District to lead their opposition and head a great popular demonstration, began on February 13 to make reservations and lay down conditions. They proposed that Ledru-Rollin should not be invited to the banquet, that a high price should be put upon the tickets, and that it should be held in the Champs Elysées; thus keeping out the working-men and maintaining its character of a pacific protest. And shortly afterwards, having been put into communication, through Vitet and Morny, with Duchâtel, the Minister of the Interior, with the cognisance of the Opposition leaders, they obtained his permission to visit the banquet-hall on their undertaking to leave it at the first summons of the authorities. On the same day Lavocat, the colonel of the 12th Legion, and deputy for the Ardennes, received the assurance of Duchâtel that the Ministry would very shortly "prove by their acts their adhesion to reform." The understanding entered into between the Government and the Opposition on February 19, 1848, was embodied in a memorandum of which Guizot gives the text in his *Memoirs*. But it was too late. On the next day but one, February 21, regardless of the advice of their deputies, and distrustful of the promises of Ministers, the people of Paris distinctly struck the note of revolt.

On that day certain municipal councillors of Paris warned the Prefect of Police that in the districts round the Tuileries, and in those of the East and West the ferment among the lesser bourgeoisie had become "general and alarming." The populace was out in the Faubourgs St Marceau and St Antoine, and on the Place Maubert; the students were out on the Quartier Latin; so far, however, the movement was not revolutionary, but only in favour of reform and hostile to the Ministry. It seems very likely that the signal for it was given to the National Guards and the bourgeoisie by an article in the *National* by Armand Marrast on the morning of February 20, which published the programme of the prohibited banquet, and an invitation to join it, in a regular and formal proclamation of an aggressive and bellicose tone, calling upon the whole population of Paris, its schools, and its National Guards, to join in an immense political demonstration. "It might have been," wrote Tocqueville, "a decree issued by the

Provisional Government which was to come into power three days later."

This programme, which was destined to turn the banquet into an insurrection through the action of the mob, dissatisfied with the concessions made by its deputies, had been composed, revised, and published without consulting the parliamentary deputies. Marrast had given only the substance of it to Odilon Barrot. It was the outcome of one hurried night's work by certain journalists and Radicals, Ledru-Rollin of the *Réforme*, Garnier-Pagès, and d'Alton-Shee. But the fact is that the breach of the negotiations between these Radicals and the Ministry which then took place was quite undesigned. The majority of the Radicals disbelieved in the success of an insurrection. Marie declared that he would not have a rising at any price; Pagnerre thought the same; and so did more ardent disciples, like Ledru-Rollin, Pierre Leroux, and Louis Blanc. They bore in mind the ill-omened reaction which followed the great insurrection of 1835, and feared lest a rising of the people, too easily repressed, should give the Conservatives an opportunity of learning their strength. And yet the heat of revolutionary passion, which their invectives against Guizot had kindled, dominated them in spite of themselves.

The resistance of the Ministry turned the flame into a blaze. The Minister of the Interior immediately met it by a proclamation, calling upon the people of Paris to abstain from any sort of demonstration, prohibiting the banquet, and forbidding the National Guard from assembling without the orders of its superior officers. The prefect also declared that he "would not allow any government to be set up by the side of the true government, violating the clearest and best-established laws." "This official declaration," said an eye-witness, "was the battleground of the next few days."

Here we have, therefore, on one side, the authorities of Paris preparing for the fray, the commandant of the National Guard distributing his forces about the District Halls, and putting into practice the plan of defence by zones devised by Marshal Gérard in 1840, the Prefect of Police assuring himself of the amount of powder at his disposal, General Sebastiani giving out rations and ammunition to the soldiers, calling councils of commanding officers, and summoning reinforcements. On the other side we see dense masses of working-men and of the lesser bourgeoisie collecting round the notice-boards, questions being asked and answered, individuals coming into touch with one another, on the dawn of the day which is to decide between Paris and the Ministry. Is Paris to have her banquet, and her reform demonstration, in spite of ministerial orders? Or is she to wait quietly without her revolt, until it pleases the higher bourgeoisie, now standing serried round Guizot and supported by the King and the troops, at its own good pleasure, at its own good time (which may be never!), to open its ranks, and resign its monopoly of power?

From the echoes of a stormy sitting of the Chambers, the world learnt that the Opposition deputies had once more fallen back before the accusations of the Ministry, charging them, in spite of the agreement signed on February 19, with provoking to riot; and in the evening a report got about that these pseudo-reformers had finally decided, on the motion of Thiers, by 80 votes out of 100, to "accept the circumstances, and to absent themselves from the banquet of the morrow." The report was confirmed by notes published in the morning journals of the 22nd. These notes, even in the republican journals, were not in the least intended to excite the anger of the people, but rather to calm it. "Men of the people," wrote Flocon and Ledru-Rollin in the *Réforme*, "beware of reckless impulse. Do not give the authorities the chance they want of reaching success through bloodshed." "To give the signal for an insurrection would be to lead the nation to butchery." At this final hour, the deputies, Radical and Liberal alike, had retreated before Guizot and his soldiery. But the time had passed for listening to deputies.

In the District of the Schools, some youthful and impetuous Republicans, to show their indignation at the cowardice of their leaders, organised committees, and sent deputations in the evening to Odilon Barrot. In the districts inhabited by the lower class, the working-men were furious at their betrayal; in the legions of the National Guard, a mixed crowd of journalists and officers proposed to reply to the order calling a meeting of the staff by simply refusing to obey and by cries of "Vive la Réforme!" "Down with the Ministry!"

Thus the rising in Paris was started without the knowledge and against the wishes of the men who had brought it to that pass. "Revolutions," wrote de Tocqueville, "that are brought about by a wave of popular emotion are as a rule more often prayed for than planned for. They are born spontaneously, a sort of chronic disease suddenly made acute by an unforeseen accident."

This was the case with the insurrection which began in Paris on the morning of February 22, without a plan, without a rallying-cry, the mere effect of the economic troubles of the working classes since 1846, and the dissatisfaction of the lesser bourgeoisie or the youthful democrats with Ministry and Opposition alike. The students marched in procession to the Chambers from the Quartier Latin with their petition. The working-men left their work, and came down from their own districts, to mingle with the bourgeoisie in the Champs Elysées, where the demonstration and the banquet were to have been held. The crowd was at first more inclined to fun than to sedition; but very soon quarrels arose. They wanted to blockade the Chamber; and the municipal police, few in number, but firm, were determined to prevent it. Some of the fighters were wounded. After having been driven out of the Place de la Concorde, the crowd became more violent, harried the police-stations, began to build barricades, to pillage the gunsmiths' shops, and to look for weapons. Next, parties of rioters spread over the outskirts of the town, always raising the same cry of "Vive la Réforme! Down with Guizot!" All this did not seem much more serious than on certain past days when the Government had found no difficulty in disposing of the trouble; indeed rather less so.

Nevertheless, there were symptoms of weakness in the course of the defence. When it became necessary, at about 2 p.m., to call up the dragoons for the protection of the Legislative Chambers, they had, on the orders of their officers, avoided charging the mob, and had been cheered in consequence; and, when an attack was made on a post in the Champs Elysées, the infantry of the Guard had turned their backs on the rioters. The conditions of peace in which the army lived, the constant relations between workmen and soldiers, the propaganda in books and democratic journals, all combined, in spite of the orders of the Government, to develop among the soldiers democratic ideas and sentiments. Another weakness, which this time came from above, was the lack of energy and unity in the directing ranks. General Tiburce Sebastiani had been given the command of the regular troops in Paris because he was brother to the Marshal, but he was a man of no reputation and no authority; General Jacqueminot, his colleague, who commanded the National Guard and was the father-in-law of M. Duchâtel, was aged, gouty, and flaccid. To crown all, with rank and file unsteady, and commanders inefficient, the King and his Ministers committed the blunder of cancelling on February 22 the orders they had given on the day before. The fact was that the capitulation of the parliamentary leaders on February 19, and above all their decision to abandon the banquet, had restored the confidence and the hope of the King, Duchâtel, and the Prefect of Police. "It is all at an end; all will go off satisfactorily," they said at Court, when in fact, all was only beginning. And on the evening of February 22, in spite of the troubles of the day, the royal circle kept up their confidence, and their satisfaction at the maintenance of order without bloodshed.

The next morning brought a cruel awakening to the aged sovereign who for eighteen years had looked for his chief support against riots and conspiracies in the bourgeoisie of Paris. The National Guard, for which General Jacqueminot was responsible, and which he had summoned for February 23, were arming, not to defend the Ministry, but to crush it. M. de Circourt, on February 22, said to a diplomatist, "You must reckon upon the National Guard not as an ally, but as an enemy. I am doing my turn of duty in this charming corps: and you may take it that mine is the best company in the best battalion of the best legion. Well, its tone is detestable!" From the evening of the 22nd onwards nothing was to be heard in the political meetings where the next day's attitude was discussed, but talk of reform, and dismissal of Guizot, "the public enemy." Petitions against the Ministry were covered with signatures. When the drums beat the "assembly of the Guard" on February 23, all the bourgeois, who obeyed the call, proceeded to carry out by common consent the demonstration which the authorities had tried to stop, by making their way to the Tuileries with shouts of "Vive la Réforme! Down with the Ministers!" "They would not have overthrown me, if they had not thought that nothing could shake me!" said the King afterwards; and it was true. These Paris bourgeois were Royalists still, though weary of the King's obstinacy in holding up a Ministry which denied them admission to municipal rights; but in the struggle between Government and People, they declared themselves on the side of the People.

And now the insurrection, which had broken out in spots only on February 22, was being methodically carried out in the lower-class districts. During the previous night fights had been going on before barricades erected round the Marais; these however had been constructed without orders from the revolutionary leaders assembled in the Palais Royal, who hesitated to take the responsibility, and dreaded the repression to follow. The smaller streets being very narrow, the insurgents were able to keep their hold on them, and when morning came, they issued from them to build barricades in the Rue St Martin, Rue St Denis, and all over the centre of the town; and they fired impartially on the regular troops and on the municipal police. Battle was now joined, and would shortly be so in the Faubourgs. In the thick of the fight, the National Guard intervened with a view of stopping it; but this only gave the populace time to consolidate their defence, and paralysed the efforts of the regular troops, whose sympathies indeed were more with the rioters than on the side of order. The mob, intoxicated with delight, greeted this intervention with cheers and renewed vigour. Soldiers and working-men clasped hands; and the staff, demoralised by the desertion and disobedience of their troops, knew no more what orders to give, or how to get them delivered across the city that was slipping from their grasp.

But a few hours had passed, and Paris had its hand on victory—if not Paris, at any rate a part of it, the lesser bourgeoisie, which had only deserted the King, in favour of the infant insurrection, to serve him by upsetting Guizot, and by effecting a reform corresponding to their own wishes and interests; and, in their honest belief, in the interests of peace. On February 23, 1848, the King declined to dispute the matter any further. Harassed by the entreaties of the Queen, dizzy and stunned by the blow that had fallen, he could not yet summon up courage to deal with the National Guard as rebels. "If I resist, blood will flow, not that of the professional rioters, but the blood of the true People, of the National Guard, of the workers and the honest folk. Can I order troops to fire on my own electors?" He was afraid to use the army, which was on the whole loyal, to inflict a chastisement on the bourgeoisie, which he hoped he might yet calm down and reconcile by decisive, if tardy, concessions; thus he might induce it to desert the popular insurrection with which it had mixed itself up, and make it once more the buttress of his dynasty. Duchâtel, the Minister of the Interior, came to the Tuileries to advise him to decide on some energetic line of action, and Marshal Bugeaud offered to direct it himself; but Louis Philippe, the Queen, and the princes all entreated the Ministers to resign; and neither Guizot nor his colleagues seem to have shown any hesitation in granting their request. Very likely they thought, as he did, that they might by resigning calm angry passions, and at the same time escape responsibilities. At half-past two on February 23 they were conversing with the King; at three o'clock Guizot, calm and pale, informed the Chamber that the King had just summoned M. Molé to the Tuileries with a view to his forming a Ministry.

It was thus, in the midst of the capital in arms, that Louis Philippe and Guizot severed the partnership entered into eight years before for the avoidance of war, civil and foreign. The rupture at this moment was a confession of impotence on their part. To the deputies under the then existing electorate, to the Conservatives who owed their elections to them and to whom the Government owed its authority, it looked like a betrayal, and was at first received with indignation. "These men," said a contemporary, "felt the wound not only in their political opinions, but in the tenderest spots of their private interests. The downfall of the Ministry jeopardised A's whole fortune, B's daughter's marriage, C's son's career. They had been living on the price of their favours, and expected to go on doing so." By thus sacrificing Guizot and his majority, the King and his family hoped at least to save the dynasty; and there seemed some possibility that the plan might succeed. Towards the end of the day, the turmoil seemed to be diminishing, and the behaviour of the mob was quieter and more playful. The general aspect of Paris was changing. The barricades were being opened, and the houses lighted up. The bourgeois, pleased and satisfied, were laying their arms aside, and strolling along the Boulevards. The parliamentary party recovered their confidence, and resumed their usual intrigues around M. Molé as to the constitution of the Ministry that was to carry out the Reform.

The change was sudden. At 10 p.m. that night a number of the lower orders who had come from the Faubourg St Antoine and were standing in groups before the offices of the *National*, singing the Marseillaise, and behaving like bean-feasters rather than rioters, came into contact with the military guard of the Foreign Office. The crowd, without any hostile intention, proposed to fraternise with the soldiers. The officer in command refused to allow it; and at that moment a musket went off, followed immediately, without warning of any sort, by file-firing which laid low more than a hundred of the other side. The news of the event, which the Republican Garnier-Pagès called a misunderstanding, but which to the still ruffled Parisians looked like an ambuscade, revived the dying embers of the insurrection. By midnight, the barricades were everywhere restored; gunsmiths' shops were pillaged; the National Guard joined the people, and surrendered their barracks to them, while a funeral car bore the bodies of the victims back to the Faubourg, in the midst of a mob shouting for vengeance.

With the dawn of February 24, the city, which had been in holiday trim on the previous evening, had resumed the demeanour it kept for days of riot and fighting. Those sudden volleys on the Boulevard des Capucines had definitively cut the bonds between the National Guard, who after the dismissal of Guizot had no more to ask for, and the power and person of the King. The night before, they had been satisfied to shout for Reform. This morning the bourgeois of Paris was beginning to cry "Vive la République!" The anger of the people was met in the councils of Louis Philippe by a corresponding awakening of energy and a desire for resistance, which at midnight resulted in the nomination of Bugeaud to the command of the Army of Paris. "His name will inspire terror," said the King, "and terror is what we want now. He will correct their mistakes; after that, we shall see!" The morning of the 24th saw the Orleanist Monarchy and the populace of Paris girding themselves for the decisive and final struggle.

At 5 a.m. on February 24, Bugeaud ordered his lieutenants, Bedeau, Sebastiani, Brunet, and St Arnault, to take energetic measures against the people on the Boulevards, in the centre of the town, and on the left bank of the Seine; and, if these had been carried out, a sanguinary fight would have taken place in the streets of Paris. The people were fully prepared for it, having made themselves masters of the barracks and the townhalls, from which they had got arms and ammunition. The leaders of the Republicans, Louis Blanc, Félix Pyat, Goudchaux, Flocon, Bastide, Martin of Strasbourg, Arago, Caussidière, Marrast, and Ledru-Rollin, though they still hesitated, were impotent to resist the call of an insurgent people crying for vengeance.

In the offices of the *Réforme* and the *National*, in the meetings of the secret societies, the Republicans were beginning to wonder whether the hour had not at last come which was to make up for their many disappointments. Proclamations, hastily drawn up and printed by Proudhon, called upon the working-men to make an energetic resistance, pointing out that they were masters of the whole centre of the city, from the Bastille to the Rue St Honoré, from the Pantheon to the Porte St Denis. The proletariat of Paris, being in arms and with half a victory to their credit, were less anxious now to fight for a mere change of Ministry and political system, than for the triumphant advent of an era of justice, fruitful of blessings and of glory. They wanted a social revolution, which should spread its doctrines throughout Europe, like that of 1789. The King's summons to Bugeaud showed that he intended to fight for his throne and his family against anarchy and revolution; thus the combatants—the King and the nation—had singled themselves out, and the struggle was at hand.

Here again, as in the beginning of this crisis, it was the National Guard and the bourgeoisie, who by paralysing the efforts of the Government, hindered the struggle, played into the hands of the insurgents, and obliged the Crown to retreat. "There," said Tocqueville, "was that middle class whose every wish had been servilely met for eighteen years; the flood of public opinion had succeeded in carrying it away and hurling it against the men who had flattered it to actual corruption." When the royal forces plunged into the streets of Paris at 6 a.m. to attack the barricades, they were met by negotiators of a very unexpected sort, in the shape of the officers and men of the bourgeois Guard, who were in greater sympathy with the populace than with the Crown. General Ducrot, who had orders to occupy the Place de la Bastille, and the Faubourg St Antoine, was at once stopped on discovering the complicity between the bourgeois and the insurgents, and obliged to make a hasty retreat to Vincennes. At the Hôtel de Ville, General Sebastiani had to give up the attack on the barricades of the District of the Temple at 8 a.m. in consequence of the pressure of the Mayor and Liberal bourgeois, who demanded that they should be left for the National Guard. And finally, General Bedeau, a soldier of African experience and a brave man, but perplexed by the shouts of the mob and the risk of responsibility for a massacre, allowed himself to be stopped by some bourgeois officers of the National Guard, to whom he handed over the duty of maintaining order—the order that he had been commissioned to restore! He even deputed a certain well-known manufacturer to visit Marshal Bugeaud at the Louvre and ask him to withdraw his opposition to the insurrection, in other words, to demand a suspension of hostilities. At 8.30 a.m. the Marshal had accepted the mediation of the bourgeoisie of Paris between his troops and the insurrection.

For this, it seems, he had several reasons. The first was undoubtedly the inadequacy of the forces entrusted to him, which struck him at once on taking command; badly fed, badly armed, and demoralised, they ran the risk of being beaten if the National Guard took sides with the rioters. In the next place he was informed that after the refusal of Molé to form a Ministry, the King had, at midnight, made an appeal to the most advanced of the parliamentary leaders, Thiers and Odilon Barrot; that he had made vital concessions to them, of which the dissolution of the Assembly was the first; and that Louis Philippe seemed to be coming back from the idea of action to that of negotiation. Finally and more especially came the advice and influence of the Duc de Nemours, who believed that the Crown and the House of Orleans might be saved by depriving the royal authority of its weapons! At 9 a.m. orders had reached all the Corps Commanders to retire on the Place Carrousel, and to leave the National Guard, who undertook to be responsible for order, to look after the policing of the city. The army retired without fighting, abandoning Paris to the rioters behind their barricade-fortresses.

From that moment neither the bourgeoisie, nor the parliamentary leaders, nor Lamoricière, who had been given the command of the National Guard, were able to hold back the mob, now in full revolution. "Reform is not enough for us now," said one of the rioters to Tocqueville, pointing to the Tuileries, "we want more than that." On the Place de la Concorde, in full view of the troops of General Bedeau and of the National Guards who were retiring on the Place Carrousel with their firelocks butt uppermost, all the police on duty at one point were murdered by the mob. At the Hôtel de Ville, the people deprived the privates of their arms, seized the cannon, and assaulted the municipal buildings and the Prefecture, which the National Guard surrendered to them at midday. The Ministers, in obedience to the King's appeals, tried to check the rioting, but in vain; Odilon Barrot, hoping for better success, went bravely through the streets of the seething city, but to no purpose. He was greeted with hostile shouts of "Down with Bugeaud! Down with Thiers! Down with Louis Philippe! No more Bourbons! Vive la République!" Like Lamoricière, he was soon driven back on the Tuileries, upon which at 11 a.m. the whole people from every part of the metropolis, having captured the Hôtel de Ville and the streets of the city, were now victoriously concentrating, armed for the final attack. The revolution threatened Louis Philippe with the same fate as Charles X; it was only a question of hours.

The first decisive attack was made at about 11 a.m., when the mob carried the Palais Royal by assault against the troops of the line, after a bloody fight which Lamoricière tried to stop at the risk of his life. The republican deputies,

Arago, Lagrange, the heads of the secret societies, Caussidière, Pilhes, Albert, no longer concealed their hopes. The republican party had come to the top; the shouts against the royal family grew louder. "In half an hour 100,000 insurgents will be attacking the Tuileries," was the message brought to Thiers by his secretary, M. de Reims. To save the Monarchy, Thiers advised Louis Philippe to retire to St Cloud, to get a force of 60,000 men together there, and to retake Paris by force. The King refused, and attempted to recover his hold over the National Guard by summoning it for review in the court of the Carrousel before himself, his sons, and his staff; but the reception given him by the bourgeois was utterly discouraging. He then offered the largest concessions imaginable, the dismissal of Bugeaud, and the appointment of Ledru-Rollin as Premier; but the temper of the Parisians grew worse as their demands increased. "The crown may still be saved for the Comte de Paris," was said at midday to Louis Philippe even in his own circle; "it is lost for the King." In spite of the Queen's entreaties, the aged King, under the pressure of the journalists, the deputies, and Emile de Girardin, who were flocking into the palace, determined to abdicate. "I abdicate in favour of my grandson," were the words he used on the formal memorandum, which Marshal Gérard, then in command of the National Guard, was instructed to lay before his legions with all speed. This document, written at the moment that he was leaving the palace to go into exile, was the last appeal made by the King to the bourgeois who had given him his crown, and who in their hearts had little more liking for a democratic Republic than they had in 1830; but to this appeal they were deaf.

The news of the abdication, far from pacifying the combatants, only increased their ardour. The National Guard insisted that the troops should evacuate and surrender the

Tuileries to them without offering resistance; and the Duc de Nemours had to concede it. At half past one o'clock they admitted a crowd of sightseers and rioters, who pillaged the royal apartments. Throughout the business, the National Guard acted as accomplices of the mob in overthrowing the Monarchy which they had established to check that same mob in 1830.

When the King's abdication took place, the Chambers of Deputies had been in session for about an hour; they had met of their own accord, without a summons from the Government. But did any government exist, seeing that in the last twenty-four hours Molé had succeeded to Guizot, Thiers to Molé, and now to Thiers, Odilon Barrot, although he had himself been appointed Minister of the Interior only that morning? It seemed that the Ministry had disappeared as completely as the King. Of all the powers established by the bourgeoisie in 1830 and now overthrown by the National Guard, the only one left to represent France, or at least the French electorate, was the Assembly; and Sauzet, the President, had scarcely the courage left to summon it. The widow of the Duc d'Orléans, with more energy than the President, inasmuch as her children's future was at stake, came with the Duc de Nemours and her son, to implore the protection of the deputies, and to ask them to proclaim the accession of her son, as desired by Louis Philippe. But, at the moment when she appeared, the chiefs of the republican party also arrived, urged forward by their victorious forces, to ask the Chamber to accept a provisional, but democratic, government, the members of which had been selected in the offices of the *National*; the list included Arago, Dupont de l'Eure, Ledru-Rollin, Crémieux, Marie, Garnier-Pagès, and Lamartine.

The hand-to-hand fighting in the streets was over; but a new struggle had begun in the bosom of the Chamber, which now had no leaders, Thiers having fled. An insurgent mob was growling at its doors; on one side men were cheering for the regency of Helène of Orleans; on the other the champions of a Republic were protesting against it in the name of the right and sovereignty of the People. The mob invaded the tribunes, and now dictated its will. It broke down the doors, and overflowed the whole precinct; an officer of the National Guard dashed into the tribune, flag in hand, and shouted: "There is no authority here now but that of the National Guard represented by me, and that of the people represented by the 40,000 armed men who have surrounded these buildings." It was in vain that Lamartine in a final speech, addressed more to the insurgent mob than to the powerless and terrified deputies, tried to put some order into this chaos, and to obtain a formal proclamation of a Provisional Government with authority from the Assembly to draft a new Constitution. The violence and insolence of the mob, not to speak of its musketry, had swept the Legislative Halls clean of all representatives by 4 p.m., and the vote for a Provisional Government was in fact passed by the National Guard and the mob. And, as if to mark still more emphatically that the victory was to be scored to Paris, the conquerors of the streets insisted that this Government should repair at once to the Hôtel de Ville to receive formal admission.

It was the story of 1830 over again. The Parisian people, supported by the National Guard of the metropolis, was imposing its will upon France; while Louis Philippe, finally beaten, and impotent to save his dynasty, fled secretly to Honfleur, murmuring to his friends as he went, "Like Charles X, like Charles X!" The bourgeoisie of Paris had utilised popular force to make him King; now with the help of the same force, which it had let loose again, it dethroned him. It was the moment to lay to heart the warning contained in the words of Tocqueville, addressed to his colleagues of the National Guard on February 23, when they were urged to overthrow the Monarchy: "If the kingdom is put into confusion, do you imagine that the King is the only one who will be injured?"

This confusion began on February 24, when first the King, next the Ministry, lastly the Chambers had all been destroyed by the revolution of Paris. Not a single representative of public authority was left in Paris, not a soldier, not a gendarme, not a constable. Even the National Guard had disappeared. The mob alone bore arms, looked after the streets by night and by day, gave orders and made regulations. It was the absolute and complete accession of Democracy. The People alone, that is to say, the classes that work with their hands, were left in possession of power. When Lamartine, accompanied by Bastide, Dupont de l'Eure, and Crémieux, and by students from the schools and journalists, walked resolutely from the Palais Bourbon to the Hôtel de Ville, to induce the People to accept the Provisional Government, he could only win his way through the crowds on the embankments of the Seine by sheer eloquence and pluck. The scene on the Place de Grève was beyond description—a confused mass of victims and victors, groups of armed men, heaps of the fragments and wreckage of battle; and through it all a singular procession, laboriously forcing its way, the members of a Government that was greeted by acclamations from one side, hostility and suspicion from the other.

The Hôtel de Ville, now held by the rioters, was being rapidly filled by a fevered mob who amused themselves by firing salvoes, cheering eminent politicians, and going into ecstasies over the speeches of the armed orators who did homage to their might. In the throne-room sat an improvised Assembly in permanent session, discussing motions, appointing Garnier-Pagès mayor of Paris, and passing outrageous decrees. This People, now master of Paris, and, therefore, by virtue of the centralisation of government, of the whole of France, being suddenly called upon to make practical use of its victory, had neither political ideas nor experience, nothing but brute passions, vague aspirations. Proudhon frankly admitted it, when he said on February 25: "In the 24th of February there was neither purpose nor idea." The victorious insurgents had not fought for ideas or principles, under the guidance of politicians and doctrinaires. They had not the capacity to create a regulated authority to take the place of that which they had destroyed with the help of their accomplices, the bourgeois. It was Anarchy, pure and simple, under the vague name of a Republic, borrowed from traditions of the Revolution.

There were men however who, throughout the whole July dynasty, in silence, sometimes in exile, had been preparing to organise democracy, though they did not expect it to arrive so soon. Most of them were of the bourgeois party—journalists, manufacturers, professors, physicians, or barristers, whose ideal was a regular government based on law, charged with the improvement of the intellectual, moral, and material condition of the people. Earnestly desiring to ensure the permanence of a democratic government in France, and to remove the fears inspired by the memories of blood and rapine connected with the First Republic, their heartfelt wish was to establish order and respect for law.

But the difficulty was evident from the very start, that these bourgeois Republicans had not, at the moment when the success of the revolution took them unawares, reached any common understanding as to the men or the methods by which this government should be carried on. One section of them was largely formed of the staff of the *National*, Armand Marrast, Garnier-Pagès, Arago, Dupont de l'Eure, etc., and was afterwards joined by Lamartine; they attached more importance to law and order than to social reform, and aspired to be leaders rather than reformers. Another section consisted of the so-called champions of the Red Republic, who met at the office of the *Réforme*, Ledru-Rollin, Flocon, Louis Blanc, and Caussidière; these men were prepared to seize upon power by virtue of the revolution in Paris, without consulting France, and were resolved to carry out a social revolution by the power of universal suffrage, eschewing violence, but refusing to retreat. The former group had looked first to the Assembly representing France for formal recognition, and next only solicited the assent of the People of Paris at the Hôtel de Ville. The second, their hands still black with powder, had met the insurgents in the office of the *Réforme* on the summons of Martin of Strasbourg; in the name of the People, they had formed a Provisional Government; but their list did not contain the names of Crémieux, or Dupont de l'Eure, whose places were taken by Flocon, Marrast, Recurt, and Louis Blanc; eventually it included also one working-man, Albert. They had already named Etienne Arago to the Ministry of the Post-Office, and Caussidière to the Police; and both of them took possession of their offices without a moment's delay.

Moreover this republican bourgeoisie, now driven by the force of circumstances to try to make a government, was splitting into sections, before it had even begun to govern. While the more conservative members, following the lead of Lamartine, went to the Hôtel de Ville to obtain the sanction of the People to their appointment, others, under the influence of Louis Blanc, applied directly to the mob in the great hall of their common building, the Salle St Jean. Here in the midst of a shrieking People bearing arms, yet incapable of turning its own victories to account, and yielding blindly to every impulse, stood the men who ought to have been its leaders, but who could come to no agreement as to the methods and form of republican government.

Seated together in the study of the ex-Prefect, M. de Rambuteau, Lamartine and Ledru-Rollin discussed the legality of an immediate proclamation of the Republic. "You must wait till you have got the authority of France," said one. "I have got the authority of the People," replied the other. "Aye, of the People of Paris," returned Lamartine; but he gave way nevertheless.

The mob insisted on having a formal proclamation of the Republic, to avoid being deceived again as in 1830. For the democracy of Paris now proposed to govern France. Further discussions of some vivacity took place as to the duties to be assigned to each Minister; and there was much debate and difficulty before Ledru-Rollin was appointed Minister of the Interior. But the principal discussion took place in the evening, when the group from the office of the *Réforme*, in the name of the sovereign People, put forward their claim to a share in the government. An actual fight might have taken place, had not Garnier-Pagès acted as mediator, and proposed to accept Louis Blanc, Marrast, and Flocon as Secretaries; and it was on the point of breaking out again when the newcomers reopened the discussion of the political programme of the Government which had been adopted before their arrival. Louis Blanc, supported by Flocon and Ledru-Rollin, demanded that the Republic should be proclaimed in Paris, and the provinces required to accept it; Arago and Dupont de l'Eure thereupon threatened to resign. Lamartine, with the help of Crémieux and Garnier-Pagès, laboured hard to establish harmony; but it was midnight before they succeeded in doing so by the use of this skilfully devised formula: "The Provisional Government gives its vote for a Republic, subject to the ratification of the People, who are to be consulted forthwith."

During the whole of that evening, the purport of these discussions filtered through to the bodies of insurgents who filled the square of the Hôtel de Ville, and occupied its passages and halls, listening to revolutionary orators who awakened their suspicion and urged them to violence. The room in which the Government was then deliberating was in as much danger as the Tuileries and the Legislative Chamber had been on that morning. There was a risk that anarchy might strike at this first germ of an attempt of the bourgeois Republicans to restore order and law. Lamartine faced the reviving disturbance with the same courage as before, making more than seven speeches to soothe their rising passions. The only chance, however, of avoiding further violence and rioting appeared to be to accept the *de facto* dictatorship of the democracy of Paris, and to effect some arrangement with its leaders to keep it quiet. Jules Simon has well summarised the upshot of these two days of revolution in these words: "The agitation was organised by the Liberals, for the benefit of the Republic which the Liberals dreaded; and at the last moment universal suffrage was organised by the Republicans, for the benefit of the socialism which the Republicans abhorred." With the threat of a social revolution before them, the republican bourgeoisie preferred to compromise with the apostles of these social theories, whose accession to power held out some sort of promise to the lower classes. Ledru-Rollin and Garnier-Pagès were the main authors of the compromise, though Lamartine got the praise for it.

On that evening a proclamation was addressed by the Government to the French nation, in the name of that nation (although no part of it had been consulted except Paris), which should be very attentively studied. "The People," it said, "shall not be deceived this time." The democracy which Paris had hoped to establish in 1830 was now realised—"a national popular government in full harmony with the rights, the growth, and the will of this great and generous people." But feeling doubtful after all of the alleged capacity of the nation to organise itself in this new shape, the bourgeois announced the formation of another Ministry, the members of which were provincial deputies, and by means of which alone "the victory of the nation could be organised and made permanent." Behind these formulae, coined on the spur of the moment amid the roar of the insurrection, two realities stood forth clear—the first, that it was Paris alone that had created, and was now imposing on France, a democratic constitution; and the second, that seeing the inability of the People for self-government it behoved the bourgeoisie to seize the reins once more, but with discretion, "in the name of the People of the provinces."

These two facts did not immediately result, as might have been expected, in a disagreement between the capital and the provinces, where the word Democracy had ever since the Revolution awakened memories of anarchy and violence, of incompatibility between the demands of the democracy and the ideas of the men who had just taken charge of public order at the Hôtel de Ville.

When, in a proclamation addressed to the People of Paris, the heads of the new administration had to point out that revolutionary enthusiasm, if continued too long, might delay the enjoyment of the rewards of victory, they suggested the importance of the service that they were rendering to Paris in its relation to the nation. The Departments, accustomed to be governed from the capital, and practically indifferent as to the form of government, regained confidence, and let things go their own way, once they knew that an authority existed in Paris charged with the maintenance of public order and prosperity. At 7 p.m. on February 24, under the rule of Arago, the postal service was working as normally as on other days, by the united efforts of the officials, in spite of the barricades. The men who occupied the high offices of state inspired confidence by their honesty or their talent—Dupont de l'Eure, President of the Council, whose whole past spoke of honour and dignity; Lamartine at the Foreign Office, who to a generous soul added the prestige of a great literary career; François Arago at the Navy, where they counted largely on his scientific reputation; Michel Goudchaux at the Finances, to which his capacity and his integrity alike pointed; Bedeau and Cavaignac, African officers, whose claims to the Ministries of War and of Algeria were uncontested; Carnot, a great republican name, at the Ministry of Public Instruction; Bethmont and Marie, barristers of mark, in charge of Commerce and Public Works. If Crémieux as Minister of Justice, and Ledru-Rollin as Minister of the Interior, were disturbing influences rather than guarantees of moderation, the Ministry, taken as a whole, was not a whit more startling than any Ministry which Louis Philippe might have selected to serve under Odilon Barrot. At any rate it formed a Government.

From February 24 onward, this Government appointed superintendents and heads of divisions in the various Ministries, to ensure the proper handling of finance, public education, military matters, and public works. In the Departments the provisional Commissaries, who had been at once appointed in the place of the Prefects who had retired without making trouble, went about organising provincial administrations. Some of these, e.g. at Amiens, Valence, Montauban, and especially at Bordeaux and Lyons, were very sourly received; but most of them, though new and very young, like Emile Ollivier at Marseilles, were accepted without protest. One of them has left on record: "The feelings with which they were met were surprise, resignation, and a vague uneasiness; but these vanished before the fact that order was maintained, and that the thing could not be undone." France of the Departments accepted the Republic, to which she was supposed to be hostile, with the resignation which for the past sixty years had made her bow to all orders from Paris, with the feeling that she was still a mere creature of the bourgeoisie, through her fear of a still fiercer outburst of democracy and her love of order.

When the next day came, on February 25, the compromise which had enabled the leaders of the republican bourgeoisie to evolve order, in its new shape, out of the Parisian riots that had overthrown the Monarchy appeared as little likely to live as the monarchical government which the bourgeois established in 1830. From the slums and poorer districts a mob once more descended, armed with muskets, wearing red cap and sash, and waving a red flag, the symbol of revolutionary violence, "of blood," said Lamartine, the flag of Terror. At Lyons, the mob took up arms against the houses of Charity, and let prisoners out of gaol; in Alsace the mob hunted the Jews. Lamartine, always in the forefront of the battle, faced the rioters, went without hesitation into the thickest of the armed crowd, and in a noble and eloquent sentence bade them "contrast the red flag dragged round the Champ de Mars through the gore of the People, in the only journey it ever made, with the tricolour flag that has gone round the globe bearing everywhere the name and the glory of the Mother-Land!" His courage checked the insurrection at the very point of a fresh outbreak. But he at once found himself compelled to make new concessions to his fellow-councillors who represented the working class and the urban proletariat. Louis Blanc insisted successfully upon the addition of a red rosette to the staff of the tricolour flag. On that evening a whole string of decrees were issued to please the socialist Republicans—one for turning the Tuileries into a great asylum for aged civilians; another for the adoption of the children of persons killed during the riots; a third for setting at liberty political prisoners.

The most important of these concessions was one

embodied in a decree dated February 25 on the "Right to Work." No sooner had the question of the flag been settled, than this one, involving the most serious consequences, came up. A tumultuous deputation of armed workmen, headed by a certain Marche, introduced the matter in threatening language at the Hôtel de Ville. Lamartine once more met threats by eloquence. "Enough of talking in that style!" was the rough reply. Louis Blanc supported the speaker. Flocon and Ledru-Rollin then combined to draw up on the spot the decree by which Lamartine and his colleagues undertook to guarantee work for workers and to give them the benefit of the profit they might earn; it further made them a present of the million francs of the Civil List which belonged to them. "Only wait till the Republic is proclaimed, which cannot be done before to-morrow." But the working-class democracy of Paris had already annexed these profits, and claimed the right to treat them as income.

It was only by virtue of this concession that the bourgeois Republicans were able to maintain for one more day the compromise which had given them the authority and the means for re-establishing order. On the next day and later they were obliged to have recourse to other measures of the same sort. On February 28, just as they were making ready to proclaim the Republic on the Place de la Bastille, a procession of 12,000 men representing a large number of societies marched in silence to the Place de Grève and unfurled banners inscribed with the words "Organisation of Labour," "Abolition of man's living upon man," "A Ministry of Progress." Louis Blanc having called upon the Government to listen to these appeals once more, Lamartine gave sharp expression to his impatience at their constant repetition; whereupon Louis Blanc, knowing that he had the support of the force in the street at his back, gave in his resignation, and Albert did the same.

The compromise was in danger when Garnier-Pagès once more stepped in as mediator, and induced Louis Blanc to give up his proposed idea of a "Social" Ministry, at the same time persuading the other side to permit the creation of a "Commission of Workers," with Louis Blanc and Albert at its head. The decree constituting the Commission and summoning it to meet at the Luxembourg Palace appeared on February 28, along with two others establishing National Workshops, and bureaus for organising the labourers on canals and railways as a preliminary. Into all this legislation the republican bourgeoisie had been forced or cajoled by the demands of the working-class democracy, whom long lack of work, dear food, and the still smouldering fever of revolution inclined to sudden and violent action; but, in the intention of the feeble Government that ordained it, it was nothing more than a method for avoiding an ever-threatening conflict.

The first working of a novel democratic system in France raised a serious question for solution; and with that solution the existence of this Government, during the first week after the fall of the Monarchy, was closely connected. Men who then called themselves Republicans were convinced in their own minds that, agreeably with the preamble to the decree of February 28, "the revolution effected by the People should be treated as made for the benefit of the People," and that the logical consequence of the omnipotence of the labouring classes ought to be an improvement in their material, intellectual, and moral condition. This proposition, which had been established as an article in the republican creed ever since 1830, was also consonant with the views which had prevailed in French society in the latter half of the reign of Louis Philippe under the influence of the school of St Simon, of Lamennais, of the young Catholics who followed Montalembert, and of Ozanam. "I do not think," said a working-man one day, "that public opinion has ever shown more anxiety for the improvement of the moral and material condition of the people."

The grudge against the parliamentary bourgeoisie, the apparent monopolisers of power, the livers at ease, was all the stronger from the tendency to compare its misdeeds with the ideals of social progress and of a common brotherhood which were now uniting every Frenchman, whatever his class or his opinions. When they had overthrown this bourgeoisie along with their Louis Philippe and their Guizot, there ran through Paris a thrill of concord and fraternity, a sort of debauch of idealism. The great bankers, Rothschild at their head, subscribed to the relief of those wounded in February. The Archbishop of Paris and other high dignitaries of the Church proclaimed their evangelic love of humanity at large. The nunneries offered their buildings as havens of rest for the victims of labour; duchesses united with the wives of members of the Government in organising aid societies and clubs for the relief of distress. The magistracy, the University, and the army offered their services for the education of the People. Church hymns alternated with revolutionary ditties. The village priest joined the village schoolmaster in giving counsel and guidance to the People. Nothing was to be heard anywhere, in feast or in debate, but appeals to the citizens to unite for the well-being of all. Democracy had now made its advent with the minimum of bloodshed, and a new era was opening for the happiness of every Frenchman, even the humblest and most wretched.

But the absence of real agreement was evident as soon as it came to the selection and use of the proper means for realising that happiness. Most of the members of the Provisional Government, being convinced of the People's lack of experience, were afraid of over-haste, fearing lest the too sudden realisation of a dream might lead to conflict and to reaction, not only for the bourgeoisie to which they belonged, but for the country in general, and even for the working class itself. While freely allowing that Liberty and Republicanism are part of the machinery of social progress, they proposed to place that Liberty and that Republicanism on a solid legal basis, mindful of the maxim "to desire the ends is to desire the means." The dream of these men was defined by Blanqui as a "bourgeois constitutionalism," while his own rival conception was "a Republic with complete political equality."

To Blanqui, the chief of secret societies, whose courage had earned him imprisonment for life and who in his prison may have despaired of a popular victory, now that the riots of February had set him free with his fellows, a Republic seemed to realise best the immediate happiness of the People and to secure them a livelihood; and any delay or postponement suggested treachery. "Was the farce of 1830 to begin again?" As to the methods selected, he cared little, "so long as the social transformation on which the future of the People depended was carried on without back-drawing or disappointment." In the teeth of the legal authority he called meetings at the Prado and at the Salle Tivoli, on February 26 and 27, to organise the might of the People, and instituted the Central Republican Society in which working-men, militant members of secret societies, literary men, physicians, barristers, socialist officials, admirers, friends, disciples, and simple comrades could combine to oppose the monarchic theory. Both logic and ambition impelled Louis Blanc and his henchman Albert, the working-man, to adopt and support at the Government board the demands of these socialists, working-men of Paris, who were alike suspicious and impatient.

The entire story of French democracy in the present era, in which its supremacy has been finally established, is involved in the two factors of political life as existing in February 1848; one being the essential harmony between bourgeoisie and People, arising from common ideals of justice, liberty, and the unity of human interests; the other, the initial discord between the two classes, the first cautious, concerned for order, and anxious to secure the confidence of the individual citizen, the second impatient, blinded by the consciousness of its own strength and inclined to abuse it, the easy victim of the allurements and incitements of theorists and adventurers.

During the first two months of the Republic, the harmony was maintained, thanks to the wisdom of the men of the *Réforme,* the radical bourgeois Garnier-Pagès, Flocon, Ledru-Rollin, representatives of the smaller shopkeepers and artisans, whose sympathies were on the side of the labouring classes, and who were useful as intermediaries between the educated and comfortable bourgeoisie and the People, with their passionate desire for immediate reforms. While Garnier-Pagès and Ledru-Rollin induced Lamartine to grant the concessions demanded by the mob, their friends Recurt and Martin of Strasbourg did their best to persuade Blanqui and the revolutionary club-men to give a republican government credit for some merit; and Blanqui, speaking before a tumultuous meeting which was taking a riotous turn, actually said, "We must avoid frightening the provinces, reviving memories of the Terror and the Convention, and recalling the King from exile. We must learn to wait." If the cautious would only learn to give, and the impatient to wait, democracy might be organised in peace.

This was the hope of Ledru-Rollin, when on March 5 he obtained the assent of his colleagues to a decree inviting the French People to nominate a Constituent Assembly by universal and direct suffrage on April 9. To induce the bourgeoisie to grant to the proletariat equality of voting power—a promise and pledge of complete political equality—and to induce the People, in return for this promise, to give up the use of violence, to be satisfied to fight with voting-papers, and to accept only such reforms as it could realise by law—this was the scheme of the Minister of the Interior. In an appeal to the People with all its risks, rather than an appeal to violence and its attendant misery, he saw the best, if not the only, means of establishing internal peace in France.

While this was going on, Lamartine, as Minister for Foreign Affairs, was working hard to maintain peace abroad, a condition equally necessary for order as for liberty. This task was not less difficult than that of the Home Minister, inasmuch as the difference of opinion between the bourgeoisie and the People of Paris was equally pronounced on these questions also. The great majority of the bourgeois in the commercial and industrial classes, and even some of the working-men, desired a cautious and pacific policy. As had been seen in 1830, the spirit that burned in the patriots of 1793 had never quite died out; and in revolutionary circles it manifested itself in the wish to see France in arms for the emancipation of nations and the triumph of justice abroad and at home. Was not the overthrow of Guizot certain to be followed by a defiance of Metternich on account of his oppression of Italians and Germans, of the Tsar on account of his tyranny over the wretched Poland, of England, because of her obstinate refusal of liberty to the Irish?

The state of Europe at the time seemed favourable to hopes of this sort, and propitious to a general revolution. Since 1847 had closed, Italy had given the signal for insurrection. The reforms granted by the Pope, the Grand-duke of Tuscany, and King Charles Albert, had hastened the movement towards unity by the gradual introduction of liberty during the past five years in that peninsula. On January 1 the people rose in Rome, on the 2nd and 3rd at Milan (against the Austrians), on the 6th at Leghorn, on the 8th at Turin. On the 12th the Sicilian insurrection at Palermo had summoned Italians to assert their independence; and while no one expected a revolution in Paris, a general rising in Italy against Austria and the Italian princes her vassals seemed positively certain.

In Germany, and particularly in the southern portion of that country, the Liberals were meeting to concert a common attack upon Austria, with the possibility of carrying with them Prussia, whose King had raised their hopes a little in 1847; on February 12 a revolt broke out in Munich. Ever since 1844 Metternich had observed that Hungary was "on the brink of the revolutionary abyss." His ears were filled with the appeals of Kossuth and Wesselnyi to the Magyars, impatient for liberty, and already craving to dominate others. He had seen the Bohemian Slavs holding a review of their forces on the occasion of the funeral of Jungmann, the patriot and philologist. "In Austria," he said, "revolution was ready, and only waited for the slightest impulse to start it."

Thus it appears that the impulse had already been given in Italy, Bavaria, and Denmark when the bourgeois and the People of Paris overthrew Louis Philippe, to the intense delight of Palmerston. For that statesman had now returned to office, and seemed fully determined to encourage revolution in every corner of Europe, in order to create fresh markets for British industry and commerce. Had republican France simply repudiated the treaties of 1815 (as Louis Blanc and Blanqui in fact wished), had she taken up arms on behalf of the nationalities which those treaties had kept in servitude, and tried to smite the return blow for which the nation had been looking for thirty years past, it would have been enough to kindle the now smouldering fire into a blaze involving the whole of Europe. Men like Emile Ollivier were never cured by the lessons of experience of cherishing the dream which, if it fired the hearts of Republicans of that day, the French bourgeoisie by the advice of Lamartine repudiated.

This repudiation and the guarantees for the peace of Europe given by the Provisional Government are expressed in the circular of March 7 which Lamartine forwarded to the representatives of foreign Powers after submitting to his colleagues for approval. As soon as he was established in the Foreign Office, he hastened to acquaint Europe and his own countrymen with the principles which were to determine the foreign policy of the democracy, conformably to the lessons of 1789 and the present interests of the nation. "The now emancipated people should use neither bluster nor violence. His own prayer was for peace among all nations, for independence with peace, for universal harmony based on reciprocal respect." Nothing could be more opposed to the exhibitions of hatred and bullying which, under the guise of liberty and nationalism, then marked the relations of the European races, Italian, Teutonic, Slav, Danish, and Magyar, than this programme, based on the reciprocal rights of nationalities, which might have been drawn up in the first years of the Monarchy of July rather than on the morrow of its decease. Lamartine laid down in this circular that "the treaties of 1815," which the Liberal and Republican Opposition had been abusing ever since 1830, "were the basis and starting-point of French relations." He condemned propagandism, holding that "the only permanent liberty was one that is born spontaneously on its own soil." Inspired by the wisdom of Mirabeau, he pointed out to the French nation, now that she was her own mistress and responsible for her own fate, the true limits of her influence and activity. "The spectacle of order and peace which she hopes to give to the world will be the only honourable persuasion that she will exercise—the proselytism of esteem and sympathy. This is not to set the world on fire; it is to shine as a star on the horizon of nations, in order to be at once their harbinger and their guide."

Noble and poetic language, and at the same time carefully considered and fruitful philosophy! If both language and policy were well adapted to reassure foreign Governments, it was not so easy to make them acceptable to some members of the French administration, Ledru-Rollin and his friends, Garnier-Pagès and Louis Blanc, who feared for their popularity. It was not in his dealings with Europe that the poet-minister's diplomatic skill was then most needed. He was in the position of Louis Philippe when he found himself condemned to please at the same time the sovereigns of Europe and the chiefs of a Parisian mob. To keep on terms with Louis Blanc and the clubs, he announced in the above-mentioned circular that "he accepted the treaties of 1815 as *de facto,* not as *de jure,* valid"; and he let it be understood, or hoped, that the non-intervention of the Republic in the affairs of Europe remained subject to one condition, that no crusade against liberty took place on the Continent. And, as if he wished to prepare for such a possibility, he strengthened the army and set up a Committee of National Defence, with Arago as president, science being once more, as in 1793, pressed into the service of the State, for the security and integrity of the French frontiers. He searched for alliances in England, in Prussia, and even in Russia.

The importance of these declarations was no doubt somewhat diminished by the reservations that the Minister found himself obliged to add; but their true signification did not escape the acuteness of such a statesman as Palmerston. "'Tis a mosaic," he said; "and the differently coloured pieces represent the various opinions which exist within the circle of the Provisional Government, some restless and warlike, others pacific and conciliatory. I will be bound that if one put the whole into a crucible, boiled off the gassy part, and took off the scum, one would find that the residuum was peace and good-will towards other countries." This was certainly the sense of the instructions that Lamartine gave his representatives abroad, when addressing them confidentially and with greater freedom. "France (he said) cannot converse with whole nations, be they Belgians, or Germans or Italians. Confine yourself to keeping me informed."

It was high time that this language should be heard abroad, and that the Republic should thereby be relieved of responsibility. For on March 13, 1848, the revolution broke out in Vienna against Metternich; on March 15 Hungary rose, Lombardy on the 17th, Venetia on the 22nd; while on March 18 the population of Berlin were in full revolt, demanding a constitution from the King of Prussia. The Republic would have been justified in telling Europe that these popular agitations, far from being provoked by her, gave her a good deal of anxiety. The revolutions let loose in Europe by the fall of Metternich did more injury to the pacific policy of the infant Republic than the Republic did to the peace of Europe. The exiles of all countries, Poles, Irish, Germans, Belgians, and Italians, flocked to Paris to seek assistance, bringing a tumultuous mob of more than 15,000 men to recruit the ranks of the advanced democratic party, who, excited by the memories of 1793, were burning to declare war upon Monarchy, and to start a crusade for a universal Republic, with a political and social transformation of Europe. On March 10, 1848, Delescluze, the Commissary of the North, secretly supported by Ledru-Rollin and Caussidière, put the "Risque tout" Society at the disposal of the Belgian patriots to create revolution in Belgium. Not long afterwards another such expedition was started on the frontier of Savoy against Charles Albert. But for the energy of Lamartine, who was determined to put down every act of aggression, the appeals of these foreign revolutionaries would have led the nation to cross its frontiers. Between Blanqui and the popular leaders on the one side and the bourgeoisie on the other, at the dawn of the Republic which they were both equally desirous to serve, the same discord existed on every point of foreign action and of social progress, one party demanding the immediate realisation of its hopes, even by violence if necessary, the other desiring a pacific development on legal lines, which can only be a work of time, method, and example.

From the beginning of March 1848 it was becoming evident that the understanding between the bourgeoisie and the People of Paris, effected on the dismissal of Louis Philippe and Guizot, ran the risk of being destroyed by these radical disagreements, by the fears of one party and the impatience of the other. Business was paralysed by the agitation in the numerous clubs, and by the audacity of newspapers which re-echoed all the violent speeches and resolutions. Workmen either could not or would not find work. The savings-banks no longer received deposits; ordinary banks could get no security. Goudchaux, the Minister of Finance, fearing a national bankruptcy, resigned on March 5. Four days later, a deputation of over 3000 bourgeois, bankers, manufacturers, and merchants, extorted a *moratorium* as to payment of commercial instruments, by the threat of a serious lock-out, and were loud in their indignation at the tenderness of the Government to the working class, which they believed would prove their ruin.

The imposition, on March 16, of an extraordinary tax, indispensably necessary to the State, was not calculated to satisfy them. The conflict grew more marked when the question arose of opening the ranks of the bourgeois National Guard to the proletariat, and of giving them a voice in the election of officers. Even the Government were shy of putting arms into the hands of the workers, and preferred to create a new paid "Garde Mobile" for the protection of the capital. The organisation of this was entrusted to General Dubourg, who had fought in 1830, and now had joined Lamartine. At this the bourgeois took further alarm; and, at the moment when Ledru-Rollin issued a circular to his commissaries in the provinces to stimulate their zeal for the Republic, the bourgeois displayed their anxiety in a movement for defending their own interests by retaining their former organisation as select companies of the National Guard.

On the following day, March 17, the working-men's clubs, under the influence of their speakers, Hubert, Flotte, Barbès, and especially Blanqui, came down from their special districts with the determination of seizing once more the dictatorship which they had lost since February 28. Their scheme was to turn out the more moderate members of the Government, and especially Lamartine, and postpone the elections, which might otherwise result in unmuzzling the rest of France and extinguishing the unconstitutional revolutionary authority of the capital. Louis Blanc and Blanqui had boldy told the People, "You cannot have any claim to represent the whole of France." Thanks to their courageous attitude, the demonstration, which numbered, it was said, more than 100,000, marched quietly through the Hôtel de Ville, though indeed it looked as if they were its masters.

A month later, on April 16, the demonstration organised by Louis Blanc, whose popularity had been increased by this preliminary exhibition of democratic force, was renewed. But this time Ledru-Rollin, yielding to Lamartine's entreaty, had mobilised the National Guard and the Garde Mobile, who received the People with shouts of "The Communists into the river!" A conflict was on the point of breaking out between the bourgeoisie and the working-men of Paris, at the very time when the French People in the provinces met for the purpose of electing a National Assembly (April 23).

As always happens in any events connected with Paris, the reaction to all this made itself felt in the elections. The provincial population, so hastily summoned to exercise a right for which they were not prepared, were not exactly displeased, but perplexed. If the voting had taken place on the morrow of February 24, they would probably have elected a Chamber agreeable to the wishes of the Provisional Government, merely from the habit of taking their orders from Paris. But two months had passed, and they were beginning to be alarmed at the audacity of the schemes and the violence of the language, some echoes of which reached them, strengthened rather than enfeebled by distance. The peasants, being interested in the idea of property, which appeared to be threatened, and forming small communities round their parish priests, often their only counsellors, came to look upon their voting-papers as weapons of defence against Paris and communism. If out of Lamartine's many supporters there were still ten Departments left to carry him by acclamation, it was most undoubtedly as the representative of order and peace. And, while at Lyons and other large towns, they chose as his colleagues a reasonable number of moderate Republicans of the same shade as himself, they were also careful to return a hundred and thirty Legitimists and at least a hundred Royalists who had sat in the Chamber under Louis Philippe. The abolition of the tax qualification which made the electors the dependents of the wealthy, the want of political experience in the public, the imminence of the danger to property, all inclined them to prefer, not pure democrats, but candidates possessing the most interest in the defence of society, men whom they knew best, bourgeois, proprietors, priests, and even bishops. Finally, in Paris itself it appeared that the People, influenced by the same considerations, had deserted the popular leaders, who also were divided among themselves, and were setting up different lists of candidates in the Luxembourg and in the Clubs. Neither Barbès nor Raspail nor Pierre Leroux, the chief of the Socialist school, succeeded; the candidates first elected were Lamartine, Dupont de l'Eure, Garnier-Pagès, and the members of the Provisional Government who had proved their moderation by their resistance to violence.

This, the first General Council of the French democracy, was certainly notable for the fact that the candidates thought it their duty to profess before it, whether sincerely or not, their desire to make the study of social questions their first care. "They occupy of right," said Montalembert in the Doubs, "a large share of the attention of the country." Léon Faucher dwelt on the necessity of putting "the instruments of labour within reach of the greatest number." M. de Mouchy in the Oise declared himself "ready to carry on the democratic work of the social revolution of 1789." M. de Dampierre in the Landes called for "a new arrangement of society." Rouher, Baroche, and Dupin, who had been Orleanists yesterday, and were to be Bonapartists to-morrow, declared themselves Republicans, and resolved that for the future "everything should be done by the People, for the People."

But all this soon turned out to be but the last breath of that great gust of "humanity and fraternity" which the proclamation of the Republic had for a moment raised in France. Its inspiration was still felt at the first meeting of the Assembly, when on a magnificent summer day the Ministers came in procession, escorted by the National Guard and greeted by universal acclamations, to restore into the hands of the representatives of the entire French People the powers that the Revolution of Paris had given them. The "father" of the Assembly, André de Puyraveau, in the name of the Assembly proclaimed the Democratic Republic; but his voice was drowned in a burst of ecstatic enthusiasm, as if on that day there had been, in the words of the ardent Republican, Trelat, "but one voice, one word, one sentiment in the depth of every heart, towards our Republic, the home of light, the accepted of all Frenchmen." As a matter of fact, the Assembly was thinking a good deal more about the defence of the existing society against the threatened violence of Paris than of the organisation of a new one. Tocqueville tells the story how his constituents in Normandy greeted his departure with tears in their eyes, feeling sure that he was running into serious danger among the populace of Paris; as for himself, he, with the greater number of the deputies elected with him from the bourgeoisie and the nobility, was quite ready, nay, anxious, for the coming struggle with the Socialists and Radicals.

The Socialists, on their side, suffering under the double rebuff, at the Hôtel de Ville on April 15 and at the elections on the 29th, were ready to accept the slightest challenge. But, as they seemed to be already beaten, the Assembly did not make its first attack upon them. They fastened upon Ledru-Rollin, the leader of the Radicals, the disciple of the "Mountain," whose conduct and behaviour reminded men of "Jacobins and the Convention." Upon the cessation of the Provisional Government, it looked as if the Assembly was going to refuse him a seat on the Executive Council, a body which it had elected to carry on the administration provisionally while waiting for the Constitution (May 9, 1848). Had it not been for the intervention of Lamartine, both in the Chamber and on the Committees, Ledru-Rollin would have been rejected; as it was, he had only 450 votes, against 725 for Arago and more than 700 for Garnier-Pagès and Marie.

On that day even the great poet whom France had been only yesterday applauding as the first of her statesmen began to be the object of a constantly increasing mistrust, which eventually cast him down from the pinnacle of his popularity, with a fall more rapid than his rise. The bourgeois Republic, which he had attempted to create in the very midst of the rioting by an understanding among all Republicans both in Paris and in the provinces, received on that day its first and very serious blow. If, instead of finding fault with him, the Assembly had given him the necessary authority to continue the work of internal pacification that he had carried on since February 24, the nation would have been spared those mortal conflicts and blood-stained quarrels which cost her her liberty. Tocqueville, who was then opposed to Lamartine, in later years did homage to his clearness of vision. Between the Conservatives of the Assembly, and the revolutionists of the People, he was beginning to be caught as between hammer and anvil. After the blow he received from the deputies on May 9, 1848, for his loyalty to Ledru-Rollin, he received another still deeper from the revolutionary leaders through his attachment to the cause of European peace in the hands of Bastide whom he had appointed Minister of Foreign Affairs on May 21.

On May 15, 1848, news having been received four days earlier that the Prussian Government had drowned in blood the hopes of the Polish patriots in Posen, a demonstration of working-men was organised by the chiefs of the revolutionary societies and the Clubs, and encouraged by Barbès and Blanqui. Barbès marched to the Palace of the Legislature with shouts of "Vive la Pologne!" and invaded the Assembly, just as the Parisians had invaded that elected by property qualification on February 24. But on this occasion the National Guard refused to play into the hands of the rioters. The legions from the wealthier districts hastened forth to liberate the Assembly, and reoccupy the Hôtel de Ville; the bourgeois of Melun, Caen, and Amiens marched out to attack the Communists. General Courtais, who had shown weakness in command of the National Guard, was deposed by his own troops; and Louis Blanc, generally regarded as the incarnation of Socialism, was ignominiously arrested in the midst of the Assembly. The Clubs under Blanqui and Sobrier were closed.

The Government and the Executive Committees were thus rescued from this new aggression of popular violence, after its first brief success. But it only exposed them more completely to the wrath of the bourgeois deputies, who held them responsible for the event and obliged Caussidière, the Prefect of Police, a friend of Ledru-Rollin, to send in his resignation. Men such as Marrast, Martin of Strasbourg, Senart, and Pascal Duprat, with Dupont de l'Eure at their head, were forming a separate group at the Palais Royal, to compel Lamartine to break away from Ledru-Rollin and the frequenters of the Rue des Pyramides, whom they believed to have been privy to the People's late resort to arms. They appeared to be secretly inclined to the Royalists of the Rue de Poitiers under Berryer, whom Lamartine himself did not favour. Unconsciously, and at the expense of the Republic, they were repeating the blunder of the royalist majority when it split into groups to ruin Guizot, and thus, without intending it, destroyed the Monarchy.

The risk to which Lamartine and his work were exposed between popular action and bourgeois reaction was made evident at the elections of June 5, 1848. The majority of the candidates elected in Paris or in the provinces at Rouen and Bordeaux belonged to the party opposed to the Executive Council and to the man of genius at its head. The Socialists, who had been beaten in April, took their revenge in Paris, electing Pierre Leroux, Proudhon, Charles Lagrange, and Caussidière. In the provinces, on the contrary, the Royalists won the day, carrying Thiers at

Rouen, Molé at Bordeaux, and Changarnier, all of whom, after having been rejected under universal suffrage, were now brought back in triumph to the Assembly. The event of the greatest moment for the future was the election in Paris and in three Departments of Louis Napoleon Bonaparte. He bid fair to take the place of Lamartine in popular favour, owing to a tacit combination among malcontents of the most opposite views, whom the policy of Lamartine failed to conciliate—working-men disappointed of their hopes, Liberal-Conservatives, and patriots, alarmed by the affairs of May 15, or angered by the abandonment of Poland. Every sentiment which then animated the nation, the passion for order, and the desire for social improvement, the passion for glory and for activity abroad, feelings so mutually contradictory that Lamartine and his Ministers had been unable to satisfy them during the past three months, threw France back into the memories of the Consulate, which the writers and artists of the last fifteen years had restored to favour.

When, on June 10, 1848, the Government proposed to issue a decree of banishment against the Prince, the reception which the Assembly gave to the proposal showed Lamartine that he was coming near the end of his authority. He had been the only one to protest against the "Return of the Ashes" in 1840, and the official recognition of the Napoleonic cult. Now in this Assembly just elected and this time by the Democracy, two-thirds of the deputies, Socialist, Royalist, and even in many cases Republican, by way of playing a spiteful trick on the Government, whom they accused of weakness and of complicity with the revolutionary party, affirmed the right of Louis Napoleon to take his seat as their colleague. With great wisdom, however, he retired, "so as to avoid giving support to disorder"; the day was coming when he would be called upon to put it down.

From that day forth, the Republic was without a government—if indeed it could be said to have ever had one. A common jibe was to call it the "Inexecutive Commission." Commerce and business, which had received a heavy blow from the insurrection of February, were now meeting daily with greater difficulties; Government Five per cents. had dropped from par to 69; strikes and non-employment crippled the world of workers and small employés; the collection of the supplementary tax of 45 centimes was the cause of disorders throughout the country; and cries of "Vive l'Empereur!" began to be heard. Obstinately opposed to terms of peace (and indeed Lamartine was no longer in a position to ask for them), the two sides prepared for a struggle that seemed inevitable, that could only be settled by force, the struggle between the People and the bourgeoisie, between Paris and the provinces, between France and Europe. The matter of the National Workshops gave, and perhaps was manufactured to give, the expected opportunity.

The Government, in setting up these workshops, after formally recognising the right to work, and deputing the Commission in the Luxembourg to ensure that right, had at first only intended to assist out-of-work cases resulting immediately from the Revolution, or from the crisis in business. The distribution of this assistance was entrusted to Emile Thomas, an engineer in the service of the Bridges and Highways Board, and differed *in toto* from the operations of the Luxembourg Commission under Louis Blanc, which aimed at the reorganisation of society. Emile Thomas was able to manipulate individuals by the wages he paid, and to win them over from the influence of the Socialists and the Clubs. "Let the Luxembourg people," said he, "worry over the sources of labour; let us consider the labourers themselves." But this temporary method of giving occupation and food to the working class was not less dangerous than the hopes awakened by the Socialist preachings. The danger began to show when the number of workmen assisted in Paris reached 100,000, and in Lyons 25,000, in the difficulty of finding them work, and in the insufficiency of the State fund out of which their wages were paid. It was felt at the beginning of May that the moment was near for taking measures for the reorganisation or dissolution of the National Workshops.

Proposals for their dissolution were at once put before the Assembly, which referred them to the Committee on Labour, instituted at one of its first sittings. The Opposition soon discovered that some drastic proposal would be an excellent way of embroiling the Government with the working-men of Paris. And from that moment, in fact, the workers in the National Workshops, who had previously been neutral or even hostile to their comrades in the Clubs and the socialist societies, began to make up to them. The threats of the bourgeoisie stiffened the ranks of the working-men.

Like the Assembly, the Executive Commission wanted to attack the problem on May 10, but it did so in a different spirit. Trelat, the Minister of Public Works, a convinced Republican, but a foe to socialist theories, had set up a Committee of State and Civil Engineers, but had declined after all to adopt its recommendations, on the ground that they asserted too positively the duty of the State to provide work. A week later, on May 24, he decided that unmarried workers between 18 and 25 years of age should enlist in the army of the Republic; that all others who could prove a six months' residence in Paris should be kept in the workshops, but paid by the piece, not by the day; and that gangs of workers should be sent into the provinces to be employed on State work. But on that day the Government came into collision with Emile Thomas, the head of the National Workshops, who, rather than see them dissolved, was now inclined to reorganise them in a fashion satisfactory to the Socialists. They then tried to force him to retire, and transferred him into the provinces; but the Executive Commission were soon warned that the workers in the National Workshops, like their head, were prepared to seek the support of the Socialists, and were obliged on May 28 to withdraw their proposal for an immediate dissolution.

The Executive Commission hesitated, seeing that it was caught between the threat of a workers' revolt and a bourgeois reaction in the Assembly. Indeed on May 28, during a sitting of the Committee on Labour in the Assembly, with Corbon, a socialist working-man, as president, the Government had to submit to attacks from the Republican Democrats, from economists such as Wolowski, and from the Royalists, and was challenged to dissolve the National Workshops forthwith. On May 29, the Committee having requested M. de Falloux, a Royalist, to prepare a decree for their dissolution, the result turned out to be nothing more than the original proposal afterwards withdrawn by the Government, for sending back into the provinces workers who had migrated to Paris in the last three months. M. de Falloux, a stout Conservative, but skilful in concealing his intentions under fairly moderate language, inveigled the Assembly into a conflict with the working class, without letting them see the danger. He overwhelmed Pierre Leroux, the official theorist of Socialism, with compliments, in which Montalembert joined, even during the debate. His tactics consisted of leaving to the moderate Republicans the responsibility for all serious attacks upon the Socialists.

It was in fact Goudchaux (who had been lately restored to the Assembly), who on June 16 definitely moved to dissolve the National Workshops, and alarmed the Assembly into so doing in spite of a last effort on the part of the Government. "If you do not settle this question," said he, "the Republic will perish, and Society will be left in a condition such as I do not care to describe. The ground under your very feet is mined." A Special Committee was immediately appointed, with Goudchaux as president, and de Falloux as reporter, to carry out the decree. In spite of the despairing cry of Victor Hugo, who predicted a civil war, and the appeals of Caussidière and Waldeck-Rousseau, the Government, yielding to the bourgeoisie, ordered, on June 21, 1848, that all workers in the workshops between 18 and 25 years of age should be enrolled in the army, and the remainder hold themselves ready to go into the country where they would all have compulsory work as navvies.

"This is going to be a fearful shock," said Emile Thomas to M. de Falloux, who had been pretending to consult him during the previous fortnight. During the night, the staff employed on the workshops prepared for insurrection. A delegation from them and from the Committee at the Luxembourg attended before the Executive Commission on the morning of June 22 to state their complaints: "We shall use force," was the reply of Marie to Pujol the spokesman of the delegation, the future commander of the mob of workers. At 6 a.m. on June 23 barricades were erected on the Place du Panthéon, amid excited shouts of "Liberty or Death!" and, later in the day, on the Boulevards. It was a repetition of the February riots, with the bourgeoisie, instead of the Crown, as their object.

In anticipation of the insurrection, the bourgeoisie had entrusted the defence of order to a Minister of War, who, though a Republican, was above all a soldier, and when fighting was necessary only thought of winning—General Cavaignac. By the advice of Generals Bedeau and Lamoricière, African officers like himself, whom the experience of the previous days had taught that the riot must not be allowed to stampede them again, he decided that the wiser course would be to send the bourgeois force, the National

Guard, against the barricades in the street, reserving the regular forces for a final stand in defence of the Assembly and the public authorities.

While the Assembly held its final deliberation, rejecting all conciliatory measures, and (on June 24) deciding to make its session permanent, the National Guard engaged the insurgents with vigour from every direction, in the Marais, and in the districts of St Jacques and the Hôtel de Ville. The Garde Mobile, which drew its recruits from the lads of the lowest class, did its duty even better. The young people of the schools pronounced in favour of the Assembly and against the rioters. The fighting, which was severe and indecisive, lasted throughout June 24, between these men, workers and bourgeois, who three months before had been on the same side of the barricades, and who had created the Republic. The workers were completely persuaded that this Republic had played them false and was plunging them into want; the bourgeois were equally convinced that insurrection was high treason towards the Republic. "The question," said Arago, "was one that could only be settled by force."

The best Republicans, men who while republican were essentially bourgeois—Bixio, Dornès, Edmond Adam, Charras, Guinard—with aching hearts but steadfast souls, and determined to make an end of the matter, surrendered their authority into the hands of General Cavaignac, to whom Lamartine and his colleagues had given up their power also after the proclamation of a state of siege by the Assembly on June 24. The General thus invested with the dictatorship appealed in the name of the country to the army, which he had at first exposed as little as possible, and had now reinforced from the provincial garrisons. And the army, under its intrepid leaders, Lamoricière, Duhesme, Bréa (the two latter killed in this action), and Négrier, supported by the Garde Mobile and the bourgeois, drove back the insurgents from the Pantheon and the Hôtel de Ville on June 25. On the morning of the 26th the soldiers thrust them back into the Faubourg St Antoine, where Mgr Affre, the Archbishop of Paris, lost his life in trying to separate the combatants. There the troops surrounded and finally crushed them.

"Order has triumphed. Vive la République!" were the last words of General Cavaignac's report of the defeat of the workers of Paris in their revolt against the Assembly. "The Republic is dead!" was the reply of Lämennais on the morrow of these bloody days by which the population of Paris had been decimated. Both judgments were true in spite of their apparent contradiction, inasmuch as they were the expression of the equally correct opinions of the two classes who had been at deadly feud—the bourgeois of Paris, convinced, with General Cavaignac, their spokesman and saviour, that order was a necessary condition for the acceptance of the Republic by the country; the Socialists, who with Georges Sand and Lamennais could not conceive "the existence of a Republic which began by killing its proletariat and the People of Paris." Democracy could not be permanently established in France unless order were respected and the concurrence of the working classes at the same time obtained. The sanguinary revolt of the latter, coupled with the clumsy threats and the necessary repressive measures of the deputies who supported the law had dug a gulf between the two which would take long to fill!

After this there was no pardon for the conquered. Special commissions were nominated to seize any rebels who had escaped punishment; Courts Martial sat to try the prisoners; and on June 27 a large number of them were condemned to transportation. The People yielded to a decisive superiority of force, but a deep-seated ill-will and class-hatred remained, which prepared the ground for the silent reception of the seed just then being sown by Karl Marx, in his attacks on capital and on the bourgeoisie. The anger of the People was also favourable to the Bonapartist propaganda, indications of which had been evident in various directions during the June riots. Lastly, the memories of the Consulate inclined the bourgeoisie to look for the Saviour of Order, of public peace, and of its own private interests, among the heirs of Bonaparte. Thus the programme of a new state of things was being outlined, a scheme which alone was capable of securing order, and at the same time giving the working classes some better consolation for their defeat than a Republic condemned to impotence, even before it came into legal existence.

The riots of June had suspended the work of preparing a Constitution to which the National Assembly should have first devoted itself. A Constituent Committee had been set up on June 18, with Cormenin as president, composed of representatives of every party in the Assembly, Republicans of yesterday like Marrast, Dornès, and Vaulabelle, Monarchists who had joined the republican ranks, Dupin, Dufaure, and Tocqueville, Socialists and workers, Lamennais, Considerant, and Corbon. It worked with such assiduity that a first report was laid before the sub-committees of the House on June 18, the day before the rioting.

The insurrection and its suppression had naturally caused divisions in the Assembly as many and as deep as in the nation. General Cavaignac enjoyed a very brief popularity, while the Republicans split into two opposed camps. One of these, on the extreme Left—Ledru-Rollin, Félix Pyat, and Flocon—drew closer to the Socialists to form the "Mountain." With Louis Blanc, they claimed the right to work, and gloried in the memories of the Convention, whose anniversary they were proposing to celebrate by a democratic banquet. Delescluze, the editor of the *République démocratique et sociale,* worked hard to restore the alliance between the democratic party and the workers' associations, while Proudhon demanded that one-third of all property should be confiscated. The moderate Republicans on the other side were naturally inclined to move towards the Conservative Republicans, who had really nothing republican about them but the name, being secretly in favour of a return to Monarchy. They allowed the Right, led by Falloux, Montalembert, and Thiers, to pass measures inconsistent with the principles of a free democracy. On July 11, 1848, they abolished the right of the great towns to elect their own mayors; they approved decrees restricting the liberty of Clubs and political associations; and passed a series of measures against the Press, which was now obliged "in the interests of property and the family" to lodge security, and admit the supervision of the authorities, and was made liable to ruinous fines. On July 15, the *Manuel Républicain*, written by a large-minded and conscientious philosopher, Renouvier, was suppressed; and Carnot, the Minister of Public Instruction, resigned on finding that his scheme for elementary education was criticised, and that he was deserted by the Republicans who voted with the Conservative supporters of Church and Monarchy.

Such were the conditions under which, in September and October 1848, the Constitution was discussed which was to decide the future of democracy, to crown the edifice of Justice, Fraternity, and Peace founded in February, and to inaugurate a new era for France. Born in the tumultuous time between the civil war and the dictatorship, it came as a sort of hurried conclusion of a drama that had severed Paris from the provinces, had sundered the classes, and even split the Republicans in twain. Armand Marrast laid it before the Assembly on September 4 with a report, the tone of which rather suggested his own newspaper articles than the responsibility of a statesman. To the deputies and the nation, distressed by sanguinary conflicts, he offered a programme of republican dogma and social politics, the vagueness of which was in singular contrast with the remarkable definiteness in the division of parties and of facts. "Revolutions," he said, "are justified by the law of progress." He defined the order of things which was based on universal suffrage, as the reign of equality corrected by liberty; as the condition most favourable to the growth of liberty of all sorts, of speech, of the Press, of associations; and as the best guarantee for the succour of the world's disinherited and poor.

The Assembly, in its turn, seemed to be ready to legislate at once in this sense. They voted almost unanimously a preamble to the Constitution so philosophically drawn up as to suggest an intention of imitating the method of Armand Marrast. Tocqueville, a member of the Committee, in one chapter of his *Memoirs,* has given us a picture of its deliberations and their objects. The text of the Constitution was first drafted by the president, Cormenin, a jurist, and underwent very little discussion except on the question of one Chamber or more. But the members of the Legislative Committee differed to such an extent in tendencies, tone, and method that their only chance of coming to a common result was by avoiding debate on all matters on which division was possible, and all questions of principle. "We were all afraid," said Tocqueville, "of getting into bitter and interminable discussions if we tried to go to the bottom of things, and we preferred to remain in apparent agreement by treating them only superficially. We plodded on in this fashion to the end, invoking large principles in dealing with small details, and putting together the whole machine of government bit by bit, without having a clear idea of the relative strength of the various wheels, or of the way in which their work was to combine."

This was the behaviour of the Committee, and, so far as

this business was concerned, the behaviour of the Assembly. The preamble first adopted stated that the Republican system would enable men to "walk more freely along the path of progress and civilisation, ensure a more equal distribution of duties and benefits, and by its laws and institutions assist citizens to reach a higher standard of morality, prosperity, and enlightenment." They recognised the existence of higher rights and duties, anterior to any written laws; but they did not say whether the laws which they were then enacting did or did not conform to this vague and really undefined code. And why talk of the benefits of free education, while they were dismissing Carnot and quashing his educational scheme? They were actually doing away with the National Workshops at the moment when they were engaging on behalf of either the State or the Departments to establish centres of public work for the unemployed. This grand but—temporarily at any rate—impossible scheme was carried unanimously, revealing the anxiety of the Assembly to discharge its debt to the People in words, being unable to agree in fact upon any fundamental democratic or social reform.

In the Assembly, as previously in the Committee, the only question which called for any lively debate was that of the organisation of the sovereign authority. The matter longest discussed was, whether there should be one Legislative Chamber or two. On September 27, Lamartine and Dupin, who were in favour of one, obtained a majority of only 40 votes against Duvergier de Hauranne and Barrot who held the other view. The Republicans were beginning to be alarmed at the notion of an ambitious dictator who might assert his authority by playing off one Chamber against the other. The only counterpoise to the single Assembly to which they would consent was a Council of State elected by the Assembly to prepare and discuss projected laws.

Had the whole republican party reasoned consistently, they would have rejected on principle the proposal of the Constituent Committee that there should be a President elected by the People, by universal suffrage. The Committee had not sufficiently considered the danger of placing face to face two powers, a President and an Assembly, with equal rights, inasmuch as both were derived from the same source, and yet without means of mutual control. Looked at thus, the Constitution was seen to be sowing the seeds of an inevitable struggle, the issue of which could only be determined by force, and therefore in favour of the dictator in command of the army. Some Republicans, especially Jules Grévy and Flocon, pointed out the danger. Lamartine's fears of a dictatorship were not strong enough to induce him to give up this point, on which the future destiny of the Republic eventually turned. He supported his views with all his eloquence, and carried them by a majority of 500, on October 2, 1848.

The experience of the United States was cited; but it was not noticed that in that country the President is elected not by the People directly, but by a special convention elected *ad hoc* by the People; and that his Ministers are not responsible to the Legislature, but that all of them, President and Ministers alike, are, in respect of the laws and constitution of the United States, controlled by the Supreme Court, whose authority and power are far beyond those of the French *Cour de Cassation.* Nor did the Republicans stop to consider—perhaps they did not even notice—the great difference between the meagre resources at the disposal of the President of a Federal Republic like the United States, and the power wielded by the Chief of a centralised Republic like France, where the head of the Executive can dispose, in the name of the People, of some 400,000 employés whom he appoints and pays, of an army of salaried officials, of all the machinery of law, and finally can rely on the nation accepting with docility the lead of the central power, to which it has been accustomed—or is content—to look for internal order, for freedom of belief, for the security of its property, and for the defence of the interests and traditions of the country in its relations with Europe.

The whole Constitution was definitely settled on October 23. With the exception of some discussions on religious liberty and administrative decentralisation, which occupied some sittings on October 18 and 19, no single question occupied the Chamber for any length of time except the definition of the presidential powers; the duration of the office was reduced to four years, and immediate re-election was forbidden.

Monarchy had been dead for barely six months, and the rule of democracy, the only one which now seemed possible in France, had scarcely begun. Already the French People, seeing their own incapacity for reconciling order and democracy, were beginning to incline to a democratic monarchy, an inclination of which the dictatorship of Cavaignac had been the first symptom. No doubt the General had resigned his extraordinary powers with perfect correctness on June 28, and, at the request of the Assembly, had formed a Ministry which seemed to represent the views of the majority. General Bedeau took the Foreign Office in the place of Bastide, who became Minister of Marine (though on July 15 he returned to the Foreign Office); Bethmont took the place of Marie as Minister of Justice; Sénart, the President of the Assembly, took the Ministry of the Interior; Goudchaux the Finances; General Lamoricière the Ministry of War; Hippolyte Carnot that of Public Instruction (till his withdrawal owing to an adverse vote of the Assembly on July 5); Recurt the Ministry of Public Works. Taken as a whole, it was just the Ministry required to serve the purposes of an Assembly building up a democratic constitution.

True, its head, Cavaignac, was a soldier, yet in the midst of the revolutionary earthquakes of Europe, it remained a Ministry of peace; indeed, it wanted a little glory to make it more popular. "There is often more courage wanted," so Bastide said in his circular of August 25, "in a country so touchy on all questions of honour, for pleading the cause of peace than for advising war." Cavaignac might, if he had chosen, have responded to the appeal of the Italians in their trouble, of Manin hard-pressed in Venice, or of Guerrieri and Ricci when sent on a mission to Paris by Charles Albert and the Lombards (July 28 and August 3); indeed Generals Oudinot and Lamoricière implored him to allow the French army to cross the Alps. He refused, backed up by Bastide, being determined not to risk the fate of France in this European *mêlée,* in which other interests were involved besides the liberty of the nations.

Supported by his Ministers, and in agreement with the democrats of the Assembly, he thought it wiser to maintain peace, and thus have time to consider the legislation required to develop the material prosperity of the working classes in town and country. Thanks to this, all the hopes that the Republic had aroused were not yet extinguished. Opposed alike to the demands of the Socialist leaders, who with their "Right to Work" were calling for a corresponding transformation in the "Right to Property," and to the conservative doctrines of economists who denied the Republican State any right of intervention between workmen and employers, Sénart carried a law for 12-hours labour in August 1848. Subsidies were granted to Societies for Cooperative Production, and encouragement given to Societies for Mutual Assistance. Tourret, Minister for Agriculture, carried a law for creating centres of instruction in Agricultural Physics on October 3, 1848: and by a law dated September 15,

12,000 volunteer colonists were planted in Algeria, the population of which was at that time increasing very rapidly. Commercial relations were facilitated by a law of August 24 reducing the postage on letters over all French territory to 20 centimes. Laws were passed for the regulation of heavy transport; funds were voted for the upkeep of country roads, high roads, and canals; and enquiries were instituted as to the mercantile marine.

If the condition of public finances prevented the members of the Ministry from carrying out their ideas of buying up the railways and of providing universal free education, they only abandoned them under pressure and in consequence of the opposition of the Conservatives, who dreaded what Thiers mistakenly called "communism," the intervention of the State for the assistance of the lower classes. They had at least the merit of actually presenting, in the form of practicable legislation, the outline of a programme which would repair the breaches made by the civil war, and help towards the welfare of the entire nation. The task was not an easy one at that moment, especially as, in the clash of noisy and violent argument, in Parliament and in public, on the political and social principles of the new order of things, nobody noticed its existence. The Government was still only provisional, and could not boast either of vitality or prestige.

On September 17, 1848, new elections were held. In five Departments the People again voted for Louis Napoleon Bonaparte. The most characteristic feature of these elections was that in Paris, where the Conservative Republicans and the Socialists found themselves face to face, out of a total of 274,000 electors the majority that voted for either Fould or Raspail, the candidates of these two parties, was larger than the number given to the nephew of the great Emperor alone. Standing between Conservatives and Socialists, and in agreement with them both,

Louis Napoleon continued to strengthen his relations with the electors. In former days he had not seemed to be destined to any great success; and his clumsy conspiracies against Louis Philippe had earned him only imprisonment and exile. But he had been prudent enough to retire to England till he had been forgotten, to wait his opportunity, and leave his friends to act. Their zeal and activity in the Assembly, in the Press, and in popular meetings had been so efficacious that the malcontents were beginning to centre all their hopes on him. The Socialists and the working-men, whose punishment for the days of June the Assembly was carrying into effect by the Commission of Enquiry of August 1848, began to bethink themselves that this nephew of Napoleon had published something in favour of the working class. Some of the democrats hoped that a Napoleon might give them a policy of glory and of Liberal propagandism, which Lamartine and Cavaignac objected to as much as Guizot. Lastly there were already signs that the Royalists were considering whether it might not suit them to use a man whom they considered to be a pinchbeck sort of prince as a docile instrument for expressing their political and religious demands.

The elections of September 17, 1848, afforded an opportunity of which Louis Napoleon, who had withdrawn from the previous contest in June, thought it wise now to avail himself. He took his seat in the Assembly, hailed by some as the champion of order, by others as the champion of democracy. He was very careful to leave the doubt unsolved, speaking rarely, and never voting on any crucial question. He reserved himself for private conversations in his house at Auteuil, sometimes with Proudhon, at other times with Monarchists. Thus he reaped in silence all the harvest of the opposition which the republican and moderate policy of General Cavaignac was exciting in the two extremes, Right and Left. With a body-guard of intriguers devoted to his cause, he got the full benefit of this coalition between the malcontents who wished for reactionary measures, and those who favoured an energetic advance.

During his last months in office, October and November, Cavaignac had become fully aware of the Prince's aims, and tried to frustrate them. Risking the displeasure of the moderate Republicans who had entrusted him with power in June, he attempted to get the support of the Royalists, so as to detach them from the "President," as they were beginning to call Louis Napoleon. On October 13, he called up Dufaure to the Ministry of the Interior, Vivien to that of Public Works, and (on the 25th) Trouvé-Chauvel to that of Finance. These were the most sensible of the men who were intriguing in the Committee of the Rue de Poitiers against the Republic, but who were nevertheless capable of giving loyal service to a Conservative Republic, if they became its Ministers. The proceeding alarmed the democrats, who on November 25, 1848, did not hesitate to charge Cavaignac with treachery; but the Assembly, persuaded of the loyalty of the General, acquitted him once more by a large majority. While however he had thus lost the confidence of the Republicans, he had not succeeded in bringing over the Conservatives, Thiers, Molé, Odilon Barrot, and many others, who were preparing to turn him out.

The General next tried to gain over the Catholics, who were disturbed by the insurrection of the Italian revolutionary patriots against the Papacy, and their assassination of Rossi (November 15, 1848). Now, though France had so far refused to intervene with armed hand against Austria, Bastide had no idea of seeing the Italian princes surrender to her at discretion. On the first tidings of the Roman insurrection, Cavaignac sent M. de Corcelles on a mission to Rome, and on November 30 obtained the authority of the Assembly for the despatch thither of an expeditionary corps, which might relieve Pius IX from the necessity of applying for Austrian help. These proceedings caused still further uneasiness to the democrats of Paris, and were not more successful in Rome, for the Pope declined the assistance of the French Republic as offered to him by the Comte d'Harcourt and M. de Corcelles, applied for aid to Austria, and took refuge at Gaeta in the company of the King of Naples on November 23, 1848. To foreigners it looked as if Cavaignac was playing false to the Revolution without gaining the confidence of the Church. The Ultramontanes, headed by de Falloux and Montalembert, were more inclined to reckon upon Louis Napoleon for the defence of the temporal power in Rome, and the triumph of their doctrine in France.

Weary it may be, anxious to make an end of it, and sick at heart at calumny and injustice, Cavaignac took upon himself to advance the date of the Presidential election. December 10 was the day on which the French People was called upon to choose a man to govern France for four years, in the place and office of the King now no more, wiped out of the memory of the nation in which he had once played so great a part. They elected Louis Napoleon Bonaparte by an enormous majority of five and a half million votes against a million and a half for Cavaignac, and 570,000 for Ledru-Rollin, on the power of whose name the democrats had counted largely. Seven thousand votes were all that were given throughout France for Lamartine, who ten months before would have been chosen by acclamation. "Victrix causa Deis placuit, sed victa Catoni," said the great poet some days earlier in the Assembly, being already resigned to defeat and to the collapse of his dream of liberty and justice.

On December 20 the "Prince President," as he was now to be called, was sworn in before the President of the

Constituent Assembly. The oath bound him to remain faithful to the democratic Republic, and to fulfil all the duties imposed upon him by the Constitution. Whatever was the real import of the popular election that had carried him to success, there is no doubt that the recollections of the Napoleonic legend, especially in country districts, the dreams "of a new era of triumphs, the fear of communism or of clerical reaction had misled the mind of a nation only too ready to accept a master." And in all the political parties there was from this time forth no other man equally competent to save democracy from its own mistakes. The defeat of Cavaignac involved the disappearance of the remnant of convinced or moderate Republicans, as the insurrection of June had involved that of the Socialists and Radicals.

At the actual moment when the name of democratic Republic was being formally recorded on the list of French Constitutions, not one of the men who had proclaimed it in the preceding February over the ruins of the Orleanist Monarchy remained in power to watch over its organisation or defence. Henceforth the only alternatives offered to the French People were, either to return to a bourgeois monarchy—the fall of the last having not so much displeased as surprised them—or to advance towards a monarchy of the People, a copy of that radiant original to which the name of Bonaparte was attached.

CHAPTER X

THE PRESIDENCY OF LOUIS NAPOLEON

"When I gave my adhesion to the candidature of Prince Louis," said Thiers to his monarchist friends, "it was not in any high hope of finding in him another First Consul. I supported him for a very simple reason, as a plank from the general shipwreck of Monarchism. I thought it better to cling to that plank, and use it to establish our present semi-monarchic, semi-republican system."

No words could better describe the transitional condition of France in the period between the election of the Prince President and the *Coup d'État* of three years later. The two authorities created by the Constitution—the one to make the law, the other to carry it out, without appeal from one to the other, and clothed with equal authority by the universal suffrage of the nation—were very soon working, the one to obtain the assent of the country to a republican dictatorship, the other for a republic under monarchist leading. The only Minister who was willing after December 10, 1848, to serve both parties at the same time in working for these two objects, the incompatibility of which three years later provoked the *Coup d'État,* was Odilon Barrot. Barrot was a Monarchist, who was now opposed to the Revolution of 1848 after having hurried it on, a man of such self-conceit as to believe himself to be, with the name of Napoleon as a figure-head, the destined chief of the

Republic, now that Lamartine had declined the offer of the Prince President, made on the morrow of his election, of a place in his Administration.

The Ministry formed by Odilon Barrot was, like himself, half-republican, half-monarchist—Drouyn de Lhuys at the Foreign Office, de Tracy as Minister of Marine, H. Passy at Finance, de Malleville at the Interior, all former adversaries of Guizot, and now, since 1848, of the democrats. The Prefecture of the Seine was given to Berger, a friend of Odilon Barrot, and formerly an Orleanist deputy; the military government of Paris and the command of the National Guard to General Changarnier, who combined these offices in spite of the law; the command of the Army of the Alps to General Bugeaud, with residence at Lyons, whence he could overawe the democracy of Paris. The Ministry were forced by the delicate nature of their task to make all use of the power which fifty years of centralisation in France had given to the Government, and were making ready to substitute for the existing Prefects, Generals, and Magistrates, men who would docilely carry out their instructions. The difficulty was that these instructions in no way agreed with the intentions of the Assembly, the majority of which, though split into "Mountaineers" and Moderates, was still purely and frankly republican. The name of its President, Armand Marrast, was a sufficient pledge of that fact. "The Assembly," said Odilon Barrot, "was our greatest and most pressing difficulty."

In the last months of 1848 the Constituent Assembly tried to prolong its own existence, although the Constitution had already been brought into operation by the election of a President. Feeling themselves threatened, both Democrats and Moderates, who had been fighting for so long, insisted that there were sundry organic laws that must be settled before they broke up, laws as to elections, the Council of State, and the responsibility of the President and his Ministers. This was the reply twice given by Jules Grévy, on December 28 and January 25, to the demands for dissolution put forward by sundry deputies at the prompting of Ministers. On January 29, by the orders of the Ministry and with the assent of the President, General Changarnier called under arms the Army of Paris and the National Guard, surrounded the Assembly with troops, without giving any warning to Armand Marrast, and summoned them to dissolve. They did so, but not without opposition, by a majority of five. The Ministry had used violence, or the threat of violence, against the deputies; and they had invited the President to hold a review of the columns massed round the Assembly, by way of obtaining the support of his popularity. He here learnt the usefulness of *Coups d'État.*

The Republic was now entering into the second period of its history; after insurrections, acts of violence on the part of the People against the Government, came the *Coups d'État,* acts of violence on the part of the Government against the People and their representatives. On that day, it was the opinion of many that Louis Napoleon might have seized the opportunity of "going to the Tuileries." "The People, the officials, and the Army were either enthusiastically cheering him, or at least bowing obediently before his fortune." But for the moment he thought it wiser to let his Ministers take the benefit, as they had taken the initiative, of the proceeding. While they fancied that they were making use of him, his name, and his popularity as obedient instruments, he kept in the background, secretly making good his road in the direction which they were opening out to him towards a democratic dictatorship.

It is desirable at this point to form some idea of the person of the dictator, and also of the aspirations of the French People. No livelier or truer portrait of the President can be given than that of Tocqueville, who saw and studied him at that time in close intimacy, and who was a man of clear and unprejudiced judgment. As a private individual, Louis Napoleon had some engaging qualities, kindly and easy in temper, humane of character, gentle and tender in sentiment and of great simplicity. Capable of feeling affection, he was also a man to inspire it. "There is a great charm," wrote Queen Victoria six years later, "in the quiet frank manner of the Emperor. Any amiability and affection shown to him has a lasting effect on his temperament, which is curiously inclined to tenderness." Moreover he could show a fine coolness and courage in moments of crisis or danger, another quality to endear him as a chief to his friends and adherents, and also to the People. His intellect was weaker than his heart, being incoherent and confused, filled with great thoughts ill-assorted, and tendencies rather than reflections, inclining him towards dreaminess and unreality through his German education and his leaning to sentimentality. Although he could certainly bring some subtlety of thought and judgment to bear on the details of a matter, his principal fault was that he had no decision or strength of character. He spoke little, for fear of having to take a side, and he practised dissimulation, which he had learnt in Italian conspiracies, and even lying, through sheer feebleness. A taste for the lower pleasures, which had weakened his bodily powers and paralysed his will, had led him into the company of dependents and servants, and even of footmen, which did not tend to his improvement. His gambler's faith in his fortune, in his star, his confidence in the future that his birth reserved for him, served him for a long time in the place of any fixed and matured plan—"a prince of chance, an adventurer," said Tocqueville, "not a statesman." In 1849 he took advantage of his opportunity, though in so doing he risked a loss. He bided his time, concealing his ambition. He used secrecy in recruiting adherents, and nursed his popularity with care.

On December 24, in the full uniform of a General of the National Guard, with white plumes to his cocked hat, and the broad riband of the Legion of Honour, surrounded by a staff of officers and friends, he held a review of the bourgeois army and the regular troops, and was greeted with cheers. Some days later, by a letter which very closely resembled an order, he compelled the two sole representatives of republican principles on the Council to resign their seats. He threw open the salons of the Elysée for brilliant receptions, which were the talk of Paris, particularly one on New Year's Day 1849, which displayed well-nigh all the pomp of royalty. The installation of his cousin Jerôme as Governor of the Invalides was purposely carried out with special solemnity, and served to assist alike the legend and the family. Editors exhibited for sale numerous works on the Emperor, and "Napoleon Albums" illustrated by Raffet and Charlet. Daily newspapers, including even the *Débats*, published "Napoleon Almanacks.' On January 29 his progress in the midst of the troops massed round the Assembly was almost triumphal; and shouts of "Vive l'Empereur!" were mingled with those of "Vive Napoléon!"

The Prince President was feeling the pulse of the nation, but was in no hurry to make his definitive appeal to it, as his flatterers were urging him to do. Being absolutely strange to the atmosphere of parliamentary debate which obscured the vision of politicians, some of whom were his opponents, others his Ministers, but who between them had made out of France two separate worlds—the country for electioneering purposes, and the country as a nation—Louis Napoleon had the wit to discern, beyond the squabbles of parties, assemblies and Ministers, the currents of opinion and of sentiment, embodying the aspirations and essential needs of the French

People, the French bourgeoisie, the democracy both of town and of country, which Guizot and Louis Philippe had ignored.

The Revolution of February had further cemented the alliance between the bourgeoisie and the Church, first by its respect for all free and sincere beliefs and its spirit of broad fraternity, and next through the fear inspired by Socialist violence. The Church leaders, Montalembert, Lacordaire, Mgr Parisis, and de Falloux, whether priests or laymen, had, each in his turn, greeted "the new era of liberty, or, after the month of June, supported the reaction in favour of order, as seemed to them most profitable to the cause." The opposition they had met with in the previous reign had been overwhelmed in the sudden storm which upset not only Louis Philippe but the parliamentary bourgeoisie, in their obstinate determination to refuse to the Church what it had granted to the State University—the right to educate the young. At the end of 1848, the vanquished side had become the zealous and active allies of the victors, who "between the two evils, the domination of the Catholics and the demands of the Socialists, chose the less." "We must show a good front," said Thiers, "to the demagogues, and not let them swallow up the last remnant of social order, the Catholic Establishment." The younger bourgeois had assembled on the summons of Montalembert, had taken their fighting orders from de Falloux, and had submitted to the discipline of Ozanam; but they had for a long time been no more than an advanced guard, until the addition of their elder brethren to their ranks gave them the status of a complete army. In their well-fortified and well-furnished camp at the famous committee-room of the Rue de Poitiers, the watchword generally came from a Catholic source. Nobles and bourgeois, Legitimists and Orleanists, side by side took the field to win recruits in Paris or in the provinces, and secure the triumph of their programme.

In this programme there were at that time only two essential articles—(1) Church Education for the democracy, now called to new political destinies, by virtue of the right to liberty of instruction given in the new Constitution and the overthrow of the monopoly of the University, the only school available to the bourgeois since the legislation of Napoleon; (2) the defence of the Holy See by France, the eldest daughter of the Church, against the attacks of Italian revolutionists. And behind this programme could be felt the activity and ceaseless efforts of the religious orders and communities, the militia of Rome, whose influence had for thirty years been the principal bugbear of Liberal and Voltairian Monarchists, but who now forsooth had suddenly become, in the eyes of these Monarchists and of the Papacy, the guardian-angels of order and property against revolution.

The French bourgeoisie, as a whole, was certainly not prepared to say with Victor Cousin: "Let us throw ourselves at the feet of the Bishops; they alone can save us." The riots of 1848, which overthrew Guizot, naturally checked the current of industrial and financial enterprise which he had encouraged as a means of diverting the minds of Frenchmen from political opposition; and the profits of bourgeois capitalists, great and small, had been affected. Money-making, however, continued to be the main concern of a section of the bourgeoisie that took less interest in the affairs of the Church and religious questions than in material interests. In Paris especially, which was now becoming an industrial town in its outskirts, and a town of luxury and amusement in its central districts, there were numbers of men of the middle class who cared for nothing but the pursuit of wealth and pleasure. The days of June 1848 were scarcely passed, before the theatres had to be reopened, and carriages were seen once more in the Acacia Avenue. It was specially necessary to get business started again after the opening of railways, in order to satisfy the demands of a crowd of young deputies, de Morny, Fould, Magne, and Billault, who had been stopped midway on their road to fortune by the fall of Guizot their patron, and the disciples of the school of Saint-Simon, who, like their master, cared nothing about politics but were intensely interested in economic progress, such as Father Enfantin, Paulin Talabot, Didion, the Pereires, Amail, and Barrault. "We must hear nothing but the clang of the hammer where powder used to speak," said Father Enfantin; "the tribune and the Press should keep silence for a time."

Whether they were religious or material, these wishes or wants of the French bourgeoisie found support among the rural democracy, the bulk of the vast mass which had been suddenly called into political life. Though startled and perhaps gratified by the new Constitution, yet still quite indifferent to its benefits, the peasantry of France soon took alarm on behalf of their land. "Fear," said Tocqueville, "had at first been confined to the higher classes, but soon permeated almost to the bottom of the lower; and an universal terror possessed the provinces." In the rural districts all proprietors, whatever their origin or antecedents or the extent of their property, combined, and formed for this purpose a single class. There was no more pride or jealousy between peasant and proprietor, between noble and bourgeois; instead of these, mutual trust and regard, and reciprocity of kindliness. Possessors of property had become, according to Tocqueville, "a sort of guild. I had never seen anything like it, nor had anyone, within the memory of man." Fear had acted on the masses of the peasantry as it had done on the bourgeois classes, and even more potently; it had brought the two closer together, and armed them for the defence of their material interests to which alone they had seemed for the past hundred years to attach any value. In a word, the French peasantry, while willing to obey any government that would assure them work and a profit off their land, were no longer sure that the Republic gave them a sufficient guarantee for these. Unable to create a suitable political system for themselves, and yet called upon to make use of their power, they were ready to give their votes to any one seductive voice, sage's or charlatan's, Bonapartist or Conservative bourgeois.

The French peasant, though scarcely a religious person, was attached to all the traditional formulae, and in many places still lived under the influence of his priest, a son of the soil like himself, the servant of his bishop, and well broken to discipline. The priest was as necessary and as respected a member of the village community as the policeman, and in his own way a protector of their hearths and homes. Between the rural population and the Catholic bourgeoisie the Clergy formed a link, or, more accurately, a net-work of relations, by means of which the confidential instructions of the Ultramontanes, coming no longer as threats of clerical supremacy, but as tokens of enfranchisement and liberty, were transmitted from Rome to Paris, and from Paris to the provinces. Obedient to these instructions throughout the revolutionary period, the country clergy, affecting the demeanour of altruism and liberty, had made an extraordinary display of activity. They supported Cavaignac against the "Reds," and brought up masses of electors to register for the benefit of Louis Napoleon, as soon as the Catholic chiefs in concert with him gave the signal, on December 1, 1848. They had still, at the beginning of 1849, great power over the village electors, who had no organisation, and even less experience or plan of action, and who, after taking up arms in a body against the revolution in Paris, were now returning with all speed to their work. This was the dominant spirit of the nation, especially in the north, in Normandy and

Brittany, and in all the west down to the Pyrenees, particularly in the Charente—in Lorraine likewise and the immediate neighbourhood of Paris.

This picture of the French nation would be singularly incomplete, if it omitted to note the progress of the democratic and republican spirit in the great towns, the workers' centres, and even in certain purely rural districts. At the date of the Presidential election, the voters in favour of Cavaignac and more especially of Ledru-Rollin were Republicans, numbering 2,000,000 altogether, out of the seven millions and a half who voted. On the eve of the Revolution of February 1848 very few French even thought of a Republic; the democratic Constitution which was then established, more by the logic of facts than by human will, did not depend upon any regularly acknowledged party. When, on the advent of liberty, this party began to group itself, by means of meetings, in Mutual Aid and Cooperative Societies, the bloody struggle of the days of June checked its growth by dividing the Republicans into two groups. The bourgeois reaction that followed that struggle, and the measures adopted by the prefects and magistrates against Clubs and political Associations, after their condemnation as dangerous by the decree of July 28, 1848, brought about some friendly overtures between the democratic Republicans and the People, the former having to admit that something must be granted to the Socialist ideal, the latter learning from its own misfortunes the danger of violence and riot.

On the union of these two forces, the democratic spirit awoke, in Alsace and all the south-east, from Burgundy and the Jura to Provence, in the south on the plains of Languedoc and in the valley of the Garonne, in the manufacturing centres of the Ardennes, at Rheims, Rethel, and Sedan, from the Doubs to Montbéliard and Besançon, in parts of La Nièvre and the Cher, in the mining and manufacturing region of the Allier and the Loire, in the Lyons district, in parts of Auvergne and the Limousin, and finally in Paris in the workmen's quarters and among the factories. It depended on the district, whether working-men or bourgeois and peasantry were in the majority; their propaganda was active, and carried on in every café by means of journals from Paris, the *Réforme* or the *Démocratie*, with some local sheets belonging to the republican bourgeoisie.

The Prince President, keeping a watchful eye on the diverging and even contradictory wishes of the various classes and groups of the French nation, anxious not to collide with anyone, and always on the look-out for new adherents, allowed the various political parties to work their propaganda, and was very careful not to meddle with them directly. During the early months of 1849, these parties were preparing for the election of the next Assembly, which was to take the place of the Constituent. The Catholic Committee of the Rue de Poitiers combined all the forces of Conservatism under the direction and for the benefit of the Church—"for the salvation of society," they said. They collected subscriptions in Paris and in the provinces, and persuaded M. de Falloux, the Minister of Public Education, to bring in a Bill on the Education of the People, and on liberty of instruction. They subsidised and distributed newspapers and pamphlets against communism, and tracts in favour of ultramontane doctrine. "Woe to the village-churches, if Socialism triumphs!" cried Montalembert, the eloquent chief of the Catholic party, who had nominated himself to the leadership of this league formed under the banner of liberty to save society through the Church.

The Republicans on their side rallied round Ledru-Rollin, who served as a point of union for the forces of the People. They preached with increased vigour among the working-men, held out new promises of social reforms, and scattered broadcast through the workshops and even through the country-side manuals and tracts on democracy. In the Assembly, they were working their hardest to keep the Catholics from getting hold of the education of the People, which was likely to fall to them through M. de Falloux' Bill, and the consequent Commission of which Thiers was president, and the Catholics de Riancey, de Melun, and Dupanloup, with a small sprinkling of University men, were members. On February 8, Jules Simon had tried in vain to induce the Constituent to pass a resolution, before it dissolved, in favour of liberty for schools, on republican principles, free from all monopoly, and protected against the interference of the Church Between the two parties who were contending for the votes of Frenchmen in the May elections, this question involved the principal stake in the game. Montalembert fought through "Electoral Committees for Freedom of Education"; the Democrats summoned the schoolmasters to their assistance in the provinces and villages.

Taciturn as ever, and skilful in non-committal, Louis Napoleon gave no opinion. Most of his Ministers, M. de Tracy, Rulhieres, Faucher, and especially Falloux, "who represented in the Ministry nothing but the Church," were inclined to favour the Committee of the Rue de Poitiers. But Odilon Barrot the Premier, Passy, and Drouyn de Lhuys hesitated, like the President, before taking a side. Louis Napoleon was awaiting the future; his Ministers wanted to secure the present.

Foreign politics and the Roman question, which at the end of December had reached the stage of acute crisis, obliged the Odilon Barrot Ministry to deal more summarily with the two parties who were bidding for the mastery of France, and to come to some decision. Cavaignac had previously been obliged to promise the assistance of France to the Pope, when driven from Rome. And, in order to secure the support of the Catholics, on the eve of his election to the Presidency, Louis Napoleon had come to an understanding with Dupanloup and Montalembert for the defence of the Temporal Power. If he had been inclined to forget his promise, he had by his side de Falloux (who had been invited to take office by their common friend Persigny and by Dupanloup), to recall it to him. He went so far as to write a letter to the *Univers* on December 7 asserting that the maintenance of the Temporal Sovereignty of the Pope "was closely bound up both with the glory of catholicity, and with the liberty and independence of Italy." It is not surprising therefore that on December 23, 1848, he allowed his Ministers to decide upon sending assistance to Pope Pius IX at Gaeta.

Against this decision, as well as against the proposal as to liberty of education, the French Republicans protested from the beginning of January 1849, invoking the precise terms of the Constitution, which forbade the French Republic to intervene in quarrels between rulers and subjects. Louis Napoleon, embarrassed between his memories of the campaign carried on in the Romagna on behalf of liberty in 1831, and his promises to the Catholics before the late election, devised a very clever method of evading the difficulty. Inasmuch as the patriot Gioberti, who was constantly pressing him through his friend Arese to intervene against Austria beyond the Alps, was also a Minister of Charles Albert, King of Sardinia, he proposed to urge the King to offer help to the Pope, and possibly to back him up with French troops, if the Austrians would not give way. "An indirect intervention, worthy of the Jesuits!" Ledru-Rollin shouted in the Constituent Assembly. But the Italian revolutionists forced Gioberti to resign at Turin (Feb. 20, 1849), proclaimed a Republic in Rome (Feb. 9) under Saffi, Mazzini, and Armellini, and forced Charles Albert by a threat of the same fate to renew the war against Austria, unsupported, on March 12. In the meantime Drouyn de Lhuys, the Minister of the French Republic, to serve the purposes of the President, invited the European Powers to a conference in Brussels, and advised Pius IX to eschew the assistance of Austria. The defeat, however, of the King of Sardinia at Novara on March 23, and his abdication, made an end of the combinations of the Elysée for helping the Pope without provoking the anger of French Republicans or encroaching on the liberty of the Romans.

What the Republicans of the Constituent Assembly would then have liked, was that the French troops should march, not on Rome, but on Piedmont, to deliver the young King Victor Emmanuel from the grasp of the Austrians (March 31). What the French Catholics asked for was vigorous action in Italy on behalf of the Pope. For a moment it looked as if the Prince President would be unable to resist the despairing appeals of the Italians, when brought to their knees by Austria in the war for liberty against the hereditary enemy for which the Liberals and the People of France had clamoured; but the Ministers Odilon Barrot and Drouyn de Lhuys now opposed him in their turn, alleging the danger of reckless action and of the revolutionary propaganda. Thiers implored him on behalf of the Conservatives to act. He did better; in an interview with Baron Hübner, the Austrian representative in Paris, he was able to persuade Austria not to invade Piedmont. On April 16, 1849, as there was no further need of interfering on behalf of Piedmont, the Ministers were free to rescue the Papacy. They therefore asked the Constituent for a credit to enable them to send an expeditionary corps to Civita Vecchia. Louis Napoleon yielded to their entreaties under pressure from the Catholics, but only on the condition that the alleged object of the expedition should be the protection of Rome from the threatened invasion of Austria, the safe-guarding of French influence in Italy, and the liberty of the people.

The defenders of the Temporal Power were no doubt satisfied with the intentions of the Ministry. But the Assembly only consented after long debate to discuss and accept the project, as an act of mediation between the Pope and his subjects, with the hope of the restoration of the former and the enfranchisement of the latter. "The idea of the Government has not been," said Drouyn de Lhuys and Odilon Barrot, "to impose upon the Roman people a system of government opposed to their desires, nor to force upon the Pope, when restored to the exercise of his temporal power, any one system more than another. The object of our expedition has been to facilitate a resumption of friendly relations, and to give to the Holy Father, and to all whether at Gaeta or in Rome who wish to cooperate, the support they will require to overcome the obstacles raised by foreign influence or evil passions."

If this was a sincere statement, their policy scarcely corresponded to the wishes of the extreme members of the two parties, democrat and Catholic, who were then getting ready for the elections on the dissolution of the Constituent. The Catholics accepted it with the intention of modifying it, hoping before long to turn this armed mediation into a crusade on behalf of the Holy See. The Republicans of the Mountain, Ledru-Rollin and Arago, would have preferred an expedition in aid of the Republic of Rome, or none at all. The Ministry had great difficulty in obtaining the necessary credits; but, having got them, they lost no time in using them. On April 25, 1849, a French squadron landed a small division under the command of General Oudinot at Civita Vecchia.

The instructions given to General Oudinot had been drawn up by Drouyn de Lhuys without reference to Odilon Barrot, and, even as drafted, involved more vigorous action than the vote of the Assembly countenanced. The General was directed to re-establish order in the Roman

States, without regard to the Republican Government, whose power was described as "irregular, opposed to the wishes of right-thinking men and of the great majority of the people." It was difficult for him not to consider himself authorised to give battle to the Republic of Mazzini and destroy it. And, when Pius IX received in audience at Gaeta the officer detailed by Oudinot to pay his respects to him, he believed that France had come to defend the Holy See, and to spend her blood and her treasure on the pious task. He fully intended, by means of this help, whatever might be the hopes of Drouyn de Lhuys to the contrary, to effect his complete restoration, unfettered by any condition or by the slightest concession to Liberalism. This was the pill—said the French envoy at Gaeta—"which France and the Assembly had to swallow without qualms."

The General expected to attain his object by a sudden attack. Having received from the Roman Assembly a protest against the French invasion, he sent two officers to Rome on April 26 with a practical ultimatum; then, urged by de Rayneval and d'Harcourt, who advised him to enter Rome as soon as possible in the name of the Pope, on April 29 he led his forces to the gates of the city. On the 30th he was repulsed by the Republicans, and retreated forthwith to send for reinforcements and siege guns from Paris. The news reached the Ministers on May 3; Odilon Barrot was in despair, and kept the matter secret for a couple of days; the public did not hear of it till the 7th, and was seriously disturbed thereby. In the sitting of the Assembly that took place on the same day, Jules Favre charged the Ministers with "incapacity or treachery." After a stormy debate, which would have brought about the fall of the Ministry if it had been responsible to Parliament, it was resolved by a majority of 100, "that the expedition should be no longer diverted from its proper object." The Assembly required Drouyn de

Lhuys to send a diplomatic agent to repair the mischief done by the affair of April 30, and to present himself to the Romans in the name of France in the character of a mediator.

On May 8 the Ministers and the Prince President entrusted this delicate mission to M. de Lesseps, whose energy and Liberalism were possibly equal to the task. Odilon Barrot himself declared afterwards that the Ministers only wished to prove their respect for the Assembly, "and to mark time, till the day came, and that soon, when the elections would free them from its interference." The Prince President did not show even that amount of scruple; as head of the army, and a soldier above everything, he could not imagine his troops standing still under a rebuff. On May 8 he supplied the *Patrie* with a copy of a letter which he had sent to General Oudinot by the hand of M. de Lesseps, stating his deliberate intention of dealing with the question as one in which their honour was pledged. General Changarnier ordered it to be read out to the troops on every parade-ground in Paris; he wished "to strengthen yet further the tie between the army and the President, and to mark the contrast between his language and that of the republican deputies who, when their soldiers were actually under the enemy's fire, could find no better encouragement to give them than a repudiation of their action." A struggle was thus started in Paris between the policy of the Assembly, to whom Ministers had made a seeming concession, and that of the Prince President, who had made up his mind to destroy the Roman Republic by force of arms.

Here was a splendid opportunity for inducing French Catholics to take up the defence of the Church: this was exactly the platform wanted by the Committee of the Rue de Poitiers. The honour of the Church as well as that of the army required satisfaction. By this means

M. de Falloux brought Louis Napoleon round to the views and wishes of his party. The alliance he had entered into with the Ultramontanes on the eve of his election was drawn closer. His letter to Oudinot was a sort of appeal to the people as final judges. While the indignant Republicans of the Assembly wanted to impeach the President on May 11, Léon Faucher, Minister of the Interior, taking up the combined cause of the Catholics, the Holy See, and the President's policy, sent the prefects, on May 12, the day before the elections, a list of the deputies hostile to the Roman expedition, with instructions to prevent their re-election. He had the impudence to describe them as "Revolutionists ready to bring back the days of June." The same charges were made in every constituency by the Catholic journals, now assured of the cooperation of the President; every public man who did not profess his agreement with the Committee of the Rue de Poitiers or seemed indifferent to the liberation of the Pope, heard himself described to his fellow-countrymen as "a Red, a rioter, a socialist, a contemner of the army and of the national honour," the latter being designedly confused with the interests of the Holy See. To the great satisfaction of Conservatives and Monarchists of every shade, it appeared that "France had only two possibilities before her, a military expedition to Rome, or a social revolution in Paris." After four months' shilly-shallying, the Odilon Barrot Ministry and the Prince President had created this situation which won them the next elections.

On May 13, 1849, the Catholic Conservatives won 18 seats out of 28 in Paris, and 450 out of 700 in the provinces—a great triumph for the Committee of the Rue de Poitiers, who had selected the candidates and supported them. While their opponents had gone into the fray united in favour of the Catholic cause, the Republicans had been split up. The Moderates, Arago, Bastide, Lamartine,

Marrast, Carnot, Jules Favre, and all their friends had refused to present themselves to the electors as allies of the combined Democrats and Socialists, under Ledru-Rollin, Madier de Montjau, and Greppo, who had united in defence of republican institutions. By this they gained nothing; under universal suffrage, flagrantly misused by the Catholics, who treated all Republicans as Socialists in spite of disclaimer, and deliberately deceived by the prefects, the nation had rejected them altogether. The collapse was complete. Dupont de l'Eure, the most popular of the party, received only 40,000 instead of 270,000 votes. This put an end to the attempt at mediation which these Moderates had carried on—with difficulty indeed—between the Democrats, passionate for liberty up to the point of insurrection, and the bourgeoisie, the main-stays of order even to tolerance of an ecclesiastical or military tyranny. From this point of view the most significant defeat was that of Lamartine. He disappeared at the moment of the triumph of the Catholic party in alliance with Louis Napoleon over the Democrats, who appealed despairingly to the people against the decision.

For in Paris only ten Democrats had been elected, the highest polling 30,000 votes less than the most favoured of the Conservatives. In the provinces 200 deputies devoted to democratic institutions had been rejected. It was a real victory for Ledru-Rollin, who had succeeded in restoring harmony between his friends and the working classes after their divisions over the June riots. He was elected in five departments and obtained two million votes, the same number that Cavaignac and he together scored for the Presidency. Entire departments in the east, in Alsace, Franche-Comté, in the valley of the Rhone, in central France, Loir et Cher, Cher, Nièvre, and la Creuse had pronounced in favour of a democratic and socialistic Republic. Even in the army, though so carefully worked upon by its chiefs, the Democrats had succeeded in gaining some adherents. After having despaired of their cause as lost through the fatal split of 1848 and the rebuff suffered by General Cavaignac, the Republicans greeted the present results as a victory. They failed to get a majority, but they could profit by every fresh step in advance effected by the activity of a compact and vigorous minority. Their great mistake was in making too violent a display of their hopes. They did not understand the tactics of their enemies in the Ministry and the Elysée, who aimed at keeping the country, already only too willing to sacrifice its liberty to its love of order and tranquillity, in a state of terror. Their first duty should have been to inspire the country with confidence. They drove Faucher into resignation. On May 19 they were very angry at a proposal for allowing Changarnier to hold the military governorship of Paris and the command of the National Guard together. "I will beat them and it shall cost nothing," replied the General. On May 22 Ledru-Rollin and Sarrans spoke in favour of an active propaganda on behalf of the liberty of the people, in fact the exact contrary of the President's work in Rome. While Changarnier, affecting to anticipate a riot, ordered all the troops to remain in barracks, the "Mountaineers" were proposing to make the Assembly declare itself in permanent session, like the Convention. But the Convention meant the Terror; and nothing suited the Conservative party better than this revival of the memories of 1793. The hopes of the Mountaineers and their provocative action furthered the designs of the Catholics, who now awaited impatiently to see the Papacy restored by General Oudinot and his troops, as the pledge and indication of their own success in France.

Amid this general fever of expectation, the members of the new Parliament elected on May 13, 1849, hailed the dispersal of the late Assembly. Only a year ago it had met, feared and postponed as long as possible by the People of Paris, then the masters of the government of France, though since despoiled of it; now the new Assembly was to give them cause to regret the old. To the late Assembly they owed their democratic suffrage and Constitution, a political liberty full of promise for the future, on the condition that they addressed their demands to a free and representative Government and were careful to avoid frightening the country by violence. The fear of disturbances, and the resulting confusion in the relations between the party of order and the Church party, were once more leading the French nation, and especially the bourgeoisie, in spite of the desperate efforts of the old Assembly and its devotion to liberty up to its last hour, towards a monarchical system less liberal even than that of Louis Philippe, a Church-supported Monarchy resembling that of Charles X, or, to go still further back, the Consulate.

The Legislative Assembly, invested by the Constitution and the vote of the nation with the right of acting and speaking on behalf of France, was destined to begin its career with a sort of crusade, in the shape of a struggle with the Romans for the restoration of the Papacy. And yet it would have been easy to avoid it. Faithful to the wishes of the Constituent, Ferdinand de Lesseps had been able, immediately on his arrival in Rome, to arrange for the submission of the Republicans to the Papal authority, on the condition that Pius IX should grant them certain liberties and a Constitution. He had experienced more trouble in staying the conflict between General Oudinot, who was determined to have his revenge, and Mazzini and Garibaldi, equally determined to stop him by the forces of the people. But on May 16, 1849, Oudinot had been obliged to accept an armistice. On May 18 the Roman Assembly resolved to despatch to his headquarters some plenipotentiaries more conciliatory than Mazzini. On the 19th, it is true, the Mazzini party had regained the upper hand in Rome; and Oudinot, animated by the arrival of reinforcements under General Vaillant, a confidant of Louis Napoleon, returned to the idea of attack. The orders brought by General Vaillant were directly opposed to the efforts of M. de Lesseps, but he was in no way disheartened. He had dared to brave the anger of the Garibaldians, and even to enter Rome for the purpose of talking to the triumvirs and supporting the efforts of the Moderates. On May 30 he signed a treaty of peace between the French Republic and that of Rome, which would have given the French troops access to the city on the one condition "that they should undertake nothing against the liberty of the Roman people."

If Louis Napoleon's only object had been, as suggested by his apologists, Emile Ollivier, etc., to prevent the entry of Austrian troops into Rome, and to secure the triumph of French influence in Italy, Lesseps' success should have delighted him. But the treaty did not ensure the restoration of the Pope; nay, it required the French army to remain neutral between Pius IX and his rebellious subjects. The alarm was given, on the Catholic side, by the French envoys, d'Harcourt and de Rayneval, and a German Jesuit who had wormed his way into Oudinot's headquarters. While Lesseps was negotiating this peace so disconcerting to their hopes, they hastily despatched to Paris a Catholic attaché of the French Embassy, the Prince de la Tour d'Auvergne. When the Prince arrived in Paris on May 27, the treaty was on the point of being signed. Drouyn de Lhuys and Odilon Barrot were still in the Ministry at the opening of the new Assembly, to which they hoped they might succeed in recommending this Convention between M. de Lesseps and the Republic of Rome, by insistence on the one condition that our troops should enter Rome. A despatch of approval was actually drafted at the Quai d'Orsay addressed to the author of the treaty, who might fairly congratulate himself upon his unexpected success, and instructing General Oudinot to march upon Rome.

On the following day, Drouyn de Lhuys' congratulations were changed into a curt order of recall. On June 1 Oudinot received instructions by despatch to attack the Roman people at once. On June 3 they began the siege of the city, and on the 30th entered it by a breach. The Catholics forming a majority in the Assembly had been able to extort this from Odilon Barrot as a concession, M. de Falloux having refused further cooperation with the Ministry except at this price (May 29). Ferdinand de Lesseps was not only recalled, but disavowed, being accused of having misunderstood or gone beyond his instructions. Drouyn de Lhuys, who knew the facts, had not the face to give the reprimand himself, and therefore handed the seals for Foreign Affairs to M. de Tocqueville. The crusade of France against the Republic of Rome for the restoration of the Pope in Rome was effected by the orders of an Administration every member of which would, in the days of Louis Philippe, have censured this Ultramontane policy.

At this time, the Conservative and Catholic majority, whose lot it was to steer France into reaction, could only carry out its object by concealing itself behind a Cabinet of republican appearance. The Prince President had originally offered the Premiership to Marshal Bugeaud, who refused it. The power remained in the hands of Odilon Barrot, who had taken as his colleagues Dufaure, Lanjuinais, and Tocqueville, all moderate Republicans, but still Republicans. This compromise suited the Monarchists, who, while united in the desire for the protection of society and for a Catholic restoration, were divided by their preferences either for Louis Philippe or for the Comte de Chambord, and moreover were anxious not to provoke either the country or the President. They were thus able, on June 30, 1849, to effect the ruin of the Roman Republic for the benefit of the Pope.

At about the same time, on June 18, M. de Falloux laid on the table of the Assembly a proposal as to liberty of instruction, which French Catholics and religious communities had been demanding for twelve years. The scheme had been drafted by a non-parliamentary commission composed of thirteen members nominated by the Assembly, with instructions to prepare a scheme "for the Union of Church and State against the Anarchy and Socialism threatening the Country." Thiers was appointed its President. On July 3, the Catholic majority, which had been delighted to hear of the return of the Pope to Rome, announced its intention of taking the earliest opportunity of starting this "Roman expedition into the interior of France," as Montalembert called it. But the Constitution of the Republic forbade the Assembly to vote on any law that had not been previously considered by the Council of State. M. de Falloux, distrusting that Council, suggested that the preliminary examination of the measure which had been going on in his office for four months should be taken as equivalent; when it was a case of securing a new advantage, the forms ordained by the Constitution did not seem to him any more essential than they did to those who brought the Pope back to Rome. The Catholic party held the power, and they made full use of it, taking advantage of the French love of liberty and dread of anarchy.

The date was well-chosen on which M. de Falloux laid on the table this proposal so favourable to his designs. It was on the day after the last attempt of the Mountaineers to rouse the People to the defence of republican institutions. On June 12 Ledru-Rollin had filed a demand for the impeachment of the Prince President and his Ministers for the violation of the Constitution in the Roman affair. "We will defend it," he said, "even by force." On June 12 he made his appeal to insurrection. On June 13 a great crowd passed along the Boulevards, but so far without overt violence. Barricades had not been yet constructed. Changarnier called out his forces, and dispersed the mob. The Republicans under Ledru-Rollin and Martin Bernard tried once more to start the rioting in the streets of Paris which a year ago had made the Constituent tremble, but in vain; abandoned by the People, and surrounded by the soldiery, they were taken prisoners or obliged to fly into exile.

This abortive attempt involved little danger to the Conservatives, and indeed was of great use to them, in enabling them to proclaim a state of siege under which the republican journals and committees could be attacked. A High Court of Justice was created for the trial of captured Republicans, Guinard, Deville, Gambon, and Vauthier, and the school-teachers who opposed the reaction. It also gave the Prince President an opportunity of appealing to the country and coming before it as its saviour. "The Republic," he said, "has no more implacable enemies than these men who perpetuate disorder. Having been elected by the nation, the cause that I defend is yours, that of your families and your possessions, that of all civilisation. I shall shrink from nothing in fighting for its success." In repudiating responsibility for the disturbance, Cavaignac was preparing for the dictatorship, and the victory of the partisans of order and the Church. Changarnier, Thiers, and Molé were then urging the Prince towards the *Coup d'État* that he carried out afterwards.

But Louis Napoleon refused. He was of opinion that, in spite of the reaction following on Ledru-Rollin's attempt, the republican cause still had a numerous and resolute body of supporters in the nation. The prosecutions instituted by Government attracted readers to the Liberal journals, such as the *National* (whose editors, Duras and Jules Simon, were feeling their way to an understanding with the Democrats), the *Siècle*, the *République*, the *Évènement* (to which Victor Hugo gave the support of his genius, with his sons and his friends, Vacquerie and Meurice), Proudhon's *Peuple*, and the *Presse*, which Emile de Girardin dedicated to the defence of liberty. In the country districts, *La Feuille du Village*, edited by a democrat, Pierre Joigneaux, carried on a very effective propaganda. The municipal and departmental elections bore witness during the whole summer of 1849 to the success of this democratic campaign. The elections to the Legislature on July 14 were even more significant. The High Court had condemned twenty-nine Republican deputies. The *Union Libérale* imagined that it could easily fill their places with Royalists, Malleville, Delessert, Ferdinand Barrot, and Ducos; but the candidates on the list of the Rue de Poitiers obtained only a very small majority in spite of the efforts of the Administration. The Republican candidates, after furious fighting and reckless lying, received nearly 100,000 votes. And in the provinces, in Isère, Haute-Vienne, the Bas-Rhin, the Saône and Loire, the Reds were elected by large majorities. Littré in the *National*, Edgar Quinet, Deschanel, and Renouvier pointed out to France, as the Liberals had done at the Restoration, and to young France especially, the dangers of a dictatorship and of the policy adopted towards Rome.

The Prince President was far too prudent a man to express any definite opinion as between the monarchist Catholic party and the champions of Liberal democracy. It suited him better to let them go on fighting, to weaken their forces, to keep their attentions mutually engaged on each other, and thus, by making his own person the centre of his policy and eschewing all embarrassing attachments, to keep the road of the future open.

His election and his change of fortune, which were

anterior in date to the growth of the views which for the past six months had been paving the way for an irreducible disagreement between Catholics and Republicans, had been due to a totally different set of influences. When the proper moment arrived, he had gathered in for his own use the whole crop of mutual dislike which had sprung up since the days of June 1848, both in the proletariat and in the bourgeoisie. Louis Napoleon did not propose to go on for ever as the tool of the Clericals, and thus lose his hold of the working classes, the peasants, and the army. While posing as the protector of order as against the Clubs and the revolutionary masses, he was careful always to assert himself as a Republican, that is to say, a stranger to every monarchist and Catholic attack upon liberty. His skill lay in figuring as a sort of powerful guardian-angel, chosen by the people to stay the triumph of the politicians of the Right or Left who wanted to bring France over to Ultramontanism or to Anarchy. "You must of necessity now-a-days," said Montalembert in July 1849, "be either a Socialist or a Catholic." Louis Napoleon was going to prove the contrary. Elected by a democracy with the help of the Clergy, he created a third intermediate party, which was eventually to serve his fortunes, thanks to the quarrels of the other two. The story of the Legislative Assembly was that of a Catholic Republic struggling apparently, but not really, with the Liberal party and the Popular Opposition. It served as a fore-runner to the establishment of personal authority, and the rule of a restored Bonapartist dynasty.

The Roman question was once again the crucial question in this political evolution. Louis Napoleon had done more than anyone for the restoration of the Pope. But, as a former defender of the liberty of the Romans, he had no notion of allowing this restoration to extend to the re-establishment in Rome of absolute power, as Pius IX was advised by Antonelli under Jesuit pressure to attempt.

Yet everything pointed in this direction. A real "White Terror," a rule of brutal reaction, had been going on in Rome since July 15 under the protection of French troops commanded by Legitimist officers, who were glad enough to try for the benefit of the Holy See methods which they would probably have liked to apply to France. The Prince President was delighted to hear that his Ministers had prorogued the Assembly from August 13 to September 30. He immediately sent his aide-de-camp, Edgar Ney, to General Rostolan, who commanded the French troops in Rome, with instructions to require the Pope to set up a Liberal Administration, to adopt the Code Napoléon, and to separate the civil from the ecclesiastical authority. Another and a still more serious demand was to the effect that the letter of instructions should be made public. This Rostolan refused to do, wishing to spare the Holy See; but Edgar Ney had it published at Florence on August 18, and, a few days later, it appeared in the *Moniteur* of the French Republic.

The letter, which had all the character of an ultimatum to the Papacy, produced much irritation in Rome. But Pius IX could not dispense with the help of their French army, which was at the command of Louis Napoleon. He issued a brief *motu proprio* on September 12, in which he promised reforms without specifying any in particular. Napoleon persisted, and instructed his envoys to demand that the Papal brief should be amended by guaranteeing that the Pontifical budget at least should be voted by an elected Assembly; but they failed to obtain even that. The letter to Edgar Ney had excited as much wrath among French Catholics as it had in Rome. The majority in the French Assembly could not forgive the President for saying, without consulting them, that "the Republic had not sent an army to Rome to stifle Roman liberty, and that he could not allow Roman Cardinals to commit acts under the shadow of the Tricolour that altered the whole nature of our intervention." In the eyes of the Catholics of the majority, France had no conditions to make with the Pope.

On the meeting of the Legislature on September 1, 1849, Montalembert made himself the mouth-piece of their indignation. "To force the will of a sovereign whose independence we had just re-established," he said, "would be a scandalous inconsistency." Odilon Barrot and his colleagues, who did not want to quarrel with the Assembly, and who were under the influence of their colleague M. de Falloux, induced Thiers to assent to a declaration that the Papal *motu proprio* of September 18, with its vague promises, constituted an ample satisfaction to France. This the Assembly actually accepted by a large majority; it also approved the maintenance of an expeditionary corps in the service of the Pope without any conditions, possibly with a half-conscious idea that it might assist the reaction that Pius IX and Antonelli looked forward to in Rome.

So far as the Prince President was concerned, the vote was a categorical repudiation of his policy. To escape this Louis Napoleon wrote another letter, addressed this time to Odilon Barrot, in which he declared himself "ready to maintain against every sort of opposition what from a political point of view he deemed to be the honour of the expedition." Barrot feared its effect on the Assembly, and, by agreement with his colleagues, refused to read it out; he would not inform the Assembly of the will of the President. The next day, October 31, the Prince dismissed Odilon Barrot and his colleagues by a simple notice inserted in the *Moniteur*. To succeed them, he appointed General Comte d'Hautpoul as President of the Council without portfolio, Ferdinand Barrot at the Interior, de Rayneval (succeeded by Ducos de la Hitte) at Foreign Affairs, Rouher as Minister of Justice, de Parieu at Public Education, Bineau at Public Works, J. B. Dumas, the famous savant, at Agriculture, Fould at Finance. They were nearly all untried men, and strangers to party questions; the President had selected them for their personal devotion to himself. His message to the Assembly was a complete sketch of personal government. "France is disturbed," he said, "owing to the lack of direction, and is looking for the guiding hand of the leader she elected in December. And this victory of December 10 involved an entire change of system; for the mere name of Napoleon is a programme in itself. Order must be restored, without injury to real liberty."

In reality, while pretending to restore authority, they were starting on their final stage towards a dictatorship. The leading spirit in this venture, the man whose talents and energy were to be devoted for the next twenty years entirely to the service of Louis Napoleon, was Rouher, a curious specimen of the Auvergnat lawyer, who had had the wit to discern in the absolutist school of politics the means of satisfying a relentless ambition. As Keeper of the Seals he had no scruple in destroying Republicans by making criminals of them, "Reds, lunatics, anarchists." In this matter he made Justice the slave of Policy. The law officers of the Superior Courts became in his hands police-detectives, whose business it was to report to him every month as to the organisation of the democratic party, its journals and associations, its secret and public doings, and to keep up a regular system of enquiry even on the conduct of officials subordinated to other Ministries, who might be suspected of indulgence or complicity towards that party.

The Minister of War, who had the disposal of the *Gendarmerie*, or armed police, exercised an equally careful vigilance over demagogues, kept the personal description of men of mark, of officials, and, above all, of school-teachers, who showed any tendency to anarchist doctrines. On December 13, 1849, de Parieu, the Minister of Public

Instruction, laid before the Assembly a proposal for an Education Law which would place the teachers in every department at the orders of the prefects. It was becoming clear that, by these repressive measures against the republican "anarchists," the President was using all his power to ensure himself an army of officials, of willing or cowed servants, ready to back him in every scheme, to accept any command he might give, an army of "order."

The Assembly, already angered by the dismissal of the Odilon Barrot Ministry for no crime but obedience to the majority in the Roman affair, was meditating measures of resistance from the beginning of January 1850. They passed de Parieu's law for the control of school-teachers by a majority of one only. The Monarchists insisted on a promise from the Ministry that the law on Liberty of Instruction should be presented as early as possible; while Louis Napoleon had on November 7, 1849, insisted that it should be first submitted to the Council of State, as asked by the Republicans.

At that moment the political situation in France was somewhat peculiar. On one side she was governed by a President whose methods were becoming daily more autocratic, who was invested with sovereignty by a popular vote, and who could command all the forces of the magistracy, of the police, and of the army, in a country where power was absolutely centralised. On the other side she took her laws from a single Assembly also invested with sovereignty by a popular vote. But those who made the laws had not the means of getting them carried out; while the Government, with all its absolute power, had no means of making the law. It was as if Napoleon and the Convention, side by side, were carrying on a joint government with two contradictory popular mandates.

If this singular system lasted for two years, from the end of 1849 to the end of 1851, it was due to the fact that the Legislature and the President were both determined to exhaust their respective mandates, each of which was limited to four years. Another reason was that they were both of them afraid of the possibility of the awakening of a free Democracy—a fear which inclined them for some time longer towards concessions.

Thus it was that the Falloux Law was carried on March 15, 1850, to the great delight of the Catholics. The principle of the law was that the right of every citizen to give instruction, already established as regards primary education, should now be extended to secondary schools. Furthermore it declared it to be the duty of the State to provide on its side for national education, following the example of Napoleon when he founded the University and the Lycées, or of Guizot in his legislation of 1833 on primary education. But for the Catholics the Falloux Law meant a good deal more, for it put them in a position to develop their denominational schools concurrently with those of the State. The communal and departmental schools, the Lycées, and the teaching staff of these schools were now placed under the control and direction of the Church. Four Archbishops elected by their brethren were given seats on the Superior Council of the University in the name of the Church, with the duties of inspecting the curricula, examining the books in use, and pointing out defects. On the University Councils of the Provinces the new law placed two ecclesiastics, one of whom must be a bishop, to superintend the teachers; in the lowest grade, the country parsons were invested with the right of inspecting the village schools. And while the Legislature thus placed fetters on the State institutions, it devised special facilities for new schools which the Catholic party proposed to scatter broad-cast. On the pretext of liberty it created privileges in favour of the teaching communities and the Jesuits, although the existence of the latter was not yet officially recognised in

France. For instance, in the staff of the primary schools, whether private or State schools, the certificate of capacity required of all lay teachers was not demanded of persons in Holy Orders; while in the secondary schools, in which principals and professors had to show a good University degree for a State appointment, priests were admitted to teach without any degree at all. Communes and Departments that provided school accommodation for free and Catholic schools were relieved of the legal obligation to provide from local funds for the needs of national education. By means of these privileges and franchises created to favour the Church, the Falloux Law, while asserting the right to give instruction to be a natural, though perhaps not an unquestionable, right, was specially and primarily enacted to make that right subordinate to the influence and progress of the Church of Rome.

If, at the time when the Falloux Law placed the docile and well-disciplined army of school-teachers in the hands of the Church, the Assembly had not already allowed M. de Parieu his Statute of January 9, 1850, putting them also under the jurisdiction of the prefects, Louis Napoleon would scarcely have been so ready to give such complete and speedy satisfaction to M. de Falloux and his clerical friends. It was a provisional compromise between the legislative and executive powers, a temporary understanding directed against the common foes—Republicans, Liberals, Democrats, and Socialists. During the first five months of 1850, the Government, in harmony with the Assembly, carried on a merciless war of prosecutions against the democratic propaganda on the charge of Socialism. Teachers were dismissed by shoals; journals were forbidden. The police and the magistracy obtained warrants for the criminal prosecution of working-men's Clubs and Cooperative Societies, Mutual Benefit Societies, Masonic Lodges, and public officials under suspicion. It looked as if

Frenchmen were to be forbidden to think or act in common.

Luckily they could not prevent them from voting. In the municipal elections, Democrats were elected to the General Councils at Stenay, in the Vosges, at Moissac, Sens, Avesnes, Bordeaux, and in the Gard. On the election, on March 10, of deputies to take the place of those expelled in June 1849, all the pressure of the prefects could not prevent the election of 18 Republicans among the 29 vacancies, in the East, the Centre, and the South, Moderates being chosen such as Ducoux and Dupont de Bussac, "Mountaineers" like Madier de Montjau and Esquiros, and Socialists. All that the Republicans had to do, in order to ensure the victory of the will of the People over the agents of Louis Napoleon and the Church, was to renew the agreement between the factions of their own party which Lamartine had advocated. The elections in Paris, on March 10, were specially notable, as the republican list, containing the names of Carnot, a moderate Republican, Vidal, a friend of Ledru-Rollin, and Flotte, a friend of Louis Blanc, was victorious over the list of the Rue de Poitiers supported by the Prince President. A prediction might well have been hazarded that the movement of 1848 would be reproduced in an exactly reversed direction—that the now reconciled Republicans would regain the ground lost. by their divisions, to the Conservative party, who now in their turn were split into Orleanists, Legitimists, and friends or foes of Louis Napoleon.

As this movement was likely to grow stronger in the next two years, the hopes of the Conservative majority and the Prince President, in appealing to popular suffrage in 1852 in the final struggle for the command of France, seemed likely to be disappointed. Louis Napoleon, thinking it advisable to give his prefects a chief who would be an example to them by his energy, and would answer for the country to himself, appointed to the Ministry of the Interior Baroche, a law officer of arbitrary temper, who had courted public notice by opposing Guizot and the Republicans in turn in 1848, and who in the month of March had been remarked for his severity in the prosecutions of socialist journals and democratic associations. Baroche would have supported a *Coup d'État,* had the President asked him. But, though some men were beginning to urge that step, Louis Napoleon hesitated, and drew back at an appeal to violence. "He would like," said Thiers, "to be assured of the support of the Legislature. You can only obtain the help of the President by offering to prolong his power. He would be a fool to accept anything less."

Without prejudice to their monarchist hopes, the "Burgraves," as they were called—Berryer, de Broglie, Molé, Buffet, Montalembert, Piscatory, and Vatimesnil—gave up the idea of a *Coup d'État* if it could be had only on the conditions demanded by the President. They offered to support a law abolishing Universal Suffrage, if the President and his Ministers would take the initiative in proposing it—a first breach, under legal forms, of the Constitution. "Unless you take the initiative," said the Burgraves to Baroche, "we shall not move." To which Baroche, on behalf of the President, replied, "You do not conceal your fear of our deserting you; and you cannot therefore be surprised if we feel the same towards you." The work of the Constituent was to be attacked, but neither Assembly nor President would take the responsibility of beginning.

At last the fear of a democratic Republic, threatened by the election of Eugène Sue in Paris on April 28, determined the accomplices to act. The Ministers of Louis Napoleon agreed to set up an extra-parliamentary Commission composed of the men of the Rue de Poitiers for the revision of Universal Suffrage. The Commission was nominated on

May 8, and on the 18th Léon Faucher laid its Report before the Assembly. On May 31 the Legislature adopted the Report after very animated debates, in the course of which Victor Hugo charged Montalembert with being a renegade to the grand Liberalism of his past, and Thiers publicly proclaimed his detestation of the "vile multitude," together with his "admiration for the great man who had found out how to keep it in order." Rouher "deplored the catastrophe of 1848." It would have been difficult for a Ministry that included Baroche to re-establish a property qualification for a vote, seeing that that fervent champion of Reform had supported its abolition in 1847. Therefore the right of voting had to be filched out of the hands of the people by requiring a residence of three years, to be proved by receipts for taxes, by an employer's certificate, or by public employment, civil or military. Three million electors were thus suppressed as "vagabonds," "criminals" or "anarchists," especially if they were proved to belong to a political association, or to have committed a political crime. The republican bourgeoisie and its adherents were deprived of the means of defending themselves. The future was reserved for the Monarchists on one side, or for Louis Napoleon, his army, and his peasantry on the other. The law was one which the Assembly had constitutionally no power to vote, and was therefore in reality a *Coup d'État* against the Constitution.

It was the signal for a vigorous persecution of the Republicans, which the Monarchists and the two Ministers, Baroche at the Interior, and Rouher in charge of Justice, described as the "defence of social order against anarchy." An order of June 9, 1850, prohibited committees and public assemblies, even during an electoral contest, also the distribution of political journals and pamphlets. Democratic deputies who wanted to consult their supporters were obliged to arrange to meet them in one café after another, with the police always at their heels. Every popular assemblage was an object of suspicion to police, magistrates, and prefects. Every association with any democratic members was reported as an "anarchist" society. The houses of Republicans were every day subjected to domiciliary visits; their journals were worried with prosecutions and penalties. Lower-class functionaries, post-men, road-men, and teachers, were dismissed in crowds on the slightest suspicion. Mayors, officers of the National Guard, and Town Councillors suffered the same fate, as soon as a formal charge was laid against them. A shout of "Vive la République!" under a republican constitution was seditious, while "Vive Napoléon!" was a passport to favour with the authorities. To wear red in scarf, hat, or tie used to be absurd; now it had become a crime.

The democratic propaganda was of course condemned in the Assembly as soon as the Republicans became a minority in that royalist body. Michel de Bourges, Madier de Montjau, and other Republicans then concerted with their exiled friends in London, Ledru-Rollin and others, to defend themselves by a fresh insurrection. But the more sensible, and therefore the more clear-sighted of them, Cavaignac, Bernard Lavergne, and Victor Hugo, would not join, confining themselves to the defence of right in the Assembly, by letting no occasion slip for denouncing the illegality and injustice of their opponents, in hopes that the nation would avenge the right. Holding patience to be the virtue of the strong, they desired to manifest their strength by their patience; they therefore decided that the party should abstain from voting till the elections of 1852 by way of testifying against the loss of freedom in voting and the violation of the law. This policy gave them this advantage at least, that, when contrasted with the selfish pursuit of private interests and the lack of scruple of their adversaries, they stood out as the party of Justice against Absolutism, Liberty against Tyranny, Constitutional Order against Civil War.

Now Changarnier's influence with the army seemed sufficient to secure it for the Monarchists; and the Electoral Law had scarcely been passed, before he was contesting the command of the nation with Louis Napoleon. The President, who wanted funds to create a party, had asked for a grant of 2,400,000 fr. instead of 600,000 fr. on his Civil List. Changarnier advised his friends to give him the money as a charity. While the prefects were pressing the Councils General in August to urge upon the Assembly the prolongation of the President's powers, or even a Life Consulate, Changarnier directed a funeral service to be held in the Tuileries for Louis Philippe (who had died at Claremont on August 28, 1850), and came to an agreement with the Legitimists who obeyed the Comte de Chambord. On October 10, the presence of the two rivals at a review held at Satory enabled them to test their respective influences with the army. The cavalry shouted "Vive l'Empereur!" while the infantry stood silent. Louis Napoleon transferred the General of the infantry to a country command, and replaced d'Hautpoul at the Ministry of War by General Schramm, a man of greater energy. In a message to the Assembly he used these words: "The army is nobody's business but mine; and it is not to be used against the counter-revolution." When the new year began, Changarnier answered him defiantly to the effect that the army was equally at the disposition of the Assembly, if the President Dupin required it.

After six months of masked hostilities, Louis Napoleon made up his mind on January 9, 1851, for an explosion. Being resolved that no authority should dispute with him the command of the army at a critical moment, and that there should be no Monk to act on behalf of the King, at least until the part of Cromwell had been disposed of, he determined to abolish Changarnier's command and divide it between General Baraguay d'Hilliers as Military Governor, and Perrot as Commander of the National Guard. His Ministers hesitating, he dismissed them on January 9, and appointed his closest friends Comte Reynaud de St Jean d'Angély, Ducos, and Magne to the Ministries of War, Marine, and Public Works. The Assembly had to acquiesce in the dismissal of Changarnier, but blamed the Ministry, who retired under a fire of invective from Berryer and Thiers—a poor consolation for so decisive a check! "If the Assembly weakens," said Thiers, "instead of two powers there will be but one; and there is your Empire!" Though the Monarchists were able to force the President to make another change of Ministry on January 24, 1851, when Vaïsse de Royer, Comtes de Germiny and de Randon, Admiral Vaillant, Charles Giraud, and Schneider were appointed, obscure men, but entirely devoted to his fortunes, their defeat was irreparable, now that they had lost the help of the army. Great in oratory, incapable in legislation, they felt that the nation was slipping away from them and turning, through love of order and of the Napoleonic legend, towards Napoleon, or, for the love of liberty, towards the Republicans.

In April 1851 Louis Napoleon, having shown them his strength, made a last effort towards an understanding with them. After all, had they not still the same enemies, the Democrats, whose zeal and self-confidence grew daily stronger, and who amid prosecutions and trials held fast to the hope that in 1852 their debt would be paid in full? At the end of his term of office, the President had but two ways of maintaining himself in power; he must either do violence to the Constitution, or get it amended. The gentler method seemed to him to be also the safer. To succeed in that and to avoid the need of force, all he had to do was to arrange something with the "Burgraves," who seemed to be reduced to cry for mercy. Montalembert advised them to give up their monarchist hopes, and devote themselves to winning over to the side of the Church the ambitious Prince now on the full flood of fortune: Odilon Barrot, Malleville, Tocqueville, Lamartine, de Broglie resigned themselves to the inevitable and would have assented but for the interposition of Thiers, who saw a possible chance of stepping into the front rank in a quarrel between the Prince and the Assembly. After many efforts Louis Napoleon was unable to find better material for a Ministry of conciliation than Léon Faucher, Buffet, and de Crousheilhes (April 10), to whom however he added Rouher, Baroche, Fould, and Magne as sheep-dogs. The bargain that he offered in April to his Ministers, and through them to the Assembly, was certainly favourable on the face of it to his ambition. It involved a slight amendment of the Constitution in the matter of the length of his term of office; but it also contained a promise to the Conservatives of a Ministry pledged to secure their re-election and absolutely opposed to the threatening advance of democracy. This would have been the "Liberal Empire" of the future anticipated by twenty years.

CHAPTER XI

THE REVISION OF THE CONSTITUTION AND THE COUP D'ÉTAT

The Ministry appointed on April 10 took every possible step to prepare the public for this peaceable solution of the crisis which could no longer be postponed. Down to May 28, 1851, the day on which the Assembly was to decide as to the revision, the opinion of the country, which had been won over by the agents and journals of the Elysée, and worked upon by the prefects and officials, was broadly favourable to it, particularly in the East, the South, and the larger towns. It was uncertain what line the various parties in the Chambers proposed to adopt. The Republicans at once took up the position, on principle, of refusing their support to any military dictatorship. But the Monarchists were a long way from agreement, a considerable section of them hoping, with Berryer and Molé, that a general revision might lead to a restoration of the Monarchy, others inclining, with de Broglie, to the alliance proposed by the President and a partial revision, others again, with Thiers and Dufaure, determined to reject every proposal as a sort of defiance of Louis Napoleon. In spite of everything, when the day for the discussion came, the majority of the Assembly voted in accordance with the wishes of the Prince; and 448 deputies, against a minority of 278, carried the limited amendment which prolonged the President's term of office. But the Constitution required a majority of three-quarters of the voters for the alteration of any of its cardinal articles; and of this figure they were short by 100.

Louis Napoleon had foreseen this difficulty, as well as the obstinate resistance of the Democrats. At the last moment, in hopes of breaking it down, he had visited Lyons, the city of democracy, to get them to listen to the language of peace (June 1). On July 8, the discussion in the Assembly having been opened on a favourable report from Tocqueville, the fiery replies from Michel de Bourges and Victor Hugo entirely disposed of the mistaken notion of the Government that the Republican party did not intend to fight. On July 19, the Assembly declined to grant the Dictator the small courtesy he asked for. "The Constitution is not to be revised," said one deputy, "but it may be said to have ceased to exist." After their vote, the Assembly was prorogued on August 10 for its two months' vacation. This gave Louis Napoleon all the time he needed to prepare for the destruction of the Constitution by force, as he was unable to effect it by legal means.

It was at this time (August 15) that, to secure men entirely his own at the head of the army, and by the advice of his aide-de-camp, Colonel Fleury, he called up to the command of the military division in Paris St Arnaud, and, later, Magnan, young African officers, brave, determined men, apt for strong measures, despising parliamentary methods, and knowing naught of parties. In the course of August, the prefect Maupas, and Morny, the natural brother of Louis Napoleon, both devoted to him and both unscrupulous, with Carlier, the Prefect of Police, met at St Cloud, and coolly discussed the best method and most convenient date for the onslaught of the army upon the representatives of the nation. The plan was arranged for September 22 by Rouher, acting as secretary to the conspirators. But, at the last moment, on September 6, St Arnaud failed them;

and his absence alarmed his accomplices, especially Carlier, who resigned his place to General Magnan. St Arnaud had not failed them through any scruples on his part, but because in his opinion the proposed measures were insufficient and ill-judged. He wanted to be free to choose his own time for action, which would be the day after the return of the deputies from the country, when they might all be taken together at one cast of the net. The President yielded to his arguments, and at the end of October appointed to the Prefecture of Police Maupas, once an official under Guizot, but stopped in his career by the advent of the Republic, and now ready for any job that would combine vengenace with his personal advancement. With these men as confidants, and these alone, Louis Napoleon secretly arranged the decisive steps to be taken at the meeting of the Assembly.

On the very eve of putting these into effect, he seemed once more to hesitate between a wish to retain power without risk by acting within the limits of law, and the fear of losing all, if he did not venture on some breach of legality. Tocqueville penetrated the real secret motive of this hesitation. "There were in him two men—the first the ex-conspirator, the fatalist dreamer who believed himself to be called to be master of France, and through her to dominate Europe; the second, the Epicurean, languidly enjoying an unwonted comfort, and the facile pleasures that his present position afforded him, and unwilling to risk their loss by attempting to climb higher." When the hour came for the last ascent, it frightened and allured him at the same time. He made a positively final attempt to induce the Democrats to vote for the revision required for the prolongation of his functions, which they had refused to do in July. He requested his Ministers to propose the repeal of the Electoral Law of May 31, 1850, and a complete return to Universal Suffrage, "with a view to improve the chance of a pacific, regular and legal solution," as he described his intention in his message of November 4, 1851.

Through fear of displeasing the Conservative majority, the Ministers resigned on October 12. The President selected others outside Parliament to support his proposal. Of course the Republicans would welcome it; but it was equally certain that the majority would be against it. Berryer at once demanded the institution of a Committee of Enquiry, directed against the President, or a Committee of Public Safety, and the Assembly made itself ready for battle.

For this Louis Napoleon had been secretly preparing, and for a much longer time. St Arnaud, now Minister of War, had made sure of his troops, and assigned his officers to their posts. Morny was superintending the final arrangements from the Elysée, and was prepared to assist the attack by taking possession of the Ministry of the Interior, then held by some man of straw. The date was at first fixed for November 20, about which time the parliamentary officials, uneasy about the future, were urging forward a law conferring on the President of the Chamber the right to call on the army for its protection without recourse to the Minister of War. The Republicans put their veto on that. Had it been passed, the Elysée would have needed to alter its plans. In the tribunes of the Assembly at the moment the vote was taken, Maupas, General Magnan, and St Arnaud were communicating by signals. Louis Napoleon postponed the date, first to November 25, then to December 2. He seemed to be looking out for something unexpected to relieve him from the necessity of using force. In the night between December 1 and 2, 1851, Morny, St Arnaud, and Maupas carried him off by force without even consulting his Ministers. On the cover of the portfolio containing the programme of the plot, Louis Napoleon on the morning of the 2nd wrote

"Rubicon." The fund in their war-chest amounted to 40,000 francs. They all swore to be "faithful unto death!" Morny said with truth, "Each of us risks his neck in this business." This was the final move in the game, of which France was to be the prize.

The essence of the operation was the proclamation printed during the night of December 2, 1851, at the National Printing Press, informing the nation that the Assembly was dissolved, and that the Prince President, the elect of the People, having taken possession, in the name of the People, of the Constituent authority was about to legislate in its stead. This was further explained by the decree at once issued, of which the first clause proclaimed the dissolution of the Assembly, the fifth the dissolution of the Council of State, the second the restoration of Universal Suffrage, while the fourth declared a state of siege in Paris.

The proclamation which accompanied the decree, in form an appeal to the People, was primarily an apology for these unconstitutional measures. It criticised alike the Constitution and the Assembly, on which the President claimed to sit in judgment on the pretext of saving society, France, and the Republic. It also proclaimed the advent of a new political system, with institutions "which survive their founders if they are men of constructive capacity"—a capacity which Louis Napoleon claimed for himself and his henchmen exclusively—the Presidential term of ten years; all responsibility to be vested solely in the President, from whom the Ministers were to derive their authority; a Council of State selected at the pleasure of the President to prepare and discuss all proposed legislation; a Legislative Body, elected practically by the President's prefects at the rate of one for every electoral district, to vote upon this legislation, but never to discuss it; a Senate to be nominated by the President—in a word, the institutions of the Consulate which had given "prosperity and tranquillity (he could scarcely add, liberty) to France," though without the glories of Marengo.

While claiming for himself and his accomplices the power to legislate, Louis Napoleon did not propose to avail himself of it except in a roundabout way suggested to him by previous revolutions. To all appearance he reserved to the People in the last instance the right to decide on the new system of government. The decree of December 2 summoned them to their ballot-boxes, and, as Maupas said, "submitted the proposed Constitution to the suffrage of the People." The Monarchy of July, the Revolution of February had done the same, immediately after the riots in Paris which had been fatal to Charles X, and afterwards to Louis Philippe. Being master of Paris by virtue of the troops he had called out on the morning of the day on which the decrees were issued (December 2), he reckoned upon the centralisation of all power in the capital for obtaining, and, if need were, for compelling, the assent of the whole nation. He invited the People "to delegate to him the powers necessary to create a Constitution."

When the Parisians, who were not expecting any move, read the appeal of the President pasted on their walls, they also found a whole army prepared to back it. Two regiments of the line occupied the Palace where the Assembly met; and the news was spread that representatives of the People, both Royalists and Republicans, had been arrested at dawn in their own houses on the absurd pretext of conspiracy against the safety of the State—Thiers and Roger du Nord among the Monarchists; in the military world, Bedeau, Lamoricière, Cavaignac, Changarnier, Le Flo, Colonel Charras; of the Republicans, Cholat, Baune, Greppo, Baze, Nadaud, Miot, Lagrange, and Valentin. Warrants had also been issued against seventy Republicans, journalists or heads of secret societies, whose resistance might "compromise the Republic." Journals, such as the *Opinion*

Publique, the *Presse*, the *République*, the *Ordre*, were suspended, and their offices occupied by the military. In a word, every man and every party that in July had refused to grant the President a prolongation of his powers was struck down and reduced to impotence—a preventive measure, which was afterwards denominated "a mere matter of police." In fact, they had been made prisoners, before any declaration of war, by an army charged by its chiefs, in the name of discipline and honour, and "with the memories of the glory of Napoleon in their hearts," to impose upon their terrified country the will of a dictator. Under the protection of his troops Louis Napoleon rode through Paris as through a conquered city.

Some members of the dissolved Assembly, both of the Right and the Left, tried to meet in one of the municipal buildings, and Pascal Duprat proposed a general call to arms; but the police, who had been watching, arrested them. The Democrats, distrusting the Monarchists, held their meeting elsewhere. On that evening they formed a committee of resistance, the members being Carnot, de Flotte, Victor Hugo, Jules Favre, Michel de Bourges, and Madier de Montjau, and agreed to meet in the Faubourg St Antoine to stir up the working-men, who did not seem inclined to follow them. On December 3 they marched through the town, then almost deserted, and tried to erect barricades; but they were driven back at the first attempt by the forces of the dictator. The day passed in ineffective struggle. Baudin, a deputy, was killed in the cause of right; and on December 4 the father of his fellow-deputy, Dessoubs, met the same fate. St Arnaud, assured of success, allowed them to advance, and at the right moment swept the Boulevards with his cavalry brigades. The soldiers had orders to give no quarter, and struck hard and sharp. Without any warning an unarmed group collected by accident or curiosity at the corner of the Faubourg Poissonière was decimated by musketry fire. By the vigour of these methods and the terror they inspired, although during those two days no real resistance was to be seen, Paris was reduced to submission and obedience (December 5, 1851).

The blow once struck, the accomplices of Louis Napoleon, and Morny in particular, made it their first business to obtain the popular vote, or *plébiscite*, which was to give them the semblance of a legal sanction. The new Consulate now reaped the benefit of the administrative machinery devised by the First Consul, which had been found so useful under previous Governments and was always ready to serve the ends of a centralised administration. A series of important changes in the official world took place after December 2; and the Director General of the Posting Department was instructed to reserve all the seats on the mail coaches for the officers travelling into the provinces. On December 4 the prefects of the departments were instructed to dismiss all justices, mayors, and other officials whose acquiescence was not certain, and to require from them an assent to the new system in writing. They were authorised to arrest summarily any would-be disturber of quiet, and to suspend any journal whose criticism was likely to affect it. And, by way of ensuring rapidity of execution, Morny made a direct and personal appeal to the sub-prefects by a despatch dated December 6, 1851, requiring them to make a daily report. The instructions issued from Paris grew more severe. All journals were placed at the arbitrary discretion of prefects and sub-prefects, who were to be sole judges of their right even to the precarious liberty that was left to them. On December 7 a list of "Suspects" in the departments, directed against members of secret societies, leaders of the Socialist party, and Republicans, was drawn up. The proposed popular conference was indeed of a remarkable nature, seeing that its members were forbidden either to read or write. "You will forbid," said Morny on

December 6, "any discussion as to the legality of recent events." It was the silence of slavery.

It was not long before the Terror was added. In spite of all precautions, the peasantry, and the republican bourgeoisie of the smaller towns rose, on the morrow of the *Coup d'État* to defend their liberties. There was no resistance in the North or West. But at Orleans, on December 4, crowds listened to the call of the republican deputies. At Montargis collisions occurred between Republicans and police. In the Allier, Democrats seized the sub-prefecture at La Palisse; at Clamecy in the Nièvre the population rose on December 5, and troops were engaged for two days in putting them down. All the South-West was disturbed; for three days, Republicans were masters of Marmande, Auch, and Mirande. At Beziers and Bedarieux, in Languedoc, and above all in Provence at Digne, Democrats organised a resistance which would have become serious, if order had not been maintained by the military in Marseilles and Lyons as relentlessly as in the capital.

These attempts were at once stigmatised as *Jacqueries* by the Government, which seized upon them as an excuse for disposing, by imprisonment or exile, of all Democrats who might have been able to thwart the pressure of the officials upon the electors. A state of siege was proclaimed in thirty-two departments, and flying columns were thrown into the rural districts to hunt down the "Reds." On December 8 a decree was issued, visiting with transportation to Cayenne or Algeria anyone breaking the terms of his police licence or affiliated to any secret society, in other words, to any political association. The mysterious organisers of conspiracy at the Elysée on December 2 did not scruple to punish as criminals the "wretches, the revolutionary leaders, who swear-in recruits and plan conspiracies in their gloomy conventicles." Between December 3 and 20, 1851, 26,000 persons were thus detained or prosecuted. "The disorders that have broken out, the approach of the day when a vote will decide the fate of the country," wrote Morny to his prefects on December 10, "must have impressed you with the necessity of securing that in every commune there should be some firm and loyal soul to second the efforts of the Government for the protection of order and of the independence of the voter."

Proscription and Terror having now set them free from any republican opposition that might have "falsified," that is, affected the vote, the Administration neglected nothing which might "secure the success of the Government idea." On December 10, the prefects were instructed to scatter broad-cast the proclamations of the President, to form electoral committees "for the guidance of right-thinking people," and to bring all the electors, those of the chief town as well as those of the smallest hamlet, within the scope of their legitimate actions. This was the essential condition under which this vote of the People was given, manipulated, as it had never been before, by an energetic and unscrupulous Minister. Morny's circular to his prefects contained one sentence which was at once a declaration of policy and a confession. "Entire liberty of conscience, but a firm and persistent use of all avowable means of influence or persuasion—that is what the Government expect of you."

Morny was not disappointed in his expectations. Louis Napoleon had reason to congratulate himself on the confidence he had placed in him at the critical moment, when on December 21, 1851, France decided by 7,500,000 votes against 640,000 (with 1,500,000 abstentions) to delegate to him the right to frame a Constitution in accordance with the programme laid down on December 2. The nation gave up its sovereign power, and placed the whole of its rights both executive and legislative in the sole hands of the nephew of the Emperor, in memory of the glory which it had once won under a Bonaparte, and in the hope of obtaining a strong and brilliant government. There could be no doubt whatever that the nation was weary of parliamentary struggles and of the impotence of party; it dreaded disturbances, and yearned for rest and security. None the less it was disheartened, broken down by the systematic pressure exerted by the Administration and by the terrorism which made a crime of every attempt at discussion or opposition, and reduced to silence by a victorious army.

It was the triumph of Louis Napoleon. He now admitted that "he had transgressed legality" by the *Coup d'État,* but he claimed that "by the *plébiscite* he had returned to the path of right." By way of giving this "consultation of the nation" the splendour of a great event, Morny ordered all the mayors of the chief towns in each electoral district to attend in a body in Paris on January 1, 1852, to congratulate the President. On that day also a Te Deum was sung at Notre Dame and in all the churches of France. Louis Napoleon left the Elysée and, as sovereign of the French nation, took possession of the Tuileries; while on the national flag the eagles reappeared, returning from St Helena, as symbols of glory and of strength.

To the quarrels which had been going on for three years between the bourgeois, the friends of order, and the People, passionately devoted to liberty, here in Paris, the master of which is the master of France, Louis Napoleon, for the furtherance of his own purposes, put a forcible end, "by claiming to create institutions conforming at once to the democratic instincts of the nation and to the universal desire for a strong and respected government." "The nation was as sick of the Reds," wrote Proudhon, "as of the Whites." On January 1, 1852, Paris accepted a political system which carried on the Republic without Republicans, and gave the sanction of a popular vote to a military dictatorship, partly from democratic instinct, partly from a surfeit of rioting.

But, even in allowing the nephew of the First Consul to seize the inheritance of Napoleon, Paris once more asserted her pre-eminence as the capital. The system established by the Constitution of January 14, 1852, under the semblance of a democratic Republic, like the Legitimist Monarchy of 1815, secured the obedience of the nation mainly through that civil and military centralisation which, for a second time, made the fortune of a Bonaparte, and through the hegemony of Paris, though it involved the tyranny of a Louis Napoleon.

BIBLIOGRAPHY

In default of a bibliography of France brought up to date, the following Collections may be consulted:

Catalogue de l'histoire de France, published by the Bibliothèque nationale in Paris (to 1866).

Caron, Pierre. Bibliographie des travaux publiés de 1866 à 1897 sur l'Histoire de France depuis 1789.

Caron, Pierre, and Brière, G. Répertoire méthodique de l'histoire contemporaine de France (annual, since 1897).

Schmidt, Charles. Les sources de l'histoire moderne de France aux Archives nationales. Paris, 1903.

General Histories of France in the xixth Century.

A complete list of the general histories of Europe, in which the France of this period is dealt with, would be impossible here. Reference to such a list will be found in the Cambridge Modern History, vols. x–xi, and in the Histoire générale de l'Europe, by Lavisse and Rambaud, vols. x–xiii.

In the following list only those histories are entered which make a special subject of French history.

Lesur, Charles Louis. Annuaire historique. 1818–1850.

Adams, Prof. C. K. Democracy and monarchy in France, from the inception of the Great Revolution to the overthrow of the Second Empire. New York, 1874.

Martin, Henri. Histoire de France, de 1789 à nos jours. 8 vols. Paris, 1879.

Challamel, Augustin. Histoire de la liberté en France depuis 1789. Paris, 1886.

Grégoire, Louis. Histoire de France. Période contemporaine. Règne de Louis Philippe: République de 1848: Empire: République jusqu'à la Constitution de 1875. 4 vols. Paris, 1879–1883.

Rambaud, Alfred. Histoire de la civilisation française. 2 vols. Paris, 1887.

—— Histoire de la civilisation contemporaine en France. Paris, 1888.

Petit, Abbé J. A. Histoire contemporaine de la France. 12 vols. Paris, 1881–1889.

Hamel, Ernest. Histoire de France depuis la Révolution jusqu'à la chute du second Empire. 7 vols. Paris, 1881–1891.

D'Héricault, Ch. Histoire anecdotique de la France: le Régime moderne. 6 vols. Paris, 1887–1891.

Dickinson, G. L. Revolution and Reaction in modern France, 1789–1871. London, 1892.

Bodley, J. E. C. France. 2 vols. London, 1898.

Bourgeois, Emile. Manuel historique de politique étrangère. Vols. II and III. Paris, 1898–1905.

General Sources of the History of France in the xixth Century.

1. Parliamentary papers: Reports of the sittings and debates of Parliament, since 1815 published in the Moniteur and partly repeated with the speeches and the appendices in the Parliamentary Records, 95 volumes, from 1815 to 1836. Index in vol. 62 for the years preceding 1830.

2. Acts of the Legislature. Published in the Bulletin des Lois, 5th—12th series, and in Duvergier, Recueil des Lois françaises.

For the Texts of the Constitutions see (inter alios):

Hélie, F. A. Les Constitutions de la France. Paris, 1879.

Monnier, H. et Duguit, L. Les Constitutions et les Lois politiques de la France. Paris, 1898.

26—2

The student will find a useful summary of the more important legislative texts in

Cahen, G. and Mathiez, A. Les Lois françaises depuis 1815. Paris, 1906.

3. Diplomatic Papers.

De Clercq, A. et de Clercq, J. Recueil des traités de la France depuis 1715. Paris, 1880.

The diplomatic records in the Foreign Office in Paris for the period 1815–1848 may be consulted there by permission. The catalogue of memoirs and papers for the period 1815–1830, and the diplomatic correspondence with Germany, England, the Argentine Republic and Austria for the same period, are all that have so far been published (Publications du Ministère des Affaires étrangères).

4. Biographies. In the absence of a general French biography, La grande Encyclopédie, 32 vols., and La Nouvelle Biographie générale (46 vols., Paris, 1857–77), will give useful information.

5. Journalism. A complete list would be impossible, but cf. the following works:

Hatin, Eug. Manuel historique de la liberté de la presse en France. 2 vols. Paris, 1868.

Hahn. Bibliographie de la presse politique française. Paris, 1886.

Histories in Periods from 1815 to 1852.

1. *Restoration.*

Dareste, M. C. Histoire de la Restauration (1814–1830). 2 vols. Paris, 1879.

Dulaure et Auguis. Histoire de la Révolution depuis 1814 jusqu'à 1830. 8 vols. Paris, 1834–1838.

Vaulabelle, A. de. Histoire des deux Restaurations. 8 vols. Paris, 1857–1858.

Duvergier de Hauranne, P. Histoire du Gouvernement parlementaire en France, 1814–1848. 10 vols. Paris, 1857–1872.

Nettement, A. Histoire de la Restauration. 8 vols. Paris, 1860–1872.

Vielcastel, L. de. Histoire de la Restauration. 2 vols. Paris, 1860–1878.

Daudet, Ernest. Histoire de la Restauration. Paris, 1882.

Weill, Georges. La France sous la Monarchie constitutionnelle (1814–1848). Paris, n. d. [1902].

2. *Reign of Louis Philippe.*

D'Haussonville, Comte J. Histoire de la politique extérieure de la Monarchie de Juillet. 2 vols. Paris, 1850.

Du Bled, V. Histoire de la Monarchie de Juillet. 2 vols. Paris, 1877.

Hillebrand, Karl. Geschichte Frankreichs von der Thronbesteigung Louis Philippes. 2 vols. Gotha, 1877–1879.

Juste, Théod. La Révolution de juillet 1830. Bruxelles, 1888.

Thureau-Dangin, Paul. Histoire de la Monarchie de Juillet. 7 vols. Paris, 1887–1892.

Weill, Georges, and Duvergier de Hauranne. See above, § 1.

3. *Republic of* 1848 *and the Coup d'Etat.*

Stein, L. Geschichte der socialen Bewegung in Frankreich. 2 vols. Berlin, 1850.

Regnault, Elias. Histoire du Gouvernement provisoire. Paris, 1850.

Stern, Daniel (Comtesse d'Agoult). Histoire de la Révolution de 1848. 3 vols. Paris, 1851.

Tenot, Eugène. Paris en décembre 1851. Paris, 1868.

—— La province en décembre 1851. Paris, 1868.

Granier de Cassagnac, A. Récit authentique des événements de décembre 1851. Paris, 1868.

Marx, Karl. Der 18 Brumaire des Louis Napoleon Bonaparte. Hambourg, 1869.

Blanc, Louis. Histoire de la Révolution de 1848. 2 vols. Paris, 1870.

Du Casse, Albert. Les dessous du Coup d'Etat. Paris, 1871.

Garnier-Pagès, L. A. Histoire de la Révolution de 1848. 10 vols. Paris, 1861–1872.

Kinglake, A. W. Histoire du Deux Décembre. (Translated from "The Invasion of the Crimea.") Paris, 1872.

Gradis, H. Histoire de la Révolution de 1848. 2 vols. Paris, 1872.

Pierre, Victor. Histoire de la Révolution de 1848. 2 vols. Paris, 1873–1875. 2nd ed. 1878.

Hugo, Victor. Histoire d'un crime. 2 vols. Paris, 1877.

De La Gorce, Pierre. Histoire de la seconde République française. 2 vols. Paris, 1887.

Mill, J. Stuart. La Révolution de 1848 et ses détracteurs. 2 vols. Paris, 1888.

Stratz, Rud. Die Revolution der Jahre 1848–1849. 2 vols. Heidelberg, 1888.

Special Sources in Periods from 1815 to 1852.

Memoirs, Correspondence, Speeches.

1. *Restoration.*

Serre, Comte de. Discours. 2 vols. Paris, 1826.

—— Correspondance. 7 vols. Paris, 1876–1882.

Courier, Paul Louis. Oeuvres. 4 vols. Paris, 1834.

Capefigue, R. Mémoires tirés des papiers d'un homme d'Etat (duc Decazes). 4 vols. Paris, 1835.

Chateaubriand, R. de. Le Congrès de Verone. 2 vols. Paris, 1838.

—— Mémoires d'Outre-tombe. 6 vols. Paris, n. d. (Edition Biré.)

Lafayette, Comte de. Mémoires et correspondances. 6 vols. Paris, 1838.

Vaublanc, Comte de. Mémoires. Paris, 1857.

Guizot, F. P. G. Mémoires pour servir à l'histoire de mon temps. 8 vols. Paris, 1858–1867.

Dupin, André (ou l'aîné). Mémoires. 4 vols. Paris, 1855–1863.

Beugnot, Comte J. C. Mémoires. 12 vols. Paris, 1863.

—— Ecrits et Discours. 2 vols. Paris, 1866.

D'Alton Shee, E. Mes Mémoires. 2 vols. Paris, 1868–1869.

Nervo, Baron de. Souvenirs de ma vie. Paris, 1872.

Guernon-Ranville, Comte de. Mémoires. Caen, 1873.

Palmerston, Life of Viscount; by Bulwer and Ashley. 3 vols. London, 1870–1874.

Ampère, André-Marie et Jean-Jacques. Correspondance et Souvenirs. 2 vols. Paris, 1875.

Agoult, Comtesse d'. Mes Souvenirs, 1806–1833. 2 vols. Paris, 1877.

Metternich, Prince de. Mémoires et Souvenirs. 8 vols. Paris, 1880–1885.

Vitrolles, Baron de. Mémoires et Relations politiques. 3 vols. Paris, 1884.

Rémusat, Ch. de. Correspondance pendant la Restauration. 6 vols. Paris, 1883–1886.

Constant, Benjamin. Lettres à sa famille, à Madame Récamier. 2 vols. Paris, 1881–1888.

Barante, Baron P. de. Souvenirs. 6 vols. Paris, 1882–1889.

Richelieu, Duc de. Correspondance avec divers (Société impériale d'Histoire de Russie, tome LIV). Petrograd, 1886.

Neuville, Hyde de. Mémoires. 3 vols. Paris, 1886.

Broglie, Duc Victor de. Souvenirs (1785–1870). 4 vols. Paris, 1886.

Villèle, Comte de. Mémoires et Correspondance. 5 vols. Paris, 1887–1890.

Talleyrand-Perigord, Charles Maurice de. Mémoires (édition de Broglie et de Bacourt). 6 vols. Paris, 1890. English translation. 5 vols. London, 1891.

Gontaut-Biron, Comte de. Mémoires (1813–1836). Paris, 1891.

Auger, Hippolyte. Mémoires inédits (1810–1869). Paris, 1892.

Laurentie, Joseph. Souvenirs inédits (1793–1876). Paris, 1892.

Monbel, Comte de. Souvenirs. Paris, 1893.

Constant, Benjamin. Journal intime. Paris, 1894.

Pasquier, Chancelier. Mémoires pour servir à l'histoire de mon temps. 2e Partie. T. I–IV. 4 vols. Paris, 1894–1895.

Haussez, Baron d'. Mémoires. 2 vols. Paris, 1896.

Mounier, Baron E. Souvenirs intimes et notes. Paris, 1896.

Broglie, Duchesse de. Lettres (1814–1848). Paris, 1896.

Pozzo di Borgo. Correspondance diplomatique avec le Comte de Nesselrode. 2 vols. Paris, 1890–1897.

Ferrand, Comte. Mémoires. Paris, 1897.

Salaberry, Comte de. Souvenirs politiques. Paris, 1900.

Reiset, Comte de. Mes Souvenirs. 3 vols. Paris, 1901.

Polovtsoff, Alex. A. Correspondance diplomatique des ambassadeurs de Russie en France et de France en Russie de 1814 à 1830. Petrograd, 1902 et seq.

2. *Reign of Louis Philippe.*

For Ampère, de Barante, duc de Broglie, Dupin l'aîné, Lafayette, Guizot, Metternich, Palmerston, chancelier Pasquier, Talleyrand, see above, § 1.

Bérard, A. Souvenirs historiques sur la Révolution de 1830. 2 vols. Paris, 1834.

Launay, Vicomte de (Madame de Girardin). Lettres parisiennes. 3 vols. Paris, 1836.

Jacquemont, V. Correspondance. 2 vols. Paris, 1837.

Périer, Casimir. Opinions et Discours. 4 vols. Paris, 1838.

Taschereau, J. A. Revue rétrospective ou archives secrètes du dernier gouvernement. (Revue rétrospective.) Paris, 1848.

Jacquemont, V. Nouvelle correspondance. 2 vols. Paris, 1867.

Berryer, A. Correspondance et Discours parlementaires. 5 vols. Paris, 1870–1874.

Thiers, Ad. Letters and papers in a work entitled "M. Thiers et les Napoléon." Paris, 1874.

—— Discours parlementaires. Vols. I–XII. Paris, 1879–1893.

Barrot, Odilon. Mémoires. 4 vols. Paris, 1875.

Heine, Henri. Lutèce (letters written from Paris). Cf. vols. IX and X of his works. Hamburg, 1875.

Doudan, Xavier. Mélanges et Lettres. 4 vols. Paris, 1876.

D'Haussonville, Comte J. Souvenirs et Mélanges. Paris, 1878.

—— Ma Jeunesse. Paris, 1885.

Bugeaud, Maréchal. Lettres et Mémoires. 3 vols. Paris, 1881.

Guizot, F. P. G. Lettres à sa famille et à ses amis. Paris, 1884.

Montagnac, Colonel. Correspondance. (Neuf années de campagne d'Afrique.) Paris, 1885.

Martinprey, Général de. Souvenirs d'un officier d'Etat-Major en Algérie. Paris, 1886.

Orléans, Duc d'. Récits de campagne. Paris, 1890.

Orléans, Duc d'. Lettres publiées par ses fils. Paris, 1890.
Talleyrand-Perigord, C. M. de. Correspondance diplomatique pendant son ambassade à Londres. (Edition Pallain.) Paris, 1891.
Melun, Vicomte A. de. Mémoires. Paris, 1891.
—— Correspondance avec Madame de Swetchine. Paris, 1892.
Veuillot, Louis. Correspondance. 7 vols. Paris, 1883–1892.
Joinville, Prince de. Vieux Souvenirs (1818–1848). Paris, 1894.
Grenville, Countess. Letters (1810–1845). 2 vols. London, 1894.
Dash, Comtesse. Mémoires des autres. 6 vols. Paris, 1896.
Houssaye, Arsène. Souvenirs de Jeunesse. 2 vols. Paris, 1896.

3. *Revolution of* 1848.

Lamartine, A. de. Trois mois au pouvoir. Paris, 1848.
—— Mémoires inédits. Paris, 1870.
—— Souvenirs et portraits. 3 vols. Paris, 1871.
—— Correspondance. 6 vols. Paris, 1873.
—— Choix de Discours et Ecrits politiques; edited by de Ronchaud, under the title "La politique de Lamartine." 2 vols. Paris, 1878.
Caussidière, Marc. Mémoires. 2 vols. Paris, 1849.
Lesseps, Ferdinand de. Ma Mission à Rome (1849). Paris, 1851.
Tocqueville, Comte Alexis de. Correspondance, dans les œuvres. 7 vols. Paris, 1864.
Audebrand, Philibert. Souvenirs de la tribune des Journalistes (1848–1852). Paris, 1867.
Merson, Ernest. Du 24 février au 2 décembre 1848. Paris, 1869.
Senior, Nassau William. Journal kept in France and Italy, 1848 to 1852. 2 vols. London, 1871.
Faucher, Léon. Biographie et correspondance. Paris, 1875.
Hugo, Victor. Actes et paroles. 3 vols. Paris, 1875.
Merruau, Ch. Souvenirs de l'Hôtel-de-Ville. Paris, 1875.
Du Camp, Maxime. Souvenirs de l'année 1848. Paris, 1876.
Ledru-Rollin, A. P. A. Discours politiques et écrits divers. 2 vols. Paris, 1879.

Sand, Georges. Souvenirs de 1848. Paris, 1880.
Falloux, Comte de. Discours et Mélanges politiques. 2 vols. Paris, 1882.
—— Etudes et Souvenirs. Paris, 1885.
—— Mémoires d'un royaliste. 2 vols. Paris, 1888.
Crémieux, Ad. Discours et Lettres. Paris, 1883.
Maupas, C. E. de. Mémoires. 2 vols. Paris, 1884.
Lesseps, F. de. Souvenirs de quarante ans. 2 vols. Paris, 1887.
Commissaire, Sébastien. Mémoires et Souvenirs. 2 vols. Lyons and Paris, 1888.
Joigneaux, P. Mémoires d'un représentant du peuple. 2 vols. Paris, 1890.
Proudhon, P. J. Confession d'un révolutionnaire. Paris, 1891.
Hubner, Comte de. Une année de ma vie (1848–1849). Paris, 1891.
Stapfer, P. A. Aus seinem Briefwechsel; edited by Langenbuelh. 2 vols. Basel, 1892.
Tocqueville, Comte de. Souvenirs (1848–1851). Paris, 1893.
Persigny, Duc de. Mémoires. Paris, 1896.
Cavaignac, Général. Souvenirs et Correspondance. Paris, 1899.
Hugo, Victor. Choses vues. Paris, 1900.
Quentin-Bauchart, Alex. Etudes et Souvenirs sur la deuxième République etc., 1848–1870. 2 vols. Paris, 1901.
Bernard, Martin. Correspondance avec sa famille; edited by Lévy Schneider. Paris, 1913.

Biographies, Essays and other Works bearing specially on the History (1815–1852) in Periods.

1. *Restoration.*

Corcelles, J. Documents pour servir à l'histoire des conspirations. Paris, n. d.
Barante, Baron de. Vie politique de Royer Collard. Paris, 1861.
Capefigue, R. La Comtesse du Cayla et Louis XVIII. Paris, 1866.

Biré, Victor. Victor Hugo et la Restauration. Paris, 1869.
—— L'année 1817. Paris, 1895.
Falloux, Comte de. Augustin Cochin. Paris, 1874.
Thureau-Dangin, Paul. Royalistes et Républicains. Paris, 1874.
Daudet, Ernest. Le ministère de Martignac. Paris, 1875.
—— Louis XVIII et le duc Decazes. Paris, 1899.
—— La police politique de 1815 à 1820. Paris, 1912.
Thureau-Dangin, Paul. Le parti libéral sous la Restauration. Paris, 1876.
Mazade, C. de. Le Comte de Serre. Paris, 1879.
—— L'opposition royaliste. Paris, 1894.
Rousset, Camille. Un ministre de la Restauration. Le marquis de Clermont-Tonnerre. Paris, 1885.
Chabrier, A. Les orateurs politiques de la France (1804–1830). Paris, 1885.
Faguet, E. Politiques et moralistes du XIXe siècle. Paris, 1891.
Rougé, Comte de. Le marquis de Vérac et ses amis. Paris, 1890.
Bardoux, A. Chateaubriand. Paris, 1893.
—— Guizot. Paris, 1894.
Spuller, E. Royer Collard. Paris, 1895.
Guillon, E. Les complots militaires sous la Restauration. Paris, 1895.
Crousaz-Cretet, L. de. Le Duc de Richelieu en Russie et en France. Paris, 1897.
Cisternes, R. de. Le duc de Richelieu. Paris, 1898.
Neuville, J. G. Le comte de Villèle. Paris, 1899.
Lauris, De. Benjamin Constant et les idées libérales. Paris, 1904.

2. *Reign of Louis Philippe.*

Sarrans, Bernard. Lafayette et la Révolution de 1830. 2 vols. Paris, 1832.
La Hodde, L. de. Histoire des Sociétés secrètes depuis 1830. 2 vols. Paris, 1850.
Cuvillier-Fleury, Alfred. Portraits politiques et révolutionnaires. 2 vols. Paris, 1851.
Castille, Hipp. Les hommes et les mœurs sous le règne de Louis-Philippe. Paris, 1853.

Bournand, F. Le général Bugeaud. Paris, 1855.

Sainte-Beuve, Charles Aug. Portraits littéraires. Vol. III. (M. Molé.) Paris, 1864.

D'Ault-Dumesnil, Edouard. Relation de l'expédition d'Afrique et de la conquête d'Alger. Paris, 1869.

Foisset, Th. Le comte de Montalembert. Paris, 1875.

Trognon, A. Vie de Marie-Amélie. Paris, 1876.

Daudet, Ernest. Le procès des Ministres en 1830. Paris, 1877.

Du Camp, Maxime. L'attentat Fieschi. Paris, 1877.

Menière, P. Captivité de la duchesse de Berry. 2 vols. Paris, 1881.

Mazade, Ch. de. Cinquante années d'histoire contemporaine. Paris, 1884.

Tchernoff, I. Le parti républicain sous la Monarchie de Juillet. Paris, 1884.

Simon, Jules. Thiers: Guizot: Rémusat. Paris, 1885.

Rémusat, Ch. de. Thiers. Paris, 1889.

Rousset, Camille. La conquête d'Alger. 4 vols. Paris, 1889.

Mirabeau, Comtesse de. Talleyrand et la Monarchie d'Orléans. Paris, 1890.

Flers, Marquis de. Le roi Louis-Philippe. (Un anecdotique.) Paris, 1891.

Thouvenel, E. Episodes d'histoire contemporaine (1844–1845–1851). Paris, 1892.

Wallace, Sir R. The Englishman in Paris. The reign of Louis-Philippe. London, 1892.

Lecanuet, E. Berryer, sa vie et ses œuvres. 3 vols. Paris, 1893.

—— Montalembert. 3 vols. Paris, 1895.

Lacombe, H. de. Vie de Berryer. Paris, 1894.

Hachet-Souplet, P. Louis-Napoléon au fort de Ham. Paris, 1894.

Thirria, H. Napoléon III avant l'Empire. 2 vols. Paris, 1895.

—— La duchesse de Berry. Paris, 1900.

Meaux, Vicomte de. Montalembert. Paris, 1897.

Laity, A. Le prince Napoléon à Strasbourg. Paris, 1897.

Charavay, E. Le général Lafayette. Paris, 1898.

Bapst, G. Le maréchal Canrobert. 2 vols. Paris, 1898.

Weill, Georges. Histoire du parti républicain en France. Paris, 1900.

Gonnard, Philippe. Les Origines de la Légende Napoléonienne. L'œuvre historique de Napoléon à Sainte-Hélène. Paris, n. d. [1906].

Cheetham, F. H. Louis Napoleon and the genesis of the Second Empire. London, 1909.

Simpson, F. A. The rise of Louis Napoleon. London, 1909.

3. *Revolution of* 1848.

Thomas, Emile. Les ateliers nationaux. Paris, 1848.

Vermorel, A. Les hommes de 1848. Paris, 1869.

Hugo, Charles. Les hommes de l'exil. Paris, 1875.

Courmeaux, Pierre Eugène. Ledru-Rollin. Paris, 1885.

Audebrand, Philibert. Nos révolutionnaires. Paris, 1885.

Grévy, Jules. Discours politiques et parlementaires. 2 vols. Paris, 1888.

Geffroy, Gustave. L'Enfermé (Blanqui). Paris, 1897.

Tchernoff, I. Louis Blanc. Paris, 1904.

—— Le parti républicain au Coup d'Etat. Paris, 1906.

Jouet, A. Associations et sociétés secrètes de la deuxième République. Paris, 1905.

Michel, Henry. La loi Falloux. Paris, 1906.

Lebey, André. Louis-Napoléon et Odilon Barrot. Paris, 1912.

Crémieux, Albert. La Révolution de Février 1848. Paris, 1912.

Wassermann, Suzanne. Les clubs de Barbès et Blanqui. Paris, 1913.

Barthou, Louis. Lamartine (1848). Paris, 1914.

Special Works.

1. *History of Religion.*

Montlosier, Comte de. Mémoire à consulter sur un système religieux. Paris, 1826.

—— Les Jésuites, la Congrégation, et le parti prêtre. Paris, 1827.

—— Le ministère et la Chambre des Députés. Paris, 1830.

Riancey, Comte de. Histoire de la liberté d'enseignement. 2 vols. Paris, 1844.

Ponlevoy, A. de. Vie du Révérend Père Ravignan. Paris, 1860.

Foisset, Th. Vie du père Lacordaire. 2 vols. Paris, 1870.

Lacordaire, Le père Jean Bapt. Henri. Correspondance avec sa famille. Paris, 1870.

—— Lettres inédites. Paris, 1874.

—— Correspondance avec Th. Foisset. 2 vols. Paris, 1886.

Thureau-Dangin, Paul. L'Eglise et l'Etat sous la Monarchie de Juillet. Paris, 1880.

Chocarne, Le Père. Vie intime et religieuse de Lacordaire. 2 vols. Paris, 1880.

Bardoux, A. Le comte de Montlosier et le gallicanisme. Paris, 1881.

Montrond, Max de. Etudes sur Montalembert. Paris, 1881.

Leroy-Beaulieu, Anatole. Les Catholiques libéraux de 1830 à nos jours. Paris, 1885.

Baunard, Mgr L. Vie du Cardinal Pie, évêque de Poitiers. 2 vols. Paris, 1886.

Lamennais, Hugues Fél. Rob. de. Correspondance avec le baron de Vitrolles. Paris, 1886.

Grandmaison, Geoffroy de. La Congrégation (1801–1830). Paris, 1889.

Roussel, Abbé. Lamennais d'après des documents inédits. 2 vols. Paris, 1892.

Spuller, Eugène. Biographie de Lamennais. Paris, 1892.

Roussel, Abbé. Lamennais intime. Paris, 1897.

Debidour, Antonin. Histoire des rapports de l'Eglise et de l'Etat en France de 1789 à 1870. Paris, 1898. Contains a complete bibliography of the religious history of this period.

Lamy, Etienne. Luttes entre l'Eglise et l'Etat en France au XIXe siècle. Paris, 1900.

2. *Constitutional and Administrative History.*

Flourens, Emile. Organisation judiciaire et administrative de la France de 1814 à 1875. Paris, 1875.

Luze, E. de. L'organisation administrative de la France depuis 1789. Paris, 1881.

Liste des Pairs de France avec notices biographiques. 2 vols. Paris, 1883–1887.

Muel, Léon. Gouvernements, ministères et constitutions depuis 1789. Paris, 1890.

—— Précis historique des Assemblées parlementaires (1789). Paris, 1896.

Hervieu, Henri. Les ministres; leur rôle, leurs attributions dans les différents états organisés. Paris, 1893.

Bourloton, E., Robert, A. et Cougny, G. Dictionnaire des parlementaires français. Paris, 1891.

Weill, G. D. Les élections législatives depuis 1789. Paris, 1895.

Caron, Pierre. Les ministères français. (Publication de la Société d'Histoire moderne.) Paris, 1911.

3. *Financial History.*

Nervo, Baron de. Les finances françaises sous la Restauration. 4 vols. Paris, 1865–1868.

Courtois, Alph. (Fils). Histoire des Banques en France. Paris, 1875.

—— Tableau du cours des principales valeurs. Paris, 1876.

Calmon, A. Histoire parlementaire des finances sous la Restauration. 4 vols. Paris, 1868–1878.

—— Histoire parlementaire des finances sous la Monarchie de Juillet. 2 vols. Paris, 1878–1879.

Wuhrer, A. Histoire de la Dette publique en France. 2 vols. Paris and Nancy, 1886.

Wagner, Adolph. Besteuerung in Frankreich von 1789 bis 1889.

4. *History of Economics (Agriculture, Manufactures, Commerce and Colonisation).*

Archives statistiques (collected). Paris, 1837.

Statistique agricole de la France. Paris, 1840–1841.

Lullin de Châteauvieux. Voyages agronomiques en France. Paris, 1843.

Schneider, Henri. Statistique générale de la France. Paris, 1846.

Mounier, L. De l'agriculture en France, d'après les documents officiels. Paris, 1846.

Statistique industrielle de la France. Paris, 1847.

Burat, Jules. Exposition de l'Industrie française, année 1844. Paris, 1845.

Colmont, A. de. Histoire des Expositions de l'Industrie française. Paris, 1855.

Audiganne, H. Les populations ouvrières et les industries de la France. Paris, 1860.

Foville, A. de. La transformation des moyens de transport et ses conséquences. Paris, 1860.

—— Le morcellement. Paris, 1885.

—— La France économique. Paris, 1890.

Dombasles, Mathieu de. Annales agronomiques de Roville. 9 vols. Paris, 1861.

Felix, Lucas. Etudes historiques et statistiques sur les voies de communication en France. Paris, 1873.

Block, Maurice. Statistique comparée de la France. 2e édition. Paris, 1875.

Mauguin, M. Etudes historiques sur l'administration de l'agriculture en France. 3 vols. Paris, 1876.

Robiou de la Tréhonnais, F. Histoire du progrès agricole en France au XIXe siècle. Paris, 1868.

Noel, Oct. Histoire du commerce de la France depuis la Révolution. Paris, 1879.

Baudrillart, A. Enquête sur les populations agricoles de la France. 4 vols. Paris, 1880–1893.

Charles, J. Ernest. Les chemins de fer en France sous Louis-Philippe. Paris, 1896.

Des Cilleuls, Alf. Origines et développement du régime des travaux publics en France. Paris, 1895.

Brandt, Alex. von. Zur Geschichte der französischen Handelspolitik. Leipzig, 1896.

Colson, Cl. Transports et tarifs. Paris, 1898.

Leroy-Beaulieu, Paul. De la colonisation chez les peuples modernes. 5e édition. 2 vols. Paris, 1902.

Schefer, Ch. La France moderne et le problème colonial. Vol. I. Paris, 1907.

5. *Labour and Socialism.*

For general purposes cf. the Bibliography edited by Stammhammer: Bibliographie des Socialismus und Kommunismus. 2 vols. Jena, 1893–1900.

Villermé, Louis R. Tableau de l'état physique et moral des ouvriers employés dans les manufactures de coton, de laine et de soie. 2 vols. Paris, 1840.

Charlety, S. Le Saint-Simonisme. Paris, 1876.
Chevallier, Emile. Les salaires au XIXe siècle. Paris, 1885.
Faguet, P. Politiques et moralistes au XIXe siècle. Paris, 1891.
Fourier, F. C. M. Oeuvres choisies. Paris, 1891.
Malon, Benoit. Le socialisme intégral. Paris, 1891.
Weill, Georges. Saint-Simon et son œuvre. Paris, 1894.
—— L'Ecole saint-simonienne. Paris, 1896.
Desjardins, A. Proudhon, sa vie et ses œuvres. Paris, 1896.
Denis, Hector. Histoire des doctrines économiques et sociales. Paris, 1897.
Bourguin, Maurice. Les systèmes socialistes. Paris, 1902.
Bourgin, Hubert. Proudhon. Paris, 1902.
—— Fourier: Contribution à l'histoire du socialisme français. Paris, 1905.
Rambaud, Joseph. Histoire des doctrines économiques. Paris, 1902.
Levasseur, E. Histoire des classes ouvrières en France. 2e édition. 2 vols. Paris, 1903.
Fournière, Eugène. Les théories socialistes au XIXe siècle, de Babœuf à Proudhon. Paris, 1904.
Prudhommeaux, Jules. Etienne Cabet. Nîmes, 1907.
Festy, O. Le mouvement ouvrier au début de la Monarchie de juillet. Paris, 1910.
Dreyfus, Ferd. L'assistance publique sous la deuxième République. Paris, 1911.

6. *Public Education.*

Chon, François. Impressions et souvenirs de la vie universitaire (1813–1879). Paris, 1873.
Buisson, Ferd. Dictionnaire pédagogique. 8 vols. Paris, 1882–1890.
Gréard, Octave. Législation de l'enseignement primaire en France depuis 1789. 4 vols. Paris, 1890.
Dejob, Charles. L'instruction publique en France et en Italie. Paris, 1892.
Liard, Louis. L'enseignement supérieur en France (1789–1893). 2 vols. Paris, 1894.
Grimaud, A. Histoire de la liberté d'enseignement en France. Paris, 1898.

Bourgeois, Emile. L'enseignement secondaire en France. Paris, 1901.

Brouard, E. Essai d'histoire critique de l'enseignement primaire. Paris, 1901.

7. *Social History.*

Reybaud, Louis. Jérôme Paturot à la recherche d'une position sociale. Paris, 1844. (3e édition. 2 vols. 1879.)

—— Jérôme Paturot à la recherche de la meilleure des Républiques. 2 vols. Paris, 1848.

Beaumont-Vassy, Ed. de. Les salons de Paris et la société parisienne sous Louis-Philippe. Paris, 1866.

Bouchot, Henry. Le luxe français. La Restauration. Illustration documentaire. Paris, 1893.

Simond, Charles. Paris de 1800 à 1900. La vie parisienne au XIXe siècle. Paris, 1900.

Renard, Georges. Les étapes de la société française au XIXe siècle. Paris, 1913.

8. *Literary History.*

In the Bibliography of French literature of the period the best and completest guide is

Manuel bibliographique de la littérature française moderne (from 1500 to 1900), completed in 1914 by Gustave Lanson. Paris, 1912–1914.

INDEX